Purchased with Library Parcel Tax funds.
Thank You San Anselmo Residents!

SEP 1 6 2014

DISCARDED

DATE DUE

NOV 1 9 2016		

Brodart Co.   Cat. # 55 137 001   Printed in USA

D0312660

TIMELESS

ALSO BY LUCINDA FRANKS

My Father's Secret War: A Memoir
Wild Apples
Waiting Out a War: The Exile of Private John Picciano

TIMELESS

Love, Morgenthau, and Me

Lucinda Franks

Sarah Crichton Books

Farrar, Straus and Giroux

New York

Sarah Crichton Books
Farrar, Straus and Giroux
18 West 18th Street, New York 10011

Printed in the United States of America
First edition, 2014

Library of Congress Cataloging-in-Publication Data
Franks, Lucinda.
  Timeless : love, Morgenthau, and me / Lucinda Franks.
    pages   cm
  ISBN 978-0-374-28080-2 (hardback) — ISBN 978-1-4299-4927-9 (ebook)
  1. Franks, Lucinda. 2. Franks, Lucinda—Marriage. 3. Women
journalists—United States—Biography. 4. Lawyers' spouses—United States—
Biography. 5. Morgenthau, Robert M.—Marriage. I. Title.

  PN4874.F6155 A3 2014
  070.92—dc23
  [B]
                                                        2013048110

Designed by Jonathan D. Lippincott

Books published by Sarah Crichton Books / Farrar, Straus and Giroux may be
purchased for educational, business, or promotional use.
For information on bulk purchases, please contact the
Macmillan Corporate and Premium Sales Department at 1-800-221-7945,
extension 5442, or write to specialmarkets@macmillan.com.

www.fsgbooks.com
www.twitter.com/fsgbooks • www.facebook.com/fsgbooks

1   3   5   7   9   10   8   6   4   2

For my family—
all fifty-one of you

Out beyond ideas of wrongdoing and rightdoing,
there is a field. I'll meet you there.
—Rumi, thirteenth-century Sufi poet

AUTHOR'S NOTE

It is always complex to write about someone you love. I am fortunate to have a husband who allowed me to do this: to talk about the personal life that he has kept so private during his forty-five years as a public figure; to divulge the unknown stories behind his major cases; to reveal the intimacies, the foibles, the highs, and the lows of our thirty-six years together.

He has never been known to dwell on the emotional or the psychological—that has been my role. Instead, he is an architect of change who never stops improving the lives of others. For him, this book was a rendering of loyalty, an example of how to stand by relationships and make them right.

I thank him for guiding me in so many ways: in sorting through the journals, sometimes barely legible, that I have kept since we met; in reading each chapter, and not just once; for the gift of his prodigious memory in helping me to re-create the moments of our life together.

His was an act of love, and it is in tribute to him that this book is written.

TIMELESS

PRELUDE

I can't get enough of you. I switch from channel to channel, trying to catch you, trying to understand your baffling persona. The husband I know has the sweet cadence of an oboe, and the husband I don't speaks with an Old Testament fury.

I am transfixed by this other you, this scowling prosecutor who makes the most hardened reporters, merciless with others, pay obeisance. If only they knew that the scowl is aimed at no one, that instead it is a superficial tic, etched on your face by years of squinting into the sun on wartime destroyers.

Out in the world, you leave a heavy footprint, but here at home you come so softly through our door, I can barely hear you. You greet me with that little smile—crescent moon against a sky of gold—then cast your eyes down and look up shyly, like a bird that cannot be caught.

I, however, have walked happily into my cage. Recognized for my journalism, I could fly anywhere I wished. But you are a public icon, and my mission is clear. "Take care of him," your cousins and friends warned me. "He is a national treasure."

How the odious matrons rebuked us! We felt young, so young, the day we met, years ago. I was twenty-six, and you were fifty-three. You were a cautious gentleman of considerable fame, and I, an undomesticated radical half your age. It was a time when such marriages were not done.

The disapproval of our friends and family brought us closer together. We were so alike in dash and spirit, no stereotype could fit us. The years between us had closed. If one day the gap widened and we couldn't love each other with our bodies, we'd love with our minds.

We were parts missing from different eras, parts that fit together perfectly. We became giddy with the concept of agelessness. We were Mayans wrapped in solar winds, awaiting the birth of a universal consciousness. We were Greeks, receiving the enlightenment, the liberal revelation that was hidden from the masses.

•

Words by the millions have been printed about you, but none have revealed your real life, your secret life—that you belong to me.

Last night the City of New York owned you, but now, as the sun rises, you are mine. Light falls upon your exquisite forehead, your extravagant Roman nose. The hand beneath your cheek rumples your lips. I gently place my fingers on your lids and feel the rapid flutter of your eyes. The wings of a hummingbird. Such are the things that make love ache.

Only when I take your craggy hand, mine so soft and round against it, when I run my fingers over the sharpness of your bones, do I remember you are twice as old as I am, twice as worldly—and twice as close to life's end.

You are the first man I have truly loved; I could lose you tomorrow. Before I know who you truly are. Sometimes, my breath skips and this excites you: you think it is passion, but sometimes it is dread. If you knew these fears that can come over me, if they were let out into the universe, they might come true.

Can I ever let go? When you give me pleasure, I worry it could be your death.

At times I've felt your heart pounding so fast, it seems as if it will burst through your chest. Terrible things happen to older men in this situation. Two ancient popes expired in flagrante delicto. So did Nelson Rockefeller, and so, incredibly, did Attila the Hun.

I always listen for your breathing. Once when I woke up, I couldn't hear a thing; your chest was still, no heartbeat at all. I began thumping on your sternum. "Breathe . . . breathe!" I pleaded. You jumped up, gasping. You thought I was crazy.

I intend to keep you alive. I will feed you what you love—white peaches dripping with juice, lobsters so fresh they snap up their tails. I will keep you moving and thinking and even teach you to shout and to curse. Everything you do will be of importance to me.

I will make love stop time.

•

How strange and beautiful it is, falling in love with someone who has lived twice as long as I have. I believe that love is no accident, no whisper from a random universe. It comes from deeper channels of longing and recognition: a collection of tiny lights that gathered force long ago. The boy with long fingers sweeping the keys of a piano, an uncle's laugh, a teacher who always listened. And the one who precedes them all. The father.

The things about him you never forget: his hands circling your waist, flying perilously in the air, sun-blinded, grains of sand rubbing against your cheek; your chubby hand smoothing back the soft bristles of his hair so they spring up again like soldiers.

Then, in a flash, you stand head-to-head, face-to-face. And he walks away, for you have become too mature, too near, a danger. Was it something you did? You are confused, guilty. An ineffable longing takes over and then eventually is forgotten.

The years go by, and one day you meet him again—the thistly chin, the bright smile, and, behind his glasses, the love that was always there. He's not your father, but he is everything you wanted him to be.

•

Seven months ago, every newspaper announced the news: Robert Morgenthau, New York County's district attorney, and Lucinda Franks, a journalist, were married in their home in Greenwich Village. The bride wore a flowing charmeuse dress and a cap made from the lace of her grandmother's wedding gown.

Now it is a time of grace. We do not sleep upon the pearly monogrammed sheets your cousin gave us. Instead, little white sheep leap about a meadow of baby-blue cotton, reminding us of our innocence, not our transgression.

Each of us thinks the other is the delightfully eccentric one. Your taste in women does not run to dusky lavender lids, moist mulberry lips, ladies who mask themselves in false mystery. In fact, you hate me to wear makeup at all. Your preference is to see me in a T-shirt that tickles the flesh above my knees. Sometimes I feel like a wobbling blancmange.

Our doorbell never rings. Most people leave us alone. We are, after all, a marriage that was never supposed to happen.

But when you go to work, you are busy and famous, surrounded by supplicants. Every day, you are making history, while I make nothing. I am a Lilliputian standing in the shadow of the giant. A lazy Buick stalled on the berm, while you whiz by in your gleaming midnight Bentley. Unwritten stories are building up inside me, but when you leave me, all I want to do is re-create you in colors more intense than can be put on any page.

Your success seems to make mine unnecessary, unwise even. What if I began to write again and failed? Or worse, succeeded? What if I joined you on your pedestal and then, God forbid, knocked you off? We have already disturbed the balance of nature; how far can we tempt fate?

.

Now, at last, you are stirring. "Who is this I see?" you say, yawning.

"It's your sweetheart," I reply, edging close.

"Oh, it's my sweetheart! What? You're wearing my knickers?" You hook your fingers under the waistband and snap it back.

You know I wear your boxers. They're a bit loose, but I wear them because they are yours.

"You're also wearing my undershirt."

These I love. They have a great deal of character. They are immortal, like the silky undergarments of royalty handed down through generations. The edges are frayed, maybe a hole here or there, but they are made of the best cotton, worn so thin they are kind to your skin. You never let anyone but me touch them.

I put my lips to your good ear. "Don't tell my husband we're meeting this way," I say and am gratified when you think my joke funny.

But there's a hint of worry in your gray-blue eyes. Do you imagine that some young guy will come along and steal me? Or has there been a threat on your life and you're not telling me? Fear runs down my back. How many criminals have you put away? Hundreds? Thousands? How many want to pay you back, and who will succeed?

"What do you love best about me?" When we play, it drives away the demons.

"You have a beautiful back." You lift up a handful of my long, messy hair, the color of honey, you say, and run your hands down my spine. "That's why I married you. For your back."

"Really? What about my mind?"

"That's nice too."

I gently punch your arm.

"No, I've never yet come into a room where you're not the most beautiful one there—and the most intelligent . . . except when you're not in the room because you're *late*."

You slide your hands under my T-shirt, making me breathe sharply.

"Did I tell you I had a great meal yesterday at that Chinese restaurant near the office?" you ask as you lay me down beneath you. "It was a pleasant change from Forlini's. They had a giant crab that was delicious."

I laugh silently. I know you better than perhaps I should. For some odd reason, when you start to make love, you chat away as if we were sitting at the kitchen table. Are you afraid of sex, you, a boy whose family seldom hugged or touched?

I cover your mouth, muffling your chatter, and plant little kisses down your belly. You are gripping my shoulders, and you aren't talking anymore—and the phone rings. Your private line.

Maybe we can make love quickly, before it stops ringing, break a record, but you have already lifted the receiver.

"Ed, hello!" you boom. "No, it's not too early."

Fuck the mayor of New York. Gleefully, I try to grab the phone, crowing, "Hi, Ed!" and you swat me away. Koch's excited voice is like a clarion, pitched somewhere above the epiglottis, while my circumspect husband's emanates from deep below his diaphragm. The two are equally stentorian, obstinate, and independent.

I can hear Koch's voice, talking about a "young rabble-rouser" who shot a guard at a warehouse. "I hear his lawyer wants a plea bargain."

"That could be."

"They're claiming insanity! Well, if you ask me, *all* of these so-called revolutionaries are insane, but that doesn't mean they don't know exactly what they're doing."

"He'll be charged appropriately," you say. "Bye, Ed, thanks."

"It isn't one of my friends, is it, this shooter?" I ask, after you hang up.

"I don't exactly know *who* your friends are," you answer pointedly and are up out of bed before I can stop you.

"Yes you do. You know they're not violent; I mean, except accidentally, when they blow up some symbol of capitalist hegemony."

You give me a mordant look and then busy yourself rummaging through your sock drawer. "I can't find any matching ones!"

I retrieve two black socks. I know where they all are; sometimes it's just too boring to put them together.

"I'm so proud of you," I say sweetly. "I know this guy has to pay the penalty, but I wonder if there are mitigating circumstances, like maybe genuine idealism. And I know you'll do what's right; you don't let anybody dictate to you."

"Except you," you say drolly. "Now where's my watch!"

"Sweetheart," I say with a laugh, "look on your wrist."

"What would I do without you?" you ask, grinning.

I pick out a nice pink-striped shirt. "Let me make you an egg," I suggest, though we both know I have not bothered to learn an art so bourgeois as cooking.

"I'll stop and pick up a bagel," you say, looking away. "I have to get to work."

"I can make some hash brownies for you to take to the office," I reply, only half kidding since you have no idea how well I can bake them. There happens to be a little bell jar in the kitchen, inherited from my last boyfriend, who was an antiwar draft dodger, filled with hay-green stuff you've never asked about. I don't use it, but perversely I don't get rid of it either. Do you think it's dried rosemary?

"Take me to work in your pocket," I say, straightening your lapels. "You can let me out when nobody's looking. I could be very useful as a spy . . . as protection. I could keep watch for attackers."

"I'll be fine, sweetheart, don't you worry now."

You kiss my cheek, pat my bottom, and then you're gone.

A haiku floating in the emptiness.

We are half of a wedding invitation torn in two. What will you take with you when you finally leave me? Twenty, thirty years? Who knows then the length of my own days? For having found you, I have become you. You left me too soon this morning, making me feel unloved, making me love you that much more.

I go to the bed and bury myself in the tangle of covers on your side. Your pillow is still warm. It smells like moss and wilting lilies. I close my eyes and begin to drift off.

•

We are walking in a glen and come upon a lush, innocent meadow of buttercups and clover. We stop to kiss, and I lean into you, taking your mouth in mine, but you are not leaning into me, you keep falling backward, and I look down and see we are standing on the edge of a cliff we had never noticed. I try to stop you, twist my waist to gain the strength, but I can't, and you keep falling back and back. Then, suddenly, you push me away hard, sending me back onto the ground, to safety. And you are gone. I look down in time to see you falling through the air, calling my name, and then breaking into pieces at the bottom. Blood filling the ditch. Your face erased, your legs splayed, and, slowly, blood seeping into the dirt.

O Lord, let me die before you.

1

The last thing I wanted to do was to marry my husband. Bob Morgen-thau was a widower almost three decades older, came with five chil-dren, a cat, and two dogs, and resided in a suburban house barely touched since the death of his wife five years before. It looked like this: On the lowboy in the hall was a mound of unopened mail that a casual breeze could have sent cascading to the floor. The chintz sofa with its fat golden flowers had gone vapid, the illusion of a spring bounty passed to winter gorse. Little crystal bowls were filled with shriveled nuts.

Not only that, this man, the stereotype of the bourgeoisie, had the power to put me in jail.

And this was supposed to be the man of my dreams?

I had barely escaped incarceration anyway, emptying balloons of pig's blood on draft files in various cities, trespassing on government property, and chaining myself to the wrought-iron White House fence.

We couldn't have been more different. In 1961, he had become the formidable U.S. attorney under JFK, sending away members of the Mafia, corrupt politicians, corporate thieves. In 1961, I was pubescent, a budding radical drawn to the black civil rights movement.

By the 1970s, I had become a young woman in a state of rage. I felt a gnawing shame whenever I thought of Vietnam, which was much of the time. An ethos of death permeated my generation. We all knew or knew of someone killed in this excruciatingly stupid war, and our heads were filled with images of what we had done: the ears of Vietnamese women sliced off for souvenirs, babies in flames, faces bubbled black with napalm. That old American men (our parents) had sent fifty thousand young American men (their sons) to die alone a million miles away because of this fallacious domino theory that had quickly collapsed on itself made me crazy. That long after we were losing the war we were still dropping almost three million tons of bombs on Cambodia made me crazy. That we had killed student protesters for no good reason made me especially crazy. I hated my country. If you were intelligent and young, you were trying to figure out how to be sane in an insane world.

It never occurred to me that a member of the establishment, a man born into the same culture as the deluded architects of the Vietnam War, would be the answer. Bob Morgenthau came from one of New York's prominent and well-to-do German Jewish families who were steeped in politics. I came from a Boston suburb that I loathed, born of an upper-middle-class New England family, thoroughly steeped in Gentile society. He was part of the status quo, and I was a hippie who, in spite of bending to the pleas of my mother to go to charm school and become a Boston debutante, was still ragged at the edges.

I let it all hang out, while he calmly kept it in. He was cautious, steady, a sloop balanced at dead center. I was guileless, eager to take risks, a catamaran racing breakneck through every channel I encountered. While he was aggressively enforcing the law, I had become dedicated to breaking it. The very notion that we should have come together was an oxymoron.

Certainly we appeared to be opposites, but in truth we were hauntingly alike. We were both born of busy parents who were oriented more toward the world than the home. Bob practically raised himself, appearing to be the good middle child but in truth secretly roaring about playing outrageous pranks. When he would confess, his mother assumed he was joking and never gave it another thought. In a more subversive way, I had done the same thing. My father, overly protective, was generally too physically absent to address this; my mother was overly strict, but only when she was paying attention. I would sneak out late at night and commit a variety of sins.

The backdrop of my childhood was the sterile, repressively elegant town of Wellesley, Massachusetts, home to the anti-Communist John Birch Society, where the men wore yellow pants and red jackets and where the lawns were cut as short as their crew cuts. On my fifth birth-

day, I remember sitting with my mother on the hot granite of our neighbor's stone wall, having seen a movie of *Uncle Tom's Cabin*. "Mom," I
asked, "why aren't there any Negroes on our street?" She looked at me,
stunned, and replied, "The only thing you have to worry about is yourself, young lady."

My father had come back from World War II broken, full of secrets,
and incapable of rekindling his love for my mother. He became an alcoholic with a wandering eye, and she gained almost a hundred pounds. My
parents had noisy physical fights. Sometimes I would lock myself into
my baby sister's nursery, fearing for us both. As we grew and my mother's
marriage further crumbled, the contempt and resentment she felt for
my father were displaced onto us. Her talent for cutting us down was
unequaled and sometimes so subtle, we didn't know what was happening. When I was nine, I began running away from home, but the police
would always find me hiding in a grove of trees that passed for the town's
woodland.

Sometimes my mother would forget to pick me up at school or to
cook dinner for us while still being intensely ambitious for me, demanding that I bring home high grades on an empty stomach. When I didn't,
she'd forbid me to go to the soda shop, pajama parties, dancing parties.
I might as well have been in a federal witness protection program.

When I was in seventh grade, I took up with older intellectual kids
with progressive ideas. To my father's amused dismay, I brought *The
Communist Manifesto* to the dinner table and proceeded to hold forth
on the virtues of Lenin over Kropotkin.

By the time I was sixteen, I had learned how to escape my mother.
At night I sneaked out with my friends to smoke weed on the country-
club green. By day, I would unobtrusively saunter around the back of
the house and then race down the block, climb on the back of my boyfriend's Kawasaki motorcycle, and roar up to Boston.

My mother sought to tame me by enrolling me in the socially enviable
Junior League. To my delight, the league had just taken on a volunteer
project sight unseen, because it was sponsored by Harvard University.
Wellmet was an experimental halfway house for volunteer students and
newly released mental patients located in bohemian Cambridge. By
day, we worked with the patients, and by night we slept together on cots
in the attic, breaking more social mores than the patients themselves.

The experiment was a success, however; we got patients out into jobs and apartments, and in spite of my mother's idle threats not to pay for my college, I stayed on at Wellmet through my senior year.

When I finally entered Vassar College, I helped found a chapter of the Students for a Democratic Society (SDS), which intensified protests against Vietnam and the draft. I had established myself in a generation whose outer rebellion reflected an inner one, a breaking away from our conventional, hypocritical, overly possessive postwar parents. When I graduated from Vassar, I felt blessedly free, a member of the exhilarating, dream-struck counterculture whose motto was "Don't trust anyone over thirty."

And then our heroes, Martin Luther King and Robert Kennedy, who had been predicted to defeat Nixon for president and finally end the war, were assassinated. With them died the hope that the system could be changed from within. Leaving America seemed to be the only choice. As soon as I graduated from college, I used the money I had saved over the years babysitting, boarded a rickety ship relegated to students who paid cheap fares, and steamed to England to live among saner people. There, I got an apartment with a bunch of fellow exiles in London. Luckily, I had already published a short story, and that helped me get a job at the major wire service United Press International.

I was the only newswoman in the organization's London bureau and was paid as much as a coffee runner. I bought a used motor scooter on which I happily drove to work. By day, I decoded cables from reporters in third-world countries, written in a shortened garble to save the company cents per word, and by night I dallied at the Anarchist Club, one of England's counterparts to the SDS. I went out and found my own scoops, and since I was not yet a feminist, my skeptical boss finally gave me praise of the highest order: "You write so well, I don't even think of you as a woman anymore."

By the time I was twenty-four, I had been nominated by UPI for the Pulitzer Prize. I was the youngest woman to win the prize and the first to get it for the prestigious category of national reporting. The award was for a series of articles that, like all top-rate stories, was the result of hard work, some skill, and, most important, a huge amount of luck.

It began in May 1970, when a Bryn Mawr graduate named Diana Oughton, who had become a member of the violent antiwar group

Weatherman, accidentally blew herself up in a Greenwich Village town house turned into a bomb factory. America was stunned; I was fascinated. Few knew that there were bright, educated children from decent families making crude bombs designed to destroy everything their parents represented. Indeed, psychological analysis might say that as products of these parents they were trying to kill themselves.

After the explosion, my mother went into one of her uniquely effective crisis modes: she had ambitions for me, and she immediately contacted a friend from her hometown of Kankakee, Illinois, who knew Diana's parents. The friend, who was a fan of my writing, told the Oughtons of my similarity to Diana in background and antiwar sentiments. They agreed to talk to me in hopes I could explain why she had turned against everything they represented.

So within a day, I packed a bag and headed back to the United States.

I stayed with the Oughtons, in Diana's room, and tried to help Mr. Oughton understand the depth of the passions our generation had against the war and the hypocrisy of the culture we grew up in. He concluded we were all in the throes of an "intellectual hysteria."

I then followed Diana's steps through the heady underground, full of safe houses and dangerous plans; I ended up identifying with her so much that I almost tossed my notebook in the trash and joined the groups that shaped her. Everything about her resonated emotionally: she was a good woman, educated, sensitive, highly intelligent, and, like me, drawn to making sacrifices for larger causes. The crucial difference was that Diana had made the ultimate sacrifice and here I was, exploiting her for my own success within the establishment she hated. I felt ashamed.

I ended up deciding not to join Weatherman and to write its story instead. I was clearly more ambitious than I thought, more desirous of pleasing my mother. The five-part series about Diana's odyssey, written with Thomas Powers, was published in some five hundred newspapers around the world. It made me even more uneasy about how intent I was to succeed in the bureaucracy that I was supposed to abhor. I got scant peace of mind by slipping stories sympathetic to the radicals onto the wires.

•

In those days in the early 1970s, I had long corn-silk hair, parted in the middle the way Joan Baez did it. I was a fair-skinned, blue-eyed blonde with a round, dimpled face, a five-foot-six-inch curvy endomorph. At the back of my closet hung the Scottish tweed suits with matching hats made for me by my Republican mother; instead, I wore sailor's bell-bottoms and sandals with straps that crossed halfway up my legs. I aspired to being "cool," but to my frustration, every tremor of my heart registered itself on my face. I put myself "out there," according to those who observed me. Whimsical and prone to doing the unexpected, I had a bent toward banana-peel humor.

I was also audacious, idealistic, and aspired to be a person of high principles.

I had heard that after Bob Morgenthau had returned from World War II, in spite of his wry, iconoclastic nature, he moved easily into his parents' powerful social and political sphere. He married, proceeded to have a passel of children, and rose quickly in politics. With a law degree from Yale, he went into private practice for thirteen years, and by the time he was forty-one, he had been appointed U.S. attorney for the Southern District of New York by the man he had campaigned for, President Kennedy.

Meanwhile, Lyndon Johnson's massive escalation of the Vietnam War inflamed Americans, and the protests and riots drove him from seeking a second term. When Nixon was elected president, Bob was investigating Nixon's dealings with Swiss bank accounts. Nixon tried to get rid of him to pick his own U.S. attorney, but Bob stubbornly held on for a year. Twice he made bold if unsuccessful bids to become governor of New York State, attempting to take on the behemoth Nelson Rockefeller. But in 1974, with a reputation as one of the city's leading public officials, he was easily elected district attorney of New York.

He was widely known as being audacious, idealistic, and highly principled.

•

In early 1973, I was about to leave for a transfer from London to UPI headquarters in New York after my father called me, deeply distressed: my mother had been diagnosed with terminal cancer, and he was helpless, didn't know what to do about her disease or how to tell her she had it. He asked me to come home, back to Wellesley. So I had asked UPI for a transfer to New York, rather than to Boston, so I could be near them, but not too near.

In London, I had found myself unexpectedly harboring a draft resister. Roger Neville Williams had called attention to himself by writing the first book telling the story of war resisters exiled in Canada and Europe. Thus, this twenty-five-year-old man from a small, unsophisticated town in Ohio was high on the FBI wanted list.

We had bumped into each other while crossing the Hammersmith Bridge in a thick, sharp fog that had trapped the coal smoke coming from the terraced houses of southern London. Just the kind of night beloved by Jack the Ripper. I was grateful when he offered to walk me to my apartment across the Thames in Richmond. We proceeded to see each other for a few months, pub-hopping on the banks of the Thames, fervently talking politics over pints of lager. Before I knew it, he had arrived at my digs with four suitcases.

When I left for New York, he followed me, uninvited. Angry and domineering, he was possessed by a loathing for Nixon, and the former president occupied the greater part of our lives together. But the sanguine side of this is that I knew he loved me; after all, he had risked arrest to return with me to America. I thought I loved him too, sort of.

Doctrinaire in his hatred of the rich, he nevertheless blithely overruled me when I wanted to live in funky Greenwich Village with the radicals and misfits; he insisted we live in the posh, established Upper East Side. I had never thought him a hypocrite, but I did now. Were others in the movement guilty of such mixed-up thinking? If so, the Cultural Revolution was doomed. As we set up house on East Eighty-First Street, Roger ordained that since we were basically political anarchists of the Kropotkin breed, we should "divide the bowl." In other words, he, who was nearly penniless, should share my bank account. I thought this sounded fair and true and practical, especially since I had never shown much interest in balancing my checking account. Roger was so highly organized, this would be an asset. I began to look askance when he ended up keeping an "Accounts" book that allocated a certain amount of money for food and a larger amount for pot.

Had I not been so adored by this devastatingly handsome and tumultuous man, I might have kicked him out. But I liked his sandy windblown hair, his scratchy, sexy mustache, his intellectual company. I even liked the fact that he was fiercely possessive of me; no man had ever cared so much. No one had ever wanted to make me his project.

•

Once I was settled at UPI's New York headquarters in early 1973, the reporters didn't look at me with the beady eyes that they had in London; I was simply the person who had got UPI a Pulitzer. No brows were raised when I was handed the plum assignment of investigating corruption in the Nixon administration in the wake of Watergate, but I didn't know where to start. I had gone to Britain straight out of college, and I woke up to the fact that I knew very little about the details of American politics.

I was a stereotype of the radicals who thought they knew it all. How few of us had studied the complex history of Vietnam's occupation or the ontology of free enterprise or the discourse of the capitalist system we loathed. Who had read Noam Chomsky or Herbert Marcuse or Nicholas von Hoffman's brilliant book, *We Are the People Our Parents Warned Us Against*? Who even knew that Abbie Hoffman, the revolution's guru, had written numerous tomes laying down his political credo. In some ways, the grown-ups had been right: we were like legions of unarmed children who had run away with ourselves. In spite of the reporter's steel I had somehow developed, I wasn't informed enough to do American government stories.

One day, Roger, who had been hired off the books as a researcher for NBC, came home excited. "I've got something for you. There's this guy, Morgenthau, a Democrat who was U.S. attorney. I just interviewed him, and he's the real deal. Nixon fired him! He found out the creep is hiding money in Swiss banks. And he knows about all his corrupt cronies. You got to go talk to him."

"I don't know. I don't know if I should start with someone so high up. So big. I hardly know anything about Watergate yet."

Roger looked at me hard. "Freak me out, you're scared! Come on, Ms. Toughie. You dodged bullets in Belfast. You risked your life in the underground. And you can't sit down and psych out a guy in a white collar?"

"Don't think so," I mumbled. He was throwing down the gauntlet, trying to teach me one of his lessons, pushing me to fight the insecurity that I had grown up with.

"So get over it. Off your duff!" he exclaimed so forcefully that I started to reach for the phone. "Get Morgenthau and stop wasting time."

•

How ironic that Roger's campaign to push me toward Bob Morgenthau would come back to haunt him, to reverse his life, and mine, forever.

I get a little thrill when I think of how one blind infinitesimal act can alter your portion, perhaps deflect the fate that binds you to the commonplace, cause plans to go cockeyed. You can wave, you can wail, to no avail. Chance will always betray the human diagram. It is perverse; it is whimsical. It often brings you to astonishing predicaments. I've had this sense of dazzling confusion only once before, and that was when I was nine, looking through my father's big white telescope, beholding Orion and the Milky Way.

"Dad, what is beyond the stars?" I asked.

"Other galaxies with other stars," he replied.

"But what is beyond the very last galaxy?"

"We just don't know. Maybe nothing."

Instead of going to sleep at night, I would try to imagine nothingness. But my little galaxy was concrete; things had beginnings and endings. Was infinity a whiteness, a blueness, some kind of nice shimmering violet? Did it move, soar past the stars and then empty out? Would I ever know what emptiness looked like? I felt enthralled by the mystery deep inside me.

And that is how I would someday feel about Bob.

•

With Roger standing guard, I dialed the number and heard the deep voice of Robert Morgenthau for the first time. He was impatient, rather intimidating, and dead set against seeing me. "I'm sick of talking about the Nixon administration," he said, "and I promised myself that this researcher from NBC was the last one."

"Well, I'm sort of desperate, Mr. Morgenthau," I said, using one of the only weapons a female reporter possessed at the time—the illusion of innocence. "Who else can I go to who knows as much as you?"

And so I defeated him. I had more power than I thought.

Since I always like to take the measure of a subject before I interview him, I gathered some information in earnest. He was clearly one of the city's most skilled movers and shakers, without compromising his loyalty and honor. He was always interceding, helping the young, molding the careers of his prize employees who idolized him and reverently called him the Boss. Eventually, those who worked for him made up half the luminaries in Manhattan; they included Sonia Sotomayor, now a U.S. Supreme Court justice, and Governor Andrew Cuomo of New York. He could assess the character of an applicant in less than an hour, but on occasion his intellectual resolve gave way to hidden passions; he was prone to hiring children of Holocaust survivors, for instance, as well as those who had the gumption to go to law school later in life and hadn't been able to pass the bar exam. They had to be smart and eager, however, for he had no time for fools.

On the morning of my interview, I slogged through an April downpour to Morgenthau's office. My hair was in strings, I was twenty-six, my white knit poncho was soggy, and my nose was raw from a cold. If this mountain of a man even spoke to me, it would be a miracle.

Morgenthau had recently started a one-man law firm, and his secretary, a sullen lady with the hint of a mustache and a slanted gait, greeted me with a series of mumbling grunts. "Sit down until he calls you," she said, and I took the only chair, a narrow Hitchcock antique with a missing rung. There I waited, looking at the bare puce walls, the brown industrial carpet, the vacant spaces where a sofa and table with magazines should have been. His secretary—I had heard she had designs on him and liked to drive away female visitors—kept looking up and glaring at me. I felt as if I were awaiting arraignment. Absently, I tore my tissue into tiny pieces. Minutes went by, then an hour. My poncho was dry, but the jig was up—I was about to be found out.

When Robert Morgenthau finally came out of his office, all six feet of him, reedy, skin of burnt sienna and a face like an elongated teardrop, he looked at me in surprise. "I thought you had stood me up," he said, and then scowled at his secretary as if he knew she hadn't told him I was there.

He ushered me into his office, which was small, smaller by far than befit his stature. His desk was covered with a three-inch strew of papers that seemed to be in no particular order. I sat down across from him, and sure enough he began talking about government people I had never heard of. He mentioned the name Wright Patman.

"Who?" I asked.

"Wright Patman," he repeated.

"Um, could you spell that?"

"W-r-i-g-h-t P-a-t-m-a-n."

"What is it he does, could you remind me?"

He stared at me. "You don't know who Wright Patman is?"

That was not the only member of the Banking Committee of the U.S. Congress whom I did not know. The consternation in Mr. Morgenthau's voice went up in increments. I was not yet flustered, though, for I was lost in his strange soaring forehead. I had never seen anyone who looked remotely like him. This oddness made me feel more comfortable, especially when I began to detect the melancholy in his eyes, in the corners of his mouth. Behind his confident exterior, he was not a happy man.

No wonder. He had just lost his wife of twenty-nine years to breast cancer, leaving two adult children and two school-age ones for him to raise alone. And now, having been thrown out by Nixon, he would surely see the cases he was developing against the president's cronies be buried by his Republican replacement, Whitney North Seymour.

I identified with him. I too faced the loss of a loved one, my mother, and in my own way I also had felt professional humiliation. When I won the Pulitzer, I was elated—until I came up against the resentment of my male colleagues, who were fiercely unhappy. Many had been driving all their lives toward the fantasy of that elusive prize and they decided that I, a naive hayseed, had stolen it out from under them. I rather agreed with them: How could I have possibly deserved this highest honor in journalism? It must have been an accident, an embarrassment. It took decades before I could feel proud of my role in the Diana series.

"Do you know *anyone* in the Nixon campaign committee?" he asked with weary resignation.

"Oh yes, I know about Maurice Stans, the secretary of commerce," I replied.

"The *former* secretary of commerce."

"Yes, the *former* secretary of commerce. And, like, I know he quit to head up Nixon's finance committee for his 1972 reelection campaign. In fact, I would really appreciate it if you could enlighten me about him. I hear he ran slush funds for the campaign and that you investigated it."

"I'm not talking about that."

"I have information on how he laundered the money, but I just need to check it with you. I don't want to print something that is wrong." *You may think I'm clueless, Mr. Morgenthau, but I am about to outsmart you.*

"No comment."

"I hear he helped Nixon hide a hundred thousand dollars."

"No, no," Morgenthau said. "More like a million."

I nodded encouragingly.

"All right, but this is the last thing I'll tell you on the subject."

Within an hour and a half I had my Watergate story, a good, detailed one too.

I rose, smiled, and offered him my hand goodbye. For some reason, his eyes were averted, and he was glaring. My cheeks grew pink with embarrassment. I thought I had been so clever, but maybe I had been obvious. Maybe *he* had outsmarted me, telling me stuff he wanted to make public. Had I forgotten the lesson that pols use reporters? I turned, bumping into his secretary, who was standing behind me, and quickly left his office. How could I have ever presumed that a Mr. Morgenthau would think well of me? I knew he had friends in high places. Would he tell them that a dense, yammering goose had interviewed him?

In fact, as I found out later, at the time of our interview, he thought I was either the dumbest or the smartest reporter he had ever met. Then, when he read my story, breaking the news that Maurice Stans was believed to have laundered campaign money through Mexico, he decided I was the smartest. He knew that I had used my naïveté to probe deeply, to squeeze more information from him than a lot of reporters could have.

Moreover, he hadn't wanted me to leave his office.

He has always said that that was the day he fell in love with me. Or rather, with my white poncho, which he couldn't get out of his mind.

For the next year, he somehow found the nerve to ring me half a dozen times, only to be foiled by Roger, who, whenever he heard that deep, resonant voice, would claim I was out, though I was twenty feet away in our tiny bedroom, writing my first book. He thought that it was an important enough book—on deserters from the Vietnam War—to keep me in a kind of boot camp. He kept friends away and even discouraged visits from Penelope, my sister, who had just graduated from college and was proud at having found an apartment in my building. Penny, six years younger, and I had a fragile bond. We could be very close and then very distant, and Roger's shunning of her, which she assumed was mine, was a mistake that caused a long rift in our relationship.

It did not occur to me that Bob had any real interest in me as a reporter, but in late 1973, eight months after I had done the story on him, he called me at the office, on the phone I shared with other UPI reporters.

"Hello, is this Lucinda Franks?" His voice detonated in my ear. "Apparently, *The New York Times* is about to be sued for not having enough women reporters," he said, as though we had been in the middle of an ongoing conversation. But I hadn't heard from him in a long time. Not a whit of small talk after months of silence. His words just came out in a rush: "So they asked me to provide them with some good candidates. I recommended you."

"Oh," I said weakly. "Why me?"

There was a silence, and then he said, "You were the only woman I could think of."

"Oh," I replied, as my blood pressure rose. I felt insulted and complimented at the same time.

"Well, that is very nice of you, Mr. Morgenthau," I said as the images came fast: my mother giddy with joy at the news, my radical friends slit-eyed at my selling out, the anticipation of crafting complex stories two columns long instead of the three-hundred-word wire service wonders. And the chance to have the most exalted job in journalism.

The next day, Arthur Gelb, the *Times*'s city editor, invited me to dinner at Sardi's restaurant. I was excited. I had never been to Sardi's, a landmark off Broadway, near the Times building, a gathering place for *artistes de renom*. I was the first to arrive. The restaurant's deep red walls were covered with excellent caricatures of famous writers and actors, some of whom swished past in full flesh to tables situated so they could be seen. I checked the buttons of my blue shirtwaist dress, smoothed my hair, which was pulled back in a neat bun, and took two deep breaths. I became self-conscious, just standing there alone, so I began studying the history of the restaurant mounted in the vestibule. Suddenly Gelb was behind me: "The caricatures were drawn by a Russian émigré of the '40s," he said. "He did them in exchange for one meal a day." The city editor was accompanied by two prominent *Times* reporters who shook my hand vigorously. I did all but curtsy.

The maître d' welcomed Gelb as though he were royalty and led us to one of the front tables. Gelb nodded at various actors and then sat down and ordered red wine and steak (which I dislike) for everyone. The three instantly zeroed in on me. "So, why do you want to be on the *Times*?" asked Gelb. "Ah, well, like . . ." I took a sip of wine and swallowed it the wrong way. As I was choking, I thought, "Do I really want to be on the paper?" How much my rebel friends, who considered the *Times* a decaying tool of the establishment, would hate me!

"What story have you liked in the *Times* recently?" the female reporter asked. "Uh, well, I liked all the stories," I replied, having not read the *Times* in weeks. I wanted to bite back my words. I could do better than this, but I always felt rebellious when I was called upon to perform; it felt as if I were in second grade, facing the kids who would pretend to be my friends and then throw insects down my dress.

The female reporter raised her chin. "How do you think we did covering the peace in Vietnam?" I had heard she had written glowing stories about Kissinger's diplomacy. I chewed my food very slowly, concentrating hard on saying what they wanted me to say, but out of my mouth popped "What peace?" They looked first at me, then at each other. "I mean, there are still U.S. advisers in Saigon," I said, "and we have bombed the hell out of Cambodia; I don't see much print about that."

The next day Gelb reported to Morgenthau. "I think she must have been on drugs," he said (I was *not*). "But thanks anyway for bringing her to my attention."

For some reason beyond me, Morgenthau wanted me to join that paper, and he pressed on, sending Gelb the story I had done on Maurice Stans. "I'd take another look, Arthur," he argued. "She did the trickiest interview with me. She's a highly equipped journalist."

So, in the spring of 1974, off I went for another interview. Trekking down West Forty-Third Street, I passed hangars sheltering giant rolls of newsprint, and then high above hung a calligraphic sign indicating that you were entering the territory of *The New York Times*. I entered an ink-scented lobby, and who should I meet but the legendary left-wing *Times* reporter Gloria Emerson, a cigarette hanging from her lips, her fingers in a nervous flurry about her coat. We both were veteran voices in the movement; once, we slept on the floor of William Sloane Coffin, the antiwar chaplain of Yale. Now, finally, she had just been fired for her insurrectionist writing.

"If you want the job," she whispered, "just tell Abe Rosenthal that the *Times* is the greatest paper in the world."

I walked into the prodigious office of Rosenthal, the *Times*'s managing editor, with its Chinese rugs and mahogany furniture. Abe, shrunk into an oversized chesterfield chair, waved me into a chair opposite him. He was a short, severe, disquieting man with a pockmarked face. I had heard how he strode up and down the newsroom, hands behind his back, inspiring reporters to type furiously as he walked by. Yet now he uttered an elegiac sermon about the paper, and I realized suddenly how insecure he was. He didn't threaten me as Gelb and the reporters did. He looked like a kid, disappearing into the chair. I realized he needed to feel as though he *were The New York Times.*

"Why do you want to work here?" he asked abruptly.

"Because the *Times* is the greatest newspaper in the world," I replied.

"You really think so, do you?"

"Yes, I do. It's the paper of record, and I would give anything to work here."

"Come on," he said, hoisting himself up, "I'll show you where you'll be sitting."

•

It was early 1974, and overnight my life had changed. I was caught up in the intensity of being a high-powered reporter for the *Times*. Though the troops were gone, U.S. advisers were still in Vietnam, and the war there raged on. Patty Hearst was kidnapped and radicalized, and I still attended concerts, burned effigies at agitprop performances, and hung out with a few of my renegade friends in walk-ups down in the Village. When former revolutionaries like Jane Alpert and later Katherine Ann

Power, wanted for bombing or driving getaway cars, finally surfaced and turned themselves in, they chose me to talk to about their lives underground. I painted compassionate pictures of these revolutionary lawbreakers, but I got such attention for the very fact they had only talked to me, I felt doubly guilty. My commitment to setting the world right was fading. I had acquired new friends, ambitious men and women whose talent and lively minds I respected. Mary Breasted had become my closest buddy; she had an irreverent sense of humor and was always teasing Arthur Gelb about the former reporter Lacey Fosburgh. Lacey frequently visited the newsroom and would saunter up to the city desk and sit in his lap.

I had left my motor scooter in London, so I bicycled to work through the traffic, winning the amused respect of my fellow reporters. I was losing my self-consciousness, getting a sense of humor. Nick Gage and a few other men in the predominantly male newsroom were constantly kidding Mary and me—mostly about sex. "Lucinda, it's time for us to go to the Ramada Inn," Nick would call out so our esteemed editor would hear it. There had been a time that I would have taken offense at this loud pretense that we were having an affair. But now I simply retorted, "Okay, let's go. I'll bring the Mazola oil." Nick could be serious, however, and he taught me how to be proud and vocal about my accomplishments. This was particularly helpful since I was working on my book and dreaded the reviews should I ever finish it. "You have to realize you're smarter than your lousy reviewer," said Nick in his persuasive Greek-accented voice. "You believe in yourself and just forge on until finally, after you write your third book, you've worn them down. They'll love it."

I had my own big metal desk, in one of twenty-three rows lined up in the *Times* newsroom like a typing pool, and an old-fashioned black phone. Working in the most influential newspaper in the nation, I quickly became accustomed to overtures from the lofty hoping to get their names in the paper. Robert Redford called me three times after I did an interview with him about his filming of *Three Days of the Condor.* Mayor Koch asked me to lunch twice, just to chat.

After about a month, I called Bob Morgenthau to thank him, and he followed up my call with several of his own. He was clearly glad to be my news source: I gave him political gossip, and he sniffed out stories for me. Bob glided stealthily through the political backwaters and unlike the other notables seldom wanted me to publish his name. He was not above using me to further his interests—leaking the unethical practices of one of his opponents, for instance—but mostly it seemed he just wanted to help me.

One day, when I had been working at the *Times* for barely two months, he phoned to say, "Look at the Franklin National Bank. Get what you can on the bank president. Jet-setter by the name of Michele Sindona: he's deeply corrupt; he's into helping the Nixon administration and the Sicilian Mafia and even the Vatican."

Morgenthau gave me one potential source: a bank vice president who he told me would drop clues and confirm or deny, but only after I had gathered as much incriminating information as I could. My experience with financial reporting had not exactly been vast, limited as it was to a color story on three-card monte games in Times Square. So Bob volunteered to brief me on money laundering, foreign bank transfers, and letters of credit, all along suggesting strategies for culling information.

I dug up an accounts manager inside Franklin who was outraged by working amid the corruption. Then, armed with some fishy bank accounts, I got myself up like a moll; I wound my hair into a bun, painted on a heavy layer of makeup, and strode past Sindona's secretaries, my heels clicking as though I were someone as important as one of his mistresses. I ended up getting a ten-minute interview that did nothing to further the story but gave me invaluable color on what the flamboyant crook was like. When I came out with my exposé, there were desperate squawks and denials from the Franklin Bank. Nevertheless, the reputation of the financial institution was going downhill, and within a few months it finally closed its heavy doors. I was roundly congratulated by the brass for my bank series, and Bob was especially pleased; I suppose it was further proof that I wasn't the dumbest reporter he'd ever met.

Arthur Gelb, the former culture editor, was unique in the annals of city editors. Arthur, who had seemed so tough and intimidating at Sardi's, was actually soft-spoken, refined, and always full of creative ideas. He would come loping down the aisle with one of his "starbursts," ideas, looking for a favorite reporter, like me, and then give the person as much time as needed to report and write it. A chunk of the staff thus worked from home, worked when they felt like it, and then finally pulled several all-nighters to come up with the blockbusters that Arthur wanted. The metropolitan section—which made up about half the newspaper— was king, full of Nick Gage's investigative stories on the Mafia, Molly Ivins's deadly funny profiles, and Mickey Carroll's incisive political exposés. Arthur and his boss, Abe Rosenthal, made the *Times* the kind of crackling, vibrant newspaper that people grabbed fresh off the presses; it was a heyday of the institution.

One day, on my own, I decided to investigate the food dyes that permeated our food supply. I found a lab worker at the Food and Drug Administration (FDA) who secretly gave me the results of a test on female rats that revealed cancer-causing effects of Red Dye No. 2. I did follow-up stories, and there was such an outcry that the dye was banned by the FDA and replaced with Red Dye No. 40. After the ban, I wrote more stories: Red Dye No. 40 was also carcinogenic, being based, like No. 2, on coal tar derivatives. My stories provoked a national red dye scare and a decline in the sale of bright red products like maraschino cherries.

Meanwhile, after my mother's illustrious Boston doctors from the Lahey Clinic refused to operate on her "terminal" colon cancer, I took her medical records to New York, to Memorial Sloan-Kettering, the world's premier cancer center. I had scouted around until I'd finally found a surgeon, Horace Whiteley, who scoffed at the Boston doctors and said he could go in and remove the tumor. He did and gave her the gift of two more years of life. Every six weeks, I would sneak out of work to pick her up at the train station and stay with her at the hospital while she had her chemotherapy. I would go to Wellesley on weekends to be with her and to help my father care for her.

But weekdays I would work overtime to find a kernel of an investigative political story. I often ran this kernel by Bob; he seemed so willing to give me advice that it was hard to get him off the phone.

I was perplexed. Didn't he have better things to do? He was now district attorney of New York County—elected about seven months after the *Times* hired me—and it was a mammoth job. He oversaw hundreds of assistants who tackled thousands of crimes.

But I suspected there was more. Did he have a wee crush on me? If so, I was sure it was innocent; I certainly didn't have any romantic feelings for him, someone *that* old. But I did like it when I picked up the phone and heard his resonating voice: "Bob Morgenthau. Got a pencil?"

After the Red Dye No. 2 story, Arthur Gelb officially anointed me an investigative reporter. Bob was so pleased it seemed as though he had been given the moniker himself. He asked me to lunch to celebrate. It would be the first time we met face-to-face since I did the UPI story on him some three years before.

He suggested dim sum at a spot near his office in the Criminal Courts Building. From the moment we sat down, the rapport we had developed on the phone disappeared. Tension pervaded our booth. I had by now cultivated several news sources, become easy with them and skilled at making them feel easy too, but there was something mystifying here. Sitting, slurping the hot juice from steamed buns, we seemed to have little to say, looking up at each other and then quickly away. I kept peeking at his wide, exquisitely formed mouth, his gracefully large nose, and his dark grayish hair, which looked as if it had been cut with fingernail scissors. Unaccountably, the sight of him intrigued me. I had always disliked the mundanely gorgeous, the male model, the movie star looks. I like the unusual, the quirky, the kind of man you don't see anywhere else.

As I walked him to his office, I assessed New York's new DA. He wore an outdated green suit with square shoulders and baggy pants that looked as if they might have belonged to his father. Smoke from his cigar, a big, fat smelly one, wafting over to my nose . . . the cigar, undoubtedly an illegal Cuban, protruding from the side of his mouth, making him look like James Michael Curley, the crooked former Boston mayor I remember from childhood.

This was the heretic prosecutor who as former U.S. Attorney was supposed to handle only New York crimes but had extended an elastic arm into international arenas? The one who prosecuted white-collar criminals who had laundered billions in offshore accounts? This representative of the status quo who was increasingly feared (friends who brought in their corporate clients hoping for leniency were disappointed; in fact, Bob's response could be particularly harsh), wasn't he a kind of revolutionary in his own right? Deliciously subversive, without fanfare or public protest.

No blown-up hair or shoes polished into mirrors. Messy desk, cracked leather. He could've cared less how he came across because he was secure and confident in his ability to slip through the cracks in the system to which he supposedly belonged. To meet someone so comfortable in

his own skin, especially when I was not, was dizzying. His scheheraza-
dian personality delighted me.

•

It was the fall of 1975. Nixon had resigned a year earlier; the takeover of
Vietnam by the Vietcong and the official end of the war had been declared. President Gerald Ford had declared amnesty for draft dodgers,
but still Roger was squirreled away in my apartment. NBC had let him
go six months after it hired him. "That's what I get for working for the
establishment: fired for being a war resister," he said at the time, but
I was not so sure that was how it had happened. The closer we came to
peace in Southeast Asia, the more the war protests waned, the more irate
Roger became. If Nixon came on the air, for instance, he would hurl my
sentimental yellow-quartz ashtray from London at the TV screen.
Finally, I threw the ashtray back at him, splitting his lip. The neighbors
complained—once they called the police—because our flimsy apartment walls reverberated with our fights. His endless curses about Vietnam finally had a deep effect on me. It made me question what really
motivated him. As I listened to the shouts of my comrades burning effigies of Gerald Ford—the only president who had provided some kind of
conditional amnesty for draft resisters—it struck me that for many,
bringing anarchy to the country was personal. If they were troubled, if
they had chaotic minds, then what better place to live than in a nation
of chaos.

I had been able to endure Roger's rage against the Vietnam War,
the draft, and the system, because he gave as much as he took. He had
always understood how much my childhood haunted me, and he knew
what to do about it. I usually avoided seeking comfort from my boy-
friends; nevertheless, those nights when I woke in a panic, Roger always
reached for me. By day, when he saw that look on my face, he knew that
if he held me often in his big bear arms, I could finally let go of my
sense of low-level dread.

•

I suppose today my mother would be labeled bipolar, but when I was a
small child, she was simply God. She saw through me to my worst side.
"I know it was you who stole half my petits fours on top of the icebox last
week," she might suddenly lash out. "Well, sister, God's going to punish

you. You're going to walk into a wall," upon which I would stomp off and promptly walk into a wall. When I was older, my beloved daddy was either away on endless "business trips" or at his workbench in the cellar, the sanctum where he could escape my mother and down his endless shots of Dewar's. When I got home from school, I never knew who she would be or why. She could meet me with a smile and a dozen powdered doughnuts or, for no apparent reason, still in her pastel satin nightgown, chase me around the house with a yardstick. I both loved her and hated her. Since she never seemed to decide whether I was good or bad, I didn't know either. This subconscious state of not knowing never left me.

Like so many berated children, I vowed to make a success of myself, and when I did, my mother switched tacks. She treated me respectfully, almost reverently. I sent her every kudo I got from editors because it made her finally rejoice in me. She subscribed to five papers in case I had an article in them; she shared them with her friends and bragged when I interviewed movie stars or went to Buckingham Palace to meet the queen. She loved every word I wrote. Perhaps I was the tool that finally gave her happiness, status even. But it was too late; she had molded me into a person balanced on the precipice, doomed to be unsure when I woke up in the morning whether I would feel like the confident, successful woman or the dorky kid who had something wrong with her. In fact, both personalities were inside me: the outer bravado of a celebrated journalist and the meekness and self-doubt of a child.

Roger wanted me to talk to Mother, resolve what had happened between us. But now that she was sick and dying, I just couldn't. So he decided he could resolve it for me. He believed he could expunge all the stuff my mother made me believe about myself through the avant-garde therapies of the moment, even the ones that were half-cracked. We tried primal scream. I was supposed to close my eyes and let out my inner anguish in a series of piercing screams. But I was afraid of our already irate neighbors, and all I could produce was a pathetic mewing.

We tried est and we tried Gestalt, both of which advocated taking the power out of memory, accepting your past, and just getting on with life. I went around for days repeating the mantra "I am what I think, I am what I think," but my contrary nature could not put up with the exercise for long. As a joke, I began to say, "I think what I am," causing Roger to fume.

One night he turned off the lights and told me to lie down next to him. "Concentrate as hard as you can on terror," he said. "Try to feel it. Be six years old again. Imagine the boogeyman crawling in your window. Imagine your mother coming at you with a knife." I gritted my teeth, made my breath come fast, tried to envision myself charged with terror. But the only charge I felt was caused by Roger's muscular thigh touching mine.

Finally, he decided to apply his creativity to reinventing my childhood. He would dissect my memories and, like a father with a child, make them into stories. But he would change the characters so that the little girl who balanced on two chairs to steal the little frosted cakes would be a perfectly nice girl and the mother would be so sane that she would laugh at the girl's ingenuity. He taught me how I became the innocent scapegoat of my mother's misery and convinced me, at least intellectually and at least for a while, that the jury was in: I was the definitive good child.

•

At some point, however, all the stories were told. It became increasingly clear that Roger resented me, his woman, who had risen far above him in journalism, a profession he aspired to. He had no job, no money, was living off me in a city he hated. Although Ford, by executive decision, had declared conditional amnesty in September 1974 for draft resisters, Roger resented the requirement that he do two years of public service and continued to be obsessed by Nixon's crimes in Southeast Asia. We were near the end of our affair. I saw finally that his passion to keep Vietnam alive was more personal than political, that he was threatened by the fact that I was no longer the victim of intellectual hysteria: the belief that the people of "Amerika" would rise up and bring on a coup. Those who had given their youth, their prospects, to these enthrallments, what options did they have left? How could they now even survive within the system? Who would hire them?

In late November 1975, he announced he was moving to Telluride, Colorado, a town in the Rockies populated by hippie refugees, ski bums, and trust-funders who were building little Victorian houses in the hills. He had visions of earning enough money writing for alternative magazines to build a little Victorian house too. He tacked a quotation up in our kitchen by the writer Richard Reeves, who left the *Times* after six years: "I'd rather be writing my novel." It was meant, of course, for me.

He pestered me constantly. "You say you want to write a novel. You'll never write a novel at the *Times*. Come with me and really do something with your life."

For a while, I ignored him. And then, in January 1976, my mother died. With her went my ambitions to rise in journalism.

2

I stayed on at the *Times* for a few more months after my mother's death, and then I abruptly quit. I decided this while standing in a hospital corridor, waiting to see if an attempted suicide by Representative Wayne Hays—hounded by the press for his carnal indiscretions—would be successful. It was June 1976, and I was in the middle of the congressional sex scandals.

The *New York Times* hated being beaten by *The Washington Post*, which had come out with a story that Elizabeth Ray, a secretary of the powerful Ohio congressman Hays, had been hired exclusively to service him. So Arthur Gelb told me and another reporter, John Crewdson, to get on a plane and not come back until we'd found our own Elizabeth Ray. We combed Capitol Hill, but people were scared, making our mission difficult. I found myself lingering on the doorsteps of female staff members, waiting to ambush them when they came home. Finally, I was led to the reluctant secretary of a longtime Texas congressman, John Young, who admitted that she had gotten a pay raise after having sex with Young. We used everything we had to get her to talk, telling her she had a moral responsibility to come clean, assuring her of how much better she would feel. Yet when the exclusive was published, I certainly didn't feel better. The loftier newspapers were justifying their participation in the frenzy as "investigative reporting" that uncovered the illegal use of taxpayers' money, but they, like the tabloids, loved a lascivious piece of anti-news; it boosted circulation. A year after the *Times* printed the John Young story, his wife committed suicide. Two years later, the congressman lost his seat. I went into the bathroom and threw up.

When I was assigned to the hospital to watch what would happen to Hays, I felt more like a ghoul than a journalist. Hays survived, but as a reporter I did not; I saw my profession from a different side of the prism. Nothing had seemed as important as racing around full of adrenaline to get the scoop of the month. Now it all seemed pointless and often destructive. My stories were too soon forgotten by everyone except the people whose lives they had ruined; the narratives I'd worked so hard to craft ended up lining the cages of parakeets.

In actuality, the only person who mattered was my mother. Now that she was dead, there was little glory in what I did. She had been so taken with my success that she introduced herself as the "mother of the Pulitzer Prize winner." She had appropriated me, but that was fine. I had been writing for redemption on a Sunday afternoon, to hear across the phone lines her peals of pleasure at my latest kudo. When the tip of my toe was blasted off in Derry, the first call I made had been to UPI dictation and the second to my mother. The acceptance in her voice finally released me.

•

It was in 1976, just after the Hays deathwatch, that I told Arthur Gelb I was going to leave the paper; it was, I said, one of the hardest decisions I had ever made. He tried to talk me out of it. Then he literally marched me into Abe's office, as if to an execution. The executive editor was nonplussed: at that time, star reporters, in fact no reporters, ever walked out on the most exalted job in the profession.

Arthur folded his arms in obeisance as Abe chastised me. "If you do this," he said, his puff of black hair seeming to rise with his temper, "if you are foolish enough to do this, you will have nowhere to go but down."

"Uh-huh," Arthur said, nodding sternly. "Down." Arthur was never stern; he had always supported me, except when he was supporting Abe.

"And I'd be surprised if you got up," Abe said coldly.

I stared at him. "Um, I'm sorry you see it that way," I said, "but . . ." I suddenly started to weep. I babbled on about my mother, cancer, death, exhaustion, my novel. The two men seemed to back away from me. Abe held out his handkerchief and I took it, stupidly blowing my nose, wondering whether I could get back into the building to return it freshly laundered. Arthur started to put an arm around me, but it just hovered in the air. They both looked stupefied, alarmed. One of their most fearless employees had become a puddle on the rug. I was scared too. I had just sealed my fate. I would be nothing without the front page of the *Times* to prop me up. Who would want to read a novel by a nobody?

Arthur dropped his arm. "Abe, she *has* had a rough time."

Abe just stood there staring wide-eyed at me. "Well," he said weakly, "we *could* make an exception, call this a leave of absence. If she wrote some freelance pieces for us, she would still be part of the *Times* family."

I wiped my eyes with my sleeves and nodded enthusiastically. "I'll write for you."

Abe stroked his dark bristled chin. "Okay, go write your book," he said, and then, relieved that I had stopped crying, he added in a near whisper, "I don't believe I'm saying this, but you always have a place here."

I tried to convince myself that I wouldn't miss the excitement of the *Times*, that I would be happy writing on my own, and that I could learn to love Roger, now that I was to become just another independent unemployed hippie like him.

The night before I was to leave to join Roger, the phone rang. I didn't answer it. I was too engrossed in trying to finish a freelance piece for *Rolling Stone*. Then it rang again. I reluctantly picked it up to the blast of a familiar deep voice.

"Bob Morgenthau," it said. "Uh, my secretary is impossible. She never tells me anything, and I was just going through some documents and I found this invitation to go to a 'peanut party' at Arthur Schlesinger's house tonight. He was a close adviser to Kennedy, you know. It's for a good cause—to raise money for Jimmy Carter's presidential campaign debts and I guess, oh, I don't know, I think it might be interesting. I thought I might go."

"Really," I said, baffled but intrigued.

"Ah, I'm not going alone. I thought you could go with me."

"Oh." Bob Morgenthau, my news source, was asking me for a date? And at the last minute! He must be hard up. I knew his reputation, had heard the joke about the book titled "People Who Said No to Bob

Morgenthau": it consisted of half a page. Well, I was about to make the book a bit longer.

"Thank you, but I can't really. I'm in the middle of writing an article and it's overdue."

"You can write that anytime," he replied in a voice so emphatic that it felt as if Jann Wenner himself were giving me an extension. Still, I rarely let myself be coerced.

"I have nothing to wear," I said lamely.

"I'll pick you up at six," he said, chuckling, and hung up.

•

And so, on that warm June evening, I found myself entering the portal of the Schlesingers' Upper East Side town house, tightly clutching Bob's arm.

Inside, a fairyland. A ghastly fairyland of flowing chiffons, feathery boas coiling around swan-thin necks, sequins flickering like fireflies, creamy shoulders beneath satin halters, noses high, eyebrows raised, eyes on the door, whispers: "She can't be wearing a Kenzo!" "How did she get into a Betsey Johnson?" Tanned ankles peeking out of palazzo pants, tiny dresses hugging anorexic bodies crowned by huge beehives. Living lollipops.

I'm in a Fellini dream sequence. Naked. Every finger pointing at me. "She's wearing a tie-dyed vest! Mud-colored bell-bottoms. Platform shoes. Is she a babysitter?" Hiding behind Bob as we make our way through the clots of glitterati—Kitty Carlisle, Diane Von Furstenberg, Brooke Astor.

I suspected Bob had asked me to the party so he could sell me on some story, and I wished he would get on with it. I slunk off to find the bathroom—maybe I could at least twist my hair up in the back—when a petite, impeccably groomed woman stopped me.

She introduced herself as Margery Oakes, wife of the *Times*'s editorial page editor, John Oakes, and looked at me curiously. "I saw that you came with my friend Bob Morgenthau. Do you work for him?"

I was saved by a commotion at the door. The elusive Jackie Kennedy Onassis had walked in. The general public had seen the president's widow only through blurry sneak photographs the paparazzi had taken of her on her new husband's yacht. After JFK's assassination, she had absented herself from society, fled to Greece, and married a Greek shipping magnate named Ari Onassis who had the money to buy her privacy. Now that she was separated from him, she would make rare appearances.

This was a debut of sorts. She looked radiant, elegant, understated in a simple white suit. The sophisticated mouths of the society ladies fell open and smiled dumbly at her.

I looked up at Bob. He was smiling too. But not at Jackie.

A weight fell through me. I took a deep breath and then another. Then I smiled back at him.

I was confused, but happily so. Being the kind of obsessive who could fail to notice that my own shadow was leaving without me, I had been blind to the purpose of this evening. Or at least I think I had. I assumed Bob wanted to propose a news story and was irritated that he had chosen this intimidating milieu to do it in.

Only in passing had I thought of Bob Morgenthau as a romantic figure. We had never socialized, and romance wasn't a consideration given our ages. But when we left the party early to eat at a restaurant that had zebras on the red walls, I knew it wasn't a news story that he had on his mind. I felt weird: the tablecloth was like velvet, the ordinary silverware had a peculiar shine, and the salt and pepper shakers made me unaccountably happy. Every time I looked up, he was smiling at me, and that smile caused me to feel a little chiming in my toes.

He had ordered a good deal of wine, and after dinner I stopped listening to him and just enjoyed the sound of his mellifluous voice swirling in my ears. I knew he was presenting some exegesis on the folly of my departure from New York for Telluride. But I was captivated by the zebras that were now jumping up and down on the walls. How dense I had been! All that attention from Bob at the *Times*, what had I thought it was about? He could have leaked political stories to any journalist in the city, but he had chosen me. He had, in his own backhanded way, been wooing me. How typical, though, of Bob Morgenthau that he would wait until the last possible moment, the night before I was to leave New York forever, to make his big move.

He hailed a taxi, and when we got to my street, I said goodbye and climbed out. As I walked down my very dark street, East Eighty-First,

I heard footsteps close behind me. I walked more quickly and then raised my hand, as I always did when I felt threatened, shouting, "Butch! Billy! There you are!"

Suddenly Bob was beside me. "You have friends down there?" he asked.

"You!" I exclaimed. He had apparently gotten out of the other side of the taxi. "No, I just heard footsteps and got scared. That's the way I protect myself."

"I just run down the curb as fast as I can," he replied, adding that I shouldn't be out after dark anyway.

And then we were at my building entrance. "Well, thank you again, Bob," I said, this time shaking his hand. But he continued to follow me through the glass doors and into the elevator. I said nothing. He said nothing. I kept my eyes on the industrial carpet beneath our feet, but when the lift reached my floor, I looked up and there was that adorable little smile.

As he followed me out of the elevator, I thought, "What nerve! I'm not falling for this," and I began devising a way to outsmart him. Maybe I could lure him down the hall, telling him there was a painting I wanted to show him, and then tear back to my apartment and slam the door. I was different from my generation in this way; I wouldn't let myself be used, especially after the first date. And then, of course, there was Roger, who was in Telluride waiting for me.

I put my key into the lock, my heart thumping. Now I suddenly felt excitement, but also a shiver of something else. What if he was a sexual predator? What if behind his ramrod-honest facade, he was kinkier than those scandalous congressmen? A politician who had left a trail of broken women who didn't dare tell about his secret mess of base, psychopathic desires? I had a passing flash of myself tied spread-eagled upside down from the ceiling. I opened the door just a crack, put my heavy shoulder bag between us, shook his hand with firm finality, slipped in, and closed the door. Somehow, he had slipped in behind me.

In seconds, he was sitting on my old brown couch, gazing at me hopefully as he pulled a bottle of wine out of his briefcase. "Do you have a corkscrew?" he asked in a small voice. I decided not to scream for help. Instead, I gave an exaggerated sigh, went to my kitchenette, and rustled around until I found a little all-purpose pocketknife.

He proceeded to talk cheerfully and ceaselessly about everything from the mayor's budget to the best way to get an illegal cigar from Cuba. This relaxed me, as organ music would, although it felt a little as if I were getting a last meal before execution.

And then the bottle was empty and then we were in the bedroom on top of my nubbly wool bedspread and then nothing more was said.

The next morning, I woke to the aroma of pancakes. On the floor of my bedroom lay a man's belt, some loose change, and a monogrammed handkerchief with a little rip in it. I laughed. For all their revolutionary pronouncements, boys my age, well, any age actually, swooped down on women like raptors. They thought sex was for them. But not this man. What had happened to me last night was a first. I looked through the door to the Pullman kitchen to see Bob at my stove, his nose almost touching the pancakes in order to watch the bubbles form in the batter. The weight of the city's safety was upon him, but there was nothing more important at that moment than making perfect pancakes, for me. I felt this sensation in the pit of my stomach and then warmth circulating through my body. Of all the bizarre things, I thought I was falling in love with him.

Once we had eaten, we returned to bed. I dreamily felt every line and curve of him. To think I had known him before only as a commodious suit! What a surprise to discover his narrow hips and flat belly taking cover under his wide, sweeping back. He was surprisingly sensitive. When I ran my fingers down his spine, I made him start. He was slow, affectionate, and careful.

Afterward, as we lay together, just the two of us, quietly, blissfully, the shadow of Franklin Delano Roosevelt suddenly crept across the bed. My bookshelves were filled with books about FDR and the New Deal, with tapes of his speeches that I had listened to so many times. I did, in fact, have a crush on Franklin Delano Roosevelt—I adored his strong handsome face—though he had lived before my time. I was sobered by how, even though he had saved us from the Nazis, saved the country after the Depression, he was still vilified by people like my parents. On Bob, I saw that monocle, the cigarette holder, the shabbily elegant home in Hyde Park; I heard that man with the warm voice reassuring the country on radio, propped up on trains, on bandstands; I saw that roguish mouth, always cheerful in the face of physical suffering. And now Bob, with his aristocratic accent—vowels stretched, r's vanishing with a flourish—and his strong handsome face, was giving me my own fireside chat.

Bob could have been of Yankee stock instead of a native New Yorker. Beside him, I was just a naive girl, born in Illinois and brought up in a rarefied suburb of Boston. I knew, of course, about his father, Henry junior, Roosevelt's secretary of the Treasury, but not until later did I realize his ancestors were prominent New Yorkers, that his grandfather had been Woodrow Wilson's ambassador to the Ottoman Empire, alerting the world to the Ottoman genocide and saving thousands of Armenians from being massacred. Both his father and his grandfather were located at the epicenter of their presidents' circles. And here I was, cuddled up to the man whose family would go down in history as one of the most august clans in America.

.

A few days after the Schlesinger party, I felt obligated to keep my promise to Roger. I went to Telluride, not only to break the news to him in person, but to be sure I was making the right decision. As I flew over the Colorado Rockies, the Maroon Bells stretched upward, their snowy caps glittering in the sun. The air was thin, crisp, cold . . . seductive. Here I flew amid God's pinnacles, a respite from the dark, smoky man-made depths of New York. Since I'd moved there four years before, I'd always had a love-hate relationship with the city; I had never felt the pure well-being that these mountains gave me.

Roger was not at his apartment, so I climbed the hills to sit and work on my novel. Instead, I found myself watching the aspen leaves spin on their laden branches, catching the sunlight like teardrops on a chandelier. I picked up my pen and wrote poems to Bob. They left little doubt. It wasn't Roger I loved. I told myself that his feelings for me must also have surely waned. Otherwise why would he have risked losing me by moving away? The antiwar movement had brought us together; indeed, to each other we *were* the movement. Yet with the movement dead, what we mistook for love had died too.

When he came home, I suggested a drive in the mountains. As we looked down at the peaceful canyon, sitting together in the faded red Beetle, I drew a deep breath and said, "I'm in love with someone else."

"Who?" he asked.

When I told him, he laughed, incredulous, and said, "You're shit-ting me." I convinced him I wasn't, and finally he stopped chuckling. His face turned black, he gunned the motor, and at full speed he took our little Bug through the treacherous switchbacks to the airport.

3

June 19, 1976

Dear Gram,

I think I may be in love, really this time. Let me tell you straight off the man I've fallen for is just a few years younger than Daddy. I know, I can hear you saying, "Oh, sweet Jesus, Cindy, couldn't you have chosen somebody suitable for once?" Well, I had no choice, Gram. This is a man even you would run after. In your time. He's quite handsome, and he has this to-die-for little half-moon smile. There's one other thing—he's Jewish, but the highborn kind. Yes, Grandma, there are Jewish aristocrats back here; his blood is as blue as yours. His name's Bob Morgenthau, and he's the famous district attorney here. I was at his office once doing a feature on him, and there were a bunch of cameras and press downstairs waiting to give him free publicity, and I know it's hard for you to understand this, living in Kankakee, but people in New York will absolutely kill to get in the newspapers. But anyway, instead of going down there, he stopped to talk to a janitor about his home back in Yugoslavia. Bob is that kind and unselfish.

There's one more thing; now, don't have a heart attack. He is a widower and he has five children, well, four really, the fifth one is in an institution for the retarded. The oldest ones, two girls, are around my age, but the youngest are Bobby, nineteen, and Barbara, thirteen. Interesting, no? He also has a wicked, hilarious, really dry sense of humor, and, Gram, you would approve of his moral standards—they're just like everything you and Mother have ever taught me. Once you get used to the idea of him, you'll know Mother would be proud. Her friends have told me that

she always thought I would be a career woman instead of the traditional
kind. Not that I'm going to marry him! But it's nice, at least for a while, to
be truly, really in love. I don't know that this has ever happened to me
before.

I can just hear you two describe him: "My, he is a man of 'fine
mettle.'"

Gram, be happy. I think my wild days are numbered. This I know
because if there's one thing Bob is not, it's wild.

Love,
Cindy

.

I had always distrusted men, even though I kept falling in love with
them. My father, when I was small, had been a coffer of ever-changing
delights. He taught me to ice-skate, shoot a pistol, ride a bike with no
hands, identify butterflies, use a soldering iron, and much more. I would
wait by the door at six o'clock, and when his old blue Buick turned in to
the driveway, I would run out and jump into his arms.

I was about thirteen when he suddenly turned away from me. I
eventually found out it was less because I had become pubescent than
that I had begun to ask him about what he had done in World War II,
which was as much a mystery as his behavior was then. That was about
the time he took out a post office box and began to answer calls in
phone booths in restaurants and disappear on long business trips. He
became remote, silent, unreachable, as he was with all adults. I realized
later that this was the only way he could keep us from probing into his
past, a past that I would have to wait until the final years of his life to
find out about, a past that would take my breath away.

Throughout my childhood, my father warred with my mother, and
my mother warred with me. Insecure and sure that others would turn
on me, I became an easy target, providing hours of entertainment to the
older neighborhood kids who would play with me one minute and hide
from me the next.

My mother figured that my unpopularity was pulling her down.
She was as lonely as I was, the family having moved to Kankakee from
Chicago when I was three, and she had set out to cultivate friendships
with the parents of the kids in my class; to be invited into their bridge

club or to be nominated for membership at the prestigious country club was a burning ambition. "What is wrong with you?" she would ask, seething. "What do you do to make your friends act that way?"

I don't think I really knew what self-esteem was until the day I was introduced into the world of violence. The older child, I became the rescuer in the family. I always thought Mom a prude, giving Dad dirty looks when he snapped open a beer. I didn't know that when he got drunk, he changed into another person. I think I was nine when I began to hear the slaps, kicks, groans, coming from their room. I started listening at night, and as soon as their voices rose, I would run in, terrified, throwing my arms around my father's waist. In truth, I hated him at that moment, hated the feel of his cold belt buckle on my cheek, the smell of the alcohol fumes coming from his angry red face. But I knew that if I told him I loved him, it would jolt him out of his rage. I would feel him relax under my small arms, and the horror would be over. The rescuer again . . .

As I grew, I developed other, less stressful methods. I learned to shame them. Pushing open their door, I would coolly inquire whether they wanted me to call the police. They grew afraid of me. The helpless child victim would always live within me, but the exterior toughness I gained then would turn out to be the tool of my success. By the time I was eighteen, I was determined to enter the real world and kick ass.

Learning how to talk people out of killing each other, I honed the twin arts of diplomacy and artifice.

•

When I began to earn a living, I would regularly bail out my father, whose alloyed-steel business had failed, forcing him to live on his savings; I continued to send my parents money for the rest of their lives.

My father rarely focused on what happened in my personal life, didn't care whether I brought home As or Cs. The only thing that interested him was my safety. If I stood too close to a train platform, he would yank me back. He taught me to use a rolled newspaper to slice an attacker's throat. When I went off to college, I found little cans of Mace in my coat pockets. He secreted guns under hats in the closet, beneath the kitchen sink, even under my bed. He was a championship pistol shooter right up into his eighties. He insisted Penny and I learn how to shoot and tacked targets on the basement wall. I never came near the target, but Penny was a comfort to him, for by the time she was twelve, she was a crack shot. I thought that this obsession with protecting us was the only way that he could show his love for us. But it was more than that. He wasn't paranoid, as we thought; he had good reason to believe that people might come after him and his family. But that was one more secret he kept from us.

One day, his obsession with my physical well-being caused me to be typecast as "the girl with the crazy father." I was on a bus to Selma, Alabama, to help the freedom fighters when a classmate shouted, "Who is that maniac in back of us? He's honking and he's practically on our fender!"

I knew without even looking that the maniac was my father. I cringed in my seat. He had forbidden me to go on this trip—Martin Luther King's civil rights march from Selma to Montgomery—fearing that I would be hosed by redneck sheriffs who had used tear gas and nightsticks on King's demonstrators. I had boarded the bus anyway, and now he was rolling down his window yelling at the bus driver to pull over. Then he swerved right in front of the bus, almost causing the driver to demolish him.

On the way home, in his Buick with its nauseating smell of new leather, not a word was spoken.

·

Bob, only six years younger than my father, was in many ways his doppelgänger—stoic, humorously ironic, unrevealing. Both were repressed members of the Silent Generation, muted by the unspeakable traumas of the Great Depression and World War II. At first, I distrusted someone as indecipherable as my father. But I quickly found that Bob was incapable of withdrawing his love and his loyalty. He trusted me, trusted that I could take care of myself.

I could talk endlessly about my childhood, while Bob would reveal his only in snippets. Yet as we got to know each other, I wanted to find out the arc of his growth, the little accidental revelations missing from family biographies. So I supplemented Bob's offhand memories with anecdotes about him that I gathered here and there.

Even though he had two siblings, Joan, three years younger, and

Henry III, two years older, I saw him as a lonely child. He was close to his brother but voiced resentment that his mother favored Henry: "She thought he would become a great musician, and she nurtured his musical talent . . . I think she felt guilty. He had fallen off a pony once, and he might have had a concussion, I don't know. But from then on she really pampered him. It was ironic because I was really the sickly one," Bob confided.

Henry's fall, when he was only six years old, "derailed the whole family," Henry wrote in his book, *Mostly Morgenthaus*: "My left foot caught in the stirrup, and at the gallop I was dragged with my head bouncing on the ground . . . I had a fractured skull and a paralyzed left leg." His mother took him south to warmer Augusta, Georgia, along with her other children, and after a winter there he regained use of his leg.

Meanwhile, she cast Bob as the solid, dependable child, the one who needed her less. He developed independence at an early age, finding a plethora of ways to assuage his loneliness. At the family farm in upstate New York, he wandered and experimented at will. He cut off the heads of chickens when he was six; used a shotgun and killed a grizzly bear at sixteen. He secretly started driving around the yard when he was twelve; unable to see over the steering wheel, he drove the car right up onto the stoop. Before anyone found out, he had jacked it up and gotten it back down to the driveway.

Bob lived such an unsupervised life, he came to feel he could do anything alone. He developed a propensity to follow his own rules; roguery bred itself into his heart. He tied sheets together and lowered Joan down from the second-story window to see if the contraption would hold. In the city, at his apartment on West Eighty-First Street, he had a pocketful of pranks. When it was raining, he would fill balloons with water and propel them out of his twelfth-floor window to see if he could collapse umbrellas below. He stole road signs and put them up on his wall; if his parents noticed the booty, they never commented on it.

•

When Bob was six, he developed serious ear problems that would plague his childhood. Doctors diagnosed his aching, suppurating auditory canal as a simple infection, but when it got worse, they threw up their hands in the face of the nasty sepsis deep in his ear. It was 1925, long before sulfa drugs and penicillin had been invented. There was simply no cure. For want of any better treatment, the doctor confined him to bed and ordered draining and hot compresses.

Bob's eardrum was in danger of bursting, so finally the doctor lanced it to ease the pressure. Before he did, however, he gave Bob chloroform, which terrified him. The staff had to hold him down so a mask could be put over his face. The compound hissed into Bob, sounding to him like a sawmill, and he thought he saw the blade coming down toward his neck. He shouted and cried until the gas finally put him to sleep.

His mother had left on a monthlong round-the-world tour with her husband and was not there to care for him. The future presidential First Lady, however, was. Eleanor Roosevelt came to see Bob nearly every day, and he loved her; she was jolly and, unlike his mother, loved to hear his jokes. He looked forward to the little presents she would bring him. One time she gave him a tan kimono, which Bob wore long after he had outgrown it.

Henry junior and Franklin, whose respective estates were only miles from each other in the lower Hudson Valley, became good friends from the time they met in 1914. Henry helped lead FDR's political campaigns for governor of New York State and then president of the country and increasingly became a trusted adviser. In the ethnically segregated society of the times, the friendship was unusual; indeed, the Morgenthaus were the Roosevelts' only Jewish friends. Elinor Morgenthau and Eleanor Roosevelt, who laughed about the different spellings of their names, grew to be close confidantes. They would ride horseback together, and the delight they experienced in the similarity of their lively minds is illustrated in an old photograph that still hangs in the Morgenthau home: their horses have been airbrushed to look alike.

When Bob was nine, another infection raged. It was so severe his grandfather Morgenthau, who lived near the family on New York City's West Side and who was now involved with Jewish charities, sat at his bedside constantly. Bob's fever spiked to 105, then 106 degrees. The doctors said he might not make it, and Janet, the chambermaid who helped look after him, couldn't stop weeping. This time his mother and father were vacationing in Spain.

Bob survived, but in the summer of 1932, when he was just thirteen, he suffered another devastating setback. This time his mother was home. She took him to his pediatrician, who declared the discharge from her son's ear was nothing to worry about; she didn't believe him and consulted a society surgeon, a champion polo player, who confirmed her suspicions. He said the infection was a serious mastoiditis that had come within a centimeter of Bob's jugular vein, and he promptly removed part of the ear bone closest to the brain. The surgeon ordered Bob to stay home for a year, skipping the eighth grade, so he wouldn't be exposed to his classmates' germs. People had died from mastoiditis, famous people such as Margaret, the crown princess of Sweden, and Sam Warner of Warner Bros., the infections spreading and poisoning their systems. As it was, Bob lost the hearing in his right ear.

But he was resourceful during his year of confinement to the farm. He wandered the woodlands with a tutor, studying wildlife, and by the time he went back to school, he had learned to identify forty birds.

In January 1933, about five months after Bob's surgery, with their children ensconced in boarding schools, Bob's parents moved to Washington so Henry junior could assume his post as FDR's newly appointed head of the Farm Credit Administration. About a year later, he would become his secretary of the Treasury. Bob's mother claimed that the town was not a good place to bring up children. She knew she would be busy with a round of balls, parties, and political events.

When Bob visited their Washington home, his mother put him to work. She had him drive around town in her Ford Roadster, complete with rumble seat, to deposit her calling cards at various important residences, including those of cabinet members like Cordell Hull and Henry Wallace. She didn't seem to care that her son, who at age fourteen had no driver's license, was breaking the law.

•

Bob wanted so badly to join the navy and fight in World War II that when he graduated from Amherst in the spring of 1941, he submitted himself for the required physical examination—and cheated on the hearing test.

He was commissioned as an ensign, then a lieutenant, and off to Europe he went. He requested destroyer duty, one of the most hazardous assignments in the war. He soon became an executive officer who often acted as captain with responsibility for an entire ship. In such a position, where following orders was a strict rule, he often followed his own sense of right and wrong. Some of his moves could have gotten him court-martialed. Once, the captain of his first destroyer, a drunk, a bigot, and a bad sailor, tried to bring a prostitute on board during an alcoholic binge and began complaining of chest pains. During the quiet of the night, Bob and the communications officer signed a statement claiming the captain had suffered a heart attack and sent it off to the admiral, who swiftly relieved him of his command.

Bob went on to fight in the Battle of Anzio in 1944. German aerial torpedo bombers came swooping down at sunset and bombarded his ship, the USS *Lansdale*, sinking it off the port of Algiers. He spent four hours in the icy Mediterranean, and though he never mentions this, he saved the life of a radar operator by giving him his life jacket. When he saw a distant Coast Guard boat, he set out on an impossibly long swim for help, but before he reached it, the boat spotted the sinking *Lansdale* and steamed to the rescue. After that experience, Bob hated to go into the ocean.

Bob repeatedly championed African American sailors. At the time, the military wouldn't let people of color be anything but mess attendants, he explained, "the theory being that if they were below deck, they wouldn't get scared by the fighting." So Lieutenant Morgenthau, executive officer, persuaded the captains of two of his destroyers to let black sailors come up top at battle stations and join the white gunnery mates in manning the 20-millimeter guns "instead of staying down making sandwiches." His last ship, the USS *Harry F. Bauer*, was attacked by kamikazes during the Battle of Okinawa, and when the smoke cleared, the white gun crew had abandoned its post and jumped to take cover on the deck below. The black sailors were still at their guns. Bob wanted to recommend them for Silver Stars, but his captain claimed that "they had been too scared to jump" and agreed only to the Bronze Star.

Bob himself, during the ship's tour, directed the shooting down of seventeen kamikazes and was awarded two Bronze Stars. The *Harry F. Bauer* received the rare Presidential Unit Citation, equivalent to a Silver Star for every member of the crew. Bob never mentions the honors and claims that he has forgotten where he put the medals.

•

Of his three children, Henry, Bob, and Joan, Henry junior was particularly devoted to the middle one. Before Henry junior met FDR, he ran the *American Agriculturist* magazine, but his first love was his 1,500-acre apple and dairy farm in Dutchess County (later the dairy farm and much of the land were sold off, and the children were left with only about 960 acres of apple orchards). Bob was the only one of his children interested in the farm. He and his father would tromp through the rows of trees, planting year-old whips and pruning the abundance of apple trees—Baldwins, greenings, Spies.

Bob was also the one who shared his father's ironic and often wicked sense of humor. In rich, bottomless voices, they would entertain the family by belting out old Broadway tunes.

For a long time, it was just Bob and his dad. That changed when Bob turned ten. Though their bond always remained strong, with his new appointment as state commissioner of conservation, his father became heavily involved with his political career. Three years later, in 1933, when FDR summoned him to Washington and he became the president's trusted adviser, Bob, thirteen, would pick him up at the airport from Washington on weekends just so he could spend a little bit of time with him.

Bob tells his father's story with pride, how he had learning disabilities that forced him to leave Cornell University, but was able to think out of the box, to become an innovator. When he took over Treasury, he helped FDR design and carry out the New Deal. He investigated corruption that caused the fall of crooked public officials and crime syndicates. When no one else in Roosevelt's cabinet anticipated that Germany was going to force us into war, Henry junior nudged FDR into taking emergency measures. By 1940, with the Nazis taking over Europe, he had persuaded the president to make a massive effort to build up the navy, army, and air force. Moreover, he helped finance this by initiating the war bonds campaign; it eventually raised almost fifty billion dollars. Without it, the United States would not have had the means to defeat the Third Reich.

Henry junior wasn't above bending the law in the service of what he thought was right. Congress was under pressure from the members of

America First to let Europe fight the Nazis alone and had passed a neutrality act. To circumvent it, Henry junior and FDR hatched a plan to secretly send tanks and planes to Britain and France: they took fighter planes up to Plattsburgh, New York, and rolled them across the border into Canada so it couldn't be said that they had been flown out from U.S. soil. Other creative actions and the increasing power of Hitler led Congress in 1941 to finally give in and approve the Lend-Lease Act, which, through loans and bartering, supplied England in its lonely fight against Germany.

As early as 1939, Henry junior was quietly acting to try to arm France. He arranged to have a French pilot test a Douglas bomber in California, and when Congress found out, it began to plan impeachment proceedings against the Treasury secretary. FDR quashed the effort.

Morgenthau protected the dollar against Nazi Germany's efforts to devalue it, and at the end of the war it was the strongest currency in the world.

The State Department was filled with anti-Semites, and Henry junior fought hard to persuade FDR to focus on saving Jews, getting him to set up the War Refugee Board, even though the president's primary goal was to win the war. Henry junior himself surreptitiously set up a Jewish refugee community in Oswego.

Bob has always expressed bitterness about what he feels was the unjust reception of the Morgenthau Plan—his father's proposal to prevent a belligerent Germany from starting another war by turning it from a military power into an agricultural state. The plan was eventually distorted by the press, criticized, pilloried, and it perished unceremoniously.

After FDR died, President Truman had a difficult relationship with Henry junior and finally removed him from office. Though Truman considered the Morgenthau Plan vindictive and strategically unwise, Bob discovered other reasons why FDR's successor disliked Henry junior.

Leafing through the papers of the former secretary of war Henry Stimson decades later, Bob would do a double take. There, in ink, was an entry from Stimson's diary, recounting the day Truman had invited him to the postwar meeting of Allied leaders in Potsdam. Stimson replied, "Is Secretary Morgenthau coming?" The president growled, "I'm not taking any of those jew boys, not Morgenthau, not Baruch."

Years after Bob's discovery, a handwritten note was found on a shelf in the Truman Library. It revealed that President Truman, a hero to the Jews for supporting Israel, had a vicious side not widely known. Written in 1947, it derided Henry junior for still trying to help the millions of displaced, sick Jewish refugees: "The Jews, I find, are very, very selfish. When they have power, physical, financial or political, neither Hitler nor Stalin has anything on them for cruelty or mistreatment to the underdog."

Henry junior was criticized by some of his Treasury staff for being disorganized and lacking executive abilities. Most admit, however, that he was generous and frank and commanded abiding loyalty from his workers—the very qualities that would eventually appear in his son Robert.

He was Bob's first hero, someone who stood up for what he believed in, who helped the little person, who always did the right thing. He was the man Bob wanted to be.

At the end, Bob was the only one of Henry junior's children who could be consistently found by his side. He visited him regularly and finally cared for him at the farm when the hardening of his arteries caused his brilliant mind to go.

This paternal devotion was in Bob's blood. Henry junior had also been deeply attached to his father, the first Henry Morgenthau. In the late nineteenth century, Henry's family had left a successful cigar-making business in Mannheim, Germany, to immigrate to America. Henry had just a few dollars in his pocket, enrolled in school, and then had to quit to help support his parents and eleven siblings. Eventually, he saved enough to go to law school, made money in real estate, and was awarded his ambassadorship to the Ottoman Empire by President Woodrow Wilson.

Ambassador or not, there was nothing more important to this distinguished statesman than his only son. He bought him a large dairy and fruit farm and instructed him on business, politics, morals, charity, and gin rummy. They were like ships of discovery riding on a grand sea. In fact, Henry junior sometimes felt so tethered, he tried to slip away to find companions his own age.

•

Henry junior derived much of his success from his wife, who taught herself to become a superior strategist in realpolitik. She was the major influence over Bob's father; she guided his moves and honed his instincts, and he was dependent on her. But she never let anyone know the role she played; she stood very ladylike behind him, but she was an iron fist in a velvet glove.

On the program of FDR's fiftieth-birthday party in January 1932, Franklin wrote Mrs. Morgenthau a poem tinged with irony about her quiet power:

> *Elinor, I want to know*
> *What makes Henry argue so*
> *Don't he get a chance at home*
> *To make his opinions known?*

By all accounts Elinor wasn't a particularly warm person, nor did she have very much of a sense of humor. Indeed, in photographs, one can't help but notice her impassive, often dour expression. It hardly revealed what I later discovered: behind that hard exterior was an insecure and tender heart.

Bob was proud of his mother's insight and articulate intelligence, which impressed even the likes of Winston Churchill. At a time when few women of her German Jewish community went to college, she had insisted on going to Vassar, where she became a talented actor. When she supported a Democrat, Woodrow Wilson, for president, her father, who, as owner of a woolen mill, was literally a dyed-in-the-wool Republican, was infuriated. Elinor took after her politically skilled uncle Herbert Lehman, governor of New York, and went on to become a speaker for the state Democratic Committee Women's Division and an advocate for women's rights. She also was active in the war effort and later became the First Lady's assistant in the Office of Civilian Defense.

Elinor seems to have been a kind of proving ground where Bob developed one aspect of his character. Frequently, he deceived her without really deceiving her. He would take out the family's Ford Touring Car, for instance, and go zooming at over seventy-five miles an hour on back roads. When he came home and told her what he had done, she didn't believe him—she thought he was teasing her. After all, he was "the responsible child."

Letters often reveal the marrow of the soul. Old letters, new letters, any letters that have been left for others to discover, are treasure. After we were married, Pauline Wais, the family secretary who became my friend, gave me a box of her correspondence with the young Bob that spanned his schooling from Deerfield Academy to Amherst College. She had saved them in shoe boxes and never shown them to anyone before. A tiny, peppy woman, unusually generous with her time, she was a stand-in for his mother; Bob and she wrote ironic notes to each other, shared confidences, and even had a secret code. It was Pauline whom he asked to send books and other paraphernalia he needed; Pauline whom he notified of his comings and goings. He once wrote a letter to her from college with this pitiful ending: "Rumor has it that I'm going to go to New York sometime between Jan 31 and Feb 4. Nobody gives a d—— but I thought you might like to have it in your files."

Henry junior was as reticent about Elinor as Bob, declining to talk about his wife even to John Morton Blum, who put together three of the *Morgenthau Diaries*. She stood like a ghost star in the family firmament.

How little we know our parents, what they suffered, how they became who they were. If we did, perhaps we could forgive them more quickly for their failings. Many years after Bob and I were married, I became curious about what his mother, behind her somewhat flat and reserved personality, was truly like. I imagined I would find Elinor's true feelings the same way I had found young Bob's—from personal letters. So I went to the Roosevelt Library in Hyde Park and read through correspondence between Eleanor Roosevelt and Bob's mother. Here I found a hidden woman, not Elinor the "iron fist," but Elinor the vulnerable woman who seemed depressed over the health problems that debilitated her until her untimely death in 1949 and who had a loving and somewhat enigmatic relationship with First Lady Eleanor Roosevelt.

I liked the Elinor I saw in those letters. Like me, she had exiled all the fancy coats her mother had given her to the back of her closet when she left home. And, like me, she suffered from periodic depression, which might have explained why she appeared gloomy in photographs.

Although Elinor has been occasionally accused of maneuvering herself into the more powerful Eleanor's life for the sake of her husband's career, the letters between the two women are unusually intimate, tender, even romantic. Elinor longed for her friend's love and reassurance.

And although the First Lady expressed genuine concern about Elinor's health and well-being, she got impatient with her resentment of her other good friends:

> Dearest Elinor,
>   . . . I have always felt that you were hurt often by imaginary things and have wanted to protect you but if one is to have a healthy, normal relationship, I realize it must be on some kind of equal basis, you simply cannot be so easily hurt, life is too short to cope with it! . . .
>   Much, much love, always.
>   Eleanor

> February 2nd On board Larovis [?]
> Dearest Elinor,
>   . . . I didn't say half what I wanted to when we were talking the other day. I've grown to love you . . . tho I can't take away the feeling you have it makes me unhappy to feel that it is worrying you and I want to put my arms about you and keep away all the disagreeable things which have made you feel this way.

> Dearest Elinor,
>   . . . It worries me to have you say you tire so easily. I wish I could give you some of my toughness! . . . Your children will all come out of any phases just as Bob has done. They are such grand people but then you and Henry have been wonderful parents!
>   My dear love, I must run to some W.P.A. projects!

> Elinor dearest,
>   —more love than I can tell you,
>   Devotedly, E.R.

There are only a few letters at the library from Elinor herself. Library archivists speculate that Elinor often used the phone, wanting to hear her friend's voice. Yet in a note hinting at her insecurity, she apologizes for inundating Eleanor with correspondence. Where this correspondence is and what it contained remains a mystery:

Eleanor dearest,

I don't mean to be deluging you with letters, for I just wrote last night, but I must send another word after reading the wonderful news of Elliott [Roosevelt] receiving the Flying Cross. I can't tell you how happy I am it is almost as if one of my own boys had been so honored.

Devotedly,

Elinor

The more I learned of Bob's mother, the more I understood him, and the more I realized that we were both cheated of the maternal nurturing we could have had if our mothers had not been such needy women.

I wouldn't have thought my mother had anything in common with Bob's mother until I compared Elinor's letters with those that I had found in a shoe box after Mother died. They were uniquely self-pitying but also similarly lacking in self-esteem. Gram Leavitt was clearly a tough mother, short on nurturing. One letter, in fact, confirms the law that the kindness a grandmother shows her grandchild is proportionate to how horrid she has been with her own child.

October 30, 1934

Dear Mother,

I was sorry to hear that you won't let me come home for Thanksgiving. All the freshmen in my dorm are going home, I imagine the whole of Sweet Briar will be emptying out since it's a holiday and everybody will want to be with their families. I guess I'll just have to stay here alone.

. . . Have a swell time in Italy.

Lorraine

I remember another letter had made my hands go cold.

April 20, 1952

Dear Betty,

How is Kankakee? It is beautiful here, yards bright green framed by yews trimmed into perfect ovals. But did I tell you

*before? These New Englanders are cold customers. They don't
even return telephone calls . . .*

*I don't know what's wrong with Tom. You wouldn't recognize
him. After all these years, he's still like a zombie. I think it's the
war, he can't seem to get over it the way other men in Wellesley
have. He pays practically no attention to me. But I guess I shouldn't
complain because he loves our daughter, our gift child, our little
package who decided to arrive after my six miscarriages. I call her
"Daddy's Little Girl."*

Fond wishes to you all,
Lorraine (Mrs. Thomas E. Franks)

The bitterness behind her words could have curled the paper. She
was jealous. My mother was jealous of me. Her own mother had rejected her, and after I was born, once again, the love that belonged to
her was taken away and lavished on someone else. She must, in a way,
have hated me.

•

The more I discovered about Bob's childhood, the more pieces I found
that explained our strange attraction. He had been the balance wheel of
his family, the peacemaker, and of course this had been my role too.
Bob's political acumen, his sleight of hand, was forged in the house
where he grew up. Unlike my voluble environment, however, Bob's family rarely shouted; they simply stopped speaking to each other. Rather
than separating them, as I did, Bob's mission was to bring his family
together.

Bob had told me that from about twelve years old, Joan didn't talk to
their mother, so their mother didn't talk to Joan. As a result, his father
didn't talk to Joan either. His father, disappointed that he didn't play
sports and had no interest in the farm, also apparently ignored Henry.
Bob tried to get them all to reconcile, and sometimes it worked and
sometimes it didn't.

One day in the spring of 1937, Bob had gotten a call from his
mother. Joan, fifteen, was about to get kicked out of her fancy boarding
school, Madeira, for locking a girl who was bothering her in a cold
shower. Joan was estranged from her mother, so Bob, eighteen and

barely through his freshman year at Amherst, went down to the Virginia boarding school for Parents' Day and showed his diplomatic best to the principal, Miss Madeira. "She's sometimes a girl who is a little too enthusiastic, even rambunctious," he said earnestly, trying to mimic the body language of a man fully mature. "But she is a good girl, and I promise you that she will never ever do something like that again." Miss Madeira was so impressed with him that she spared Joan. On the way home, Bob was both angry at and amused by Joan. He identified with her rebelliousness and was intrigued that she had clearly come into her own, wild and kicking.

•

If I was unwittingly looking for someone like the father of my childhood, Bob seemed to be searching for a second wife *not* like his mother. His first wife, a Smith undergrad whom he began dating when he was at nearby Amherst, was a woman of her generation: as family oriented, reserved, and discriminating as Elinor. But by the time Martha died at the age of fifty-two, sexual stereotypes had changed. Women had careers; they were idiosyncratic and, to men like Bob, startling in their independence. He had his pick of these exotic feminists of the 1970s. Having been an editor of his college newspaper and always a frustrated journalist, he dipped into New York's vast river of female writers.

They weren't always suitable: there was a thirty-year-old scribbler whose conversation consisted of prattling on about friends who told friends things of stunning triviality; a beatnik in her forties with a messy apartment that smelled of old sneakers; a prominent author whose main activity consisted of making cards for her Rolodex containing the names and accomplishments of every person she met (upon which she promptly forgot about them).

Then he met me.

•

After our first non-date that blossomed into something of a saturnalia in June 1976, we stayed in my apartment and played house. When he was at work, we began speaking on the phone twice a day, and when he wasn't, we lit fat colored candles, listened to old Buffy Sainte-Marie albums, debated the Israeli raid in Entebbe, found farm-fresh vegetables, and bought sprigs of lavender so I could put them in the pillows. We liked making fresh hummus, dripping the oil into the blender and watching it whirl through the chickpeas and tahini.

Love creates itself from the tiny things that plant themselves in your memory. His sweet awkwardness when he first kissed me; the way he ends his jokes with that infectious laugh; his romance with food—watching him savor every bite long after others have finished and then start eating the leftovers from their plates; his pride in his two excellent baritone notes that make him break out in song at the most surprising moments; how he wakes me up at night by tickling my back; how I turn to see his handsome, mystifying face, his adorable smile like the sliver of a moon, how his dimples deepen and his eyes crinkle, a smile he saves for me, how our love is the love of two eccentrics.

I love when the sensitivities he hides so well suddenly spring up, the wet streak on his cheek when I recite the Statue of Liberty's inscription "Give me your tired, your poor . . ." or he hears a reading of Lincoln's Emancipation Proclamation. I love deeply his devotion to helping the downtrodden not only in words but in life-changing actions, the way he always takes the moral high ground no matter how strong the temptations are to do otherwise.

What does he love about me? He loves me, he says, because I am beautiful, I am daring, I am unpredictable, I am different and a little bit offbeat. I keep him on his toes and inspire him, and he enjoys the fact that being with me is like going on Mr. Toad's Wild Ride.

•

A month after we had started dating, Bob asked me home to dinner. This was perhaps the most significant step he had taken to declare his interest in me. Our common friends had confided in me that he had never brought his other girlfriends home so soon. I realized later that the invitation was primarily to see how his daughter Barbara, fourteen, and I got along.

I felt as if I were being brought home to meet his parents. Barbara was the most important responsibility in his life, and her opinion of me, though I didn't realize it then, was crucial.

His other children were not living at home. Bobby, nineteen, was away at Amherst College, and the two older girls, who were close to my age, had their own houses. Since Martha's death, he had tried to become all things to his youngest child: he knew the names of her teachers, knew that she talked to an imaginary squirrel, researched the type of skis she needed for their winter holidays together.

He would always take her calls. "There was this big, important conference at his office, and he suddenly excused himself," said Ken Conboy, his executive assistant at the DA's Office. "He was asking her about her new jeans, how they fit, what color they were, did she like them . . . The mayor was waiting on him. I was amazed."

•

The night of the dinner, I found that Barbara was a cute, lively girl, and I immediately took to her. She and her cousin Ellie Hirschhorn giggled helplessly through the London broil and baked potatoes. Even her father's look of warning could not stop them from cracking up. Initially, I was embarrassed into silence. Then it struck me how funny it must seem to a teenager, her ancient father bringing home a date who looked as if she could have been a college babysitter.

Well, I could hold my own here. "Why did the banana go out with the prune?" I asked loudly.

They stared at me as if I were from another planet. Finally, Barbara replied, "Okay, why?"

"Because he couldn't find a date!" I went into a paroxysm of laughter, and in spite of themselves they joined in. I could see the look of relief on Bob's face; he proceeded to smother his potato with sour cream and contentedly demolish his steak.

•

As the glories of age and youth converged, we had, in a sense, taken custody of each other. I exposed him to my world: concerts in the park, offbeat plays at the Cherry Lane Theatre. He exposed me to the excitement of murder trials and exclusive art auctions, where we looked for the works of painters collected by his forebears and became addicted to the lightning-fast honeybee drone of the auctioneer, taking as a bid the swipe of a fingertip across someone's nose.

From the start I wanted to be wherever Bob was, so I went to every political event. They were, at first, horrifying.

•

*The hall smells of perspiration and male pheromones . . . dark suits scatter
like ants, foraging alone. Each ant for himself. Bob comes in, and they
line up to devour him. Invisible hands brush my fingers, greeting me
invisibly. Who could I be but someone's girlfriend du jour . . . an obsta-
cle to men of purpose. The eyes on the tops of their heads scan the room
for more important prey. Ah, there's the light, just beyond. They push
past me to get to it, link antennae, make deals, seal them with hearty
handshakes.*

*Those who have walked away from me do not know that I am the
light, the most important predator in the room, the one who with a stroke
of the pen could leave their careers in ruins. Yet I stand alone as though
the room were empty, a thistle among the birds of paradise.*

*Thankfully, Bob's arm shoots out from the crowd to gather me in. At
times, I try to slip away and hide in a waiter's nook or linger in the ladies'
room, but he always finds me.*

•

"Introduce yourself! Tell people who you are, give them your byline.
They'll talk to you then."

"I'd feel like an impostor."

"What?"

"I mean an operator," I replied. In truth, I could hardly operate myself. Lucinda the hard-driving reporter inevitably became Lucinda the
pimply pubescent. These were bigger, more distinguished parties than I
had ever been a guest at. I was terrified of what might come out of my
mouth. Not that it even mattered, for I made his colleagues uncomfortable with my miserable habit of looking through them instead of at them.
I would study the ways their hands moved, the sets of their mouths, the
angles they held their hips, anything that told me who they really were.
When I was expected to respond to their questions, I just stood there
frozen-tongued, because I hadn't heard a word they'd said. They would
drift off, even flee, for I reminded them of someone peeking through
the blinds before they were fully dressed.

"The problem is that I can't make small talk," I said.

"It's easy. Listen." He proceeded to arm me with an arsenal of amusing stories that I never could remember. "Then talk about the weather, the ambience, the speakers, the balloons," he said. If I didn't know someone, I was to avoid discussing politics, because I could be talking to the man I was talking about. If I did know him, I wasn't to ask how his work was going, because he might have been fired that morning; nor about his wife, because she could have just asked him for a divorce.

I gradually learned the rules, reined in my bare face, and acquired the refinements of the superego. That's when I began to find the events dreadfully boring and simply stopped going.

•

My turn to help Bob came when we were in jarringly noisy environments. Not only was he deaf in the right ear, but he had diminished hearing in his left; as with my father, the nerves were damaged when big war guns went off beside him. If I thought he had not understood someone, I would whisper or mouth out the words.

And then I did what no one else could do: I persuaded him to say farewell to the commodious suits of his tall, much larger-boned father. We went to Bloomingdale's Men's, and because his attention span for shopping was so limited, we bought four suits in half an hour. To everyone's astonishment, he showed up more like Maurice Chevalier without a hankie peeking from his pocket. "If you had dressed like that in 1970," cracked his good friend and gubernatorial campaign manager, Pierre Leval, "you would have been governor now."

•

For us, being in love fell wide of sheer enchantment. We suffered anxieties and second thoughts. There was the contradiction in how we lived, for instance. I loved my little rental apartment in Manhattan, my five pairs of jeans, four turtlenecks, three blouses, and two skirts. I loved the fact that this was all I had. Bob, on the other hand, took pleasure in his spacious home in the elite New York neighborhood of Riverdale, his acres of fruit orchards in the Hudson Valley, his Volvo, his thirty-two-foot fishing boat, and his Border collies. He had a six-inch mattress and a maid to tighten up his linen sheets. I had a comforter wadded up at the end of a futon that Roger found propped up in the street.

We both knew that life together was a strong possibility, though the complications would be so great, the differences so vast, we avoided talking of it. I went cold even thinking about it.

·

I will have to wear pumps. Style my hair. Put on relics of my adolescence, like skirts and horrid tight panty hose. My legs, not my finest asset, will get cold. A little pocketbook will dangle from my wrist. I will peek longingly through heavy drapes at marchers passing by, protesting the multitude of things still wrong with our country—the thousands of homeless, the disenfranchised, de facto segregation. They would all leave me behind. The high of a long day yelling myself hoarse would never again be mine. What else would you expect of me, my love? Would my lifestyle turn over on itself? Am I to be a homemaker, a stepmother to five, a decoration on the arm of a public official? Do people become how they act and not in a dinosaur's age? Does your behavior, if you change it, quite quickly and subtly rework you inside?

·

When I brought up the possibility of marriage to my closest relatives and friends, they only magnified the things I was most afraid of. "What will you do when he's seventy-five?" asked my beloved eighty-nine-year-old grandmother. I had visions of pushing wheelchairs and finding lost canes . . . or one day discovering my deepest love had left forever without being able to say goodbye.

But when he came into my presence, like sun through a rainfall, these ugly visions would vanish. He was young, vigorous, my savior. He would be supporting *me*, this man who was able to finally anchor me to the ground. I couldn't imagine him any other way.

Ironically, our attraction to each other was related to the chasm of time. Bob had rounded a corner and stumbled into the neoteric, into an existence he thought was no longer attainable: a fresh moment, another chance at surprise. Was he up to it? Would having a young wife befuddle him? The men of his generation were largely servants of their age, impervious to change, too old to start again, even if they wanted to. But Bob was an incongruity. Once we had a gathering of his neighbors, and one of his older daughters, Anne, asked, "How does it feel, Daddy, to be so much younger than all these people who're your own age?"

Within his young body was an old soul, and I was drawn to its harmony. What a refreshing change from Roger! He did not try to control or mold me, his credo being that if you told someone not to do something, he or she would go and do it anyway. Of course he followed the credo himself; anybody who tried to tell him what to do or what to say went to hell and back.

4

"So tell me about your past, your sex life," I said as we were walking over the rough cobblestones of SoHo. I cringed. No, it hadn't seemed the right thing to say just after I'd said it. Was I testing him? Seeing if he would give up his sense of delicacy in order to get with my way of being? The question was simmering; I felt compelled, driven even, to ask it.

He was taken aback. I probably was too blunt. But how else could I have brought up the subject, which, after several months together, we bloody well should have shared before? And after he, who on a first date that I didn't even know was a date, had almost pushed down my door to get at me? Hadn't I waited long enough to find out who else had been the object of his rabid appetites?

"I mean, let's start with how *many* you've slept with?"

He gave me a wintry look.

"It's a perfectly legitimate question! At the *Times*, I was told you had bedroom eyes." I smiled encouragingly.

"Pure rumor," he replied, laughing.

"I've also heard you've gone through women like wine."

He gazed up at the buildings. "Look at this architecture," he said, the November winds almost blowing off his tweed cap, surely a relic from some ancestor.

"Every building different, gargoyles, mansard roofs, gables, pillars. Incidentally, these cobblestones are really Belgian block, they . . ."

I squeezed his hand. "Bob, we've shared everything else. Why won't you answer me about sex?"

"It's my business." I saw a hint of a smile. "If you're so eager to talk lovemaking, why don't you tell me about yours?" he asked.

"Okay, sure. Let's see . . ." I made a show of counting on my fingers. "I'd say I've been to bed with about forty lads."

It took a minute for him to get that I was joking.

"Oh, it hasn't been a lot really. They're not worth mentioning. You know about Roger, and maybe I should tell you about the two famous older men I went with."

"Yes, you should," he said, suddenly interested now.

We were getting near this old café I knew, a remnant of the Beat days. The sun had risen above us, hot. He had taken off his cap, and his hair floated in the air like strands of silver.

"They were national icons. I think you would have done the same thing in my place."

"Undoubtedly," Bob said. "A once-in-a-lifetime opportunity."

I was feeling brave now, even loving this. Gone was his deadpan expression. He was a challenge unlike any I had encountered; I couldn't ruffle him, until now.

I whispered in his good ear. "*Nobody*, not a single person, has ever made me happier than you do in *every* way." And that was the truth.

•

We had finally reached the literary coffeehouse; trudging up a steep flight of listing stairs, he bounced on ahead of me, taking two steps at a time when he reached the top. Pretty lively for a fifty-seven-year-old.

We squeezed through the narrow room, taking stools at a little round table. The ceiling was an elaborate design of beige-painted iron, and on the bare plaster hung crooked photographs of poets from the late 1950s.

"Look, there's Philip Whalen and William Burroughs, and I think over there, that one is of Lawrence Ferlinghetti. I went to his City Lights bookstore in San Francisco once. Have you read *A Coney Island of the Mind?*" I deepened my voice, rolled out, "I have heard a siren sing at One Fifth Avenue . . ."

•

He's not listening, not even looking at me . . . he looks disheartened. Shit. I blew it. You're not like men of my generation, Bob Morgenthau. When I

told Roger about my past, he just smirked and tried to one-up me. But
you, I can't tell you about things like sex without your getting offended.
What else do you consider so private you can't talk about? What else can't
I tease you about? Nothing can ruffle you, I thought, but I was wrong.
You are sensitive, and I didn't see it. Why did I have to open my big
mouth? I made you feel unsafe with me.

•

"All those guys . . . sleeping around . . . it, it meant nothing," I said, suppressing the urge to reach out and touch him. I couldn't stand it if he re-
buffed me. "Look, my generation, a lot of people, we felt like we'd grown
up in prison cells, and when we were old enough to break out, we just
did. We broke every rule we could, including sex. We were drunk on
freedom.

"But I don't expect you to accept that," I added. "My generation is
not yours . . . I was insensitive."

"You're young, I'm old," he said finally. "I've never gotten so close to
someone so different."

"But I'm not that girl anymore. I was sending her up. I've changed."

"You know, I'm old enough to be your father. Maybe you'll feel
about me like you felt about your parents."

"Of course not. You're not exactly a jailer," I said, and then laughed.
"Well, I guess you are. But not with me.

"Besides, I'm sick of chaos; I want structure," I half lied.

We suddenly heard a trilling voice. Up on the café stage, a slight
man with a ponytail and a voice like Tiny Tim got up and read Allen
Ginsberg's "Howl," the intense obscenity-filled poem emblematic of both
the 1950s and the 1960s. The reader had passion and, unfortunately, a
lisp.

"Who let themthelfs be fucked in the ath by thaintly motorthyclists
and thcreamed with joy."

I looked nervously at Bob, but he was suppressing a smile. "I'll take
you to a better place next time," I said.

"No, I thought that was a howl."

I sighed; he had forgiven me. "You're always such a good sport. I
mean, it wouldn't matter if I took you to see an aqueduct, you'd think it
was great." We were sharing smoked oysters on saltines.

"Nothing about you is uninteresting. We're compatible."

"Why?"

"I don't know. I can't dissect the reasons."

"Try, or I won't believe you."

"Because we both like chocolate," he said, digging in the bag of truffles we had picked up at Li-Lac, the best chocolatier in the city.

"No, come on, be serious."

"I loved that Indian rug you wore when I met you."

"Very funny. It was a white knit poncho!"

"Whatever it was, you're different. I like how you think, and I like those fringes and bright colors you wear."

"I can't imagine why. You hate showiness."

"And you have a strong sense of morality. I like that."

I slipped my fingers between his. To the pulse of a dark Anne Sexton poem, I watched him eyeing the room. Looking for one of the dozens of mafiosi he had jailed? Protecting me as he protected so many others—his family, his employees, the poor and underprivileged.

People are like the houses they build. When asked to tell their stories, most stick to the bare beams, but others happily rev themselves up until they are describing elaborate pillared mansions. Bob was a beam man. But I had already done my due diligence and put in the walls. I had parsed out his childhood by looking through the *Times* "Morgue" and picking up tidbits from friends and acquaintances we had in common. I suspected that he had drawn a similar bead on me.

But I wanted more. What about his youth, his early career? What kind of a human being had he been? Would he be too modest to tell me about his achievements? Too reticent to admit his failures? Would he talk at all?

"So," I said, trying to act blasé. "I hear you pretty much knocked out Tammany Hall when you were first in office." Which was 1961, when President Kennedy had appointed him U.S. attorney of New York.

"I'm not *that* old," he said, frowning at me over his glasses. "Tammany Hall was gone by that time, only a few remnants left."

"But Charlie Buckley was a powerhouse remnant, and I hear you gave him the proverbial finger," I said with a smile.

"You know who Charlie Buckley was?" he asked, surprised.

I gave him a withering look. Since my first embarrassing interview with him in 1973—he didn't get the courage up to ask me out until three years later—I had done my homework on U.S. political history. "I hear he was a friend of Wright Patman," I quipped, and was rewarded with an appreciative smile.

"Then you know Buckley was one of the last bosses in the Democratic machine—Bronx congressman, Bronx Democratic county leader, and head of the congressional Committee on Public Works, and that was a patronage bonanza.

"A group of us new young Democrats were trying to end the Bronx machine system that was still under the control of powerhouses like Charlie Buckley and crooks like Carmine De Sapio."

"You were a social troublemaker. Kind of like me."

"Buckley got me back," he continued. "When Jack Kennedy won the presidency, he used his influence to hold up my appointment as U.S. attorney for three months. Then he tried to move right in. On my first day in office, it was January 1961, I got a call from his crony Jim Healey, another immensely influential congressman, pressuring me to hold up the indictments of two constituents who'd been selling shrimp from China—this was against the Trading with the Enemy Act. He said, 'Kick it around for six months, Morgenthau. That's what your predecessor did.' So I looked the case up, and indeed, just as it was about to go to the grand jury, the former U.S. attorney had pulled it six different times, forcing the investigation to be started all over again."

"Don't tell me, you laughed in his face."

"I put the case before the grand jury and got an indictment within forty-eight hours." He started chuckling. "Healey called me screaming: 'Damn you, Morgenthau, why couldn't you have waited thirty days so I could collect my fee!'"

"Weren't you afraid of all these Buckleyites? They could have squashed you under their feet."

"Huh," he grunted. "After I'd been hit by German bombs and sunk in the ocean and shot down Japanese suicide pilots, I wasn't about to let a Charlie Buckley kick me around."

I pursed my lips to hide a smile. I had goaded him into it, but still, he was enjoying trying to impress me. He was building the mansion, connecting the crossbeams of his legendary success. And most delightful, he was the kind of storyteller who could keep you enthralled by his

own stories simply because *he* was so enthralled. He was not so different from other men who, no matter what their station, gloried in their
victories.

How could he do all this talking while simultaneously eating? In
fact, I thought, he elevated his enjoyment of food to a political skill. I
watched, fascinated at his gustatory ballet—bite, bit of story, bite, more of
story. I saw how he could command the attention of a table, keeping his
listeners in suspense.

"Even Bobby Kennedy"—chew—"was obligated to Buckley for his
support of JFK. He was JFK's attorney general then"—chew—"and he
didn't dare come to my swearing in."

"Amazing. You were close to him; you were with him when he got
the news his brother had been assassinated! What was that day like for
you, by the way?"

He pushed his plate away and speared an untouched oyster from
mine. "I was stunned. I didn't know what was happening. There had
been nothing like that before in my lifetime. We all thought that it was
a conspiracy. It could have been the Russians, the Cubans, the Republi-
cans, the Texans, none of us knew. We were afraid of who would be
next. After Oswald was shot, Bobby ran around for months trying to find
out who really was behind it."

We were both silent, and then I asked, "Did Bobby pressure you on
behalf of Buckley?"

"Shhh. Your voice is too loud."

I narrowed my eyes. "Guess why?" I felt like saying. Everyone I have
loved has been hard of hearing. I had to scream at my beloved grandmother, blast like a bugle at my deaf father, and now here was Bob, with
a single working ear. Once again, I sounded like a PA system.

I mischievously repeated the question in a near whisper.

"What?"

I repeated it again, loud and, by now, hoarse. I was destined to go
through life sounding like a tree frog.

"Yes, Kennedy put the arm on me back in 1967," he said quietly.
"He was just a senator from New York at that stage, and he called me
about my indictment of Louis Wolfson. Wolfson was a crooked financier and big contributor to the Democratic Party, but Bobby told me,
'Bob, Stanley High, the mayor of Miami, is a friend of ours, and High is

a friend of Louis Wolfson, and Wolfson wants his case transferred to Miami.' Bob looked at me as he continued his story:

"And Bobby was firm. 'You could do that,' he said.

" 'No I can't.'

" 'Why not?' Bobby asked. He had gotten a little edgy.

" 'Because he wouldn't get a fair trial, he would fix the judge,' I replied.

"Then Bobby said, 'Be serious.'

" 'I am perfectly serious,' I said.

"After that, I began getting calls at least once a week from the assistant attorney general in charge of the Criminal Division, accusing me of 'abusing' Wolfson.

"I ignored them," Bob said. "And in 1967 and 1968, we ended up convicting Wolfson of security violations, perjury, and obstruction of justice."

"That's amazing, but what I can't believe is that you were so young and new in the job and you dared defy a Kennedy! Kennedys are known for never forgetting. How did you dare?"

He thought about it and then he laughed softly and said, "I guess I did have a lot of balls."

.

His second order of smoked oysters arrived, and that made him even happier, examining a plump brown mollusk and swiping it up. It made me remember the moment I fell in love with him. I woke to see him bent over a skillet in my Pullman kitchen, ascertaining that the pancakes he was making for me would be perfect.

And then I suddenly smelled waffles and remembered Daddy's delight as he lifted the lid and found that the one he'd made for me was perfectly, evenly brown. I was happy on those Sundays, truly happy, because he was happy. The rest of the time he was serious and secretive, as though hiding something. Well, he was. For one thing, screwing another woman. Would Bob do the same to me? How could I know?

"There's something I want to ask," I said hesitantly. "Did you ever do something big on the sly? Something you had to hide from your friends . . . your wife?"

He looked at me appraisingly. "I might have."

"Some clandestine affair?"

"Two of them."

I could feel the flush creep up my neck. Was he telling me he had cheated on his wife, twice?

"There was Abe Fortas."

"A man!"

"*The* Man, one of the greatest men, or so everyone thought. He was revered; he'd been nominated by President Johnson for chief justice of the Supreme Court in 1968. What people don't know is that I was the one who discovered that Wolfson was paying him twenty thousand dollars a year for life. I worked hard behind the scenes to get him off the court."

I gave a silent sight of relief.

"Then, the second thing was I found out that Arthur Goldberg was"—Bob stopped to dip his napkin in water and dab a spot off his shirt—"an unwitting spy.

"During World War II he was a captain in the OSS and had an affair with a female who he didn't know was a Soviet courier. She became a witness and helped us make a case against Robert Soblen, who was a leading member of the Soviet spy ring.

"We never made it public. I didn't think it was right to crucify a man for a crime he didn't know he was committing."

"Very noble," I said with a tinge of irony not lost on Bob. The truth was I was starting to wonder if I should be amused or put off by the self-congratulatory tone of his anecdotes.

"Maybe 'noble' isn't the right word. It's just that I was wondering who influenced you, who made you a man with such high values. Besides your father, of course."

"Judge Robert Patterson," he answered without hesitation. "He had been secretary of war from 1945 to 1947, and later joined the law firm Patterson, Belknap & Webb. He hired me right out of Yale, and I soon went from being his clerk to his right hand. I researched and wrote drafts of letters and briefs.

"He was an independent Republican, but we took loyalty cases when no big lawyer in New York would touch them—they were too afraid of the McCarthy hearings. We represented Edward G. Robinson, who had been blacklisted by the entertainment industry."

Bob gently put down his fork. "Talk about noble, Patterson wouldn't even take clients if he smelled a whiff of guilt. He'd shun the fancy restaurants and eat at the Automat with the people. I modeled myself after him. He liked me, and he liked to have me travel everywhere with him.

"Commerce tried to bring a physicist in front of the Loyalty Review Board. I defended that physicist. And I won."

Of course he won. Did this man ever seriously stumble? I knew of only one instance. He had developed three corruption indictments against Roy Cohn and failed to get a single conviction. That was not a good record against a rabid Communist hunter who with his boss, Senator Joe McCarthy, had ruined countless lives in the 1950s.

"Ah, I was wondering about your indictments against Roy Cohn. The newspapers said you were out for vengeance because he investigated your father."

"He did *not* investigate my father. That's a gross distortion," he said, scowling at me. "There were reasons we never got a conviction on Cohn. The first trial ended in a hung jury, and at the second trial we were pretty sure Cohn or one of his cronies got to one of the jurors.

"You know Bobby Kennedy tried to stop me from prosecuting Cohn, while the *grand jury* was deliberating. I was on vacation in Martha's Vineyard, and he summoned me to Hickory Hill on Labor Day weekend."

The way Bob uttered the rather precious name of Bobby's Virginia estate, enunciating every syllable in his crisp, provocative voice so that it sounded as if he were poking fun at Bobby without doing it at all, got me laughing so much, I swallowed the wrong way and had a coughing fit. I decided I couldn't care less if Bob was the hero of all his narratives. He was priceless.

"Bobby said a columnist had accused me of persecuting Cohn. I laid out the evidence against him—bribery, conspiracy, and blackmail. By that time, Bobby knew I wouldn't follow orders. So he just sighed and told me to do whatever I thought was right. The grand jury deliberated for sixty seconds before they brought in an indictment."

"Then at trial there was a hung jury," I said sympathetically.

He nodded. "But you know I convicted Carmine De Sapio. And I wiped out a lot of the Mafia—operatives of the Bonanno and Lucchese families—as well. A lot of gangsters."

"That's extraordinary," I said.

"President Roosevelt was a huge influence on me. I hate to hear people say he should have bombed the Nazi concentration camps and done this or done that. He had a war to win. And he transformed this country.

"When he died, I was stationed out on a destroyer, and I cried for the first time in my adult life."

"He was your friend. He was family."

"He was my commander in chief," Bob said with finality.

I got goose bumps, the way he had said those words: duty and sacrifice before anything else. He was the kind of man they didn't make anymore. I pushed my plate of smoked oysters toward him: "You have the rest."

The man across from me was for real. Many have the intention to do good, but Bob Morgenthau had actually succeeded. The politicians I had interviewed, with their fishy faces and well-oiled egos, would never be in his league.

I had a shiver of recognition. Today he was a fine man, but someday he would be a great one. Would he want to marry me? The thought was terrifying. How could he choose a rebellious, insecure kid with a veneer of bravado? I would be a poor political asset, even a liability. Did I even have what it took to stand by him, to put myself aside and help him achieve his destiny?

•

My apartment was so cold when I returned home that I put the oven on, wrapped myself in Aunt Kit's afghan, and watched the dazzling orange sun as it dropped below the horizon. It had been a lovely interlude between us, but then a web of cracks spread over the gloss. The magic was gone.

When we had left the café, I followed Bob down the stairs, feeling warm and loving, missing the shadow that had fallen over him. Then he rather rudely pushed through the door ahead of me, letting a blast of wind hit my face. Something had pissed him off. Was it that I had brought up Roy Cohn? Or all the men I'd been with—was he resentful, or did he think it in bad taste? Either one, I had gotten my first hint of his exquisite sensitivity.

Outside, the sun had lost its brilliance. Grumbling about the lack of taxis in this woebegone place, about feeling tired, he seemed like an ordinary man in baggy pants wanting his nap.

That evening, having seen this new petulance in a man whom I thought as unflappable and gentlemanly as my father, I decided there were many sides to Bob. Did I miss, for instance, a certain vindictive streak? Did he always use his power for good, or at times was he motivated by a personal animosity?

I knew who he had been as a child, as a youth, but what about afterward? I only knew his public persona by reputation. He wasn't the mea culpa confessional type; in fact, though I did encourage him to brag, today he had portrayed himself as the hero of all his stories. But was he? And did I have the moral right to find out? To muckrake about a man I was devoted to?

I had butterflies all afternoon. But then, when the gloom of evening descended, I couldn't help myself. I picked up the phone.

I called my friend the book publisher Victor Temkin, a Morgenthau devotee. At first, he parried my questions but finally admitted, "Let me put it this way: I'd hate to have Bob Morgenthau for an enemy.

"He's always known where the bodies were buried," Victor added. "He liked to say, 'Never get mad, just get even.'

"Look, Bob could intimidate you. Just being in his presence was scary. But his independence and defiance of the status quo was mind-blowing. People thought the Boss was God, they had been given a tremendous chance in life, they came out of his office with their knees shaking."

Their knees shaking? Mine hadn't. Yet.

I was more than curious now about the Cohn controversy, so I called Bill Safire, the *Times*'s famous conservative columnist and Roy's pal. "There's no doubt in my mind that Roy was hounded by Morgenthau and that afterward Cohn was never the same again," Safire said flatly. "He is a loyal and a kind man and a great lawyer. He's been tortured. Ruined by these indictments. I'd suggest you look at the October issue of *Commentary*. A very interesting article by Irving Younger . . . he witnessed Morgenthau's persecution of Roy precisely because he was part of it."

I got hold of *Commentary*, which had become a neoconservative magazine, and found a long mea culpa article by Younger, confessing that he had been used by a spiteful Morgenthau as a tool "to get Roy Cohn."

He wrote how Morgenthau had summoned him with a buzzer that

linked their two desks. In Morgenthau's office was the attorney general, Robert Kennedy, who seemed as enthusiastic about bagging Cohn as Morgenthau was. Younger said Morgenthau appointed him to lead the investigation and then sent him to Zurich on a complicated goose chase involving machinations with other parties who he hoped would help corner Cohn. The article went on to list a number of the Boss's misuses of prosecutorial power in pursuit of his quarry.

I put the magazine down, shaken. But I smelled a rat. Bob had told me Bobby Kennedy, far from encouraging him to go after Cohn, had tried to *stop* him.

I called Arthur Liman, who had been one of Bob's big guns at the U.S. Attorney's Office, to get his opinion on Younger's narrative. "It's full of outright lies and exaggerations and preposterous conclusions about Mr. Morgenthau's integrity. A lot of assistants and members of the Justice Department can't believe it was published. Younger makes up a good story about a noxious office none of us recognize."

There were those who thought the law's pursuit of Cohn, on any pretext, was justified. "He was the greatest scoundrel of the twentieth century," declared my friend Dorothy Samuels, who worked at the ACLU and would later become a *New York Times* editorial writer. "Bob Morgenthau could have indicted him three more times as far as I'm concerned. He'd wave his arms against homosexuals while being gay himself; he was evading taxes, taking bribes, you name it. Meanwhile, he made himself a celebrity, throwing these lavish parties for everybody from Norman Mailer, Abe Beame, Andy Warhol, to men like Carmine De Sapio."

Okay. So yes, Bob's assistants refuted the Younger accusations, and yes, people hated Cohn, but I felt as if this were just scaffolding. What was the inner story of Bob Morgenthau and Roy Cohn?

Victor was always good for the rich stuff. I invited him to lunch at the Oyster Bar at Grand Central Terminal. He was a former assistant. And he was also the kind of person so brusquely honest he'd give you answers to questions you wished you hadn't asked.

He was a character: a handsome, stocky, and ebullient figure who got on his stationary bike and pedaled furiously for two hours a day. He ordered a salad, which he picked at as we chatted. I finished my popcorn shrimp, and then, twisting a bottom corner of the checkered tablecloth, I asked the question. "Was there any serious mistake you think the office made? Like Roy Cohn. Was he plagued?"

Victor started to shake his head, but then he looked away.

Finally, he turned to me. "I think we *did* go too far with Cohn," he said. "Sil Mollo tried to convince him to stop, but Bob just hated Cohn, just *hated* him. His motto was 'prosecute without fear or favor,' but I think he stretched things with Roy."

I let out my breath. So Bob wasn't perfect. He had told me he didn't want to crucify Arthur Goldberg, but according to some he had crucified Roy Cohn. Bob was human, maybe even as human as I was. And that made me love him even more.

It was time to change the subject. "So do you miss the office?" I asked cheerfully. "What was it like working there?"

"Oh Lord, we were a motley crew from all over the place," he said, laughing. "There were Irish Americans, Italian Americans, German Americans. Sil Mollo, his chief deputy, was a shrewd, diminutive man who looked a little like a muskrat and wore white short-sleeve button-down shirts. Arthur Liman, with his rumpled suits and hair half tumbling down his narrow forehead, had not only brilliance but, like Bob, total recall. He went on to become a prestigious criminal lawyer, you know; he shone as chief counsel to the Senate committee investigating the Iran-contra affair.

"Bob once crowed that Liman could 'take a witness's socks off, leaving his shoes still on and securely tied.'"

I laughed. "What was he like when Kennedy appointed him, when he first came in as U.S. attorney?"

"He did the complete opposite of what was expected. Instead of hiring the white-shoe boys from Yale and Harvard, he'd take hungry imaginative students of minor law schools like St. John's in Queens, train them relentlessly, and set them free. I was just a kid from the boondocks of the Middle West!"

Under Bob's direction, Victor went on, they wiped out the torpid traditions of previous U.S. attorneys who had given free passes to crooked lawyers and big financiers who should have been indicted for tax fraud or corruption. With the approval of the new Kennedy administration, Bob's office took away the virtual immunity enjoyed by the high and mighty. His closest employees, like Steve Kaufman, Pierre Leval, and Frank Thomas, ran circles around them.

"He was aloof to the disgruntlement of the lesser guns," Victor explained. "They complained that he played favorites, and he did. He worked the city making alliances while he groomed his best assistants to become judges, partners in law firms, heads of corporations. When they were ready to move on, they could do just about anything they wanted.

"My gosh, half the judges in Manhattan owe their posts to him!" Victor spoke exuberantly. "The office became so famous that Bob could move mountains. How do you think I became head of Bantam Books? Bob gave me a lifestyle I never would have had otherwise.

"We were paid less than fifty thousand dollars a year, but we were so cocky we helped him develop the prosecution of white-collar crime like it had never existed before. Lucinda, the office was a playground! And it was filled with a panorama of nobodies who would one day be known as among America's best and brightest.

"There was nothing like it," Victor said wistfully, pushing away his plate. "Nobody like *him*, before or after."

5

I love you, love you, love you.

For the last month, we had said the words, acted out the words, immersed ourselves in their meaning. If we separated for a day or two, we began to get that strange hollow sensation, like people who are thirsty before they know it. It was just too much being together and too much being apart. It was early January 1977, and we had been together for about seven months.

When he was hospitalized for one of his particularly stubborn ear infections, our separation was unbearable, so we wheeled his IV into the bathroom and shut the door, an experience all the more sweet for the imminent possibility a doctor or nurse would come in. Later, he found an excellent ear specialist who pierced holes in his eardrums so any infection he got would drain out, thus ending a lifetime of misery.

As inextricable as we were, I had my own life, and Bob continued to accept it without complaint. He didn't say a word when I continued to put myself at risk by participating in agitprop demos with the Black Panthers, the White Panthers, the Purple Panthers, whomever, or hung out with the straggle of hippies left over from the early 1970s. Truthfully, no one paid attention to us. After the war ended, we lost support. Unless they're bleeding, Americans are too lazy for outrage. And we had already managed to engender change in the culture: blacks and women gained some rights; people were less repressed, lived freer, and even truer, lives.

But living in the real world, loving Bob and watching how he changed the culture in his own quiet way, had affected me. As I joined feminist "Take Back the Night" vigils and I lit straw dummies representing

President Ford, I began to feel embarrassed. Feminism was worth fighting for, long overdue, but nice old Ford wasn't worth putting a match to. He wasn't a fascist. It was the hardened and by the way *sexist* revolutionaries of my generation who were the true fascists now.

My friends and I had believed in absolute simplicity, the workability of the pure idea, but man is just a tiny step above the animal, and the mores and restrictions of society that we have been battering against probably hold us together. The circular nature of life lets us change the world very little. The Weathermen, who threw homemade bombs at empty banks, corporation warehouses, military offices, did not move forward in a straight line; they moved in a spiral, coming no closer to overthrowing the establishment than they did when they began.

We had been simpleminded, so idealistic, so gullible.

·

At dusk, the diminished people sit
In caves and sing songs that are not heard until
The sun slips beneath them and they recede
To watch the birds tuck
Up their wings and drop like stones.

·

I had one or two friends left who were still true believers. Bob even agreed to visit them and sat eating tofu on a water bed, but when he came out of the bathroom, having had to wipe his hands on towels made of American flags, he looked dour. Though he didn't discourage me from visiting, he never went there again.

Nor did I. I didn't want to sleep on icy stone church floors anymore. I was ready to feel safe, sheltered. I wanted to get my grandma's Victorian bed out of storage and cover it with a Wedding Star quilt. I wanted to watch old movies, have roses on my table, and feel a familiar shoulder beside me on which to lay my head.

I knew that Bob, after five years of being unmarried, wanted this also. We lived like a couple, at my apartment, at Riverdale, and, since he had to have a Manhattan residence as DA, at a rental on Central Park West. We were in a marriage without being married. The question circled above us but was never asked. I naively fantasized: maybe he was trying to decide on a ring, or maybe he was worrying over where he should ask me. It could be in the bathtub, for all I cared, or in a noisy restaurant; he could even do it in his office while he was reading an indictment. Just so long as he did it.

But the question did not come.

Even his first wife's friends in Riverdale told me I had healed him. "You're strong, you're ebullient," said Nan Leneman, a family friend in Riverdale. "I've never seen him so animated. If he hasn't asked you to marry him yet, he had better do it."

But he didn't. He still didn't.

So, one day, I simply asked him. "Wanna go to Vegas and get married? We could honeymoon at Caesars Palace. Play the slot machines. Sleep in a round bed with black satin sheets and a mirror on top."

He laughed, then looked away. "We should do it, I know. Let me ask Barbara what she thinks."

•

You'd think he was marrying Barbara, for God's sake. But then . . . Barbara isn't just an ordinary child. She's extraordinary, because she's motherless. I know how lousy that feels. And I was an adult when my mom died last year, not a little girl. I can't imagine how it must have hit her, how confusing it must have been not to know, down deep, what dead even means. All you really know is that Mommy left you, not why. I didn't know why, really, it had happened to me. We were both of us too young to lose each other. But Barbara lost her mother when she was nine, and at that age the world is magical. Did she worry whether it was something she had done? And now, if he marries me, she'll think she's lost her father too.

•

A week went by, then two weeks, and Bob didn't mention marriage again. As hard as I knew this must be for him, I began to think that perhaps his youngest daughter was a blind. Maybe he loved me but didn't love me *that* much . . . or maybe he was simply terrified. I gave him the benefit of the doubt and decided he was terrified.

More time went by. He began saying he would ask her tomorrow, but tomorrow followed tomorrow until there was no tomorrow, only today.

We were walking in the park through the balmy spring air from the Great Lawn up to the Conservatory Garden to an abundance of yellow daylilies, scarlet peonies with their big black eyes, hollyhocks. I wanted to make a particularly good impression on him that day: I wore a white sundress cinched at the waist, and I had pinned my hair up in back, leaving strands to fall over my neck.

"Bob," I said as we sat under the bower of violet wisteria. I crossed my ankles and smiled up at him sweetly. "Could we discuss getting married, I mean really discuss the whole thing seriously? Decide some things."

"Not again. Can't we just enjoy ourselves? Look at the beautiful gardens?"

I swallowed back the tears. "You say 'not again' to me, even in the middle of all this beauty! I thought you were more romantic."

"I am a romantic; I'm very romantic in fact."

"Could we at least talk about your problem talking to Barbara about us?"

"I don't have any problem."

"Then you've talked to her?"

"Not yet. Give me some time."

"You've had lots of time. Listen, I'm a very simple and innocent person."

He made an exaggerated cough.

"I think in equations. One and one make two. If you love someone as deeply as we do, if you want to spend the rest of your life with them like we do, you just say, 'This is what I'm going to do.' And then take everything else as it comes."

He laughed and put a bloom of wisteria in my hair. "You're right."

"You can't romance me off this topic. It feels like you don't really care about me."

"I do, of course I do. It's just there's never been the right moment."

"What moment are you waiting for?" I said warmly. "The moment when she sits down and says, 'So how's Lucinda, Dad? When are you going to marry her?'" I turned my back so he wouldn't see my tears and went down the steps to the bright green lawn. He followed. I put my face in the fountain spray.

"I know what I'm doing," he said evenly. "Just get off my back."

"Get off your back? Get off *your* back! You know what you are? You know what I never realized? You are an emotional wimp!"

He looked dumbfounded, as though he hadn't the least idea what I meant.

I stormed off: "And I don't even know if I want to marry you anyway!"

•

For the next week, the phone rang and rang, and it sounded to me exactly like his ring, so I didn't answer it. Finally, the intercom buzzed. I picked it up and shouted, not too agreeably, "What!" But to my chagrin it wasn't Bob at all but an Irishman named Ted Smyth, the head of PR of the Irish consulate. I had met him on a story, and he was killingly handsome—lean, taller than Bob, thick dark hair, a big sexy smile—and he said clever things like "What is public relations? You throw out a bone and see who picks it up."

So I let him come in, and he promptly asked me to dinner. "Well, why the hell not?" I thought. The next night he took me to hear Irish music, which I love with a passion, and the following, he took me for a buggy ride in the park. The night after that, having reserved a table near the harpist at the Palm Court, we went to the Plaza for high tea. Afterward, we walked along the park, and he leaned over, his hair lit from the back by an old streetlamp, and kissed me. Then, in his fetching Celtic brogue, he whispered, "You're a fine thing, Miss Lucinda Franks."

For the next two weeks, I dated two *Times* men, one of whom I asked out myself, but mostly I went out with Ted. He was kind, romantic, and shared my love of Ireland, about which he talked incessantly. He knew things like the best Guinness (double X) and where to get it. And when I was with him, all I could think about was Bob, who had never taken me on a buggy ride or to hear Irish music, who thought the Plaza was for tourists, and who, next to Ted, was a scrawny old man.

One day, I was sitting chatting away with Mary Breasted when I noticed a cigar butt sticking out between her sofa cushions. It had been smoked down to a mere inch. I knew only one person who did that.

"Mary, what's this? Has Bob been here?"

Mary reddened.

"You've been seeing him, haven't you?"

"Just a couple times. It's nothing. We're friends."

"Right, well, you go right ahead and see him. I couldn't care less."

One lazy Sunday about a week later, I was lying back in my bean-bag chair, watching the sun twinkle on my fire escape, morosely day-dreaming about whether true love existed, when my five-alarm doorbell jolted me awake. I got up and looked through the peephole. I took a deep breath. It was Bob.

"I'm not here," I said.

"I understand you've been dating Ted Smyth," he replied through the door.

"It's a free country."

"Can I come in?"

"I don't know."

"I talked to her," he said. I could hardly hear him.

"Who? . . . Barbara? You talked to Barbara?"

"Yes."

I threw open the door. "I thought you didn't love me!"

He was grinning. "It's fine with her. She said, 'Okay, Dad, but if you get married, can I have a horse?'"

I hugged him. "She can have five horses," I said.

When I let him go, his smile dissolved to a frown. "I don't want any more nonsense with this Ted Smyth."

"Okay," I said, flipping my hand. "Will do . . . unless I find another cigar butt shoved into Mary Breasted's couch."

6

If there is anything harder than being the stepmother of children of divorce, it is being stepmother to children whose much-loved mother has died an untimely death.

Martha Pattridge was the daughter of a trade magazine publisher in Minneapolis and, like me, of Gentile heritage. The pictures placed around the house when I first visited show a handsome woman with the short curly brown hair of her son and a happy, grateful smile. Friends say she was kind and gracious but could also be diffident with those she didn't know. The family was close, doing the things that normal suburban families do: planting different kinds of roses round their white gabled house, swimming at the neighborhood pool, playing tennis at the Riverdale Yacht Club.

In 1969 she was diagnosed with breast cancer, had surgery, and was treated with chemotherapy and radiation. During her recovery, she hired Renia Hylton, a Jamaican housekeeper, to help her, and the stalwart woman became almost like a member of the family.

Barbara was born more than five years after their son, Bobby. Martha was devoted to her last baby, keeping the child close by her side, as if she had a premonition that she wouldn't have another chance.

Then, in the summer of 1970, when Barbara was seven years old, Martha's breast cancer came back. Friends told me she didn't tell Bob, she didn't tell the kids, she told no one about the recurrence because she didn't want to ruin their August vacation in the Vineyard, where they always rented a house. Bob had told me that Martha's mother had died of cancer and that she thought treatment would be futile.

When they returned in September, the disease had spread. She fought it for two years, then spent three or four months in the hospital. That is a long time in the life of a little girl. Barbara could not have fully understood what was happening, just that her mother was not there anymore and was very sick. Renia recounted that Martha called her youngest child a week before she died. "She said, 'You don't sound so good, Mommy,'" and that was the last time mother and child spoke.

On October 5, 1972, Martha died. When Bob came home from the hospital, his two youngest children, Barbara, almost ten, and Bobby, fifteen, had been waiting. Bob put his arms around both of them. "I'm sorry," he said, his voice breaking. It was the first time the children, who never forgot that moment, had seen him cry.

Bob went up to his bedroom, according to Renia, and seldom came out—a workaholic who didn't go to work, a sociable fellow who didn't socialize, a telephone addict who seldom answered the ring.

•

The last few years had been a cascade of misfortune. In 1969 he was fired by Nixon in the middle of investigating the president's hidden Swiss bank accounts; in 1970 he began to run for governor of New York for the second time but had to drop out when the Liberal Party said it would support Arthur Goldberg instead. After that, he declined a position at Patterson, Belknap & Webb. With his wife's breast cancer and harrowing posttreatment, he wanted to spend more time with her and the family. So he opened his own law office where he could make his own hours. Then, in October 1972, came the worst blow of all. Martha finally passed away. Some people thought he would never fully recover. A spirit of malaise pervaded the house in Riverdale. Barbara was, of course, stricken and depressed, but Renia wouldn't let her give in. She got her up every day and took her to her nearby grade school, Fieldston Lower.

When he finally began to leave the house after his wife's death, Bob frequently visited the Kaufmans, partly because he knew they would never mention Martha. Steve Kaufman, one of his chief deputies at the U.S. Attorney's Office, was a more outgoing, openly giving man, but in his avoidance of the personal, the emotional, he was Bob's twin. Steve knew he didn't want to talk about Martha and had told his wife, Marina, never to mention her name in front of Bob.

The only one who seemed open to talking about her, this woman whose loss had almost broken him, was Renia, who had become my best friend in the household. She was a self-deprecating woman in her late forties who referred to herself in the third person. A sterling housekeeper, a fine cook, and an old-fashioned Caribbean woman steeped in her culture's superstitions, she had been quietly cheering me on since the lily I brought her one Easter kept unaccountably blooming throughout the winter. To her it was a sign that I would be her new mistress.

As we sat in Riverdale one day, she told me more about the late Mrs. Morgenthau than perhaps I wanted to know: "You listen to me now, there is a ghost walking here, scaring poor Renia half to death. The curtains move, things aren't where they're supposed to be. Maybe she's looking for something, I don't know.

"That day, that terrible day for Barbara, it was clear out, completely clear, and suddenly rain came, and then the shower just ended, and I knew this was the moment Mrs. Morgenthau passed.

"Mr. Morgenthau is a fine man, but," she said, leaning toward me and lowering her voice, "he wouldn't let me put sheets over the mirrors. The dead don't like to see their reflections in the mirrors, you know; you've got to cover them for at least three days. Otherwise they never rest."

I loved Renia, but I excused myself and left the kitchen, feeling chilled.

·

I liked to dream about the little nest Bob and I would create, just the two of us, huddled against the cruelties of the world. Then, pop, the dream would disappear as I realized it wouldn't be that way at all. His twenty-nine-year union with his first wife had kept him busy. There would always be many other people in the nest, children I didn't choose and who didn't choose me.

If Bob had wished for a passel of attractive, intelligent, and talented children, he had gotten them. The third of the five, whom they named Elinor after Bob's mother, turned out to be severely mentally disabled. She had to be put in a special home in Rome, New York, when she was a toddler, and though Bob still went up to see her, she never recognized him.

Bob was steadfast, and, like his father and grandfather before him, he expected his children to be forever nearby. When they reached college age, he told them, "You can go anywhere you want, as long as it's within two hundred miles of New York City." And they complied. They all had gone to school in the adjacent state of Massachusetts. Jenny, at thirty-one, the oldest and in fact older than me, went to Smith. Annie, twenty-nine, to Radcliffe, and Bobby and Barbara to Amherst, their father's alma mater. When the two oldest girls got married, they came to the family home for dinner most Sundays, and two out of his four children ended up living nearby in Riverdale.

Bob often found them jobs, apartments, and even husbands. Annie, who worked for her father in the U.S. Attorney's Office, had met and married an assistant attorney named Paul Grand. Jenny's second husband was to be another former assistant U.S. attorney, Gene Anderson. Both men were bright, ambitious, and destined for success. And much older than their wives. Thirteen years older in Annie's case, and eighteen in Jenny's. Ironic, I thought, given the two daughters' later objections to their father's marrying a younger woman.

I first met Bob's oldest two children, Jenny and Annie, at his home in Riverdale, an enclave of the Bronx that reminded me all too well of Wellesley. Annie and Jenny were tall, slender girls, graceful as swans. Jenny had a magnetic, slightly roguish smile, and Annie was a fair-skinned beauty with her father's prominent aquiline nose. We were of the same generation, but the similarities seemed to end there. They clearly kept their own counsel. They were as self-possessed and contained as I was prone to revealing anything that came into my mind. I went into phobic mode. I had never been able to pull off being cool. Feeling gawky and artless, I chattered away nervously. They must have felt as if they'd entered the subway at rush hour.

At first, I was a question mark to Bob's youngest child, Barbara, but we became increasingly fond of each other. She was a delight: smart, honest, funny, with thick ginger hair and her dad's glowing, mischievous smile. I bought her a Siamese cat, whom she named Peter Rabbit, and we giggled together at his hilarious habit of jumping about the house like a hare. She was careful about being loyal to the mother she still loved, but sometimes she would let me take her shopping or pick her up at school. Much later, in her senior year of high school, we went white-water rafting on the Colorado River with a friend and her mother, crashing through waves by day and lying in the sand watching stars by night.

As I got to know the older girls, I grew to like them. Jenny, who was newly divorced, worked for underprivileged children in a city job. Annie, the mother of Hilary, five, and Noah, two, had once been freewheeling and independent at Harvard. I came to respect them for their similarities to as well as for their differences from me. Annie and I would talk one-on-one and laugh easily together. One time, she told me, "I'm glad that Daddy is finally dating someone who's real."

Barbara had a superb athletic body. A field hockey player, she fearlessly butted into her opponents and got butted back, scaring Bob, who was afraid she would get knocked out. She was also a runner, and I would sit with her siblings in the school bleachers at track meets, cheering wildly as she rounded the course, her legs spinning like wheels, her chest thrust out, a look of agonized perseverance on her flushed, sweat-drenched face.

On occasion, we talked about her feelings. She was often insecure—how could she not be, having lost her mother at such a vulnerable age—and complained that she wasn't any good at running. "You might not have come in first," I remember telling her, "but I thought you ran better than anyone else. Like a gazelle."

The other child based at home, Bobby, nineteen, was a sophomore at Amherst College. Physically, he resembled his mother with her thick brown curly hair, but his gestures and dry wit were all his father's. I had first seen him when I was a reporter and attended a celebration of Bob's 1974 DA election victory. Sticking out of the crowd was a voluminous dark Afro belonging to a lean young man with pale skin. I did a double take when I found out who he was; my respect for Bob, clearly a liberal father, grew exponentially. One day, this independent teen finally cut his hair down to a normal length, giving Bob secret relief.

Bobby had the integrity and sharp, discerning eyes of his ancestors. He was also an athlete, an expert skier who spent time working at the Alta, Utah, ski lodge. I admired his mathematical acuity and his ability to absorb and remember things as arcane as the net drag of a hurricane that occurred a decade before. A faded photograph of him still hangs on our wall; hair rising up three inches or so, he leans back, a contemplative look on his face.

As the only boy in the family, Bobby had a special status: Bob recounted how he always got the biggest slice of steak or the only ticket to the basketball game. After his mother's death, he grieved by retreating inside himself, but his father coaxed him out with a new and important responsibility. "Bobby, you've got to help me with Barbara," he said, and Bobby did. The two became close partners.

And then, suddenly, as if from a genie's bottle, I materialized and took his place. I was now the one at his father's side, absorbing all his attention, the one who took the bedroom next to his dad's, and he must have felt as if he'd been summarily dismissed. He accepted it grudgingly at first but then in time with grace.

At first, he was cool, but he never shunned me and gradually came to respond to my efforts to engage him. We liked to debate the merits of a news article or a current event, with Bobby automatically taking the opposite side. If I cited an Op-Ed piece giving evidence for Israel's rightfully belonging to the Israelis, whether he believed it or not, he would argue that it was called Palestine and was the homeland of the Palestinians. Being far more clever than I, to my secret delight, he would usually win the argument. I figured it wouldn't hurt him to one-up me.

The summer of 1976, I went to Martha's Vineyard with Bob and his children for the first time. We shared a big rambling house overlooking Menemsha Bay with the two youngest kids, Bobby and Barbara, and the mother's helper, who became a close companion to Barbara.

The house was always full. Jenny and Annie and her family came frequently. Our days were routine—breakfast, work, lunch, beach, showers, dinner. For me, the odd man out, it was rather like J. Alfred Prufrock measuring his life out in coffee spoons. This was Bob's time with his family; he seemed to have little time for me save an hour every afternoon when I would join him during his "constitutionals," an old piece of family humor that really meant he was taking a nap.

At night, the family would sit on the porch and eat lobsters, laugh, chat. I would watch them. They were having such a good time; I felt almost part of the fun, except that I didn't know what the fun was about: the family mythology, the cast of Vineyard characters. Bob and I had been so close but now he had detached himself.

On these crisp moonlit nights, one by one, everyone eventually made for their beds while I sat on a wicker chair and listened to the spit of toothpaste, the gargling of mouthwash, the mass flushing of toilets. We didn't want Barbara to get the wrong, or rather right, idea about us. So my bed (a cot, really) was officially downstairs until the house was silent and I would tiptoe up to join him.

One night, lost in an article on killer whales, I forgot to join him until an hour had passed. By then he was asleep. I put on my warm Lanz nightgown and gazed out the window at a full moon sending a fountain of light over sea and sky. It was irresistible. There was no choice but to meet the challenge. I went into a hidden pocket of my suitcase and got out a small bag of Nepalese hash, good relaxing stuff. Then I hesitated. I shouldn't be doing this. I would feel so guilty, it wouldn't even be fun. But then I thought about "Prufrock" again. My favorite poem, it had taught me not what I should be but what I shouldn't:

"Do I dare?" and, "Do I dare?"

I tiptoed downstairs and walked through the backyard until I reached the cliffs. Then I carefully made my way down through the rose hip bushes, dirt sliding, to a flat-headed rock. I lit a joint and inhaled deeply. Bob's two Border collies were watching me, sniffing curiously, keeping guard from the edge of the bluff. The sand below looked delicate and soft, peach-colored, like a baby's skin. The loneliness I felt was so profound it was like a dark rapture. I had bodysurfed during the day, and now the same waves had come up so strong they looked as if they could kill you. They rode in like stallions, manes flying, then suddenly broke, spilling over into a million pieces, routed, fooled, disintegrating, their ends a foamy nothingness. I was about to take out my pen and notebook when I heard an angry voice above.

"What are you doing down there! You'll fall," Bob shouted crossly. He was wearing his blue robe with the navy piping.

I scrambled up to the top.

"I've been looking all over the place!"

I put my shivering body against his. "I couldn't sleep. I didn't know you'd wake up. I wouldn't have frightened you for anything."

He softened and rubbed my shoulders as we climbed the stairs. "You're a fucking wild woman."

"Love your language," I whispered. The curses of the youth culture had rubbed off on him, at least now and then. Having been formidably fluent with swear words in the navy, he had refrained from bringing the impolite words home. Until now. When we argued, let the house be empty and "asshole!" in a basso profundo issued from the eaves.

"I suppose I can never expect you to act conventionally," he sighed.

My teeth were chattering; I had gotten colder than I thought. My nightgown was streaked with dirt. He wanted to put me in a hot shower, but I shook my head and put my icy hands under his nightshirt. He jumped.

He scowled but didn't move a muscle. Did I see a little glint of amusement? We took off our nightclothes, and, with salt on my face, frigid as an ice block, we made love as we never had before.

•

Wellesley, Massachusetts, had long ago closed its portal to Jews, and in my pure-blood secondary school I had been too intense, too emotional, and too spontaneous to adopt the required air of Waspy indifference. Once in college, I discovered a kinship with my Jewish friends. Mostly born of Eastern European stock, they were intellectual, voluble, clever, antic. I began to think of myself as a Jewish soul in a Gentile body.

And then one day, in Martha's Vineyard, where Bob vacationed, I encountered a very different breed: the elite German Jew. Meeting Bob's extended family—cousins, nieces, nephews—I experienced once again the languid handshake, the drooping palm, the greetings to loved ones that consisted of a grazing of the cheek, a pecking the air. In other words, they were more Waspish than any Wasp I had grown up with. They were often mercurial, sometimes snooty, other times quite interested in me—but always aloof. And there were so many of them of various removes that it felt as if I were meeting the UN General Assembly.

That summer, I was a curiosity. Martha's Vineyard was replete with the prominent and the moneyed, and two of Bob's closest cousins, Nan Werner and Margie Lang—the grandes dames of Chilmark, who had little crushes on Bob—invited him to a stream of dinners and cocktail parties to meet and psych out this young woman who would steal him away. To my surprise, I was declared fit and worthy, and soon found myself at great homes, chatting animatedly with authors such as John

Hersey, William and Rose Styron, and Diana Trilling and Lillian Hellman, who had begun their famous literary feud.

A few people were dubious about me and played picador. "This must be a very heady experience for you," said Dan Lang, Margie's husband and a prominent writer for *The New Yorker*, "being here with Bob Morgenthau and meeting all these famous people."

Newly confident, I replied easily, "Oh, not really, I've interviewed any number of these people for the *Times*."

•

I suppose the Morgenthau children might not have objected to me because they thought I would come and eventually go; before me, their father had mostly dated women ten or even twenty years younger, but not some *thirty* years. They probably assumed that this was a pleasant dalliance that would end in my acting sensibly and moving on. They never sensed the danger.

We were faced with an impossible conundrum: We were in ways as suited to each other as a giraffe to a baby kangaroo. But we loved each other passionately, in every possible way. Bob finally made one of his iron decisions that he would never go back on: that no matter how anyone reacted, there was only one solution. The thought of leaving each other was intolerable, so we decided not to. Instead, several months before we got married, Bob and I began to tell people about our plans. The reaction was swift and acerbic.

Parents of my friends called their children and declared, "Look what she's done now!" My friends themselves thought he might drop dead on me at any moment. His relatives thought I might walk out on a whim.

Cousin Nan urged him to see a psychiatrist.

Cousin Margie stopped speaking to him.

Joan, his beloved sister, maintained an eerie silence.

The names of therapists of various modalities were sent priority mail, some anonymously. Behavioral therapy, hypnotherapy, eye movement desensitization and reprocessing, and even Scientology were suggested.

"You'd think the pope had declared he was marrying Squeaky Fromme!" I remarked to Bob.

When we were simply dating, eyes were raised, but mostly people smiled at the sight of the sedate DA on the arm of a gay young girl in a peasant blouse. Everyone deserves a little fling, after all.

But a marriage? Between a public figure of the establishment and an outspoken peacenik some thirty years his junior? It just wasn't done. The mid-1970s was an era of divisiveness, of ageism, a time when the young still blamed the old for sending them to die in a useless war. We were a walking morality tale, an assault against nature. No matter that we were just normal folk with noble professions, we evoked shibboleths of incest, of dirty old men and moneygrubbing minxes, titans with their trophy wives.

My phone stopped ringing. I called the operator to find out if there was a problem. There wasn't, at least not on the lines. I could feel in its silence the contempt of my radical buddies.

We felt like Romeo and Juliet, albeit a hoarier version. The silly attempts to thwart us only brought us closer together. In fact, they gave me an icy thrill. Iconoclasts that we were, we met our accusers with defiance. We began to plan our wedding. It would be in August of this year, 1977, and we would honeymoon in Greece, because both of us were eager to see the place where intellectual civilization began. Nick Gage, who came from the mountains of Greece, insisted on planning a trip for us.

Nick and my other friends from the *Times* were among the minority who gave us their blessings. "I think it's very cool that you are marrying the district attorney," said Marty Arnold.

"I don't know why he chose *me*," I quipped.

"Are you kidding?" said Joe Lelyveld. "I can just see him running down the street shouting, 'She said yes, she said yes!'"

Gloria Emerson waxed lyrical. "Oh, Lucinda, he is a poem. That hair, those lines on his face, that mouth. The sex appeal!"

Even Mary Breasted was pleased. That was at least in part because I had introduced her to Ted Smyth, and, in an abundance of irony, he promptly married her.

In my presence, Arthur told a *Times* executive, Jimmy Greenfield, that I was marrying Bob, and Jimmy asked if I was going to stop writing. Good old Arthur, the champion of talented women, retorted, "Why don't you ask Bob if he's going to quit *his* job."

My father approved of the marriage. Like Bob, he is a master of understatement, yet he knows how to separate what is of value from what isn't. "I like Bob," he said in a deep soothing voice. "He's a nice guy. If you're happy, then I'm happy. I don't think the age difference should figure in your considerations at all."

Bob broached it with Annie and her husband, Paul, and they were supportive. Paul thought that "kids are seldom wildly excited by their stepparents, but Barbara likes and respects Lucinda." Always the optimist, Bob thought the other children would accept it, even if it took a little time.

Meanwhile, on the weekends, we went up the Hudson Valley to the pillared Georgian-style Morgenthau home, with its cracked old tennis court, its brook-fed cement swimming pool, a huge ancient oak, expanses of green, and, in spring, an endless field of daffodils. There, Bob took refuge in the surrounding 960 acres of apple orchards now owned by his siblings and him. It had become a working operation called Fishkill Farms, with a store and a pick-your-own business at harvest time.

"The best kind of fertilizer is the imprint of the farmer's boots," Bob would say with relish as we tramped through the rows of Macs, Paula Reds, Golden Delicious. He told me how his father had taught him to graft a branch onto a tree to get a different variety. "In those days, they would bury dynamite to make a hole to plant new trees, and he'd always let me pull the plunger."

When the bloom came, in early May, you would stand up at the farm store and look down into a sweep of white, like snow. I sat among the trees just staring at the blossoms, sometimes writing about them, trying to find words to describe those tiny bunched flowers, as delicate as a baby's hand.

Bob loved the Georgian home where he had grown up, with its shabby elegance and multitude of rooms containing canopy beds, Early American furniture, and claw-foot bathtubs. There was even a mural painted across one wall of the large dining room depicting his family—Henry junior, Elinor, Henry III, Bob, and Joan—picnicking in a soft viridian field.

One Sunday in October 1976 we were sitting in the leather chairs in his father's cozy den when I heard the crunch of gravel and the slam of a car door. One of his older daughters, Jenny, suddenly appeared, carrying a big bowl of chopped tomatoes and basil. It looked yummy. "Oh, that looks so delicious, Jenny!" I said. She made for the kitchen without a word.

"I'll walk you to my car," Bob replied, uneasily. "You can drive it home."

"Why?" I asked, incredulous.

"Uh, well . . . it's a special day. We honor Martha."

I quickly made for his old green Volvo. I was just as anxious as he was to get me out of there before the rest of his children arrived. I drove down the Taconic State Parkway, my cheeks burning. Bob's older girls seldom came to the farmhouse, and it must have been infuriating for Jenny to find me sitting in the den with my legs over the arm of her grandfather's chair, perfectly willing to horn in on the special day that the family had always spent together, on the private sadness they felt for a mother lost to them. Had I been told of this, I never would have come that weekend.

This was typical Bob; he seldom tells anyone what is going to happen, until just before it happens; it doesn't matter whether it's a major controversial event, like the anniversary of her death, or just a simple political affair. His father had been the same way: for instance, when Henry junior once made a historic trip with the legendary Israeli prime minister Golda Meir, Bob was never even told about it.

Bob didn't want to lose his children, and he didn't want to lose me. In between lay a colossal lack of nerve. It was as though he were dangling somewhere between the prosecution and the defense, unable to do his job, unable to decide who was right, finding himself faltering where he had always had a strong, steady hand. Perhaps he thought he was trying to protect me, but it seemed more likely that he was protecting himself.

Was he some kind of silent aggressor?

The next day, he came to my apartment so early I was in my nightie. He sat down at the far end of my couch, forcing me to choose whether or not to sit next to him. I didn't.

"I'm sorry about yesterday," he said. "I just forgot."

"You forgot that your children were coming to memorialize the death of your wife?"

"I didn't mean to put you in that position."

"Oh, really?"

"You told me once that Freud said sometimes a cigar is just a cigar," he said hopefully.

As if on cue, he took out an illegally obtained Cuban Montecristo, clipped off the end, and leaned back, as though he were at his club.

He took a long puff. I stared at him. "Comfortable? How about a snifter of brandy?"

"What? At this hour?" he asked, my sarcasm lost on him.

The room was filling up with smoke. These illegal Cuban cigars he somehow obtained were hideously pungent. I hated the smell. "Look, Bob, I need some time to myself. Let's do this visit another time. Could you leave, and take your cigar with you?"

He looked at me in surprise. "I'll put out the cigar," he said, but I shook my head and pointed to the door.

Very slowly, he got up, stood there while I ignored him, and slowly went to the door. He had on my favorite shirt with the purple stripes, but in back it was drooping down his derriere; I wondered whether he was so eager to get here that he had forgotten to tuck it in. He looked so disheveled, it almost made me cry. And when he was gone, I did.

A week later, I applied for a space at the MacDowell Colony, the nation's oldest retreat for artists, in Peterborough, New Hampshire. To my delight, I was accepted, and in March 1977, I packed up for a month-long stay.

"I wouldn't go up there," Bob said gloomily. But I was determined not to let my love life take over my professional one and felt obliged to show my independence.

MacDowell was one of the most sought-after retreats for writers, painters, musicians. By day, it separated them and provided a quiet environment for work, free from distractions. But at dinner, they all came together and shared everything from gossip to problems with their works of art. It was an Amalthea's Horn of disparate creative individuals helping each other along, giving tips, even reading parts of manuscripts in progress.

I was ushered into a lonely cabin where I was to glue myself to my Olympia electric typewriter, which had been easier to carry than the lead-footed Remington. The only noise in the woods was the thump of the picnic basket, complete with red-checked cloth, delivered at lunchtime. I sat down, and at first the words came faster than I could type them. Then they suddenly stopped. A yellow warbler outside my window resonated louder than the low hum of my Olympia, and its melodious song invited me to move to my little bed and daydream about the story I was working on. Just for a few minutes. Only the minutes turned into hours and the hours into days because I couldn't think about my writing, only about Bob. I would wrap myself in the patchwork quilt and reenact our moments over and over, as if we were in a play that ran every night. The time his face came peeking out of a row of China-town pig carcasses just a block from the offices that knew him as the austere DA; the night we accidentally fell out of his bed; the wry, unhurried way he told his jokes, which made them funny no matter how many times he told them. He was so vividly there in my cabin, with his ironic smile and his deep, echoing voice, that I hardly ever missed him.

But he missed me and was uneasy about our separation. One weekend, he just showed up. The first night, I took out some weed Roger had left me and dared him to join me in a toke or two. He refused but was eager for me to go ahead. Clearly, he wanted to watch what would happen.

We soon ended up on the floor doubled over with laughter. I was too stoned to make love.

"Meet me halfway!" he complained.

"I can't. I can't move."

"Look," he said, sitting up. "I want you to exercise. Get down on the floor and do butt crunches. You know the stories about older women teaching young men how to have sex? Well, this is a case of an older man teaching a younger woman how to really do it."

"How to *really* do it? Your split infinitives are killing me!" I went into a laughing fit. "And what's this antiquated 'have sex.' Did you mean 'have a good screw'?"

The next day I felt like a jerk. "I acted ridiculous, didn't I?"

He nodded.

I teased him for not joining me.

On Sunday, the author Nora Sayre, who had come to the end of her stay, hitched a ride back to New York with him. As soon as she got home, she called me excitedly. "All he did was brag about your accomplishments the whole way down to New York."

If only Bob could see my formidable accomplishments now. I gazed at the rolled-up page in my typewriter, tore it out, crumpled up the twenty other pages I had written, and left the cabin that symbolized my failure. It was too soon after the death of my mother to write about my crazy childhood; I had no distance, no sense of irony. My mother and I had come to a kind of peace, but we had never talked about her erratic mothering, about my explosive teenage rebellion against her, never resolved all that had gone before. As a result, it didn't matter how successful I had become; I was still trapped, still that somnolent child surrounded by peril.

•

If I couldn't write about my childhood, I could certainly try to connect it to the present. Why *had* I fallen in love with a man who doled out his comfort sparingly instead of one like Roger, who gave me more reassurance than I needed? The answer was obvious. We marry our fathers. They might have given the world to us, but it was never enough; they posed questions they didn't fully answer; they left us with a sense of never having known them. My father, who adored me, had still drawn away from me when I was about thirteen, and all my life I had been trying to find out why. All my life I had been trying to figure out why he wasn't there, why he would never reveal himself to me.

"Your father and I understand each other," Bob would say later, after we were married, rather understating the fact. The six years that separated them belied their uncanny similarities; it was as if they had been born at the same minute. Both were lieutenants in the navy, heroes who cared too little about their own safety. With their deadpan demeanors, they were both taciturn, unflappable, touched by the unfortunate, and often tongue-tied with those they loved. They were not only noble characters; they shared a myriad of other trivial oddities: conducting activities in slow motion; taking an interminable time to finish a meal; pausing to think before answering a question; and donning weekend clothes whose conditions they seemed to ignore.

•

One Saturday, not long after I had left MacDowell with typewriter and blank paper in hand, the doorbell rang. I was reveling in the quiet of the snug nest I had created for myself, but then who would just come over uninvited except Bob? So with a little frisson of pleasure, I got up to answer it. There he was, grinning. As soon as we sat down, he put his hand in his jacket pocket, took out a little blue Tiffany box, and thrust it at me.

Inside, on a puff of ebony velvet, was a ring with a sapphire flanked by two smaller diamonds. "Oh," I said, my breath catching. I touched the glistening stones. "Oh!"

I held it up to the light. "Oh, sweetheart. Oh. It's exquisite." It was delicate, lovely . . . and the band was the size of a dime. He must see me as some petite Bo Peep, I thought, and was so touched by this that instead of shattering his illusions and trying to force it over my bony knuckle, I put it back in the box.

"Try it on."

"I will. I believe in delayed gratification." I went over to my record player and dropped "Hey Jude" on the spindle.

I sat beside him and folded my fingers into his. "I didn't expect this."

"I didn't mean for you to expect it."

He looked so pleased with himself. A sunset somewhere beyond the skyscrapers turned his skin rosy, and he smiled the smile I love, the curve of a half-moon.

"I love you," I said and nestled into him. The last light drifted in and flickered over his finely furrowed hands. They were the most beautiful hands I had ever known.

He lay back, and we were still except for the rhythmic circling of my fingers on his wrist. Soon, his arms began to slip from around me. They fell to his lap. I tried to relax, to doze with him, but I felt the pressure building in me. The old pictures. The old beliefs. *When the good comes, the bad will come quicker.* I tried to head it off. *Head your mother off before she shows her other face.*

But I couldn't. "What will all the kids think?" I asked softly. "What will they think when I wear this ring?"

Silence.

"I want to know," I said. "You must have talked to all of them by now. Tell me, please."

I felt the heave of his chest. "Can't we just enjoy the moment for once?"

But the moment was gone.

"They don't want me to marry you," he said.

"What?" I sat up. "I thought they liked me!"

"They don't want the marriage."

"You mean they don't want it right now."

"They don't want it, period."

"That can't be right. We all get along! We share a lot," I argued, though I knew the only thing we shared was their father.

"Can't you speak to them, convince them this could be a good thing?"

"I've been speaking with them. For a considerable length of time."

"What have you been saying?"

He fixed his gaze on a corner of the rug. He looked worn down. But I couldn't stop. I couldn't just keep paddling around in some gray marshy water. I couldn't keep not knowing what was going to happen. "Talk!" I said.

He turned his deaf ear to me. I heard my voice rising and was ashamed. Over and over, I was asking the same question, hoping to get the answer I wanted.

"Maybe you haven't been definite enough," I said. "You can be evasive, you know."

"They want you to sign a prenup."

"A prenup? What's a prenup?" It sounded like a diaper for old people.

"Doesn't matter, you're not signing it."

"Like, what is it?"

"It's about my assets. They don't want you to get anything. We're not signing it anyway."

"I don't believe it! They think this is all about money?" The room tilted. I felt dizzy.

"Forget about it, the issue is over. Your voice is like a razor."

"Well, damn it, Bob, this is gross. I know you love me, but why do you let them manipulate you? Why not just shout, 'Quiet! I'm not taking any more polls. I'm marrying her. Period.'"

"I have to let things take their course, do this in an orderly fashion."

"This is not an indictment, for Christ's sake. We're not in the grand jury."

Suddenly his chin began trembling. He put his head in his hand. Then I saw a long tear roll down his nose.

"Sweetheart, what's the matter?"

"I can't have all of you yelling at me at the same time." His voice broke.

I sat frozen. I had never seen him cry like this. I had never seen him cry at all. I stood up and held his head in my arms. I had been a bitch. "I'm sorry," I said, crying too. "I'm sorry. I didn't know you were hurting so much." I stroked his hair. "My beloved, I'm so sorry."

7

Over the next few days, I meditated on Bob's paradoxical personality. By day, he was nonchalant about criminals who threatened to kill him, and by night he became paralyzed by his children. The man who was brought to a pitch of agony by a personal crisis was the same one who regarded shady corporate giants with hard, unmerciful eyes, recommended the maximum sentences for rapists, and was immune to city power brokers petitioning him to go easy on corrupt politicians—the man who'd taken me to Rao's restaurant in East Harlem and introduced me to a rough fellow who gave him a big smile and a vigorous handshake. "That was Matty the Horse," he'd told me. "I put him away for ten years."

How could his family turn him into such a different person altogether? I mused. But then I thought about their own feelings, the desperation they must have been experiencing. Although it had been five years since their mother died, it must have seemed like five months. They had all lost her at young ages. It was easy to see how powerful an instrument Bob was in their lives, how much they must have felt they had to lose. He had been a beacon in their lives, and here I was sucking up all the light.

Now it seemed he was about to leave them for another woman. Bob advised me against it, but I decided to talk to the kids, one by one, to let them vent, to tell me how I could help. I put on a dusty-rose wraparound dress and conservative block heels and tied my hair back, hoping to look older than I was.

I started with Bobby. We went into the old playroom in Riverdale, sat down, and stared at the bookcase in front of us. It was full of Modern

Library classics that his mother had subscribed to. There were pictures of her everywhere: she and Barbara in Fair Isle sweaters, the family on the deck of Bob's boat, Martha laughing in a bathing suit, she and Bobby as a toddler.

"So what are you doing marrying a fifty-seven-year-old man?" he asked, his fingers holding up his chin.

"Uh, well. I love him."

"Are you, like, going to have children?"

Was he worried that a whole other family of five would sprout up while he wasn't looking? "Oh, well, not a lot," I said. I held up one finger. "Maybe just one." I held up a second finger. "Or two at the most."

He was quiet.

"I'll be here for you, Bobby. I'll be as good a stepmother as I can be."

"Well, that we *don't* want," he replied.

"Well, then I won't interfere," I said, my hands slightly shaking. "Is there anything else I can tell you, anything else you were wondering?"

"No," he said and got up to go, not looking very reassured.

I was told that it would not be helpful for me to talk to Jenny. But she was known to feel that the only way I could help would be to leave the premises in a hurry. She feared I might be a fortune hunter, out for the Morgenthau money, such as it was. Since Bob's grandfather made a fortune in real estate and other investments, the original funds had dwindled. She was intent on protecting what was left, however, and on convincing her father of who she thought I was before he married me.

I called Annie's husband, Paul, a tall, handsome lawyer who met his wife while they were both working for Bob. Paul, an honest and witty individual who had been particularly friendly to me, looked and acted more like a Morgenthau than a Morgenthau did. "Yes, of course they're concerned about a second family," he said. "They feel like their father thinks they're not good enough. Otherwise, why would he want more children. And who can blame them?"

I was more hopeful as I walked over to Annie's large turn-of-the-century house, a few doors up from Bob's Riverdale home. Annie and I had always had something nice to say to each other. And I admired her because she had been a lifesaver for Barbara, particularly with her two young children. Barbara loved sprinting over to Annie's house; her older sister was her adviser and comforter, and she loved playing with the kids and being part of their family.

I sat at Annie's kitchen table as she leaned over the sink, washing dishes—making it clear she didn't want to look at me. I could hear the clock ticking, moving toward the time she must leave to pick up Hilary from school. I finally found the courage to ask her if my marriage to her dad would be problematic for her.

"I wouldn't want to be in your position," she said, turning around. "Not for one minute. People are very emotional about this."

"Please tell me what I can do," I said. "I want to help everyone adjust."

"Jenny broke up with her boyfriend a little while ago," she said pointedly, "because he had two children and she felt she couldn't do anything for them."

"I feel I can do things, especially for Barbara," I said.

"It's really Barbara that we're all concerned about," she replied.

"I understand and I will do the best I can by her."

She looked at me hard. "It's her father she needs. She doesn't need anyone else. Just her father." The rims of her eyes were red.

"I will give them plenty of time alone," I protested.

"Frankly, whatever you're prepared to give them I don't think will be enough."

I sighed, exasperated. What did she expect me to do, obliterate myself? Well, of course she did. "I would think his children would want their father to be happy," I said.

"I think they are more concerned about themselves right now," she replied.

I was startled. My head began to pound. Bob had devoted his life to his kids, nurturing Barbara in spite of his own grief.

I was about to walk out the door when, surprisingly, Annie asked if I would like to come with her and get Hilary from school. Hilary, now five, was perhaps my best friend in the family, probably because she had no idea what was going on. When the Grands came up to the farm, we would put blankets and cups under the big oak tree so I could invent little tea parties for her where we pretended to be proper "Cambridge" ladies. Now, when I saw her bounding out of Fieldston and into the car, I gave her a big hug.

Annie dropped me off at the bus stop. I looked around, saw no one, and hid behind a tree to have a full-blown cry.

I went to our apartment on the West Side, which Renia happened to be helping me clean out. I must have looked hangdog. She shook her head. "Don't you trouble now, Mrs. Morgenthau, I mean, Miss Franks.

"You're to take care of Mr. Morgenthau and don't bother with anybody else . . . Listen now, you make him happy. I never thought anyone would again.

"You should see what my own son Bill's gone and done to his family. Children, they only think about themselves. But what can you do? That's the way it is.

"I think," she said, lowering her voice, "they hope if they're rude enough to you, you will walk out that door and never come back."

•

Later that afternoon, I sat on my bed, so dazed that I jumped at the trill of my phone. It was an unexpected call from an old radically active friend, inviting me to a mass antinuclear protest in New Hampshire. Things always happen for a reason. I thanked her profusely for remembering me, even though I had renounced protest politics. Just for a day, I needed to get far away from those who thought me unworthy; just for a day, I needed to feel the warmth of people who forgave me for leaving them and remained loyal and kind.

The next morning, I was lying down in the muddy marshland of Seabrook, New Hampshire, blocking workers from entering a nuclear energy facility under construction. An accidental nuclear explosion was, by the law of averages, certain to happen. It was a cause I believed in. So I found myself once again linked arm in arm, part of a large but tight community, waving placards, handing out leaflets to the workers trying to climb over us.

I joined in shouting insolently at the police who were dragging people by their legs into buses they'd made into holding cells. Suddenly a big beefy cop hauled me up, and into the arrest line I went. Word traveled fast; the demonstrators who got caught would be held in a national armory for days and days. Now I was scared down to the soles of my Doc Martens. I had always welcomed being arrested, but that was before

Bob. I could see the headlines across the front page of every tabloid: "DA's Fiancée Arrested and Incarcerated!" I might lose my first true love forever.

As the police were writing down names, I saw my chance. Along with a man from New York, I broke away and sprinted as fast as I could before we were noticed. Thankfully, we ran to a road, put out our thumbs, and were immediately picked up by a trucker. As we bounced along, I could hear the sound of sirens right until we crossed state lines. In a few hours, I was home.

•

Two days later, on Monday night, I was both relieved and not relieved to be sitting with Bob in the cozy comfort of my apartment. I hadn't told him a thing about Seabrook. It would be my secret, my exhilarating assertion of independence, the comforting knowledge that I had somewhere to escape to if the complications of this relationship got too much for me.

"So where did you disappear to this weekend?" he asked.

"You know, I never did read you that Frost poem that I love." I jumped up and took my Frost omnibus out of the bookcase. "Let me do it before I forget." I read him the all too relevant "The Road Not Taken," then I launched into the provenance of the framed knights on my wall, carrying on about how I spent many happy hours in Westminster Abbey on my knees rubbing the brass with black or gold wax, then I popped into the kitchen to make him a treat I had ordered from England. I knew he'd never refuse food. "Your Majesty, your crumpet," I said in Windsor English, flashing my engagement ring. By now, I had surely diverted his attention.

"Was it my children? Did you go away because of them?" he asked, sinking his teeth into the buttery snack. "You didn't tell me how your talks with the kids went."

I picked a thread from the hem of my pink sweater. I knew how exquisitely vulnerable he was to reminders of the children and me, and I vowed not to add to his pressure. "Oh, fine. It was no big thing," I said cheerfully.

"It wasn't very nice of you to abandon me like that," he said plaintively.

"I didn't go far. Just visiting some friends in New Hampshire."

"You could have told me." He was studying me with those blue eyes, sharp as surveillance cameras. I knew he was taking my measure. Then he raised his eyebrows and reached out and touched my cheek, and I burst out crying.

He put his arm around me, and I got the English lavender shirt I'd ordered from Turnbull & Asser all wet. He pushed back my hair, and when I had wiped my eyes on his shirt, he tickled the sensitive inside of my hand, causing me to smile.

"How's November?" he asked.

"For what?"

"For the wedding. And before that we can go to Greece, like we'd planned."

"Our wedding? But, Bob, what about . . ."

"We are going to be married," he said firmly. "You're not leaving me again."

"Sure?" I nuzzled his prickly cheek, taking in the fresh smell of his collar.

"Yes, I'm sure," he said, feeling my engagement ring. "I love you so much." Over his shoulder, my brick walls were brilliant red, the dull brown stripes of the couch had gone deep chestnut, my humble apartment was a riot of color. Had I never noticed this before?

"I'm not concerned about what anyone says. I'm marrying you."

•

We were in JFK airport, waiting for our plane to Greece. It was August. I held Bob's damp hand. We had sat here for an hour, and by then he knew the men's room nearest Gate B28 intimately. He hated to fly, hated to be on planes whose mechanisms he didn't understand, especially for eight hours. He was doing this for me.

As we boarded the plane for Athens, I uttered soothing words: "Planes are just like birds; planes *want* to fly."

Myself, I loved the experience; I grew up on a wing, a leaf batted about in a capricious home, and then a frequent flier to investigate UPI and *Times* stories. Bob, on the other hand, had such deep roots that were seldom disturbed; he must have felt as if I had unceremoniously yanked him out of the earth. As we took off, he gripped the armrests as if to hold the plane steady; once in the air, he immediately fell asleep. I watched him, the shine on his forehead, the crown of hair that had been a mass of curls in his boyhood, his strong mouth with its upper lip, feminine, vulnerable. I loved him. He was mine. I could not run away now or switch or disengage. The cogs were locked.

I sipped a second glass of wine and watched the dimpled skin of the Atlantic Ocean below, the clouds wafting like bits of dreams.

In mid-flight, Bob woke. "Hello, my love," I said. "Would you like my pillow, my blanket, my shoulder . . . my body?"

"I want gum," he said, and took two sticks of Dentyne from my hand. "Thanks. You're a lady and a scholar," he murmured, his favorite rejoinder.

As the Swiss Alps appeared below, I told him to lean over me and look out the window. He wouldn't; he was afraid to look down.

"Not me. I love danger," I teased him. "Okay, I'll tell you what they look like. Veins of white are running through the valleys, veins pulsing white blood, and the peaks are sticking up like knives, so close it looks like they could puncture the plane." His chin went down, and his pupils rolled up to the tops of his eyes, a particularly murderous look I had not seen before. "I'm joking, I'm joking, we are miles above the mountains," I said quickly.

"But it is so vast out there," I went on, "the universe is so vast, and we are so little, but with these little brains we can imagine, we can deconstruct the universe. Sometimes I think, 'What are we, anyway?' Have you ever wondered, 'Hey, what am I?'"

"This is a big plane, isn't it?" he said, apparently ignoring me. "It's a McDonnell Douglas DC-10. Three engines, that's good."

After we landed in Athens, we went to Nick Gage's house and were so tired, he showed us straight to the guest room. We sat down on the intricately carved antique bed, and it promptly collapsed beneath us. Nick came running in, saw us on the floor, and started laughing uncontrollably. For years, he dined out on various ribald renditions of our dramatic arrival at his home.

I was discovering new things about my man: he could get as crazy as I could. We were trying to find our way about Athens, driving moderately slowly, when a car started riding our bumper. Finally, Bob revved up and got ahead and then just stopped our car. He stopped the rental car in the middle of a little rotary and took out his city map. "Sweetheart!!" I yelled at him as the driver behind us leaned on his horn.

"I'm tired of these Frogs crawling up my tail," he said calmly, studying the roads.

"They're not Frogs; that's the French. Please, start up the damn car!"

So he did, and we didn't speak for ten minutes. To break the tension, I began exclaiming over the scenery. "Look, they tie their cows to poles!"

"Yes, I suggested that the last time I was here," he replied. "I said, 'Look, you've got all these telephone poles, why don't you do something with them?'"

"Sweetheart," I said, giggling. "You're mad." Bob's sense of humor struck when you least expected it. I loved how his extraordinary mind worked.

One day we discovered a deserted beach with fine gold sand that slipped through our fingers. The sky was soft white, and palms bent toward the silvery-blue Aegean. The gentle waves broke like bodies somersaulting, melting into yards and yards of sugar foam. "Come on." Bob took my hand and trotted into the ocean, stopping at his waist so he wouldn't get water in his fragile ears. I was paddling around his legs when he shouted, "Stop pinching me!"

"What? Oh my God, run!" I yelled, seeing a swarm of red-dotted jellyfish.

When we got to shore, I saw what we had missed before—the dead blobs lying on the sand. Bob tiptoed through them as if he were mounted on hooves, making me giggle.

"*That's* why there's no one on this beach," he said, laughing. "Now what shall we do?"

"Something that's perfect," I said, getting out the camera and telling him my idea. "It's for posterity. A record we wouldn't have any other way."

"What I do to please you," he grumbled.

"Smile!" I snapped a couple of gorgeous shots of him au naturel.

"I figure that if you leave me for another woman," I said coolly, knowing that he was constitutionally unable to do such a thing, "I can sell them to the *Post*."

•

We loved to linger in the tavernas, eating taramasalata, homemade yogurt, mullet, calamari, and Mediterranean lobsters grilled with olive oil. We sipped deadly shots of ouzo or mixed it with water and watched the anise-flavored liqueur turn white. We asked to sit side by side because we couldn't bear to be more than a foot away from each other, and the waiters obliged, peeking and smiling indulgently when we sneaked kisses.

One night, thoughts were like sparrows fluttering around my head, keeping me up. When Bob sleeps, he hibernates. I snuggled up to him but couldn't even get under his arm. Finally, at midnight, I got up, opened a window, took in the salt air, and wrote a poem to Bob and put it on his bedside table:

> When you wake
> See me, a squash blossom
> Lying obediently
> Inside your palm.

The next day, we drove through fields of fat melons and almond trees in Delphi and climbed the road through hazy blue hills laced with waterfalls. Then we sneaked through a restricted area to make the long climb up to the holy sanctuary of Apollo, the god of truth. Far from the modern Athenians, honking, drilling, shouting for their dollars, we stood in the holiest place of ancient Greece, where the oracle prophesied to commoners and kings. I felt a ripple of awe as I ran my fingers down a huge Doric column, standing lonely on the horizon. The sun sparkled off its smooth pink stone. I am actually touching the work of men who lived four hundred years before Christ, I thought. I looked at the mountains rising up like Praetorian guards, and I felt the infinite presence of the only civilization ruled by the intellectual elite, the state that inspired Sophocles, Plutarch, the giant Socrates, his brilliant student, Plato, and Plato's student Aristotle, the short-bearded, long-winded scientist-philosopher. I hadn't prayed for a long time, but at that moment I got on my knees in the sanctuary ruins and prayed for peace that passeth all understanding. In the middle of my prayer, I heard a voice boom, "I wonder where they parked their chariots?"

I stood up slowly. "Isn't anything serious for you?" I said quietly. "Is everything meat for a wisecrack? This is a sacred place, a spiritual one. I wouldn't blame Zeus if he struck you down."

Bob lowered his head. "I'm sorry. You're right. But I do feel it. It gives me . . . ah . . . a feeling of the endurance and expanse of the human mind. It's hard for me to put into words. I'm not like you."

"All you have to do is imagine. Imagine the statue of Apollo, so grand and white and beautiful . . ."

"I don't know that I can do that," he said. "The only thing that's beautiful to me is you. When I imagine beauty, you are all I can see."

Back at the hotel, we cuddled up in the middle of our sagging bed. Suddenly he began to emit a mock moan and laid his head on my chest. "Tell me I'm a good boy."

"What?"

"You got mad at me today," he said plaintively. "Tell me I'm a good boy."

I looked at him, startled. I didn't know what to say. This wasn't my stoical husband. It was a strange child I didn't know. But where had it come from? I had a flash of his upbringing, how he had once thought that no one gave a damn about him. How little he must have been coddled and praised. Did his parents ever notice that he was a good boy indeed?

I brushed away his wisps of gray hair. "You *are* a good boy," I said, kissing his forehead, "a very good boy."

Then I reached for my cigarettes. "Why don't you think you're good? Tell me about it." I was eager to seize this opportunity to know him better.

He took my cigarette away and ran his finger over my mouth. "I'm jealous of those things. They take your lips away from me." Then he distracted me by undressing us both.

Afterward, he studied me in the bright light coming through the arched window, looking for freckles, noticing the vaccination scar on my arm.

"Don't look at me, I'm too plump."

"Mine is on my thigh," he said, twisting around so I could see it. "My mother didn't want me to have a scar.

"I don't want you to lose weight," he added. "I love you the way you are."

He put kisses that were barely kisses on my nose, eyes, hair. He gently rubbed his cheek against mine. "We're going to be side by side, two as one."

"Oh yes," I answered, with a little smile.

•

On the plane back to New York, Bob lay back in his seat, holding my hand loosely, easily. Away from the haranguing world, we had become inextricably tethered. In the clarity of the Greek sun, air, water, we had stood exposed to each other, stripped down. His hard exterior had given way to the poetic, and I had received the intimacy I craved. He had become an uncertain child in my arms. He had studied the geography of my body, as though by knowing my identifying marks, he could claim me as his. We knew the intensity of the problems that lay ahead, but we knew we could handle them together, that they would no longer unravel us. We were married now, if not yet wed. We experienced even short separations as unsettling.

Unsettling, and perilously irresistible. Love had made me blossom and wither at the same time. Until then, I had mightily resisted what I knew would tempt me, obsession with the concrete reality of another that would overwhelm the urgent obsession I had for my own abstract perfection. Love had undoubtedly empowered Bob, but the female capacity for sympathetic identification, for total absorption, threatened to erase those boundaries for which I had fought so hard. For me, a dangerous state of bliss lay ahead.

"I'm so happy," I said as the plane floated up into the sky. "I've never been this happy in my life."

He nodded. "Never happier."

•

Once back in New York, Bob suggested that when we were staying in Riverdale, I use the dressing room of his master bedroom to write in. Bob was not known for being foolish, but there were exceptions to any rule. The room had been Martha's. Her things were everywhere. How different she had been from my mother, how secretive about her illness. Mother had announced her cancer to everyone. A dynamic, outgoing woman, she had a stream of visitors, little trips to Cape Cod, the finest chocolates, back rubs, gourmet casseroles. Most important, she had my estranged father, who came back to nurse her for the last two years of her life. Shortly after she died, we cleaned out her wardrobe and her drawers and her desk until all visible signs of her were gone.

But Martha's possessions—and such a private woman she was—had been left out for any workman, any passing girlfriend, to see. Her dresses, surely bearing her particular scent, hung in the closet still. The closet had double sliding doors, and one door was not quite closed, a beige satin sleeve sticking out. I set up my electric typewriter on a little table next to her desk, my back to the sleeve. One day, worrying over a sentence, I got up and paced. Back and forth, past the sleeve, back and forth, past the sleeve. Finally, I took a peek inside the closet. Beautiful brocade jackets, paisley blouses, chiffon dresses with pleated skirts. Clunky pumps. A mother's garments.

On the floor were boxes and stacks of papers—amid the paraphernalia, a folded piece of light blue stationery stood out. I returned to my electric portable typewriter and typed out a couple of lines on my short story. Then I went downstairs to see if Barbara had gotten home from school yet. Even if she was being a moody teenager, I thought it was important that a living, breathing being was there when she came home.

The days went by, and each time I sat down to write, I gazed at what I assumed was a letter and then quickly gazed away. Reporters, I'm afraid, are born snoops with searing curiosities, and on the fifth day smoke was coming out of my manuscript. I strode over, picked up the letter, and unfolded it. I looked at the salutation: "Dear Bob." I dropped the letter. The writing was uncannily similar to my mother's: not too small and not too large, perfectly legible, perfectly conventional, each line ruler straight.

A day later, I picked up the letter again and discovered it was dated about a month before Martha died. I put it back, wondering if it would still be there the next day. It was, and with rain blowing about so hard it rattled the windows, with my chest going up and down, with visions of being found in a dead faint, the letter on my breast, I started reading. As I recall, it said something like this:

You will want a wife and you should have one. Then you can finally have a complete marriage. She should be a nice woman, who is attentive to you. She should be someone who fills the house

with people, your friends and neighbors, because you need people
around you.

The children won't like her, at least not at first, because they
won't have chosen her. She will be a stranger, but she should be
someone who is good to them.

I sat on the floor, the letter shaking in my hand. Bob had never
talked about Martha, never shared any stories, never told me what it
was like to lose her. I hadn't pressed him, because I thought it forbidden
territory.

And now I was hearing her very voice. I read the letter over and over
so that I could get a sense of her. She had given Bob permission to love
someone else, but she might as well have chosen the woman herself.

Could she have chosen me? Could I be what Bob needed? Would I
fill my house with people? Cocktail parties spilling out onto the patio?
Dinners with guests balancing plates on their knees? Friends dropping
in uninvited?

Would the fact that I couldn't meet Martha's criteria set in play
some metaphysical justice? Would I suffer the misery of the new bride
in *Rebecca*, haunted by the ghost of her husband's former wife?

I heard Bob arrive, bags bulging with press clips, indictments, and
unread mail bumping against the front door.

After we sat down and were sipping wine, he asked me why I looked
as if I'd been crying.

"Do you love me for who I am or for what you think I'm going to
be?" I asked.

"What?"

"If our home is not full of people, will you still be glad you married
me?"

"What *are* you talking about?"

I took a deep breath and gave him the letter. "I found it in her dressing room. It was sticking out of a box. I'm sorry for reading it."

He perused it. "Well, I haven't seen it."

"No?"

He folded it up and put it in his pocket. "She must have written it
and just never given it to me."

"Or left it for you to find," I said.

•

A week later, a month before we were to be married, he was still wearing Martha's wedding ring. "It's for the children," he explained. "I don't want to upset them."

"What are you going to do, wear two rings at our wedding?" I asked. "Bob, please . . ."

He nodded and pushed back a strand of my messy hair. "Don't worry."

But on the next day and the day after that, it was still on his finger. I told him it hurt me.

The next day, his left finger was bare. And the day after that, he called his children to empty Martha's wardrobe.

While the children sorted through the dressing room upstairs, Bob called downstairs to me more than once: "Lucinda, what do you think they should take?"

At first, I couldn't answer. Why was he asking me this? "They should take whatever they would like," I called out, unable to think of anything else to say. I realized at that moment that to some degree Bob had switched his allegiance. His late wife's closet now disassembled, he had moved from being protective of her and her children to being overly protective of me. I felt happy, a bit guilty, and nervous all at once. I didn't know if I wanted anyone, even my true love, to lie prostrate at my feet.

We set the wedding for November 19, 1977, a year and a half after we fell in love.

•

"I want a small one," I said, curling up to Bob in the living room. Earlier that summer, I'd fantasized about the wedding: "Maybe we could go to Provence! We could take our vows in a field full of lavender."

"That's—that's not possible, love. I have too many people here that really have to be invited. Colleagues, friends, acquaintances. It's the kind of situation where if you invite one person you have to invite another."

"But I haven't the foggiest idea how to do a big wedding. And I don't even have a mother to help me!"

"We'll have it at Charlton Street," he said definitively.

During one of our jaunts to the West Village, we had fallen in love with a three-story Federal house from the mid-nineteenth century that had wide floorboards, elaborate double doors, and a sweet, rather large garden in back. Before we knew it, we had put a deposit on the lovely grandam. We would put the Riverdale house on the market and move out of my rental apartment. He would be able to give up Central Park West, the apartment that provided him with the Manhattan residence required for the DA. Charlton Street was to be our first and perhaps only home.

Bob immediately picked up the phone and dialed Marina. Like so many people, she would do anything for Bob Morgenthau. The wife of Stephen Kaufman, she was a Moroccan-born woman with a unique forcefulness and such trademark abundant hair grazing her ribs that she mesmerized people. As Steve, a forceful lawyer in his own right, joked, "I'm known as Marina's husband." She was a rescuer, always there for people in crisis, and within a few weeks she had organized virtually every detail of our traditional ceremony—the flowers, the decorations, the wedding cake, the food. She spared Bob not a penny. Workmen lumbered laden around the house as windows were turned into French doors and a wooden spiral staircase was erected from the parlor to the garden so that I would have someplace to walk down the aisle.

Sweet little eighty-year-old Miss Wais, our secretary, wrote out the invitations on creamy Strathmore watermark paper, and to my horror Bob had them mailed to a list of 250 people. I knew only 30 of them— Mary Breasted and a few other friends from the *Times*, a couple of broad-minded radical friends, and seven near strangers from my new woman's group, invited to swell my little camp.

Thankfully, in flew my loyal sister from Chicago, complete with an elegant maid of honor dress. From overseas, Irona and Greg Jensen, my good friends and surrogate parents, came and forthwith obtained a supply of sentimental Valpolicella. UPI London, with its drinking culture, had inspired us to consume magnums of this *vino ordinario* together on many a cold gray evening.

It was like a pajama party at Charlton Street. By night, I played guitar and we sang and chattered. By day, Irona and Penny accompanied me on my quest for a wedding dress, which ended up being an old-fashioned ivory chiffon with tiny buttons running down the back. We had the Belgian lace from my grandmother's gown made into a little wedding cap.

Two nights before the ceremony, I had my panic attack, a frequent ritual of brides-to-be. I had heard of some who ended their nights in strange places: crumpled up in a sloop at the Seventy-Ninth Street Boat Basin or hanging off a horse at the carousel in Central Park.

But I had Greg Jensen, who had been a surrogate father to me in London, to keep me in one place. An elegant writer, Greg was a tall, blasé man of few words and no nonsense. He could also be grumpy. Sensing that I was getting jittery, Irona plopped Greg, me, and two bottles of wine in my study tucked away in the top floor of the town house. She warned everyone to stay away.

We sat on either side of a futon I'd covered with madras. Greg, wearing one of the thrift shop shirts he favored, puffed on his pipe.

I sat cross-legged, facing him. "Sometimes I wonder whether marrying Bob is doomed to failure. I mean, like, I just idly wonder."

"Why would that happen?" asked Greg. "You've succeeded in everything you've set out to do."

I rolled my eyes. "Methuselah marrying Little Bo Peep?"

"A lot of people have done it before you."

I filled our goblets again. "Mother would have admired Bob, but he wouldn't have been in her plans for me. A nice Waspy businessman or a doctor from Wellesley, that's what she wanted. You know how she was a social butterfly. She wanted me to 'come out' in the worst way. I finally agreed, and that thrilled her, and with her dying so young, I'm glad I did do the debutante thing. But it was ridiculous. Daddy had to wear a tux, and he did look so cute, but he had to bow to the queen of the ball, and I had to curtsy almost to the floor.

"She wanted me to do charity work, like the garden club, to knock the rough edges off me, and to her horror I not only volunteered but disappeared into a halfway house for students and mental patients!"

"Hmm. What were you, a student or a patient?" He emitted a belly laugh.

"Greg, I just love the way both you and Bob find only your own jokes hilarious.

"You remind me of my mother," I continued. "Like when I was ten, she forced me to join the church choir. So we sang 'Jesu, Joy of

Man's Desiring,' which was such a beautiful hymn that apparently I began to sway to the music. She was furious; I had embarrassed her in front of the other mothers. I had loved choir practice, but I never went again."

"Well, forget about your damn mother, will you?"

"You know, Greg," I said, trying to enunciate my words crisply. Heat waves were radiating from his head, and he'd become blurry. Maybe I'd had too much to drink. "I've never once seen you without that pipe. I think it's your pacifier."

He glowered at me. "I thought this conversation was about you."

"It is. You know, I worked really hard to get out from under all that haut monde stuff of my mother's. Now I'm back onstage. And I don't belong there. I'll probably get in political fights at dinner parties with people like William F. Buckley who'll never speak to him."

Greg opened another bottle of wine. "So if you're so unsuited to him, why didn't you think of this before, instead of two days before your wedding?"

"I *have* thought about it! A lot. But love can destroy you. Look at Romeo and Juliet. They were perfectly happy—young, carefree—until they fell in love. Then they ended up dead."

"In case you've forgotten, that story was made up.

"Tell me the reasons you shouldn't marry Bob," Greg said, tapping his pipe on the palm of his hand. "And I mean the real ones, not the superficial pap you've given me so far."

"Greg, you're like a father to me. So I have an important question." I leaned over and whispered in his ear, "When men are old, can they still have sex?"

He gave me a withering stare and laid his blackened pipe beside him on the couch. "Look at Pablo Picasso, Charlie Chaplin . . ."

I sniffled. "If I'd only loved him, I could have married a young man, like Roger." I knew Greg had disapproved of Roger.

"God help us," he said, but before he could go on, I had fallen over, dead asleep on his pipe.

•

The day of my wedding, I was late. I couldn't find my good panty hose; I was having a bad hair day; Irona crawled across the floor looking for my other wedding shoe. And finally, dressed and ready, I just sat on my bed, unable to move. Icy waves keep traveling down my left arm. "I think I'm having a heart attack," I said to nobody in particular.

"No, no, it's all nerves," Irona said. "Just sit quietly a minute. Collect yourself."

So I did. And then tears gathered in the corners of my eyes. My mother, the social butterfly, had won. I had been outmaneuvered. The roots of my childhood had come up like weeds to overwhelm me. My carefully constructed empire had been sacked—all my people, my privacy, my friendships with men, my rides on elephants, packing suitcases, taking trips, sitting on fire escapes, dancing naked on the roof, my walls, my floor, the nails in my floor, the capacious old shower, the only thing that knew the beauty of my crackling high Cs . . . I would give all of these things up, and though I might long for them, I would never get them back.

Just then Marina came in. "Time is up!" she announced, clapping. "Your father came up here, your sister came up here, all to see what was going on. I told them to go away, you were having a 'private moment.'"

"I still am," I replied as Irona finished dabbing my face with a cold washcloth and adding a little powder.

Marina threw my wedding cap across the bed and said, "Okay, I am going to go downstairs and tell the guests that the wedding is off." She sashayed out the door, and I heard her thumping down the stairs.

I ran out after her to find that she hadn't moved.

"I'm ready," I told her. Of course I was ready. I had always been ready. It didn't matter that this was a relationship that shouldn't have happened; it had happened. Bob had given me joy where there was none, and all the rest was irrelevant. I was ready to go down to pledge my troth to him for the remainder of our days.

As we made our way downstairs to the parlor, we ran into our friend Susie Temkin, who took one look at Marina and gave her a Valium and a glass of vodka.

My sister, Penelope, the maid of honor, stood at the top of the wooden stairs, looking radiant with a flaxen bob and a rose-colored dress held up by one diagonal strap. She turned around and saw me. "At last, here comes the queen," she quipped.

My father gave me his arm, and we started down the raw and slightly rickety wood stairs. I heard the chatter hush. My dress reached just below my toes, and I moved very slowly. Then, suddenly, my high heel caught in the gap between two slats and I was going down. My father, looking straight ahead, tensed his strong arm and swiftly lifted me back up, hopefully before anyone noticed.

It was chilly outside but snugly warm inside the tented garden, thanks to the space heaters Marina had thought to place around. As we reached the bottom of the stairs, we heard a little shriek: "My husband's robes are on fire!" Sure enough, smoke was billowing from the back of the voluminous garments of Bob's close friend Judge Sidney Asch, who stood at the end of the garden, ready to perform a combination Jewish and Episcopal ritual. He had backed up too close to a heater. Someone threw wine on the flames, which only intensified them, and then glasses of water were tossed until the last spark was extinguished, while the judge stood smiling, acting oblivious to the fuss.

My father waited until this interlude had concluded, then gave me a little nod, and I continued the fateful walk. The appropriate "aahs" rose from both sides as I walked down the aisle. I was too nervous to look anywhere but straight ahead, but I glimpsed the family up front. I was prepared to see them staring at their feet, unwilling to witness what they feared most. But Barbara, Annie, and her husband, Paul, all wore smiles on their faces. And then there was Bobby, standing next to his father, bearing the ring. To our surprise and pleasure, he had agreed to be Bob's best man, and he looked handsome and proud. These glimpses calmed me, made my spirits rise so that I was ready for my beloved father to deliver me to the altar.

Bob looked pale, but when he saw me, his gaze was like light breaking through a haze. I looked back at my sister, and she looked back at me full of emotion. Everyone was happy. Everything was as it should be.

"Do you take Lucinda as your chosen wife?" the judge asked.

Bob did not answer, and I held my breath. He stared at me with a look of astonished admiration. The woman whom he remembered wore turtlenecks and men's shirts. He gave me one of his rare ear-to-ear smiles. "I do," he boomed.

And then, in a single moment, it was over. Two hours later, we licked wedding cake off our fingers, left two hundred people still dancing, and sneaked off to our suite at the United Nations Plaza Hotel. Our lives finally intertwined, we entered our room and immediately fell asleep.

.

"Hello, sweetheart," I said with a yawn the next morning.

"I can't find my left shoe," he said sweetly.

We searched the room, and finally I pointed at the bathtub. "Well, what is it doing there?" he asked. "Did you hide it from me?"

I closed my eyes in mock disgust and had hardly opened them when I found myself inside the tub. I must admit I had never imagined that I'd be conducting my honeymoon rites in an empty porcelain Jacuzzi, but it was no less engrossing, given that I didn't even feel the shoe that lay beneath me.

We took a short flight to Jacksonville and then a raft to Cumberland Island, a primitive landmass off the Georgia coast with soft sand beaches, wild horses, crumbling mansions, and bike trails through trees dripping with Spanish moss.

It was the kind of place we both loved. We found a stream with banks full of protruding oysters, and Bob promptly removed his shoes, climbed down the muddy sides, and filled his socks with them. It was a beautiful and horrifying sight, my hero, my new and forever husband, having used his bloody feet as a tool to bring me back this mountain of pearly-white oysters. That evening, we put them on a grill and, as they popped open, slurped them from their shells.

8

We returned home to Riverdale in late November, dreamy and besotted, to the aroma of Renia's roast chicken and a blast of cold air. Bob wanted to see Barbara right away; he had missed her, and she came down the stairs with a little smile. He put his arm around her shoulders and kissed her on the top of the head. I went to give her a hug, and she turned around and ran back up the stairs.

The big armchair in the living room sighed as I fell into it. Had I ever truly woken up to the fact that Bob and I had caused a huge, cataclysmic disaster for his children that might never be repaired? Of course they bitterly resented Bob and blamed me. I had already taken away half the love that their father had lavished on them, and now I was chipping away at the other 50 percent. I would leave them with nothing. *Really* nothing. To them, I was a vampire of fortune after their inheritance. They would never know me, know that I lived frugally, that I saw money as corrupting America. I would be Sisyphus, rolling the boulder up, only to have it roll down again.

After we returned from our honeymoon, I had to deal with the hundreds of gifts we had received. I sat buried in crystal decanters, silver tea strainers, odd abstract vases, meditating on the concept of wifedom. How was I supposed to be as Mrs. Morgenthau? What was I supposed to do?

A voice from the Great Mother in the Sky dictated that first I must write my thank-you notes. I've always hated writing thank-you notes. But I knew that this was what Martha would have done. And Martha, without ever being spoken of, only seemed to gather power in Bob's home.

This was a hazard of marrying an older man and a widower. I was drawn both to identify myself with his late wife and to identify her with my own mother.

Martha found it regrettable that I didn't take a broom and attack the dust on top of the door lintels, that I didn't know a vacuum cleaner from a UFO, and that I didn't dare enter the kitchen and make yet another subpar meal. Thank goodness for Renia: she made such good, wholesome food. If I hadn't been in residence, his older girls, who were superior cooks, might have come and cooked him gourmet feasts.

Martha's eyes seemed to follow me as I went from her living room to her dining room, up to her bedroom, to the queen bed that we bought to replace the twins, watching as I flipped up the half-drawn window shades to let in the light, judging me as I put away all of her pictures, replaced her throw pillows, plumped up my new ones. Nothing I did to change Riverdale really weakened her presence.

Her friends dropped in to take a peek at me, sometimes while I was writing thank-yous to them. A few found me refreshingly young and lively; others whispered that I could use a lesson in propriety: I hadn't even visited the neighbors with gifts of homemade jam or place mats.

•

Easter 1978 came too soon. It had always been a glorious holiday in my home: the day of the Resurrection, when Christ rose from the dead and saved men from eternal suffering for their sins. "Christ has risen" were the first words our mother would say to us, whereupon Penny and I would reply, "He has risen indeed." At church, I bowed before the big gold-gleaming cross and sat mesmerized by candles flickering everywhere. We wore new Easter bonnets and dined on paschal lamb, praying together around the table.

The Morgenthaus, on the other hand, had lost many of their own traditions—bar and bat mitzvahs with their big parties, Hanukkah candles and chocolate gelt and a present every day for the children. Their ancestors, the pioneer German Jews who emigrated in the late nineteenth century, dropped the trappings of their religion in order to be accepted into the culture of Christians, many of whom were anti-Semites. They kept their Jewish identity, however, building Reform synagogues, socializing with each other, celebrating major Jewish holidays such as Passover and Rosh Hashanah. They also added some Christian ones as well—but only the ritualistic parts. I had been trying to get Bob to go to an Episcopal service with me since we met, but he made one excuse after another. Then I learned that most Jews simply didn't go into churches. In fact, after centuries of persecution by the Christian religious establishment, it was almost an insult to ask.

Even when Penny and I were teens, my Easter Bunny mother had hidden jelly beans, and wicker baskets full of goodies were waiting for us in the living room. So before the holiday, I asked Barbara if they'd like an egg hunt and a silly giant blown-up bunny. She looked at me blankly. Easter in its commercial jollity was clearly not a holiday that had made the cut.

I had been an unusually spiritual child. I talked to Jesus and loved him, so I wept at the thought of the pain he felt when nails were pounded into his hands and feet. Kneeling at the Communion rail, sometimes I felt a large hand resting softly on my head. For a time, I thought I'd be a nun. I also believed that the son of God would answer my most fervent prayer: that my parents would stop fighting and love each other. I stapled together books of construction paper promising that I would be incredibly good if only he would give me a real family. Sometimes, when I squeezed my eyes and prayed hard, to my delight, I would go floating out of my body. I thought I would meet God. Once, a blazing light did break through the dark, but it hurt my eyes and pulled me toward it; I guess I didn't want to meet him after all, for I was afraid that when he came, he would come for me.

Time went by and the family deteriorated, each retreating into his or her separate room. By the time I was fourteen, I had lost interest in Jesus, who as a man-God knew my suffering and had refused to help. How naive I'd been.

Now, more than a decade later, I might have been an agnostic, but I still loved the Easter traditions. I woke in a festive mood that day. We were at Riverdale with Barbara, and since she had declined the Easter Bunny, I gave her a little present. And I vowed that I would communicate my good spirits to Bob's children, no matter what; you had to remember the essence of giving is not to expect anything back.

Bob was carving a fillet of beef, while I stayed in the hall to greet his older girls. When they arrived—dressed in flouncy skirts in contrast to my new, rather stiff spring suit—they walked by me as if I weren't there. "Hello!" I said to the backs of their heads, but they passed on into the dining room, gathering around their father, advising him on how to carve the beef.

•

The brown sphere seems to be hurtling over the sun, arcing straight for my head. "Move back, move back!" I hear the shouts of the team. But I cannot move. Cannot bring my foot up to kick the ball. I cover my face, waiting for the horrible moment to come when this weapon will crush my skull. It smacks into my face and bounces away.

"Jeez Louise, you're off the team," yells the captain, a nasty boy named Shotsy Moore. I stick my tongue out at him and, reddened, stride over to the jungle gym. The tar is burning through my Keds; the steel bars are scorching. I'll show them; I will climb up high and swing from bar to bar. I can do it! I will make them look at me with awe.

I climb the first rung but quickly get down. What if I hurt myself? No one will notice. They won't even bother to laugh at me. Nobody dares talk to me, for nobody wants to be me. I am just invisible.

•

Bob put me at the other end of the dinner table, where the mistress of the house sits. They were quiet. What could they say to this interloper? If I had been a turtle, I would have pulled in my head. I too couldn't think of a thing to say.

I cleared my throat. "I've never tasted Renia's gravy before, it's wonderful," I said in a neutral voice.

But they were chatting among themselves now; their witticisms and stories of the past going back and forth like tennis balls. I could barely follow them. But I did notice, at that meal and at ones to come, that the person always absent from their tales was their late mother. How could the whole family not even mention her? Were they trying to guard her memory or keep their own at bay?

And then it came to me. They *were* grieving. Of course. That would explain why they had trouble looking at me, listening to me. I was sitting, healthy, full of life, exactly where their mother should have sat.

I wondered whether they had ever *openly* and thoroughly mourned Martha. For many years after she died, I certainly hadn't mourned my own mother.

I lay awake the night she passed away. I don't think I was sleeping. I felt my body changing. I panicked. I was becoming my mother. In life, she had smothered me, and now she was trying to take me with her. "I don't want to go with you," I cried out, and she left as quickly as she had come. I was wheezing badly, gulping in breaths, but I was myself again.

The next day, my father and sister sat immobilized. They looked on dumbfounded as I went scurrying about, drunk on denial, arranging the funeral, working the phones, putting death notices in newspapers, and reporting her passing to relatives and friends. "She went quickly," I would reply reassuringly to all the tears and sympathy.

Before the week was up, I went back on the presidential campaign trail for the *Times*, working twelve-hour days covering Sargent Shriver, an eccentric candidate who dished out delicious copy. I hardly thought of my mother at all. Until five years later, when she returned with a vengeance.

The dead may pass out of this world, but they don't let go so easily. They wait patiently for their due; for you to ponder what they gave you and what they took away, relive the wonder of their lives, the terrible wonder of their deaths.

Had the Morgenthaus been dealing with their mother's loss as I had dealt with mine? Pretending outwardly that it didn't happen and inwardly unable to express it, hurting that much more?

I had compassion for them. When my father had started going out with a woman not my mother, I thought she was dreadful; I saw only a sharp freckled nose, a mean mouth, a Boston Irish accent that made me wince.

When I got used to her, I realized she was attractive and rather nice. Pat's ability to make Dad happier and less lonely was a God-given gift that made my Oedipal objections look petty. And in the long run, she had lifted me from the burden of being a parent to my parent.

The Morgenthau family gatherings continued to get more onerous. I was not the only one the children had trouble talking to; they also seldom addressed their father. I knew he must have been suffering, though he never showed it. He'd just trade little smiles with me across the table as though we were the only ones there.

"I think you and Bob are quite good with Barbara," Margie Lang remarked one day as we went looking for antiques together. "You know what the problem is, don't you? If she likes you too much, she feels like she's betraying her mother. So she gravitates to her older sisters."

Teenagers were a puzzle to me, perhaps because I had repressed my own dreary adolescence. One day, Barb would sulkily walk away when I approached her, and the next she'd chatter away with me as though I were her best pal. Instead of taking her moodiness in stride, I got upset and felt I had failed her in some way.

I broke my nose twice in my first year of marriage. If that had some Freudian significance, I didn't know it. I only knew that I was in a daze all that year and kept ending up in the hospital. The second time, Barbara sent me a card that read, "My mom keeps breaking her schnoz. What am I going to do?" I smiled and felt miraculously better. I still have the card pinned to my bulletin board.

My father lived three hours away in Massachusetts. My sister, Penny, who worked as a special assistant to a number of movie stars and producers in Hollywood, hated to fly; thus we were seldom together. I was never happier than when Bob and I went out to dinner with Bobby and Barbara alone. Bob could raise everyone's spirits by telling old jokes; uttered with perfect timing in a voice like a kettledrum, they sounded uproariously new. Even if silent, we felt peacefully complete, one unit, meshed together in some spiritual way. How I had longed for this! My childhood home had been a place of impending disaster, like the night before the Battle of Gettysburg. When I first met the Morgenthau children, each so different but so much the same, quipping and laughing and delighting in each other like characters from a nineteenth-century novel, I felt a surge of hopeful anticipation.

Family. A fortress. Faithful and abiding. Louisa May Alcott's *Little Women*. The five little Peppers. The dozen Gilbreths. Contented clans gathered by the fire as the icy winds beat against their windows.

Family. The incarnation of perfect love imagined in an attic on a lonely Sunday afternoon when the mother was in bed and the father wasn't to be found. The young forever dancing round and round on a Grecian urn that brightened Keats's drooping heart.

But if I thought that I would be a link in their chain, a rock in the rampart, that I would even be allowed to enter their lives, I was dreaming the dreams of my youth.

If only I had been like my aunt Kathleen, my own family's interloper. She had been through much worse. When my uncle Billy brought home an older middle-class woman named Goldie, my proper Victorian grandmother was horrified. As a condition of their marriage, Gram made Goldie change her name to Kathleen. Well, Goldie simply ignored Gram's anger and chattered on to her as though she were Gram's best friend, until finally that is exactly what she became.

Bob tried to make me feel better by downplaying the tension. "I thought it was a very successful dinner," he'd say. "Everyone seemed to get along well."

I thought Bob the smartest man on earth. He must be right: I always *have* exaggerated things.

Then he began to up the ante on me. "You're imagining it," he'd say, cross and fed up when I tearfully complained about the kids. "You're a pessimist; you're too sensitive."

"Well, you're *in*sensitive!" I said in a voice so loud I thought I might have cracked a glass. He put his hands over his ears. I upped the decibel level. "I see now that you've been making me feel worse by not acknowledging I was being hurt. And you're wrong. Finally, I see through you. You only pretend you're infallible!"

He walked away and began to loosen his tie, take off his jacket, examine the receipts stuffed in his pockets. I was history. I went dead calm and regarded him. I had remembered reading that women can easily calm their emotional outbursts; the flush, the tears, the screams, the rapid breathing, are dispatched at meteoric speed. On the other hand, men are left at high pitch: their heart rates take much longer to return to normal. Maybe it was his body rather than his mind that avoided confronting things.

•

Cousins Margie and Nan, though tough dames, had by now veritably adopted me, fussing over me at their parties. And when Nan, an environmentalist who wrote under the name Anne W. Simon, came out with a new book, I offered to throw her a book party at our Charlton Street house. Nan, a very rich woman, was a rarity who had overcome her plain looks with her glamorous gestures and slow, mesmerizing voice. She was not without arrogance and edge, but I was used to it. At one of her Vineyard extravaganzas she asked me, "Where did your sylphlike body go?" and at another she remarked, "Your sweater is pilling."

It seemed appropriate, then, that her new book was called *The Thin Edge: Coast and Man in Crisis.*

I had moved the antique furniture given to me by my grandmother into Charlton Street, and the rooms were spare but rich. Nan's party was the first social gathering I had hosted as Mrs. Morgenthau, and I was nervous. I handwrote invitations to sixty people and arranged to festoon the house with flowers from the flower market. But I didn't know what to do about the food. Should I make it myself?

"Lucinda, you're not a cook," said Marina, a master of understatement. She was lounging on the worn velvet love seat my grandmother had sent me. The tufts were coming apart, but she looked like a Goya spread out on it, with her flowing cream silk tunic and long, lustrous dark hair.

"Well, what can I do!" I fretted. "I've never given a fancy party."

"Have it catered, silly," she said, giving me an indulgent smile. She was raised in an extravagant Moroccan family where she was treated like a princess. "Call up Giorgio," she said. "Giorgio DeLuca—he's just opened a fancy food boutique. He'd die to do a party for you."

So I sat down with Giorgio at Dean & DeLuca. He suggested six different hot and cold hors d'oeuvres, including truffle rounds, beluga caviar with crème fraîche, and hand-smoked Scottish salmon. I thought it sounded swell.

On the night of the party I miraculously felt calm. When Nan entered the room, she immediately looked at my legs and cried, "Boots?!" I didn't even flinch, much less run upstairs to put on heels. Instead, I smiled and told her this was the latest fashion (if it was, I didn't know it) and mingled among the guests with ease. I was proud of myself. I had repressed my shyness and acted the perfect hostess. The party was a great success.

A few days later, I came into Charlton Street and Bob was holding up a bill from Dean & DeLuca. It was for $700, which in 1978 was probably more like $2,513.87 in 2013. He was angrier than I'd ever seen him; his voice thundered so, it sounded like cymbals banging in my ears.

"What on earth were you thinking of, spending this much on finger food!" he held up the bill, printed on conspicuous eight-by-ten pink paper. "Do you think we have that kind of money?"

"Oh, shit, I'm sorry. I didn't realize. They just brought the food. I didn't ask how much it would cost," I said.

"Well, that's the most stupid thing I've ever heard from you."

"I'll pay you back. I'll go out and sing on the street corner. Anything."

"I'm not amused." He threw the bill on the Queen Anne hall table he had recently bought.

"But everybody loved the canapés," I said lamely, "don't you think?"

He turned to face me, eyes like stones. "You're going to go through money like Sherman through Georgia, I can see that. You'll have me bankrupt in a year."

The brass pendulum of the grandfather clock hammered its rods six times, and they felt like Bob's voice, each gong going through me like electricity. I sat down on the hall stairs and put my head in my hands.

He went upstairs, and I quickly headed for my study to get my savings account withdrawal slips. I had taken the pink bill off the table. He would never know what happened to it.

•

When you first marry, you become so emotionally blind you expect your spouse to bend to your every wish. For years you can fail to know him as well as you do the least of your friends. Instead, he becomes a mirror, reflecting all your needs and assumptions. Sometimes it takes years for you to overcome your narcissism and wake to see your loved one as he really is.

If I assumed that Bob equated money and love, he assumed that I equated money and opportunity. We had joint checking accounts, and although his secretary paid most of the bills, every time the charge card bills came in, I quickly paid them myself. I wanted to drown out his accusatory voice about what I spent on the party. I didn't spend a nickel more than I had to and shrank from the elegant way the women in Bob's world lived. I didn't buy any more suits at Brooks Brothers for Bob. I began shopping for clothes at Alexander's, trolled the aisles of Kmart for slipcovers, and only occasionally visited the forbidding Saks.

Still, I obsessed about Bob's furious response to my spending too much money on the party. He had been unfair and unforgiving of my youth and naïveté. But really, how *could* I have been that stupid? I, who had hoarded the money I earned at summer jobs so I could move to London after college? Who had been sending part of her paycheck to her parents since her father's alloyed-steel business collapsed? Who *always* asked the price of every purchase she made? Had my disgust with conspicuous consumption collapsed under the stature of being Mrs. Robert Morgenthau?

•

The party for Nan Werner had been our goodbye to Charlton Street. We had rented an apartment on the Upper East Side so Barbara could be nearer her school, Fieldston, in Riverdale.

The loss of Charlton Street was the loss of my dream house. Its neighborhood had been my hood with its avant-garde culture and funky shops, and it was close to Bob's office at the courts area in lower Manhattan. The thought of living in a penthouse on Park Avenue and Eighty-Eighth Street, even though, thanks to a real estate friend of Bob's, it was a rent-stabilized apartment, was stupefying: pretentious bankers, stores that sold baby dresses for a thousand dollars, and of course the formidable ladies who lunched.

Our new home, in fact, was a rather spectacular dump. The paint was peeling, the floors warped, and the rooms marched one by one around the building in the form of an enormous railroad flat. It was said to have housed the maids of rich tenants a half century earlier, but now the walls of the warren had been knocked down, making way for bigger rooms—a spacious dining room, a living room, a study, three good-sized bedrooms, a maid's room, and a laundry room. It was quirky to the extreme, though not my kind of quirky. Steel doors and windows reinforced with wire mesh gave off the aura of a minimum-security prison. The hall leading to the rooms was dark and oddly narrow, and outside there was a wraparound industrial terrace where workmen were constantly wandering, peeking into the bedrooms. Bob told me to stop making self-pitying wisecracks because most people would kill for a terrace so large. Well, he was right. And at least it was not some pretentious luxury pit with pillars, sponge-painted walls, and spotlights on the Andy Warhols. And it was located near the Metropolitan Museum, the

Guggenheim, the Frick, and many other little cultural gems, which would be good for Barbara, for all of us. It was also a relief to think that Barbara could stay for after-school sports and not come home in the dark.

It was the summer of 1978, and the time had come to say goodbye to Riverdale as well. It was hard for Barbara to leave the home in which she grew up, and as the movers hauled out the last of the cartons, she lingered. There was only one thing left in her bedroom, and that was a picture of a horse tacked up on the wall. It was so good I had thought of asking her to have it framed. But she wrote a message under the horse, perhaps for the girl who would claim her spot, closed the door, and left her childhood room forever.

I felt sorrow for her, I wanted to take her in my arms, but she had distanced herself from us.

When we arrived at our new home, we assumed that Barbara would arrange her room, make it her own. I had bought new sheets and some things to help decorate it. It was a sweet room, and she had her own bathroom with old-fashioned brass fixtures. The movers, however, had hardly gotten the first load of furniture up to the tenth floor when one of the older girls arrived; I can't remember which one. She looked around. Her nostrils were wide and her eyes pooled.

She watched us roll out the carpet in the dining room. "Have a nice life," she called as she ushered Barbara into the elevator.

I don't know which one of us felt worse.

9

We were standing on the terrace, watching that ephemeral light that precedes sundown set the work of our hands aglow. The petunias and marigolds, the pots of eggplant, the purples, the yellows, the browns, glistening perfection. "Isn't that a beautiful sight?" Bob said and tenderly brushed a speck of dirt off my nose.

We had been planting as if our wacky terrace, with the cracked red tiles and fat shingle-topped sides, were a rich black field. The previous year we tried to grow green peppers, but they turned out looking like miniature Quasimodos. We blamed it on the black gusts of smoke that continually blew onto the terrace from some nearby furnace. I looked up fearfully, as I always did, at the huge rickety water tower that sat above our bedroom. If it collapsed, at least the eggplants would be well watered.

The sky was so creamy blue and Bob was in such a mellow mood that I wondered if he would open up about the one subject that divided us, that prevented my stepchildren from giving me a chance—the inscrutable woman whose clothes had hung untouched in her closet, whose ring had stayed on Bob's finger until almost the eve of our wedding, and who lingered still. What you don't know scares you, and really, I had never known why.

"Bob," I said casually, loosening the soil in a pot of petunias. "I wonder what Martha would think of our garden. She liked gardening, no?"

He nodded. "Flowers."

"What was she really like?"

"She was a very private person, and she would want to stay that way," he answered emphatically, as though she were standing in the next room. He dripped water into the pots of plants.

"Look, maybe you don't get the impact this has on me. It feels like she's a secret lover that you're protecting. Or someone whose name you can't utter or you'll be struck down."

I followed him down the hall, through the bedroom, and into the bathroom, which was so small two people could hardly be in it together.

He spread shaving cream on his face with an old-fashioned badger-hair shaving brush. Then he took his straight razor, jutted out his chin, and very carefully ran the blade down his cheek.

"You still must be so much in love with her," I said quietly.

"I had five children with her," he replied.

I turned around to leave and closed the door behind me. I went into the kitchen and splashed water on my face. Then I felt a hand on my back.

"Take it easy, Mrs. Morgenthau, take it easy now," said Renia. She usually didn't intrude, but she had something to say: "They were feeling bad about themselves in that house, the house in Riverdale, after she passed. I saw it." She nodded her head. "They were angry too. She was a good person, but no saint, don't even think that way. Never mind about anybody else. You just take good care of Mr. Morgenthau and you'll be happy. You can do it. I know you can." Then she went back into the kitchen and put the London broil under the hot broiler.

What was Renia telling me? That the children felt bad that their mother took on her cancer recurrence alone so they could have a good vacation? That would be a reason that Bob couldn't face talking about her. Maybe he thought that in spite of her hopeless attitude, if only he had known about the recurrence, he could have somehow saved her. And the anger Renia cryptically referred to?

Then it suddenly occurred to me. How could I have been so dense? Bob was so careful not to hurt people's feelings. He was a sensitive man, and he must have known that anything he shared would make me feel inadequate. If he said she grew gorgeous sunflowers, it would reflect on my own ignorance of gardening. If he told me she was a great cook, I would feel like a bad wife. Given that most of my balls went out of the court, how could he say if she was a crack tennis player who won championships with him?

And there was something else I had to understand: he was protecting me further. I didn't need to know anything more about Martha. I now knew the secret I had been dreading. He still loved her, and always would. But that was all right—I could accept it, because I knew he loved me too.

I gave Renia a hug. When Bob sauntered into the kitchen, I looked at him apologetically. "Thank you for tolerating me," I said.

He was bewildered—not for the first time. "I thought you were mad at me."

"I'm sorry I invaded your privacy—and hers."

He took my hand reassuringly.

•

I have never understood how some people live their lives in utter stillness and restraint. They seem to float in the nests of mythic halcyons, who tame the gales into calmness. I need a halcyon. I whirl around in a maelstrom of exhausting epiphanies, odd moods; certain sounds and sights, no matter how trivial, disturb me—an overly bright sun, a car going too slow, pants with grease spots—I screen out very little.

How I wish I could put that agitation and energy into making my old Remington move. My warhorse, its ivory keys sticking up on metal necks, the letter *u* missing, had been my best friend through hard news, investigative pieces, profiles. But now that I'm trying to write fiction, it is my enemy.

My Pulitzer for national reporting had given me both a lifetime calling card and a lifetime curse. I wasn't alone. Many Pulitzer recipients went on to failure (the talented Anthony Lukas ended up killing himself) and never could write anything afterward that seemed good enough.

Deadlines, editors eager for your copy, that makes it easy. But on your own, writing is a capricious obsession. Sometimes, it will be pure pleasure, even euphoria, and others, utter misery. Writer's block is a condition whose symptoms are restlessness, a bad conscience, and an incremental increase in self-loathing. It is like entering a black hole of impossibility from which you might never emerge. There is a void that only writing can fill, but if the fragile writer manages to write and doesn't like what he has written—which is probable—then in comes the void again.

Aside from a few articles, I had hardly produced a word of value

since I began to date Bob two years earlier. And I knew that the longer
I didn't write, the longer I wouldn't.

•

"Bob, I'm a vegetable."
  "Hmm?" said Bob, lost in his *U.S. News & World Report.*
  "I'm a vegetable."
  "You mean you're vegetating."
  "No, worse." I flopped down next to him on our denim-covered sofa
in Park Avenue. "I mean I'm a vegetable."
  Finally, he put his magazine down. "Well, what are you going to
do about it? What about trying to become a lively, enterprising reporter
again?"
  "And also a lively, enterprising wife? I take care of a public figure,
get involved with his cases, look after a teenager, a big apartment. I go to
events at night, conferences on the weekend, speeches, dinners . . ."
  "Don't blame me for your writer's block. I've been very supportive of
your career. Who pushed you to go to Northern Ireland to get the Peace
Women story?"
  He was right, he had nurtured my talent. In a sense, I was his proxy.
Bob was as much a frustrated journalist as I was a frustrated detective.
In fact, he had been editor in chief of the *Amherst Student* in the late
1930s and had distinguished himself throughout his three years on the
staff by writing unsigned editorials against the school's president, Stanley King, for his conservative leanings; to be particularly mischievous,
he formed the Amherst Political Union, inviting King's nemesis, the
liberal First Lady Eleanor Roosevelt, to be the first speaker.
  It was 1939, and Amherst, reflecting the rest of the country, was divided over the question of American involvement in the European war.
The majority of the students, a broad spectrum from liberal to conservative, were vigorously against having anything to do with a conflict so far
away.
  "When she arrived, she said, 'Bob, I'm scared.' The First Lady, the
wife of the president, about to address a bunch of green undergraduates,
was scared! She was so human and honest," he said.
  "I thought she was beautiful. I never understood the stupid remarks
about her being homely."

Mrs. Roosevelt's talk was a success and, according to Bob's thank-you letter to her, "won over many who have feared the so-called dictatorial tendencies of the government."

Bob also said he thought her talk would make Amherst's president, a conservative businessman, more thoughtful about the interests of students: "President King . . . has been trying to use the war as an excuse for imposing restrictions on them. He does not seem to realize that, as you said, students must have the privileges of citizens when they are in college if they are to make good citizens later on."

Mrs. Roosevelt replied that Bob had been "a perfect host, even to the sherry and oranges, and I enjoyed every minute."

Emboldened, Bob put an anonymous note into the *Amherst Student* in Latin: "Beware the King lest the people rise up and the kingdom fall!" He ended by urging people who wanted more information to dial "80"—President King's personal extension.

•

Now Bob wants me to do the writing for both of us, wants to see my name on the front page of the *Times*. But since I quit the newspaper, the name I had made for myself is fading, the fan mail is down to a trickle. My husband was attracted to me in large part because I was a star in journalism; I wonder how he feels now that the blockbusters with my byline are no longer on the front page of *The New York Times*.

"Sweetheart, I think you fell in love with *The New York Times*, not me."

He looks up, frowning. "Don't be ridiculous. I'm trying to get you to write again because I think it's important for your morale. It's not about me."

It is June 1978, and the heat is already brutal; we are both sweaty. I pick up my Dante. I'm reading *The Inferno*, and I feel as if this month has been a *contrapasso*, a "divine revenge" for the widespread complaints about the constant snowstorms and rain and drizzle of last winter. The only bright spot is the election of Carter. He has halted work on the neutron bomb and given official pardons, a step beyond simple amnesty, to Vietnam War draft dodgers. Roger, wherever he is, must feel vindicated. As for Bob, he feels betrayed by Carter's weak support for Israel.

"Be my wife," Bob says suddenly. "Just be my wife."

"What? You think I shouldn't be a writer anymore?" Sitting in the gloom of quick-falling night, I feel hurt and bewildered.

"I didn't say that. I just don't want you to beat yourself up."

And in truth, Bob *had* been trying to help me write again. I can picture it so clearly, that day almost two years ago:

•

I am staying the night at Riverdale. He comes in from work looking glum.

"I've lost my cap!"

"Oh no, not your DA's cap!" I say with exaggerated sadness. "Not the old, faded one you've had for how many years? With the top all crushed down. Is that the one?"

"Nobody likes a W.A., as my father always told me."

He reaches in his pocket. "No, I'm sure they're going to be big." If he starts a sentence with "No," it can mean he is continuing a conversation he has had only in his own head; it can also be about a conversation he's carried on with others some time before. Jenny teasingly calls it Daddy's "return to original subject."

"What are you talking about? Who's going to be big?" I ask.

He hands me a little *Daily News* clip about two women, a Protestant and a Catholic, who've gotten together to help bring peace to Northern Ireland. One had a husband killed in the fighting. "It's the perfect story for you," he says.

I can hardly speak.

"I've already booked you a ticket. You can leave for London on British Airways day after tomorrow."

My competitive juices begin to run. "But I'd have to leave you alone." We've never been apart for more than a day or two.

"That's all right," he says. "Let's have a glass of wine."

Even if it wasn't all right, he wouldn't tell me.

"I'd be gone for a week or two. How will you get along?"

"I don't know. I'll just have to manage somehow," he says plaintively.

I rest my elbow on his shoulder, kiss his lips. It occurs to me that by temporarily plucking me out of his life, he has ironically taken charge of it. It feels sexy.

"I never can tell what you're really thinking. Maybe you'll resent it if I go."

"I won't."

"You don't care?"

"No, I do care. I'll miss you very much."

I can already hear those lilting Northern Irish tongues, feel the tart breezes, the gladdening music, the story I'll write. I run upstairs to pack; with all the gun fighting there now, maybe I should get a Kevlar vest. I only realize when I get to the top that I never poured him his glass of wine.

•

I arrive in London and take a train, then a ferry, to Belfast as I had done when I first made this trip years ago. I want to hear the waves slap against the hull as we enter the harbor, smell the peat smoke, hear the clang and crack of shipbuilding from the ancient Harland & Wolff shipyards. Going to Ireland is always like going home.

I hadn't been to the North since the early 1970s. During my three years in London, UPI always sent me here when trouble broke out. Though I was in my early twenties, they knew I could beat the pants off the jaded male press who had seen it all. They would hit the pubs, waiting for the mild British press releases that they would rewrite and file as their own stories. But I was raw and shamelessly ambitious. Typical of the young, I had no fear and would happily hotfoot it out into the riot-filled, tear-gassed streets, happening onto stories the British press would never let out. The saddest one was going up to Strabane in Derry and finding the neighbors and parents weeping over the body of young Eamon McDevitt, an innocent deaf boy who was shot by an overzealous soldier. They said he had a gun. Some were still milling around, and I looked at a particularly menacing soldier with disgust. He pointed his gun at me. I gave him the finger.

Now, giddy with the sharp cool air and the hills so green they almost hurt your eyes, I walk into Belfast. It is almost unrecognizable—burned-out houses, the sound of gunfire, empty streets. Britain has sent troops in, and they have become each side's enemy. Every time a soldier is shot by an IRA gun, troops stage night raids, knocking down Catholic doors and dragging off suspects to internment camps.

"The women have become like a second army," I tell Bob on the phone. He's fascinated. "They bang garbage can lids to warn their men the troops are coming and then make a chain around them. Boy, I would get the biggest rush pulling out my Glock and protecting you from some rampaging mafioso."

"You don't have a Glock," Bob says, chuckling a bit uneasily.

En route to the province, I meet a freelance photographer lugging a conglomeration of equipment that is almost bigger than she. A pair of biceps bulge like tennis balls from her slight arms. She invites me to share a double room in her hotel, which turns out to be a simple affair— algae-colored walls, splintered wood floors, but only a ten-minute jog from the tumultuous city center.

I walk down an alley that links the Protestant Shankill and the Catholic Falls Roads, and I find a mixed cluster of women who look hopeless, afraid; they have collapsed their bones on kitchen chairs outside their small brick row houses. When they see me, they go silent.

I persuade them to talk to me. Speaking softly, they tell me that the paramilitaries on both sides control them like medieval trade guilds. They extort money and deal out punishments; they have become the law in their respective neighborhoods.

But now, today, the women of the province get up and speak out. Here are Catholics and Protestants, who not long ago spat at each other across the barricades, embracing under banners calling for an end to the province's sectarian war. Betty Williams, a tall, raw-boned Protestant, who lost a cousin, and Mairead Corrigan, whose sister lost three children, tell me the young children of the province have been forever infected: "Our kids don't know how to play. Give them a book, and they draw tanks and guns on it."

The IRA and the Ulster Volunteer Force hate the women, but still they have succeeded in frustrating the gunmen and winning the hearts of people. Today, I am covering a march that has brought thousands out onto the perilous streets. No one has seen anything like it. Perhaps they really can bring peace where others have failed.

When I come back to the hotel, windblown and excited, my photographer friend is sitting cross-legged on her bed, running her hands through her hair, which rises like a tea cozy on top of a teapot.

"Wasn't it the greatest?" I ask. "Bet you got some great pictures."

She glowers at me. "I dropped my film in a gutter of water."

"Oh no!" I sit down across from her. "Oh, dear . . . I'm so sorry . . .

you could get other pictures; I mean, the two of them together would be nice, with men, maybe. No one's talking about the movement's men . . ."

"I know my profession," she snaps.

I retreat. "Of course."

We are so tired that night that we order dinner from room service. I dig into a plate piled with bangers and mash—the English version of bratwurst and whipped potatoes. She picks at an arrangement of raw vegetables. "What's your favorite food?" I ask in a lame attempt to make conversation. She looks at my sausages with barely disguised distaste. "I always like a nice big salad."

I feel like we ourselves are on the verge of a sectarian war. She is a bad sleeper—I bet it's because she's hungry all the time—so she goes to bed at 8:30 p.m. I wait until 10:00, hoping she has fallen asleep, and bring the phone into the closet to make my nightly calls to Bob. But just when I begin to whisper endearments, she starts loudly clearing her throat.

The night of the march, I stay up until 2:00 a.m., writing on the stairwell so the light won't disturb her. Then I go downstairs to the hotel phone to call Bob. The line is faint. "Tell me what you think of my lede," I shout. "I talk about these women, huddled under their brollies, looking like a great long centipede coming down the road. Then it reads like this":

On the stone walls lining the street, they are watched by boys with chopped-off bell-bottoms, boys with deep swampy eyes and hollow cheeks . . . they take stones from their pockets and hurl them at the women. As they raise their umbrellas to shield themselves, they smile at the boys—unsteady, tightly pressed smiles. As the stones hit their arms, legs, heads, the line does not break. The march goes on.

"Very nice," the nearby pub owner weighs in with a Northern Irish accent.

"That's great," Bob says. "Terrific."

I smile at the guy, who's now filling a glass of Guinness from the spout. "Oh, good, I wasn't sure . . ."

"You know I envy you," Bob said. "I was there during the war, and I knew why they called it the Emerald Isle . . . green even in late November. But the wind was so raw it's understandable why the Irish like their shot of whiskey."

"I didn't know you'd been here!"

"I was navigator of the lead destroyer taking a convoy of fast tankers into Belfast harbor, and we went up the river Foyle to Derry.

"There was a USO reception for us in Derry," he continued, "and the girls were more interested in eating the sandwiches than talking to us. Except for this RAF sergeant. I took a walk with her."

"Oh?"

"We stopped under a bridge and I kissed her."

"What?" I was startled and tantalized. He had never admitted having a romantic attachment before he was married. "Did you do anything else to her on this first date?"

"Oh, I think so but not much. We weren't there that long."

"Did you see her again?"

"No, we shipped out the next day. I don't even remember her name. So when are you coming home?"

"You kissed her, hmm. I suppose it was too cold to make love under the bridge."

"When are you coming home?"

"Well, uh, I wanted to interview this Protestant today, but I lost the whole afternoon. You see, after the march I wanted to get some reaction, so I went up to Strabane and got caught in sniper fire. But everything was fine. I dove under a car, and the only bullet that hit me went through my boot. It kind of took off the tip of my toe. Lucky I was wearing my Doc Martens."

Silence. Then a burst of tinny anger comes over the line. "Why did you do a stupid thing like that? What do you mean, *the tip of your toe?*" My husband is angry rather than solicitous? I'm about to get mad myself when I remember Bob telling me how furious his father was when one of his kids got hurt.

"It was no big deal. I went to the infirmary, got it sterilized and bandaged."

Suddenly I know someone's behind me.

It's the photographer. "Look," she shouts. People at the bar are looking at her. "Can't you wrap this up? I can't sleep not knowing when you're going to come in and wake me up."

The connection suddenly gets strong, and Bob hears the woman. He knows how difficult she's been. "I'd get out of there as soon as you can," he says. "Don't you already have enough material?"

"Yes, I've got plenty."

The next morning, I catch a flight to London and then on to New York. When I arrive, Bob holds on to me tightly and for a long time.

Weeks later, when the article is published, he acquires a pile of *New York Times Magazines* and liberally gives them out; my story is on the cover.

10

I sit down to dinner one day in the spring of 1978, and though I am thirty-one years old, I learn that I have now reached adulthood. I know Bob loves me deeply, but he has a mind that divides facets of certain individuals' characters into a number of cabinets, sometimes unjustly. I have, for instance, been locked in one that reads, "Dreamy, innocent, often unable to keep a secret."

Therefore, he withholds from me the meatier aspects of his cases, which is partly his fault. Last summer, for instance, we were renting a house in Martha's Vineyard belonging to John and Margery Oakes. John was the genteel, famous, and rather fusty editor of the *Times* editorial page, and Margery, his wife, was the woman who had assumed I was Bob's employee when she met me at the Arthur Schlesinger party. I had just put potatoes on to boil for salad when Bob said, "Hey, let's take the boat to Cuttyhunk and spend the night." I was thrilled. Bob didn't do a lot that he hadn't prepared for, and when he decided to do something spontaneous, he wanted to do it right then. Bob loved the wooden Bass fishing boat, and when we were here, we went out for blues at dawn. Before he changed his mind, I threw a few things in a duffel bag, and we beat it out the door so we'd get to this quaint little island before dark.

We were halfway there, I, sitting in my usual place, the tip of the bow, enjoying the spray, and thinking about my husband and how I had brought out the free spirit in him. I mused about whether our marriage had helped peel away his layers of caution, which made me suddenly remember the potatoes. We sped back to port at twenty-five knots, but by the time we reached the little kitchen, it was full of smoke. The pan, the stove, the soot-covered walls, were destroyed. Margery, a woman who hated things to go off plan, was not pleased. It was the way she muttered "That was a very expensive potato salad" and then stalked off that made us both break out laughing, even though we knew a new kitchen would cost Bob a great deal of money indeed.

Then I made another stupid mistake. We were dining with friends, and, excited with pride in my husband, I was praising his daring as a DA, and before I realized it, out of my mouth came classified details of a murder investigation. Bob looked darkly at me and I stopped short, but the damage was done. As a reporter, I knew that leaking grand jury deliberations was verboten, and if they got out, it could sabotage his trial. As usual, I had been distracted and indiscreet.

Recently, however, we went to a political fund-raiser, and I covertly watched Bob covertly watching me as I dodged the questions of friends trying to wheedle out information about the indictment of a well-known company CEO. I really hadn't been as skillful as he thought since I didn't know anything about it anyway. Still, I hadn't talked, and this was apparently enough for Bob.

"So," he says the next night, after I give him the biggest piece of swordfish on our gold-rimmed wedding platter, "there's no doubt that this Argentinean banker, Graiver, committed massive bank fraud."

This, as though we've been talking about old Graiver forever. I sit very still.

"It's very confidential, this case. You mustn't mention it to anyone."

"No, no." I shake my head vigorously.

"This character, David Graiver, held a controlling interest in American Bank & Trust here in New York, and we think that he transferred, oh, some fifty million dollars to an affiliated Belgian bank. Then he withdrew the money, and pocketed it, and left the American Bank & Trust to collapse.

"And then he disappeared . . ."

"Wow," I exclaim. "Did he . . . ?"

"Just listen, let me finish. His associates say he was killed in 1976 when his chartered plane crashed on its way to his home in Acapulco."

"Oh, so he's dead."

"I'm not so sure. Actually, I don't think he is. I think it's a ruse for him to avoid prosecution. He took that plane shortly after he looted the bank. And then he was reported walking through an airport some time after the crash. But his family insists he is deceased.

"The point is, can I indict an alleged dead man?"

I can't believe he is asking me, but I don't miss a beat.

"Well, Bob Morgenthau can do anything, even indict a dead man! But seriously, if you don't do him now and then he reappears when the statute of limitations has run out, he walks. If he did something wrong, and as far as you can determine, he is *not* dead, I think you have to go ahead and prosecute him."

"That's exactly what I thought." He nods appreciatively.

"Was the plane found?"

"Yes, in the mountains in Mexico," says Bob, sweeping up the last of his peas and eating them off his knife. I repress the urge to scold him, as my mother would have done had I ever breached good table manners that way.

"But his body was not identified," he added. "Why wouldn't Graiver have taken a regular airline? Rather than a charter? It would have been more comfortable and quicker. The Mexican authorities haven't investigated the crash, and Americans combed the area and never found a black box."

"So the whole thing is suspicious."

"Very damn suspicious. American Bank & Trust was the fourth-largest bank failure in American history. I think I'm going to go ahead and gather evidence to present to a grand jury."

"Does the jurisdiction of the New York DA include Belgium?"

He chuckles. "No. But since it all started here, I think we have a duty to the now-defunct American Bank & Trust to find out where their money went."

"You devil. It's the U.S. attorney's territory. What are they going to say, or worse, do?"

"They'll probably be mad as hell. But if we turn over the case to them, they'll most likely forget about it."

I am witnessing the first of many high dives that my husband will be making as DA. His restless arm has begun this day to stretch into a faraway place where a local DA is not supposed to go. It won't stop here. White-collar crime incites him. He sees it as the root of society's evils. He sees the consequences that the little guy suffers—drugs, for instance, imported with laundered money that end up in the school yards of New York. I foresee that he will use any Manhattan connection, no matter how slim, to go after international white-collar crime. He will probably get death threats from feds enraged at his incursions into their territory.

A few days later, Bob comes home grinning. "We've cooked something up, and I want your opinion."

He sinks into our cushy sofa for our ritual cocktail hour, which is really Bordeaux hour since he likes to drink different vintages from the region. I wait patiently until he has selected, uncorked, poured out, and savored the wine of the night, a 1974 Pomerol. Only then do I say, "You've cooked up what?"

"We have to get the records of this Belgian bank, and the banks there only hand over their internal accounts to representatives of the U.S. government. So I got Jawn Sandifer of the New York Supreme Court to sign an order—that's called a letter rogatory—to the bank. The order authorizes Pierre Leval to receive the bank's records."

Bob suppresses a laugh. "We're going to stamp the seal of New York on it to make the order look more official. Then we can attach a ribbon at the top for good measure.

"Do you think we should do that?" he asks me. "Or is it overkill?"

"Hell yes, do it! You could just bull right through and make them think you're the most powerful law enforcement officer in the city—Le Dernier Cri."

"You know, that just might work."

And indeed it does. Pierre goes to Brussels with the fully beautified order, and Bob waits anxiously to hear from him.

After Pierre calls, Bob tells me of the conversation: "Apparently, the Belgian bank officer was very, very skeptical of the order; he kept insisting he'd been expecting it to come from the U.S. attorney.

"Then Pierre told him, 'Oh yes, Mr. Morgenthau was a U.S. attorney when he was a young man.' Implying that I was more powerful than any U.S. attorney, that being the DA was a step up. The bank manager turned over the records."

Armed with the evidence, the assistant DAs persuade a grand jury to indict Graiver, and the judge, Arnold Fraiman, refuses to dismiss it.

When the bank president finds out Pierre has gone behind the back of the U.S. Justice Department, "the Belgians almost made it an international incident," Bob tells me.

"We got that indictment on a wing and a prayer," he says, chuckling, and then he smiles and adds, "And on your good advice."

A frisson of pleasure runs down my back, and I can hardly look at him.

Unfortunately, however, the following January, with no visible sign that the defendant is still alive, Judge Fraiman reluctantly dismisses the indictment; he encourages the state to reindict if it gets further evidence that Graiver exists. Bob's fearlessness in bringing the case in the first place has only enhanced his reputation. And I had begun, in a tiny way, to be part of the game.

In the first two years of a marriage, you discover that you're not going to conduct your daily life the way you had hoped, or even the way you were used to. Life becomes not only about romance but about survival of the fittest. Rules are set down by each party that remind you of the hated curfews of adolescence. You can no longer smoke in bed or read by lamplight; pity to you if you're late or forget to shave beneath your chin. There are the struggles over little things. Take the bathroom sink. It has been divided so you have an equal half for your toiletries. Soon, however, your Oil of Olay begins inching toward his half, until one day you find that all your vitamins and creams have been rudely shoved into a corner. You like a cold room, and he likes it hot, so you alternately open and close the window, with the result that neither one gets a good night's sleep.

The bigger bids for power, however, can get bloodier. A person married becomes a person unveiled, slouching about in his or her raw authenticity, the facade of utter charm gone. You can be blissfully happier than you've ever been in your life and suddenly find yourself in a fight to the death.

Monday, November 19, 1979, was our second anniversary, and it should have started with a haircut.

I wanted Bob to look smart for this sentimental day, but there was no place to cut his hair, save the toilet seat. Every other surface in our New York City bedroom was covered with Bob's bricolage—a mess of old magazines and catalogs he's never going to read, old mail, new briefs, old briefs, ear drops, eyedrops, books on the destroyers of World War II, unpacked tote bags, and much more. Our bedroom was suggestive of a front yard in Appalachia replete with used refrigerators and the hulks of cars. I begged him to clean it up, for me, and to my delight he agreed.

Then my sister, Penny, called to wish us happy anniversary, and I put the phone on speaker. "Penny, you should see the mess your sister has made," Bob called. "Junk strewn everywhere, brassieres drying on the lamp shades. I've pleaded with her to clean it up to no avail. I wish you'd speak to her . . ."

"That's a lie! I'm pin neat!" I cried, my husband's sloppiness having driven me to the opposite extreme. I could hear Penny cracking up. We have cultivated a good-natured teasing that never hurts. "Oh yes, Bob," she drawled, "it's been a problem for us for years."

Yuk, yuk, Bob and Penny.

This day had to be wonderful. We liked to haunt antiques stores, thrift shops, auctions, and we had bid on and won a unique lamp, a brass dog in the shape of a wiener with an adorable little buckle collar and dangling name tag. Light was given off by its illuminated torso. One of the younger children saw me polishing it and scoffed, "What a piece of junk."

"It's Lucinda's," said Bob, selling me out.

"I thought so."

Now, today, after Bob cleared up his stuff, he volunteered to make good on his rather moldy promise to read my short story. It was a funny piece about order and disorder in a man's life, and I watched in vain for any sign of appreciation or amusement, but his facial muscles remained frozen.

"What did you think?" I asked anxiously as he put it down.

He shrugged. "I don't understand the point of the story."

"But the point is obvious! Did you like the descriptions, the similes, the metaphors?"

"Well, I just don't know what you're trying to do here."

It occurred to me then that the kernel of this story had risen from Bob and his sloppiness. Well, that, of course, would be a good reason for him to dislike it. What possessed me to even share it with him?

A little later he came up behind me, sifted strands of my hair. "I didn't mean to hurt you; the story was promising, really. I knew if I read it, it wouldn't be a good idea, husbands just can't be objective. Arthur Gelb told me he never reads Barbara's work because if he so much as questions a comma, she gets annoyed."

We packed up and set off upstate. Since the vast old mansion at the farm was owned by Bob and his two siblings and often full of family, we decided to go away for our anniversary. We would stay over until Tuesday at an inn in Millbrook, up the valley from the orchards and full of beautiful pastures and horse farms. Someday, I didn't know when, we would build our own house on Apple Pie Ridge, the highest point in the apple farm. Until then, I would continue to dream about it: I would create a paradise of color, a profusion of buddleias, lilies of the valley, peonies, trumpet lilies, and herbs. Scents would ride on the breezes, and I would watch the buds creep out, changing every day.

Our room was a sweet Victorian treasure with a canopy bed, located above the front door of the Millbrook inn. It looked out over a pond crowned in burnt-orange leaves, the shade of its green water shifting with the autumn sun. I threw open the window and sat Bob down. Time to cut off his hair. He complained bitterly, as was his custom, but now that his locks were tickling his collar, he grudgingly conceded that my rates were cheaper than a fifteen-dollar barber. As I held the shears over his head, the baby fuzz on his neck sent shivers down me. I had to rub his leg; I loved the feel of smooth khaki against the swell of a man's thigh. Most particularly, this man's.

Because his head was buried in the newspaper, I had to clip away in a hit-or-miss fashion, like painting a mural with my eyes closed. I tried to work carefully, but then I was caught by the shadow of a swan soaring across the white billows in the sky. I loved clouds, and these moved like satin petticoats, length upon length of silk, a woman's skirt riffling in the gusts. The swan landed and picked its way down to the pond like a cat, sniffing, looking both ways, dipping a webbed foot before the plunge. Then it sank its head into its round white chest like an angel resting on a pillow of clouds.

"Lucinda, are you paying attention? You're cutting a hole in my hair. I can feel it."

"Oh! Sorry." There *was* a little swatch missing. My dreamy nature was not helpful as a hairstylist. I spread Grecian Formula through his new coiffure to darken the white, and he grumbled, as was his custom. "That's not going to make me any younger," he said pointedly.

We dined at a romantic candlelit restaurant, and Bob, who had quickly forgotten his ordeal of emasculation through haircutting, ordered a very expensive Château Latour. I suggested we toast our two years together.

I looked at him lovingly. "You have touched me with your honesty, and I mean more honest than just saying I won't lie, steal, cheat, but saying I'm going to help people and do the right thing. Your humanity is global."

He clinked his glass against mine and said, "And your humanity is personal. It's a part of you. That's what you have more than I do. You're loyal and compassionate, the way you come to the aid of friends in trouble, like when Jessica was sick and you were there every day."

"Thank you for your stability . . . your equanimity in the face of my *moody* humanity," I replied.

He raised his glass. "Thank you for bringing adventure and creativity to my life. I couldn't get bored with you, ever."

"I'm remarkably lucky."

"*I'm* remarkably lucky."

We ate a sumptuous Dover sole, periodically reaching for each other's hand under the table. Professing that we would let nothing interfere with our loving each other, Bob ordered a second bottle of fine wine, a 1971 Saint-Émilion.

Then he wanted to introduce me to Calvados. We had two snifters each, made silly toasts, and clattered our glasses together until we couldn't stop laughing.

By the time we got back to the inn, the excessive spirits had made Bob, on the other side of sixty, dizzily tired, while I, half his age, was flying high. "Let's play in the shower," I cried, "it's only ten o'clock, and it would cap off the evening," but he shook his head.

"We didn't exchange presents yet," I exclaimed.

He reached over to his carryall and pulled out a silver pin in the shape of a question mark without the dot. I've never worn pins, but it was certainly beautiful. I gave him my poem:

> You are a hundred suns lighting the water
> Silver dolphin arcing over me

> *From the joining of*
> *Our minds*
> *Sea pressing against sea*
> *From this great power*
> *Is squeezed the delicate*
> *Glitter-finned fish.*

> *I will love you til the end of time,*
> *Your Sweetheart*

"Nice." He let the handmade paper I had gotten in Italy waft to the floor.

"Bob, I know you're very tired, but is that all you can say?"

"I'll read it again tomorrow," he said, yawning. "Come to bed, silly bill."

All day I had suppressed my anger at his reaction to my short story, but now, with his disregard for my poem, it seethed up again. "You won't like it any better tomorrow.

"I feel I have to earn your love, but it doesn't matter what you do, you can smell or be foolish, and I still love you. I still love you, even though you don't like my writing, you don't like my haircuts. I love you even if you never take me to the Plaza for tea."

Bob lifted his head. "You're choosing now to list all the grievances you have against me?"

"Bob," I said, pacing the floor. "It's been bugging me for a long time. You are so withholding, you won't talk about deep feelings, and you won't even recognize them! I don't think you're even in touch with them. Or mine. I spent days writing a love poem to you. But do you appreciate the effort? No, you'd rather drop it on the floor."

"Don't be ridiculous. Stop your bellyaching, I want to go to sleep."

I picked up his trousers and threw them at his head. "There's just too many years between us. The generation gap, that is our quintessential problem. You are like on the cusp of the Silent Generation, and I come from a culture that keeps no secrets."

"And in the process you don't care who you hurt. You just pound away at me and make out as though I'm inadequate. You think that's the way to get me to talk?"

"This is not how I thought it would be. Marrying someone who communicates with the grunts of a Neanderthal."

"I didn't know you knew such a big word."

I gritted my teeth. "I'm calling my father! I'm going to go stay with him. At least he doesn't diminish me."

"Oh, please, not that threat again," Bob said with a withering look.

So I picked up the phone and, for the sake of my credibility, actually dialed Daddy. He told me to go to bed, get up tomorrow and have a cup of coffee, read the newspaper, and everything would be fine again.

I hung up. "Bob, did we make a mistake?" I said very gently. "Maybe we weren't meant to be married." I expected him to soften, tell me that we certainly were.

"You are a horse's ass of considerable dimensions," he said, flicking out the light and turning over on his good ear so he couldn't hear me anymore. "And no lighting any candles," he added, nestling into his pillow. "The *Harvard Health Letter* says you need a completely dark room to sleep."

I stood and stared at him, a lump in the bed. Since I couldn't talk, I had to write. But I had no light, so I decided it was a good idea to crawl out the window onto the inn's awning. I paused for a minute when I realized that all that wine Bob had ordered had put me in some stage of inebriation, but my qualms quickly passed. It was a nice strong canvas anyway, brightly lit, and the smell of cigarette smoke wouldn't wake him up. So I grabbed an ashtray and pen and paper and climbed out. Then I began to write:

> Mind racing like a runaway train. Why can't I be more relaxed and understanding? Why is everything an emergency with me? I know there is no perfect marriage and I want everything my way, perfect. But when he didn't throw me on the bed and lock me to his body on this anniversary that will never come again. His parents undoubtedly taught him that a proper hug might break you in pieces.

"Lucinda! What the hell are you doing? Get back in here!"

Bob had woken up. "I don't want to bother you," I called icily.

"You'll fall through the canvas!" He was pleading now. "It won't hold you."

"You think I'm *that* fat?!"

"I'd come out and get you, but then it really *would* cave in."

I ignored his pleas and commands until, exasperated but defeated, he finally went back to bed.

When I was tired of writing, I inched up to the window on my belly, climbed through, got in bed, and curled up behind him.

•

The next morning, we woke feeling like caterpillars in the pupal stage. We had never drunk as much as we did the night before.

"My back aches," Bob croaked.

"My stomach hurts," I moaned.

"Do you know why your stomach hurts? Because it was next to my back."

Then his face clouded. "I'm glad to see you're still alive."

"Oh God, don't remind me." I buried my face in his hand. "I'm sorry, I'm sorry. I don't know how you can possibly love me. All I do is make your hair stand on end."

He thought for a moment. "I'm afraid that's *why* I love you," he said, then picked up my poem and with a sweet little smile began to read it.

11

In June 1980, we are sitting on our terrace in T-shirts, watching balloons of black smoke pump from an ancient stack next door, when Bob quite casually says, "Why don't we circumnavigate the state of New York in our boat?"

"What?"

"Let's sail the canals and lakes. We'd go west, then north, then east, then south. Make a complete circle."

"Are you serious? What a superlative idea!" Bob does not love adventure traveling, but he knows I do. He knows what I need to be happy. The power of his love comes over me, and I feel him, feel him as though I *were* him; it must be in moments like these that a couple really achieves oneness. Not in lovemaking, not in the exchange of language, but in the act of forsaking our own desires in order to identify with the desires of the one we love.

I feel so close to him now. I can hear him thinking, hear him, behind his strong, confident words, wondering, "Can I pull this off at the age of almost sixty-one? Am I up to it? Yes, I better be. Her excitement will inspire me. If I learn to love the things she loves, I'll always have her."

"You will always have me," I say. I kiss his arm from his fingers to his elbow and feel him shiver. I hear him say to himself, "It feels like a caterpillar's inching up my arm."

"You're tickling me," he says aloud.

"It could be dangerous," he warns. "Lake Ontario can turn rough as an ocean."

I kiss him again, this time on the lips.

This is what the boat we will travel on looks like: a thirty-two-foot wooden Bass boat with a large deck, half of which is taken up by a diesel-engine box, and a miniature galley with a tiny head, a tinier sink with no faucet, and one and a half bunks. It is seventeen years old and painted a pale pinkish orange.

The boat leaves Cape Cod in August and comes steaming into the West Twenty-Third Street pier like a big Creamsicle, its hull freshly painted gleaming black and the deck a rosy ivory. I am beyond excited. But when the boatman docks it and I step down below, it looks like nautical salvage: everywhere are little plastic lures with rusty hooks, reels, spinners, rods, dirty sponges, and an oily outboard motor lying on what will be our bed.

That night, we sit down with an atlas, and Bob solemnly traces our route: up the majestic Hudson, through the Erie and Oswego Canals, across Lake Ontario, through the Thousand Islands in the St. Lawrence River, past Montreal, up the Richelieu River to Lake Champlain, through the Champlain Canal, and back down the Hudson. This will encompass more than a thousand miles, four canals, sixty locks, four lakes, three rivers, and two countries. And it will take, he says, a great deal of skill.

"But you've manned huge destroyers in the war, big fishing boats, little Sailfish, and, in the Vineyard, you've gone eight or so miles out to Nomans Island. And don't forget me. I'll help. I ran Daddy's boat while he was up on the flying bridge spotting swordfish. We went twenty miles out deep-sea fishing in a boat six inches bigger than yours."

Whoops. I bit my lip. I just compared him with my father. Big mistake. I wait for a reaction now, the scowl or something, but it doesn't come. Or at least not then.

The next day, when we board the *Souvenir*, he is wearing an old blue captain's hat complete with gold braid. Without a word, he goes up to the bridge and installs a new radiotelephone, radio direction finder, and depth finder and lays out parallel rulers, a barometer, and a pile of charts, or maps, of the waterways. He has also brought aboard a carbine with cartridges the size of carrots, and that is one toy he is not taking. Period.

I ponder how a boat is a man's playground—a place where he can empty his mind of work and worries and absorb himself with fiddling and charting and moving pieces back and forth. He begins writing in the ship's log, so I take out our first chart from its waterproof sleeve and study the channels of the lower Hudson.

"What are you doing?" He yanks it away. "Don't touch the charts or the log. Look, there's going to be some danger out there. You've heard that a ship has only one navigator, one captain, and on this ship that's me."

I begin to argue, but he interrupts. "When I instruct, you're going to follow. Now go clean off the gunwales. Go on, get abaft with you!"

And so I go, wondering where the man I married went. My father had treated me as an equal nautical partner. Why was I being demoted by my husband?

But to my surprise, I find myself yielding to him. I slip too easily into the role of first mate. My back aches when I scrub the deck, my fingers go numb as I wash oil from his shirts in a bucket of cold water, I am constantly wiping out water bugs and spiders that dangle like drop earrings from the portholes.

The truth is, I find the experience of his being my lord and master oddly appealing. No, I find it downright sexy. And allegorical. Sometimes we see only one facet of our spouses. But now I see a work in progress, a man kaleidoscopic, mercurial. He liked and respected women; he hired so many that one day soon they would make up half his staff of lawyers. He was a friend to females one minute, and the next he was a medieval knight holding them down with his robust, beautifully veined foot.

Does the modern liberated woman have some prehistoric memory in her genes: the memory of her favorite Homo erectus dragging her off by the hair? I'll have to talk to Betty Friedan about this.

My surrender to Bob's domination has put an edgy excitement in the air. He is usually a gentle lover. But one day, he simply kills the engine, drops anchor, and summons me to the bow, ordering me to strip off my clothes—fast. He doesn't even bother to take me below.

I think how much relief his overtaxed mind is getting on this trip. From morning to night, he tinkers. He tinkers with the engine and the lines, peers through binoculars, and uses the radiotelephone every chance he gets, especially when we pass a Coast Guard station. "This is the yacht *Souvenir,*" he says in his basso profundo. "Are you reading me? . . . Roger. Over and out."

The Hudson is ravishing: silvery, winding, and wide. The smell and the sound of freshwater on the tarp, like a thousand birds landing. Eventually, we reach Albany, and the water lifts 568 feet. Once in the Erie Canal, or the Barge, we navigate the many cobweb-filled locks. Locks are like big bathtubs that raise or lower a boat in a canal when there is a sharp change in the elevation of the ground.

On one of our last locks, we are exhausted and grouchy. We had been stuck in the previous lock for two hours, and now, almost immediately, we have to deal with another. Bob has made fast the bow and stern lines with Schenectady hitches, and we wait our turn to enter. Then the big iron gates creak open to reveal slimy stone walls that are so high the lockkeeper above looks three feet tall. It is dark and dank, and to add to this infernal aura, the heavens open up and the sky bugles with thunder. We maneuver toward the port side and kill the engine. The gates, like dungeon doors, close behind us.

"Untangle the knots in the stern line!" Bob yells at me.

"Would you like to explain how?" The lines are a point of contention between us. He has them so overly long that they keep tripping me. And getting knots.

"Then get the hell up and get the bow line! Hook the first rung you can."

I reach out with the long boat hook and successfully hook the ladder embedded in the wall. Then I am pulling the long boat hook with all my might so I can loop the bow line over a rung of the ladder.

"Pull!" he shouts. Bob has already thrown his line around the stern ladder and is holding the boat with difficulty against the rising, swirling currents.

"What do you think I'm doing!"

"Harder, dumbbell!"

Just as I finally get to the ladder and grab it, the wind tears Bob's fingers from his own line, snapping it back into the boat. The stern swings dangerously outward, and I suppress a bubble of laughter. Inappropriate, for sure, but not only is Bob's temper a new and humorous thing; the order of command on the *Souvenir* has been suddenly and delightfully reversed.

"Jerk, you have the IQ of the Little Moron!" I call. The boat is all mine now. But then another violent gust comes up, and I panic and let go of my bow line, and the boat hook goes flying into the oily waters.

"Pinhead!" he yells. "You're the dumbest woman I've ever met!"

"Oh, that's right. Assassinate my character, that's typical Morgenthau!" My indignation gives me strength. I am able to grab a rung and climb up the ladder with my hands, rung after rung, holding as tight as I can, the water rising quickly.

The toothless lockkeeper, who is getting bigger and fatter as we get higher, sits grinning, no doubt because of my predicament. The direction of the gale keeps changing and is now pounding the stern against the wall: Bob has been thrown flat on the deck. I know he is all right because he is roaring out instructions I cannot hear. I keep pulling the boat to the ladder, lightning cracking around me, a single bow rail the only thing that keeps me from plunging into an eddy of dead fish. I ignore Bob. "Hand over hand," I say to myself, gritting my teeth. "Just hand over hand, that's all you have to do."

Suddenly I see alarming fountains of water spurting through leaks in the gates ahead of us, and I wonder if they have ever yielded to the pressure, letting the water rush in and wash us away.

And then, just when I think I'm going to lose my grip, I'm at the top. Out of this hell comes Arcadia. The rain has stopped. I am mesmerized; balls of mist rolling off the towpath, revealing emerald pastures, a tiny red lock house, sun lighting the silver hair of the lockkeeper, the last of the wind gently batting pink roses back and forth.

The lockkeeper glances at me with reluctant admiration and ties the line to a bollard while I run along the gunwale to Bob. "Are you all right?"

"Fine," he says gruffly. "Just a bruised rib."

"You were hit by a tornado! Nobody could have gone up against that," I say, trying to be comforting.

"You should have gotten that line over as soon as you'd hooked the ladder," he says gruffly. "Good thing I put extra fenders down, or the boat would be in splinters. It's a miracle we got up."

"No, Captain, it was not a miracle," I reply. "It was me."

He looks at me grudgingly. "I never thought you had that much muscle."

Then I notice his body and start to giggle. He looks like Jack in the Beanstalk, his arms poking out of the too-short yellow sleeves. The storm came so suddenly that we must have mixed up our slickers, and my cuffs hang halfway down my hands. It dawns on me that this is why I was able to hold on so long: his cuffs had protected my hands from the punishing rusty rungs.

"Look at yourself!" I say, and when he does, he chortles. Then he flaps his arms, sticks out his tongue, and sends us both into paroxysms of laughter.

Outside the lock, I am bleary-eyed in the gray pink of the morning, and I see rowboats everywhere. This is Theodore Dreiser country, and for a moment I am inside *An American Tragedy*, sure that I see a young man try to drown his companion by pushing her out of the boat.

That night I have a dawn nightmare.

The locks get harder and emptier, the ones that lift us up and those that take us down. As we are holed up in them, cobwebs actually form on our spring lines. It is 102 degrees. "The Amazon couldn't be as bad," I kvetch. If we must wait in a long line of boats, we must smoke cigars to ward off no-see-ums. By the time we enter the Oswego Canal near the Canadian border, however, we feel immune, river-hardened salts with that russet tan achieved only on the water.

We eat pots of creamed tuna in the rain, uncork some table wine with an ice pick, the corkscrew having abruptly jumped overboard, and then fall into the bunk, rocked to sleep by the music of rope rubbing against wood.

•

When we enter Lake Champlain, there are multiple storm warnings. We try to find berths at several marinas, but every boat has gone in and they are full. So my husband steams ahead into the wailing sea, huge waves smacking us around. He knows the direction and force of every oncoming swell and cuts through the turbulence until we are out of it. We finally find a deserted steamship pier, throw our line up over a bollard, climb the ladder to the top, and walk across a bridge into the state of Vermont.

Too soon, we are bouncing back down the Hudson in twenty-five-mile-per-hour winds, waves arching and lifting us up and whacking us down, depositing spray everywhere. Then the Manhattan skyline rises before us, and, oddly, the waters go quiet. The end of our adventure.

We disembark and take one last look at our boat. He gently puts his arm around me, and we turn and walk up the dock. The genteel, tractable husband whom I married reclaims his body. But what was with this dictator who sprang from the river?

"I've been thinking," I say, swallowing, trying to keep my voice light. "This whole captain thing, all that ordering me around, were you trying to send me a message? Should I be doing things for you that I'm not doing, more wifely things? Do you want me to learn to cook and be more demure, put your cardigan over your shoulders, your briefcase in your hand? Is that why on the boat you put me in my place, where you thought I belonged? Unconsciously anyway."

He drops his arm. "Do you have to psychoanalyze everything? Boats are a dangerous business! A boat can go down in a minute if you don't know what to do and quickly. That's why they invented executive officers. It's basic boatmanship. Nothing more complicated than that."

The light is golden now; the boats look as if they were painted by the brush of Vermeer. He catches up with me and hooks my arm, and I know that he is trying to make it up, becoming cute and loving, as he always does when he thinks I'm pissed off.

"Look at that," he points at the silvery crescent on the horizon. "See the new moon? See how it has a faint blue ball around it as if it was full?"

"That's called earthshine," I reply. "I learned it from my dad. It usually happens in April or May; this is unusual for August. When sunlight is reflected from the earth to the moon, which is beamed back to the earth and then up to the moon again, the light is sometimes powerful enough that you can see a faint whole moon, even when only a sliver is bright." We stroll up toward his detective driver, who is waiting with a city-issued Chrysler. "It's called the new moon holding the old moon in her arms."

He gives me one of his half-moon smiles, and then he surprises me, as he is apt to do. "I think we're like earthshine," he says, with feeling. "We reflect light onto each other. I might be the old moon, but I'll always hold you in my arms."

•

Before the boat trip, Bob had held my wanderlust at bay, so hating to fly that he naturally hated to travel. But because of his international cases, invitations had flowed in for him to visit foreign countries. The one that most interested him was the country that his father had raised millions of dollars for, the one he himself had always helped by being active in huge charity organizations. Israel. I had watched Bob develop a deep respect for this little country, built by the kinds of Jewish Holocaust refugees that his father helped to save.

"We have to go to Israel someday," he remarks idly, as he's reading a book about the Yom Kippur War by Chaim Herzog. I believe windows of transformation open suddenly in our lives, and if we don't go through them, if we put them off, they never open again. The things we have waited to do are often the things we have lost. Thus, the day after Bob's idle remark, I purchase two tickets to Tel Aviv. I also buy Bob a book that contains statistics about how it is rarer to die in a plane accident than it is to die from a bee sting.

His passion for Israel heightened the day in December 1979 when he met the man who captured Adolf Eichmann, the architect of Hitler's Final Solution. Peter Malkin, a former Mossad agent and accomplished artist, had wrestled the Nazi war criminal off a bus in Argentina and spent days in a hotel sketching him, befriending him, and trying to find out what had motivated this nice guy to harbor such evil.

Malkin, a tall, battle-worn man, was also a magician who delighted children by taking quarters from behind their ears. He became a good friend and would regale us with stories about trapping other war criminals and thwarting Palestinian terrorists. Peter had also helped Bob make a sting on an international arms terrorist, Frank Terpil. Bob arrested and turned Terpil over to the feds, who injudiciously pushed the judge to let him out on bail. The arms dealer had fled and disappeared into the Middle East.

We leave for Israel in the fall of 1981. During the flight, I hold Bob's clammy hand; he has read my optimistic material, but like a moth drawn to flame, he has also collected articles on plane crashes and knows that takeoff is the time when the plane is most in danger.

The air in Tel Aviv is balmy, sweet. We are met at Ben Gurion Airport by Uri Dan, the international journalist, as well as Malkin and Rafi Eitan, who was part of the team that captured Eichmann. Peter gives us a party with a guest list that includes the present and former heads of the secret intelligence agency Mossad.

There is hardly a day during this visit when we're not moved by the plight of these extraordinary people who have made such sacrifices in the face of their terrible histories. We see the incarnation of their post-Holocaust ideals; they have developed strong, dynamic, and ingenious Jews who will never again fail to fight for their lives. We see barren deserts blooming, and the kibbutzim and moshavim that are built by diverse self-sufficient communities that grow their own food and engender national spirit.

In Jerusalem, I walk the rough stone path of the stations of the cross, feeling awestruck as I put my sandaled foot where Jesus did when he walked, stoned and jeered, to his death. Meanwhile, Bob pushes a note of gratitude between the stones of the Wailing Wall. Is it a prayer to the Jewish God? He won't tell me.

We stand on the Arab West Bank, looking down, imagining PLO terrorists aiming rocket launchers from this spot at the Israeli towns up and down the coast. We go to the southern end of the West Bank, which overlooks Ben Gurion Airport, whose planes are also vulnerable to attack. We visit some of the controversial newly built kibbutzim in the occupied West Bank and meet the nervous but tenacious inhabitants, who endure constant attack by terrorists. Many of them are young. Many were born in Israel and are called Sabras, after the prickly cactus that is rough on the outside but soft and sweet within.

We travel ten kilometers into turbulent Lebanon, where terrorists, operating from Palestinian refugee camps, regularly launch rockets at Israeli kibbutzim. We enter a pro-Israeli Lebanese Christian enclave to meet a family who lives in a bare whitewashed home with bullet holes in the plaster. Outside, men are sitting on benches smoking hookahs, and inside children are arrayed on pallets. Terrorists use explosives to attack the enclave, and a baby in a crib is covered with heavy mattress material to protect it from grenades. On the walls are bandoliers filled with ammunition. They are excited to see us, for they love Americans and insist on giving us cup after cup of bracing bitter tea from their one valuable possession, an old etched samovar.

We drive south and meet up with our Israeli guides, who take us deep into the Sinai. As we bump along in their jeep, they are silent, solemn, suspicious. I guess that this is because they don't know why we have been given special permission to climb Mount Sinai, which is now closed to most people. Much to the resentment of many Israelis, the Sinai Peninsula, which was seized by Israel during the 1967 war, is in the process of being returned to Egypt as stipulated by the 1979 peace treaty between them.

We arrive at the fourth-century Greek Orthodox monastery of St. Catherine's, where we will spend the night in separate monks' cells before we climb Mount Sinai the next morning. This granite monastery, one of the oldest in the world, which owns codices and manuscripts dating back to the fifth century, is in a gorge at the foot of the mountain. The beds are hardly wider than our bodies and we don't sleep well apart, so we begin our ascent the next morning bleary-eyed. But soon into the rocky journey, we feel the pull of this sacred peak and stride past our surprised Sherpa, who scurries after us.

Reaching the top more than two hours later, we stand speechless, breathing thin air but beholding mountain ranges for miles, even glimpsing what we think is the Red Sea way back in Israeli territory. We walk to the cave where the Ten Commandments were given. It is cold up here, but that's not why I'm shivering. I am standing in the place where God is said to have spoken to Moses, and the sunrise has turned the sky into a flag of bleeding yellow and blue and orange.

How I wish Bob could share the wonder of this moment with me. But I had asked him so many times whether he believed in God, in prayer, and he had skillfully avoided answering me. I didn't know anything about his relationship or lack of relationship with God, and I was afraid I never would.

"Remember that beautiful passage in Exodus, when God's voice comes from the burning bush, commanding Moses to lead the Israelites out of slavery in Egypt?" I ask hopefully.

"God made a good decision," he said, standing behind me.

"You're being flip. Bob, we're on holy ground, *Hebrew* ground. Have you read Exodus?"

"I certainly have." He is taking in the glowing rock formations and the dry cypress trees and the dirt beneath our feet. His eyes are welling up. I feel a terrible sinking inside. I have again missed who Bob really is. What Israel has done to him. It comes back in flashes: how shaken he had been in the West Bank, imagining Arab rockets obliterating Jewish cities below, how thrilled he was riding in the fighter planes, how astonished by the moshavim and their young farmers who had devised a way to irrigate the parched desert. This man's religion was based on Moses-given commandments. How could I have assumed he was still the old wisecracking Bob? I saw now that the passions he never showed in life, he was putting into this precious land of resurrection. Here, he had met survivors and Sabras and boy soldiers ready to give their lives. And most of all, he had met his father.

I take his hand.

He strokes mine tenderly. "Do you remember when Moses asks God his name? That's in Exodus 3. God replies, 'I am who I am.' That's something to think about."

•

We travel several miles down the Red Sea for our final adventure and camp out in the middle of a Bedouin tent community on the bank. I wake in the morning to a long, bumpy nose almost touching mine; the Arab has ruddy brown skin layered with sand particles, cracked lips, uneven teeth, and a beautiful red-and-white tasseled kaffiyeh over his head. He seems to be studying my long, uncovered hair curiously. I give out a startled scream and he flees the tent. Then I want him back, want to look at him, talk with him, for I know that it is not the fragile ivory-skinned image in the churches that really depicts Jesus, but this, this rough, unbathed Bedouin. He could have been living two thousand years ago, a holy rabbi who wandered with the coarse and the poor and the outcast and slept under a roof of goatskin.

I never see my Bedouin visitor again, but he has touched me. As a child, I discovered an old Christian songbook in Gram Leavitt's house, and I would go into a grove, where I thought no one could hear me, and sing "He walks with me, and he talks with me" over and over. Now, every once in a while, when I'm alone, I get both a comforting and an unsettling sensation that someone is behind me, watching. Sometimes I think I feel a warm breath on my shoulder.

We then hike for miles until we finally see a stream and gaze at it thirstily. Our guide says it is perfectly clean. I decide not to partake, but Bob dips his cup in and drinks it down, eyeing me cheekily. A minute later, we see a goat defecating in the water. We leave the next day, and on the plane Bob is struck down with a mercifully short-term abdominal malady.

When we return home, we feel like different people. I have been touched by the trip, but Bob has been transformed. The survival of Israel has become and will remain one of the most urgent things in his life.

It has made its way into my heart too. I have flashes of memory that explain to me the depth of my feelings about the Holocaust.

•

I am eleven. My friend opens a book she has hidden under her bed. On the pages are children who are so skinny their bones stick out, and they have horrible huge heads. My friend makes me promise not to tell anyone. "A bad man starved them. They're real, it really happened." I go home and cry for a week; I tell no one and then forget what I saw.

I am fourteen, already a raving liberal, and I am in my bedroom, arguing with my father. "It's in the Bible, Daddy, the Arabs are the sons of Ishmael, Abraham's firstborn son. They have as much right to be in Israel as the Jews!"

"You don't know anything. What the Jewish people have gone through," he says. "You will never, ever be able to imagine it." His cheeks are slick with tears I've never seen before. When he leaves, he leaves a stranger. I cry.

I am eighteen. If I had ever met a Jew, I didn't know it. Yet at the mention of the Holocaust, something unsettling occurs. My father's angst has worked its way into me. He has seen the real children. Their eyes too big, their dug-out faces, squatting grimy and sour-smelling, in the first concentration camp discovered by the Allies. He never told me he had been a liberator, but he has given me his sorrow anyway.

•

Bob and I talk endlessly to our ultraliberal friends, many of them Jews, but they won't be parted from their self-hatred, their conviction that Israel is an aggressive militaristic state that has seized Arab land out of greed rather than self-defense. They won't budge, even refusing to believe in the historical fact that the Arabs have started the wars. When they claim the PLO manifesto to drive the Israelis into the sea is just empty rhetoric, I give up on them in disgust.

One night, we go to a party and meet Francis T. P. Plimpton and his wife, parents of the celebrated writer and editor of *The Paris Review,* George Plimpton. The event is full of dignitaries, and, intimidated, I cling to Bob. He seems to like it when I do. But after I consume quite a few glasses of fine Côtes du Rhône, the rich and famous seem to shrink as I get bigger. I am feeling almost cocky when I hear Mrs. Francis T. P. Plimpton say, "Why must the rest of us support Israel when all those rich Jews should be the ones to give them money?"

Now, Mrs. Francis T. P. Plimpton, the wife of the U.S. representative to the UN, is old society, the daughter of the aristocratic botanist Oakes Ames from Boston, the land where "the Lowells speak only to the Cabots, and the Cabots speak only to God."

She is settled in a wing chair, legs elegantly crossed. I'm sitting Indian-style on her carpet. Bob is somewhere behind me. I look at her stony face that tilts slightly skyward, clear my throat, and say, "I'm a Christian and I support Israel. That's because I've read about the Holocaust. I think it's everybody's duty to help build a homeland for those who've suffered so much." Thus begins a bitter argument, with a number of guests apparently drinking it in as though we were a peep show. Bob is just a yard away. A guest who is the director of the FBI steps in, but retreats when he sees this blood feud.

"Do you know how tiny Israel is? It's a fingernail in a fist of Arabs. It's littler than New Jersey, and it's surrounded by enormous Arab countries that fire rockets on the kibbutzim and farms," I declare, and she rebuts: "What concern is that of ours?" I go on and on, about social responsibility and political compassion. Eventually, she closes her mouth and doesn't say another word. Bob raises his eyebrows at me, the signal we use if one of us wants to leave. I feel suddenly sober and mortified. I shake Mrs. Plimpton's limp hand and we get in the elevator.

Who was I back there? When I step outside my reporter's persona and into the public, I still never know what will happen. But I normally don't pick a fight with the hostess of a party. I can't see Bob's face—he is getting our coats now—but I can hear my mother's voice saying, "Shame on you."

I finger my earlobe nervously and suddenly notice, with horror, the absence of one of the emerald earrings Bob had given me. It is probably irretrievably lost in the thick pile of the Plimpton carpet, justice for my crude behavior. I will never have the nerve to call and ask Mrs. Plimpton to look for it. I will not even tell Bob. As soon as we leave the apartment building, I peek up at him. I see a proud grin. "That," he exclaims, "was your finest moment."

"How Lucinda put Mrs. Francis T. P. Plimpton in her place" becomes one of his favorite stories. I imagine his love for Israel blinded him to the deficit of refinement in me—until I found out that refinement wasn't what he wanted at all.

12

By the early 1980s, the old Morgenthau homestead, which had been in the family for half a century, had been sold. The relationship between Bob and Henry, who had been so close as children, temporarily soured around the decision to sell the house and divide the property. Henry was the only one of the three siblings for selling, and only when he himself found buyers. Then the apple orchards were divided into three parcels of about three hundred acres each. Joan, keeping her share of the orchard for her children, let it go to seed, and Henry sold his for development. Bob, the farmer at heart, kept the property that included the store, the barns, the tractors, and all the other farm equipment.

When it came time to empty the homestead, Bob shrank from the trauma of dividing his parents' possessions and sent me up as his representative. Asserting what they believe belongs to them is always acrimonious among siblings, but less so for a sister-in-law. So off I went alone, his surrogate.

Joan and Henry were waiting inside the cavernous hall among a plethora of needlepoint rugs, four-poster beds, popcorn bedspreads, Henry junior's time-honored desk, Windsor chairs, fine old lithographs, and furniture made at Val-Kill, Eleanor Roosevelt's little furniture factory in Hyde Park. To my relief, we divvied things up with equanimity. Only a few items were debated, one of which was a big fur lap rug that was used in the days of open carriages. I knew Bobby loved that. When I gave it to him, he was so pleased I had shown concern for him that he was never again simply tolerant of me; he became my friend.

And so the other children followed. In the words of Yeats, the widening gyre had been turning, but instead of falling apart, the center held. After five years, the children had gradually made peace with our marriage. It didn't hurt that I had written a humorous and tender article for the *Times* about my husband, the cook, who never looked at a recipe but poured farm-pressed cider over everything; each weekend we ate his invention, Chicken and Apples in the Pot, which bubbled in a cast-iron cauldron over our open fireplace. "How could your stepkids doubt that you really love him after that?" asked Susan Sarnoff, one of Barbara's closest friends.

My stepchildren and I now smiled, even laughed together. At least once, Jenny, two years older than me, had the courage to introduce me as her stepmother. Annie and her husband, Paul, and I would joke around. After my father died, Paul wrote me a poignant letter about what it was like losing his own dad.

·

There were many reasons I loved my youngest stepdaughter. I loved Barbara's irrepressible laugh. I admired her quick wit and her independence and courage—surviving and thriving in spite of losing her mother so young. I loved her fine sensibility, the integrity her father undoubtedly passed on to her. I was grateful for the way she affectionately called me Lucille and bought me some handsome journals to write in. She didn't mind at all if I was moved to do a turkey walk around the house, singing, "Alley oop, oop, oop, oop oop." She decided both her father and I were weird and relished telling us so.

Barbara could crack me up. One day at dinner, Bob was subjecting her to complicated family history—how the Lehmans related to the Fatmans and the Morgenthaus to the Strauses and the Wertheims to the Guggenheims. "Now, Mayer Lehman had eight children, four girls and four boys," Bob explained. "There was Harriet and Herbert . . ."

"Oh!" interrupted Barbara, aged thirteen. "If Grandpa and Grandma hadn't spent so much time fornicating, it would be easier to understand this family."

Barbara's graduation from Fieldston came all too soon. I cried when she stepped up in the spring of 1981 to get her diploma. As she went off to Amherst, her father and brother's alma mater, I reflected on the last five years with her. Bob loved her with a deep, transcendent love unique to them. If I had taken away some of her time with him, it was just a matter of time before she took herself away from him. Strong, self-sufficient, and nineteen, she had been taught well by her father. I had loved her, laughed with her; she had given me both delight and exasperation. Hopefully, I had brought some noise and laughter, some light, into the dusky place where she had lived.

·

The Vineyard in August 1981. Barbara and I, shoulder to shoulder, making a mean tuna *niçoise*. Hot, humid. The smell of boiling water. Steam coating already sweaty faces. Scrabbling about in a sink full of olive pits, celery stalks, a fountain of scallions. The tick of the clock above the stove: intervals calm, predictable, dreamy.

One night after dinner at the Kaufmans' home, Barbara and I were clearing the table when she whispered, "I have a boyfriend. Serious." The leftovers nearly slid off the plate I was holding. Barbara had never confided in me about anything so personal. I responded casually, and the confidences kept coming. She hardly needed my advice, but the boy was professing his love, so I told her to be cautious. I was happy for her, and happy that she had felt comfortable letting me into her life.

Bobby had also acquired a summer girlfriend; I caught glimpses of them hand in hand, faraway little figures guarding their privacy. I think they knew I had seen them. Nan, Margie, and assorted relations and friends pumped me about the liaison, but I held them off, claiming that the two were just friends. Bobby was a very private individual, and I had absorbed some of the family's restraint. One weekend, when he went to visit friends off island, he gave me a grateful peck on the cheek.

At last, I felt included and was the mistress of my home. That summer, I could hardly remember the time when I wasn't a part of anything or anyone. When I simply tried to survive.

·

The mind is tissue paper on which experience is written with a shaky hand. What a difference in your perception of things, when everyone seems just beyond your reach. Every little gesture is greater than itself, everything a symbol that re-creates your past or predicts the future. Rejected,

you walk stiffly, measuring each sentence, hearing every word resound as
though you had never said it.

Then, one day, you find you have come unstuck. You climb off the flat
black line you've drawn in mid-nowhere, penetrate the membrane of the
circle, and float now and forever through its streaming dimensions.

•

Our rental was a little clapboard house at Stonewall Beach in Chilmark, so close to the bluff it looked as if it might fall off at any moment.
Barbara and her friends wandered in and out, leaving empty Coke cans
and bikini tops everywhere. I loved an orderly house, but I loved this
more, having signs of her being around us. I tried to do my writing in
the cellar, but it was too dark, so word of my predicament traveled, and
before I knew it, a lady from one of the old island families was offering
me her fishing shack as a studio.

Bob loved the village atmosphere of the island. He loved people.
That summer, I got a new appreciation for the way Bob cared for them.
If the sea was too choppy to sail, we sometimes lounged around the boat
with guests or family. He would slip down the dock to the Galley and
suddenly reappear toting big bags of lobster rolls, crab cakes, clam
chowder, just when people were suddenly hungry for lunch. He liked
passing out the food. "Does everyone have what they want? Noah? Lila?
Paul? No clam chowder, Annie? Here." He would give up something he
loved to eat so he knew everyone was satisfied.

When he was free from the stress of work, Bob's aloofness would
melt away. He would grin at me mischievously, as though he were letting
me in on a secret that had surprised him as well.

One night, we went to a dinner party at the home of John Hersey.
People were talking to him about his historic piece on the bombing of
Hiroshima that had taken up a whole issue of *The New Yorker* after the
war. But I was sneaking looks at Bob, observing the happy creases in his
cheeks, the flash of a smile in his eyes. "He's sooooo cute," I said to Margie
Lang. "Adorable," she replied.

Finally, one day I couldn't help asking, "Why are you smiling all
the time?" My husband wasn't one to bring me flowers or bend me over
in a fervent embrace. But I would have traded all of that for the answer
he gave me.

"When you're happy, so am I," he said.

There was another reason. That summer we decided to have a child. Before we married, Bob had agreed to this, and after four years together we figured it would be nice to add another. We had stopped birth control, and I had stopped smoking, for we expected to become pregnant soon.

At the thought of becoming a father again at age sixty-two, he behaved like a youngster, leaping toward the waves and riding them in, not caring about the water flooding his delicate ears, hair slicked down like a wet cat, wanting only to have fun and show off for his delightedly clapping wife. The sand was golden white, and by the end of the summer it would look old and rusty, streaked with iron red and black, the stones having washed down to cover the beach. But now they were banked, and we would gaze at the frothing high tide crawl toward them, moving like fingers into the crevices, stretching for that extra inch. Their rumble was mesmerizing, like the clattering of herons and gulls, a thousand voices at once, the muffled screams of people trapped in a tunnel.

We would emerge from the beach sun dazed and pickled with salt, and then we would hop into our whites and play tennis with a friend whose spouse was as poor a player as I was. We didn't win any competitions, but we had a jolly time of it.

Noah, Annie's second child, asked Bob, whom the grandkids called Hoppa, and me to watch him take his first tennis lesson at age six. We cheered him on and then tossed balls across the net to him. Life was a round of Humphreys fresh doughnuts, trips to the red-and-gray-clay Gay Head cliffs for breakfast, antiquing, fishing trips, catching crabs, eating lobsters, buying slabs of pink swordfish that had come right off a trawler just returned from sea.

City dwellers love their anonymity, but the price they pay is the loss of spontaneity. Here, on this bygone island of gnarled scrubby oak, full of apple-green pastures rolling down to the sea and trails fragrant with horse buns, anyone anytime can arrive at your door. Bob, for instance, became renowned for delivering a couple of bluefish he'd caught to his cousins and friends; the only one who cared whether the fish bled all over the fridge was me.

Community flourished, even community you didn't want. People you hardly know and you will never see in the city press you to come to dinner. Exhausted by four parties in a row, you can still be lured to a fifth with the dangled bait of distinguished people you've always wanted to meet. Bob needed to see charitable people who would donate to the Police Athletic League (PAL). I was excited by the prospect of simply laying eyes on redoubtable writers like Lillian Hellman or John Hersey or William Styron.

When Lillian Hellman asked me to sit down beside her, I was terrified. She had the reputation of being an irascible, scathing person who, it sounded, could cut you down faster than my mother. She was having a nasty feud with the writer Diana Trilling on the other end of the island, and people had to be careful not to ask both of them to the same party. "So I hear you're a fan," she said. "Tell me how you liked *Maybe*," a story that had just been published. I told her I hadn't read it. "Well, some fan you are!" she replied. I quickly started talking about her play *The Children's Hour*, and she rasped, "Everyone's read that. I've heard too much about it. Tell me something interesting." I blanched, and she began to laugh. "Don't get upset. I'll tell you a secret. People think I'm a bitch, but I'm just pretending. If you're going to be a writer, you have to be bitchy. You've got to scare the reviewers!"

Years afterward, one party I attended was to have a major impact on my life. In August 1997, Bill and Hillary Clinton began coming to the Vineyard. One night, we went to a party given by Bill Rollnick, a founder of the Mattel toy company, and his wife, Nancy Ellison, a talented photographer of Vineyard scenes. We sat at round tables near their beach, and I was surprised to see that I had been put one seat away from the First Lady, whom I had never met. She was warm and charming, without pretension. She made me feel as if we had known each other before. At the table, two newsmen of some repute were loudly dominating the conversation, discussing television politics, when an aide came and spoke into Hillary's ear. I saw her eyes fill. I thought I saw her hand shake, and finally I put my hand on hers and whispered, "Is everything all right?" She shook her head and, looking unsteady, rose from the table. I took her arm and walked her inside. We went into the Rollnicks' television room. Bill Clinton was gazing at the set, at flashes of Princess Diana, fresh-faced and smiling, on her wedding day. "She's dead," he said numbly. Hillary sat down. She watched, in shock, as we all were, while newscasters gave the bloody details of the car crash that had killed their friend.

"You've been very kind," she told me before she left. And she never forgot it.

•

By the fall of 1982, I had gotten used to leaving Bob's side at large functions. Through our popularity in the Vineyard and my presence at his political and charity events, I had lost my habitual frozen stare and learned the art of bonhomie. It wasn't easy. Bob was a pro, so socially relaxed he could talk to anyone about anything. And everyone knew him, and if they didn't, they pretended they did. I, however, had to concentrate in order to shake each hand vigorously, to dare give a bold, shining smile to anyone, to look into people's eyes with such interest they felt important. It was kind of exciting, but at the end of the evening I was often depleted.

We began to owe hospitality to the political and cultural czars of the city, but could I pull off a party, and would they even come? "We can ask anyone we want; they'll come," replied Bob. "Don't forget, you're also famous." I told him he was off-the-wall.

It was early October 1982, and in the city was Israel's defense minister, Ariel Sharon, who had caused an international outrage in June by invading Lebanon and allowing a right-wing Lebanese militia to enter the Sabra and Shatila refugee camps, where they massacred some eight hundred Palestinian women, children, and the elderly. I thought it would be interesting to begin by giving a party for him.

Sharon's invasion and occupation of Lebanon had wiped out the infrastructure of the PLO, which had long been shelling settlements in northern Israel. He had thus become a hero to pro-Israeli conservatives and a criminal to liberals. I love a good brawl, so I invited prominent people from both sides of the controversy. There was Iphigene Sulzberger, the elderly mother of the publisher of the *Times*, who recounted that she had been in Palestine in 1937; Robert Semple, the paper's evenhanded Op-Ed editor; Steve Ross, CEO of Warner Bros., and his wife, Courtney Sale, who at the time was an art dealer; Uri Dan, Israeli correspondent for the *New York Post* and Sharon's good friend, who had been such a dynamic host to us in Israel; Victor Temkin and his wife, Susie; and

Arthur and Barbara Gelb—Barbara was a fine writer and a blunt, out-spoken, and occasionally oppositional personality.

Most of the guests were sipping wine in the living room when Sharon walked in like a jolly Santa Claus, leading with his big belly. Barbara, who wrote for *The New York Times Magazine*, was not charmed, however, and started right in on him: "Minister Sharon, I mean General, can you tell me why you ordered your allies, the Christian Phalangists, to go into those refugee camps and murder men, women, and children?"

Sharon smiled indulgently at her. "Call me Arik. We were on the perimeter of Sabra and Shatila. We thought they were rooting out terrorists; we didn't know that they were killing non-terrorist elements."

"Elements?" Barbara replied, her eyes hard as marbles. "You mean the boys who got scalped and castrated? The women whose throats were slit, who were found lying in their tents with their skirts up and their legs spread?"

"Let the man sit down and have a drink," Uri Dan said in his slow, insinuating drawl.

I hurried to get Arik and his protective wife, Lily, comfortably seated on the couch and poured him a glass of wine made at Tal Shahar. "This was made at a moshav that's named after Bob's father, they . . ."

Barbara interrupted me. "The invasion has only enhanced Israel's reputation as a militaristic state," she said in a gravelly voice.

"Why did you really invade Lebanon anyway?" asked Arthur, who could often be found deferring to his wife. "I think the murder of your ambassador in the U.K. was a weak pretext. He wasn't even killed by the PLO. It was the PLO's enemy Abu Nidal."

"Abu Nidal, PLO, PLF, PIJ, they are all the same. All of them are committed to shedding Israeli blood," Sharon said quietly, his English becoming more heavily accented. "The murder of our ambassador was the last straw in many aggressions toward us. What if Mr. Dan here started to throw Molotov cocktails in your window? Would you sit on your hands and say there is no pretext here for retaliation?"

"But you killed thousands of innocent refugees in Lebanon for what, twenty-four Israelis killed by bombs in the kibbutzim?"

"Twenty-six," Sharon corrected her. "They were busily tilling their land, hugging their children, and, poof, they were gone."

Bob uncharacteristically cut in with his resonant voice. "Barbara, there are a lot of American Jew-hating Jews who criticize Israel for not just securing a buffer zone but going all the way up to Beirut. But wiping out the whole PLO was the only way to ensure that they wouldn't start up again. Alexander Haig gave Arik the go-ahead. The American government was behind him. It was a great achievement."

Sharon nodded. "I'm proud of it. I just wish I had killed that rat Arafat on the way."

"Oh!" Barbara closed her eyes and groaned in disgust.

I looked at Bob, horrified, wondering whether I should do something to shut Barbara up. But he was just sitting there, smiling.

Sharon looked pointedly at the *Times* people. "This is off the record. I have not spoken about the Lebanon War before, and I don't intend to. But we found underground tunnels dug by the PLO filled with more large weapons than they would ever need. Huge numbers of tanks and rifles of Soviet manufacture. Next, they would have stockpiled long-range missiles."

Arthur was listening closely, looking as though he would give anything for a notebook and pencil. Sharon said, "Mr. Gelb, remember, you can't write about this. No, no, not for background, not for anything at all."

Bob had an impeccable sense of timing, whereas I had none, so he was the one who stood up and subtly ushered everyone into the dining room. Once they were digging into Renia's roast quail, which was tender as butter, Sharon was left in peace. He ate heartily and laughed often.

Then, after people had stopped eating, he took out maps of Israel and used a knife to point out the Golan Heights, where Syria had shelled Israeli territory below, and how close the Palestinian terrorists in Lebanon had inched down to Israel. "See this castle on the border. It was built by the crusaders, and now it's a PLO headquarters."

As the Gelbs were leaving, Barbara, looking chastened, turned to Sharon: "I apologize for hounding you. I was out of line."

"Not to worry," said Uri Dan, carrying a roll of the defense minister's maps, "he's used to answering all kinds of questions."

"It is important that people understand us," Sharon said, smiling flirtatiously at Barbara. "You see, my job is to defend Israel not only from those who would annihilate us but from beautiful American women who like to argue."

As Lily was going through the door, however, she looked over her shoulder at Barbara as if she were an agent provocateur from the PLO.

•

Joyce Carol Oates sat shyly in our living room with her husband, Ray Smith. They had enviably straight posture. Joyce and I had become friends after I did a story for *The New York Times Magazine* on her new novel *Bellefleur*, which moved her into the popular culture. She had come from Detroit and was teaching at Princeton.

Ray was a gentle man who ran their literary magazine, *The Ontario Review*, while Joyce, striking with her dark bobbed hair and huge brown eyes, had to sometimes discipline herself not to write.

Conversation was stalled until Bob came to the rescue. "These Tylenol deaths are very odd," he said as if he had a window into her mind. "They still don't know if it was accidental or the work of a criminal."

And indeed, he hit the right note. "Oh, I think it was murder!" she said. "Someone injected poison into the pills, I'm quite sure. I just received the galleys about this new book on the jilted boy from Yale who killed his girlfriend with a hammer," she said, shaking her head, "but I can't bear to look at them. It's so tragic, so gory . . ."

"Were you a detective in a prior life?" quipped Bob. "You have the imagination of a sleuth."

"Well, I have so many hypnagogic experiences, seeing images between sleep and waking . . ."

Ray cut in. "The night Joyce was inducted into the American Academy of Arts and Letters, I asked Howard Nemerov what he thought of Ted Weiss's new epic poem and he threw up in his soup!"

"Oh, Ray," she said with a tilt of her head. "It was only that he had had too much to drink.

"Ray makes delicious bread," she said, changing the subject. Yesterday, I walked into the kitchen and he was covered in runny dough and his bread—he's very sweet about his bread—had fallen, and he acted like he just didn't want to live anymore."

"I know what you mean, Ray," said Bob. My husband was a good cook who used no recipes.

"Well, it was a time of a great low for me," he replied. "This was the last straw."

"How is your novel coming, Lucinda?" asked Joyce. "Are you still in the grasp of writer's block? She reassured me that she too suffered from this paralyzing condition, which I took as a well-intentioned prevarication. At age forty-four, the woman was as prolific as Simenon, having published more than two dozen books by 1982, with many more stacked in a chest; her publishers simply couldn't keep up with her. She had even written a number of other books under a pseudonym.

Suddenly the Siamese seal point I had given Barbara jumped up on Joyce's lap.

"Peter, get down," Bob said, but Joyce was delighted.

"Actually, we do have to get back to Princeton now," she said, stroking Peter Rabbit.

"We have the five cats at home."

Ray nodded. "They'll be fretting about us. And they'll want their meal."

"And I have to vacuum," added Joyce with a glint in her eye. "I love housework, it makes you feel like you've really *done* something . . ."

•

The next time they visited, the elevator was broken, so they took the freight elevator and walked smack into Renia taking out the garbage. They wandered around calling us, but we had just gotten out of the shower. Bob padded out in his bathrobe to apologetically greet them. I threw on my clothes and followed. Bob was standing there staring at Joyce, and I did a double take. She was as transformed as a character in one of her novels; far from falling into the abyss, however, she looked almost Olympian. A mass of becoming curls now framed her face, brightened with eye shadow and lip gloss. Gone were the sweet flowered dresses made by her mother upstate in Lockport. Instead, she was wearing a rakish blue pleated blouse from Issey Miyake. When I complimented her, she looked away modestly, but her voice was more sonorous, more definite: "Oh, well, it's only that Gloria Vanderbilt has become a friend, and she sends me all these clothes."

•

A few years before, I had persuaded my adolescent hero, Eudora Welty, to come up from Jackson, Mississippi, to speak at the first fund-raiser of the nonprofit Writers Room, which I had helped found. It provided communal space for professional writers who couldn't afford private offices; it allowed them to work in a peaceful, silent atmosphere far more conducive to creativity than noisy home environments full of phones, doorbells, and family talking or walking over their manuscripts.

I had first met Ms. Welty when she had visited my senior creative writing class at Vassar, which was taught by her friend the college's legendary English professor Bill Gifford. She was as quirky as Sister in my favorite Welty story, "Why I Live at the P.O." Professor Gifford had picked her up at the Poughkeepsie train station, and on the way to the college she had cried, "Oh! There's a squirrel leaning on its elbow." During class she advised us that if a tornado struck, stand under the lintel of the doorway and you won't get blown away.

Though much different from Joyce, she had the same diffidence. But when she smiled, she did so with such an inviting radiance you felt as if she had brought you home. She lived and wrote alone, in the quietude of her late mother's house, and in her talk to the crowd she gave a hearty salute to our big space full of desks and dividers and freedom from chaos.

•

Bob liked to have parties, so since I was not writing at the time, I kept having them. There were the occasional faux pas and near disasters. Once I seated Teddy White, author of the distinguished *Making of the President* books, next to Christopher Lehmann-Haupt, who had just panned his new book in *The New York Times*. On another occasion I asked Mayor Koch, whom I had sat next to me, what he was doing about the homeless. "Let's talk about serious issues," he replied dismissively. "Most of them don't help themselves."

Koch began to wax passionate on the need to fix the city's potholes. I, on the other hand, was passionate about the need to help America's destitute. "What about the families who've been evicted, Ed?" I interrupted, a little too loudly. "Hungry children, overcrowded placement

An eighteen-year-old debutante. And a dashing young Robert Morgenthau

One of the high points in our lives, literally and figuratively:
reaching the pinnacle of Mount Sinai, just before it was returned to Egypt

On the trail of a story

An early high point—finding out that, at age twenty-four, I'd just become the youngest woman to win the Pulitzer Prize, and the first woman to win for national reporting

Three generations of public service—from left to right: Bob's brother, Henry Morgenthau III; their father, Henry Morgenthau Jr; their grandfather Henry Morgenthau I; and Bob himself

More illustrious company—from left to right: New York governor Nelson Rockefeller, Italian ambassador Sergio Fenoaltea, President John F. Kennedy, Bob, and Mayor Robert F. Wagner of New York City, at the Columbus Day Parade in 1962

Bob riding through New York City with JFK in 1962

Bob, an early supporter of the civil rights movement, meets one of his heroes on the ferry to Martha's Vineyard

Interviewing Robert Redford on the set of *Three Days of the Condor* in 1974

Never scared of a little controversy, Bob and I were always full-blown supporters of Israel. Here we are in 1983 with Ariel Sharon and his wife, Lily, on their farm; and here I am, shaking the hand of Shimon Peres, the then–Israeli prime minister, while Bob and Ed Koch look on.

Sometimes you have to go to great lengths to get your story, literally: on a plane to Africa with Hillary Clinton in March 1999, in pursuit of an exclusive interview

Our son, Josh, and I providing Bob with a bit of support on the campaign trail as he faces his first challenger for the office of DA

But it wasn't always business. Here we are, with Josh and our daughter, Amy, happy and off duty, in the apple orchards at the idyllic Fishkill Farms

Josh and Amy, then
eighteen and twelve, make
us proud

The whole Morgenthau clan: from left to right, Paul Grand, Annie, Jenny,
Barbara, Noah Grand, Hilary Grand, Harry Morgenthau, Bobby, Susan, Josh,
Amy, me, and Bob

And one of our closest friends, Marina
Kaufman, who organized virtually
every detail of our wedding ceremony,
and stuck by our side throughout the
marriage that followed

Bob and me at a dinner dance during the early years of our marriage

Still in love after all these years

offices, shelters so violent the homeless would rather sleep on the street!"
A smiling Bob was egging me on; he still loved to see me get publicly
feisty about a cause he believed in. But the mayor clearly did not; he
abruptly turned to chat with his other dinner partner.

And then, on January 28, 1982, President and Nancy Reagan invited us to a formal dinner. The White House! But Ronald Reagan's
White House? I worried over the hypocrisy of shaking the hand of the
man who was against gun control, abortion, universal health care—and
the general well-being of the people. Jack Newfield of *The Village Voice*
would kill me. Yet it would be my first time in the presidential mansion.
The old conflict. My political principles versus the social splendor
Mother tried to groom me for. When Bob booked us into the Hay-
Adams, the oldest, most exclusive hotel in the city, I crossed the line.

On that memorable night, we were welcomed to the White House
by a brass band as we processed down a red carpet that was flanked by
marines in full uniform. Nancy's much criticized formal redecoration
of the rooms—"so that all Americans could be proud"—was elegant,
cool, and immaculate, like Nancy herself. As she received her guests,
however, she seemed less gracious than tired, resigned to shaking hands
with an assembly line. Every smile has a message, and hers said, "You're
below my element." Behind her highly designed veneer, though, I thought
she seemed like a minor factotum in the Junior League.

The marine officers were eyeing everyone, shadowing those who
peeked in closed rooms, accompanying others to the bathroom. I
thought how Mother would have savored all these details if she had
been alive for me to tell her. We strolled through the crowds and came
across Alistair Cooke and other British journalists I had known in
London. I stood with them, fascinated by Cooke's stories, and before I
knew it, Bob was gone. I went looking for him, but then a marine hooked
my arm and ushered me to my table.

I was, to my surprise, at a table of heavyweights, undoubtedly seated
there for variety. Joseph Alsop, the former dean of conservative columnists, was giving the table a sharply enunciated monologue about
our cowardice in Vietnam. My unusually quiet dinner partner, Teddy
Kennedy, who had just gone through both a divorce and a defeat in the
presidential primary, took Alsop on and I joined in. The argument was
getting heated when Bob came up and squeezed my arm, hard. "I'm

tired. I want to go home," he whispered. I excused myself and followed him into the hallway.

He didn't look happy. "I don't think it was a good idea to attack someone as influential in your profession as Joseph Alsop," he said in a cool tone.

"But everyone agrees Vietnam was a terrible mistake," I declared. "Alsop was arguing as if we were back in the Stone Age. I think he's past his prime, don't you?"

"I don't know. I don't make personal remarks about people."

Something was clearly wrong. It was usually Bob who was surrounded by admirers. Maybe he had felt left out. "Why did you leave me when I was talking to Alistair Cooke? Why didn't you just stay and join the conversation?"

"I don't know. I couldn't hear you—or anyone else."

"Sweetheart," I said, steeling myself, "you *need* a hearing aid."

"Don't start, just don't start."

"You act like a stubborn little boy who doesn't want to wear his galoshes. And all I'm trying to do is help you.

"I would think you'd want to listen to what people are saying to you," I added.

"Then I'd have to listen to you. Harassing me."

I kept my temper. I didn't want to spoil his evening, our evening.

I hugged his arm as we walked out together: "I wish we had been at the same table. I missed you. You're my anchor."

He patted my hand, and we talked about the evening as we crossed Lafayette Square to the Hay-Adams.

"I like Ronnie. He's smart, you know," Bob said. "He remembered meeting my father in July 1943 at a war bonds rally.

"I couldn't believe he could call up that brief meeting, with the date, forty years ago," he continued. "People who call him senile are just ignorant. He has a better memory than me."

"Impossible," I exclaimed. Of course, I was one of the people who had called Ronnie senile, not once, but many times.

"Well, sweetheart, this was an unexpected pleasure, to be at the White House. Just so long as this is the last we see of Ronald Reagan. We're Democrats, Bob, we have no business with a die-hard Republican like him."

"You're right."

Back at the hotel, we went right to sleep, exhausted by the events of the evening.

When I awoke the next morning, Bob was gone. I saw a note propped on the bedroom mirror: "Sweetheart, gone to see the President—8:10." I stared at it, unbelieving. Then I looked at my watch: 8:11. He must have just left. I rushed out the door and down the hall, but the elevator was cold and unmoving. When did he get an appointment with Reagan, and why didn't he tell me? I went back to the room. Still clad in T-shirt and boxers, I found that of course I had locked myself out. "Oh, damn it to hell!" I shouted.

The door opened. "What are you doing out there?" asked Bob quaintly, shaving brush in hand.

"But, but . . . oh you, you . . . you!" I took in his little smile. "You knew exactly what I'd do when I read that note. Someone could have caught me out there half-naked!"

"I was watching you. Why didn't you think to look for me in the bathroom? You always have to rush into things."

I crumpled up his note and threw it at him. "One of these days I'm going to stop believing your little teases."

"Who says I was teasing?" he replied innocently.

13

In the 1980s, the same politics that had brought us together now separated us. Bob had become more and more of an independent, and sometimes conservative, Democrat. Like so many Americans, he was affected by the malaise of the country: low economic growth and high inflation, poor foreign policy, the spectacle of our servicemen being paraded through the streets of Tehran with bags over their heads. He joined the majority of Americans who thought President Carter had botched the Iran hostage crisis, and Bob personally thought him anti-Semitic. Thus, as the presidential election loomed, the polls rose for Carter's opponent, Reagan, who was promising to bring a new conservatism into the country.

But, faced with circumstances beyond his control, Carter, in his leadership, seemed almost valiant to me: He hadn't lost his liberal values under the pressures of realpolitik. He had remained a humanitarian, and he was a leader who had inherited the problems with Iran from previous administrations.

Bob and I usually went to PS 6 holding hands, but on the morning of November 4, 1980, we entered the voting booths hardly speaking and emerged looking at each other with superiority.

I knew Bob, though characteristically secretive about his vote, had pulled the lever for Reagan, who was strongly pro-Israel. Bob had come to put almost all other national issues aside for the sake of supporting this tragically beautiful land, encircled by enemies; its children, fathers, grandfathers, lifting guns to save the only homeland their people had ever known. Most of us repress the impact of the state-ordered Jewish genocide; its multitude of horrors can hardly be comprehended. But the continued suffering and struggle of the survivors in the Middle East was a cataclysm never far from Bob's mind. Or mine. We had shared this from the beginning: deep anger and sorrow over Hitler's Final Solution. The concentration camps only had to be mentioned and we would both well up.

Bob was seldom impressed by eminent people, but meeting Holocaust survivors was an exception for him; he was gentle, awed. His living heroes were people like Peter Malkin, whom he asked again and again to recount his capture of Eichmann. He refused to buy anything German: cars, coffeemakers, even the Rieslings that he secretly loved. When we went to Washington's Holocaust Memorial Museum and saw the vast pile of shoes taken from Jews at the camps, his face stayed set, but inside I could see his anguish.

Not that I really understood how this led him to love Reagan. I sat down to breakfast one morning, and on my plate was the *Times*, folded to a column that mocked the thinking of those who rejected Reagan's draconian economic plan as undeveloped. I was exactly such a thinker. I believed in keeping Social Security intact, giving ample unemployment benefits, subsidizing housing for the poor, protecting the environment. And to deem these the rights of all people, a philosophy that was good enough for one of our greatest presidents, FDR, seemed to have no value to my husband, who dismissed my opinions as if they were the dreams of a child.

"What's happened to your concern for the underdog?" I asked Bob one morning, slapping down the paper. "Who do you think his trickle-down economy has trickled down to? To the rich, so they can get richer. Not the families who are destitute."

"You don't know what you're talking about."

"Well, all you know is what you think you know," I replied. "All you care about is how many F-16s are sent to Tel Aviv, not the quality of the leaders who send them."

He picked up the paper and pretended not to hear me.

This weapon of his infuriated me. "I give up all my radical beliefs and my radical friends and my lifestyle to stand by you, because I believe that at bottom you share my beliefs! But now I find you supporting mediocre ultraconservative politicians.

"Have you forgotten the liberal legacy your father left you?" I kept on. The more he ignored me, the more excited I became.

"Your father *believed* in taxing the rich for the sake of the poor. He helped FDR build the New Deal! He gave people back their dignity and self-worth. What would he think if he saw you now? Letting your vision shrink to a fraction of his! Betraying what he believed."

The air seemed to go out of the room. I had brought the father whom Bob revered into our dispute, not a good idea. I had accused Bob of not living up to his father's high ideals. Words I couldn't take back.

Bob's father had in fact suffered greatly for his ideals, and no one was more sensitive to his father's pain than Bob. The only Jew in the cabinet and in FDR's group of principal advisers, Henry Morgenthau Jr. never believed his efforts had saved enough Jewish refugees. After the Morgenthau Plan was rejected, even by Jews, he left Washington an exhausted and depressed man.

The experiences of Henry junior's father, Henry senior, were eerily similar to his son's. So driven was Henry senior in publicly condemning the Ottomans for the Armenian genocide—which resulted in the massacre of two million Armenians, Greeks, and Assyrians—that he irritated the Wilson government, jeopardized relations between the Ottoman Empire and America, and left his ambassadorship defeated.

And I had been utterly unfair. Bob, in fact, cared deeply about the poor. He believed that they should receive the same opportunities as the more privileged, that they should have avenues that kept them away from the law. Like his father and grandfather, he wanted to give back some of what he had received. He had a special feeling for young people and for those who had struggled to make it. Once, an African American boy, a ten-year-old whom PAL had rescued from the streets, opened a fund-raiser by singing "The Star-Spangled Banner" in notes so pure and resonant, Bob's eyes glistened.

As long as I had known him, Bob had been active in Jewish organizations and soon began meeting regularly with Sharon and the Mossad, joining them in making cases against terrorists who wanted to topple the little country. He was appointed to lead a commission by Mayor Koch to build a memorial to the Holocaust in New York. And when other members of the commission finally became discouraged as the project failed to raise money—many Jews thought it destructive for Jewish persecution to be publicized—Bob stepped in. One weekend, I watched him make cold calls to millionaires—some he knew, like Steve Ross of Time Warner, and some he didn't, like Steven Spielberg. One of the moguls left an important investor to take his call. "I was so happy I wasn't going to be investigated," he said, "that I immediately sent a contribution." By Monday, Bob had raised several million dollars, and plans for the museum suddenly took life.

I wondered if Bob was unconsciously trying to save the Jewish people whom his father, his hero, was unable to. The museum would forever remind people of the Jewish genocide so that it would never again creep up, disguised and hidden, to overwhelm a nation.

Now Bob got up to leave the table. I said "Wait" very faintly, but he had already gone into the bedroom and almost but not quite slammed the door.

When he came home that evening, I was afraid to even mention the morning's fight. But he wasn't. He told me I was naive; I said he was a stuffed shirt; and on it went. Finally, we got tired and a little ashamed of thinking up vitriolic things to say. We became very polite with each other. But something was different. Being in the same room with him was like being alone.

The only time we were close was in bed, and even then I felt a little as if we were mechanical dolls in a sex education class. You see, there was another simmering issue dividing us. We had tried for two years now and hadn't gotten pregnant.

•

I was not alone. My doctor said urban women in the 1980s were simply not getting pregnant. Not in the Northern Hemisphere, anyway. They worried too much, worked too hard. Their fallopian tubes must have shrunk with the tension, their frightened eggs hiding from the tide of agitation. Bantu or East Indian women who whiled away the day under a lazy sun had babies they didn't want, and desperate working women in London or New York City didn't have them at all. Why else would men have invented in vitro fertilization? Why would clinics devoted to infertility be opening all over the place?

Each month of barrenness had pulled us further apart. Failure permeated our marriage. We were embarrassed. I hid the nakedness that was once so natural. I forsook the intimacy of my husband's T-shirts and wore my own nightclothes. Making love became akin to paying a tariff.

Sometimes Bob got into bed and, forgetting to even say good night, just turned his back on me. We were secretive: we never shared our ordeal with anyone, nor did we talk about it ourselves. We had been strong enough to hold up against the fury of family and friends at our marriage. How could our bond be breaking now?

•

Then came Bobby's wedding in West Virginia.

On June 25, 1983, at 3:00 a.m., the fire alarm at our motel in Charleston was accidentally tripped. We stumbled, scantily clad, out into a soft summer night until a megaphone informed us it was a false call. Afterward, our blood still stirring, we crawled into each other's arms, and somehow, in our lazy, unpremeditated lovemaking, a spermatozoon wrestled down one of my eggs.

We had been so excited by the prospect of Bobby's marriage that we had recently declared peace, deciding that this existential estrangement was silly and agreeing to disagree on politics. So we merrily drove through the Blue Ridge Mountains, bound for Charleston, West Virginia, to the home of Bobby's intended, Susan Moore, who was twenty-four to Bobby's twenty-six. We sang endless verses of "There's a Hole in the Bucket" as we took turns driving our eccentric diesel-fueled Peugeot, which happened to have been, in another life, a bright yellow New York taxicab. Bob thought the color was witty, but I was afraid people would try to hail us down, so I prevailed on him to paint it blue.

During the trip, I defied my gynecologist by assaulting my ovaries with forbidden caffeine, and at the wedding I drank wine and boogied the night away. In truth, the celebrations were an excuse for us to escape the little ruinations of infertility.

Just when the tension had become a foreboding, the Almighty took pity on us. In the Old Testament, Gideon, trapped in darkness, was told by God to break all his clay pots and the light would shine through.

When I didn't get a period the next month, we were slightly optimistic. But how on earth? Had the earsplitting fire alarm roused my stubborn fallopian tubes? Since we had decided to take a vacation from scheduled intercourse during the wedding festivities, if we were indeed pregnant, the embryo must be spectacularly determined.

One morning, Bob stays home from work because we are waiting for the results of a pregnancy test. It is July 6, 1983. I am only a few days late, but I feel odd, physically tender, so for the hell of it I ask the doctor to give me a pregnancy test. We haven't much hope, for there have been many of these tests, all negative.

I jump up when the phone rings. The doctor speaks. I drop the receiver. "Bob," I scream, "I'm pregnant!" He comes charging out of the bathroom in his T-shirt. He stands there, staring, and then embraces me. I feel him shiver; I think he is shivering. In my dreams, our marriage has appeared like a Grecian urn, neglected, crumbling away. Now, in this moment, the pieces are put together again, the cracks seamless. Everything seems new, awash in clarity. The sheets, so crisp! And the gray-tar tops on the terrace walls, which I have always hated, flash with bits of sparkling crystal.

During the next weeks, we are joyful, certainly, but even greater is the relief. We have returned to normality. I feel like sending a thank-you note to Bobby and his bride for creating the magic that created the baby.

•

I had first met Susan five years earlier when I was a visiting professor at Vassar and she was rooming at the college with Bob's niece Elizabeth Hirschhorn, the daughter of Bob's sister, Joan. Elizabeth often brought her to the old Morgenthau homestead in Fishkill, where we spent weekends, and Susan and I had immediately taken to each other. She was an English major studying writing, as I had been, and we talked about the short story that she was working on. Susan was an original, almost a paradox. She was so striking with her flawless skin and strong features that she didn't need to be as nice as she was. But she had established special relationships with everyone in the family. She made it her project to bring our blended brood together. She encouraged me to make overtures to them and went out of her way to sit next to me at family gatherings, ensuring that I was included in their conversations. Susan and I took long walks through the orchards, advising each other about the exigencies of being a married woman. Though she was loved by all Bob's kids, she joked that we were the fellow outlaws of the clan.

I don't think she ever forgot the party I threw one summer that would change her life. It was a joint celebration for Bob, Annie's son, Noah, and myself because we all had July birthdays. Elizabeth decided to bring along Susan. Our terrace was aswarm with Bob's extended family, but I noticed that Bobby, who usually had feet to the ground, was talking to Susan, bedazzled.

Less than a year later, they were married.

•

My obstetrician has put me on a disgusting diet, poached egg whites in the morning, naked tuna at noon, and fish and spinach at night. Starches and sugars are never to pass beneath my nose.

"It's your fault I'm ten pounds overweight," I grumble. "When I first got pregnant, you told me to eat everything I desired, and now you want to starve me." Once she gets used to putting her legs in his stirrups, a patient and an obstetrician sometimes develop a flirtation, no matter how oblique. In this case, I am a wise-ass and he is deadpan. One day, Bob, my proper, modest husband, announces he wants to come in while I am being examined. The doctor stares at him, surprised, discombobulated. I guess he's never encountered a husband who wanted to see what he saw. I am moved and amused by Bob's jealousy but have to suppress a laugh. Finally, the doctor shrugs and says, "She's your wife. Come in." As the examination proceeds, Bob is very quiet, and afterward I notice that his face, which I hadn't dared look at, is a bit pale.

•

A beautiful hell, this is my life. I cannot satisfy my urge to skip round the terrace or bend over to pick up a pin. I cannot take an aspirin or any other pill, cannot drink even a soupçon of wine, cannot subject my body to a hot bath, nor in any manner, any manner at all, sweat. And I must drink gallons of water, which, with no exercise, blows me up like a balloon in the Thanksgiving Day Parade.

Nevertheless, Bob and I, without much physical exertion, manage to become cyclones of energy. He takes up the Graiver case again, targets the heads of American Bank & Trust who had colluded with the crooked financier, and proceeds to prosecute the largest and most complex bank swindle in the history of the office. On a whim, we buy a neglected nineteenth-century house on a historic street in West Tisbury, Martha's Vineyard. I teach as a visiting fellow in the Appalachians. Then, with my pregnancy in its seventh month, we fly to Israel in the dead of winter for another visit in swaying helicopters and rocketing jeeps, and after that I write another magazine cover story.

But before all that, we lie low, living in a bubble, never closer; sometimes Bob leaves the office to bring me dumplings from Chinatown or just to make sure I'm resting. We don't challenge the gods by going public until after my third month, when I'm less likely to miscarry. I do tell one person who is about to leave on a book tour, though, and that is Judy Rossner, my mentor and the well-known author of *Looking for Mr. Goodbar.* This is because some part of me believed she conjured up my pregnancy by putting a little bronze fertility goddess above my desk. "I have goose bumps," she says, hugging me. "This will be the most wonderful and complicated adventure of your life."

I never knew what it was like not to live with an undercurrent of dread. These days I feel a peace so unfamiliar it's almost scary, a quiet joy that carries me along on a dream. When I lie on my stomach, I think I can feel her, or him. I love this baby so much, even now before it has given me reason to love it; it goes achingly deep, deeper than the lovemaking that merges you with another. Nothing interests me except this life that depends only on me. Dinner parties seem interminable, cocktail parties positively deadly, and movies and TV that I used to like seem silly or maudlin.

I refer to the baby as "him," and Bob retaliates by calling it "her." He thinks a girl would be nice because it would look like me.

The Morgenthau children suddenly think me fascinating; I shine with happiness. It is reflected back on Bob, and he shines too.

But then I summon up instant disaster movies, as is my wont, reel after reel playing inside my eyelids. Will the baby have all his toes and fingers, will he ever grasp a spoon, be able to hold a book? Will he be part lizard, all Morgenthau nose and no chin?

•

October 14
  He moved! It wasn't a fetal flutter, like they say, but the shaking out of a silk handkerchief or maybe a mouse stamping its feet on my sacroiliac.

•

I am in my fourth month, and it is time for the dreaded amniocentesis. I lie on a table where they baste my stomach with cold jelly. I have to crane my neck back to see the sonogram machine, where everyone is marveling at a blurry black-and-white picture.

"There it is," says the doctor, slowly moving the wand over the jelly. "Looks like a healthy baby. No gross deformities."

"I can't see it!" I say. "It's like a nature film of water currents!"

"Look, right there," Bob says. "It has your nose, love!"

Then I see it: a leg stretching, clenched fingers waving back and forth, a heart beating like a little tadpole. "Oh my Lord, he's all head! He has your head, your big lovely head," I say, weeping.

"At this age, all fetuses are mostly head," the doctor says dryly. Then, wearing sterile gloves, he pours Betadine over my stomach. Bob, who thinks he's really a doctor, is holding my hand behind me and reaches over and pats down a gauze pad that is catching the drips. The doctor raises his voice: "No, no, no! That was sterile. Now I'll have to replace all the pads." I was laughing, so I didn't even feel the big needle go in and extract the fluid that will tell us if the baby has any hidden diseases. He asks us if we want to know the sex, and Bob says a strong no: "I'm superstitious. I don't want Lucinda and me interfering with the natural order of things; we want to be surprised." I tease him about being a Luddite, wanting me to give birth in the desert where there are no machines to tell the sex.

There is little doubt in our minds, however. He will be a boy. And we will call him Joshua.

We go to Hopkinton to tell my father first. He is the most visibly undemonstrative man I know—well, Bob's a close second—and sinks himself in his myriad of hobbies. I am touched to see him wipe away a tear. He says he would prefer it if I had a girl. I look at him suspiciously. If Joshua is a girl, I tell him, he can teach her about the stars and the butterflies but not about guns. "No guns?" he says plaintively. "No guns," I say firmly. When I was five, I shot a hole through my mother's fashion wig, set out to dry on the porch rail, an event he thought hilarious but that deprived me of a week's allowance.

Next, south, to Barbara; it is her response that really counts. A junior at Amherst now, where her father and brother went before her, her world revolves around things very far from us. When we enter, we trip over a mélange of khakis, books, and sports equipment.

She looks skeptical when we tell her, and then, unaccountably, she starts laughing. She looks up at me and laughs, looks down, laughs, looks up, and finally reddens. She gets up and says she's hungry. At the cafeteria, she finally looks at me, and eyeing my slice of Boston cream pie, she says, "You better not eat too much or you'll have triplets."

If all the relatives and nosey parkers shook their heads at poor Bob's being forced to have yet another child, they should see him singing songs to my stomach, bellowing "Give My Regards to Broadway," with his two or three brilliantly resonant notes.

There is a reason Bob has had so many children. He cannot stand it if a little person is not circling around him, entertaining him with antics, begging to be picked up. He likes it when they inevitably attach themselves to him—sometimes too much—in a way his busy parents never did with him.

•

After the grand old house was sold, Bob told me we couldn't afford to build a weekend house, but we could live in a trailer instead. It actually turned out to be very cute, like a dollhouse, and nicely tucked into a corner of the orchards overlooking a quirky pond that had almost silted over. On the weekends, we behaved like Hansel and Gretel. We walked in bare feet on a rug of shiny brown pile and ate on the floor, our plates balanced on a pink-striped futon couch. The bedrooms were about six by eight feet, and the ceilings almost grazed Bob's hair. I loved our Lilliputian mobile home, even without central air-conditioning, which Bob thought too expensive. Until I got pregnant. Three months gone, I was suffering through a hot September. So he bought an inflatable baby pool that we called the rubber ducky.

"I'm too hot," I said one day, wiping the sweat rolling down my cheeks.

"Go sit in the rubber ducky," he suggested.

I gritted my teeth. "If you don't get me central air, I'm not going to have this baby!"

The following weekend, I walked in to a blast of chilled oxygen. I embraced him and plopped down on the couch. I dozed, dreaming of the Arctic, and then woke to see him walking by, smiling at the sight of me. It was a moment I wouldn't forget. Wonderful and sad, for somehow I knew that this was one of the last times I would experience such deep, sweeping love for him. Those moments would not be his anymore; the baby inside me would claim them.

Bob and I would sit together in love's rocking chair, holding hands, attached but not merged, smiling out at the one who had taken the light: the longing, the agony, the passion that was once ours, his everlasting legacy.

•

I have been crying all day. I have written six letters to Gram telling her about the baby and my plans to visit her. Today, they came back unopened. Then I saw the note from Uncle Billy: "Don't bother coming here to Florida. Your grandmother won't recognize anyone." He wrote that she was frying bread in bacon grease when she suddenly left the kitchen and went to bed. He said all she talks about is her past—her beaux back in Watseka, flying around the dance floor in her feather boa. My quick-witted, strong-willed Gram! Could he be lying to me to keep me away? He always disliked me, the crazy nitwit. I need her. I think how sad and awesome if the life I so cherished in the past is ending while the one that I will cherish in the future is about to begin.

•

Dear Gram,

I hope that Billy is reading this to you. It's Cindy, Gram, and I love you so much, and I wish I were there to tell you that I am going to have a baby. It's barely the size of your hand, but it has a spine, a brain, and the beginning of muscles. This fragile, evanescent thing cuddled inside me is your posterity.

Our best friends are so excited. I've had four showers, a stork cake, and a slew of fancy little dresses. Wendy Gimbel, she lives near us in Martha's Vineyard and she's a romantic. She wants to buy a wicker carriage and stroll the baby down Music Street. It will wear your bonnet, the one you saved for me. I can see you rocking your grandchild, softly singing "Caro nome" like you sang it in the Chicago Opera House.

*Our good friends the Kaufmans will be the godparents. And you,
Gram, will be one of the most special people in her life, just as you were
the most special in mine. Gram, listen, I could come down and get you;
you could come here to live with us. We'll play bridge and buy maternity
clothes and go to the opera. I'm beginning to believe in God now, and I
know he is sitting there next to you. Do you hear me praying for you? I am
on my knees praying as hard as I can.*

Much love,
Cindy

•

I have none of the symptoms of a pregnant woman: no nausea or diz-
ziness or fatigue. Bob, on the other hand, has developed morning sickness. He also drinks so much water he has to pee all the time. It is a
constant race for the bathroom. I have promised Bob that I will do
everything I can to get him through this pregnancy as comfortably as
possible.

•

Winter. Apples lying on the ground up at the farm. A sad time. Orchard
stripped and a dull, dusty green. Garbage everywhere left from the pick-
your-own customers.

Penny is working on the *Cheers* TV show now, but she may get
away for a visit. She is one of many, including Bob, who claim to have
brought in the baby: my sister, a Buddhist now, chanted Buddhist
prayers.

We went to a dinner party last night, and I sat between William
Safire and Bernard Malamud. Safire asked me what I was working on,
and I told him I was very excited about these two plain lamps that for
only $1.60 I had bought from the dime store and stenciled with pigs and
giraffes. I don't think I expected him to fall off the chair in admiration
of my creativity, but he didn't have to turn to his other partner so
abruptly. That's when I saw Malamud chuckling at me: "You better stop
stenciling and get all your writing done because you'll never do it once
this creature comes." We talked about his book *The Fixer* and how Tony
Lewis is always writing *New York Times* columns criticizing Israel. He
called Lewis one of the "neo-self-hating Jews." Malamud is one of the

country's greatest writers, but he looked old and very tired, so I talked about all his books I'd read and praised every one for something. I hope it didn't sound too much like a eulogy.

During coffee, Mayor Koch and Charlie Rangel offered to babysit.

The *New York Post* ran a cute little story headed "DA Morgy to Be a Daddy Again at 64": " 'It's her first baby,' the DA said joyously."

How could I ever have doubted how deeply Bob loves me? How many times now do I remember that when I am down, so is he? So this is marriage: the happiness of one springs from the other. It is a beautiful thing.

We bump bellies in the shower. He put a pillow beneath his under-shirt and had Renia take pictures of us. He continues to be super kind and gentle and loving to me, doing things in public he never did before, stroking my cheek, twirling my hair, as though saying, "This fine speci-men of womanhood belongs *to me*."

Not so long ago, I was called a turncoat to the liberation movement for becoming the wife of an older, prominent man. And indeed, my life was so subsumed by Bob's, I felt like an antifeminist. But Betty Friedan had faith in me; she wrote that soon I would get tired of self-subjugation. Now, suddenly, I am a harbinger of a new type of woman. "I love the symbolism of you guys having a baby," says my journalist friend Ellen Fleischer. "You've blown away the old assumptions and conventions. Let's go tell Gloria and Kate Millett, 'Hey, we *can* have a career and a husband and a baby. We can have it all.' "

•

We've had a mini snowstorm, and I am out walking the orchards, hitch-ing up Bob's wool-lined khaki pants. I roped them as if I were a hillbilly, but I hardly needed to since, at six months, I fill them out nicely. The pants, his flannel shirt, they make me feel restless. This energy, I can't contain it. I kick up the thin, crusty layer of snow, rhythmic as the chug of a choo-choo train, like William Carlos Williams naked, spiraling round his study. I am doodling in the cornfield, yodeling "La donna è mobile." The odd apple hangs shriveled on the tree, and the faces of the snowdrifts are pleated like ancient skin.

Bob's shirt has his own familiar, yet unfamiliar scent. Sweat . . . tobacco, maybe. I pat my cheeks. I feel like him. I have borrowed his stately face, his loopy body, his careful footstep. We have remade each other, become a tribal couple. Bob has begun actually putting away his clothes, lining up his comb and brush on the bureau. I have come to own his fear of the ocean.

Did we both always have the habit of dreaming off, listening to certain people with a glazed eye, and then, when asked to reply, getting rigor mortis of the tongue? I have made his calmness mine, become less volatile, learned to be more subtle, make people fear me. When I don't like what someone says, I let the person know it, gently. Bob gets excited or silly or mad in a way he never did before. His occasional tantrums befuddle him; he says he hasn't had one since childhood.

We still have our moments of puppy love. I call him Tart—short for "Sweetheart"—so he occasionally calls me Tartlette. He is so easy, he would do anything to please me: I have begun to take advantage of it just a bit, like now, wearing his best lined pants over my big belly and messing around in the snow. When two people make a baby, the trust they have is unique.

I decide to practice my Lamaze breathing and pant until the bracing air turns white. The trees are twins, triplets, quintuplets, each the same, swirling toward the half-light of the sun. Apple trees are the most beautiful of all trees with their short blue-gray trunks and bumpy, curling branches.

There are the little things where we mimic each other. Bob now washes his hair every day because I do; I used to hate the smell of his once-repugnant cigars, but now I love them, taking in their rich, warm heady smell. If I eat a treat, like an ice cream cone, he has to have one too. Then there are the bigger things. We are adopting each other's inner thoughts. Bob's past must play like a movie across his eyes, and though I don't know what he's seeing, I'll shake my head too.

•

December 2

Almost six and a half months and I can't put my hands in my pockets, for I'll lose my balance.

People regard me with such awe, as though I accomplished something like peace with China.

Bob and I are in dark, aggressive moods. I have the nightmares I had as a child, the Red Wolf chasing me around the Burning Balcony, the Bicycle Race to the Death, and I wake up screaming, and Bob holds me until the terror subsides. He also revisits his childhood, remembering cutting the heads off chickens at the age of six.

He likes to watch westerns, and he loves Clint Eastwood. "I'm going to teach this child to be tough. I'm not having a weak-kneed child, boy or girl. It's going to get a hatchet as soon as it's born."

I guess I'll be raising a Morgenthau whether I like it or not.

14

It is when I look like I have swallowed a watermelon that Bob suggests we get on a plane and go to Israel again. How can I maneuver through the Old City alleyways pushing a wheelbarrow? Josh is probably walking up and down my uterus by now. Does my husband care if I pop out a baby in midair? Or zoom through the hairpin roads in an open jeep with the crazy Israelis? I picture the helpless fetus yanked from his placenta and sloshed around in a tidal wave of amniotic fluid.

I worry that Bob is sixty-four. When our child is eighteen, he will be eighty-two. Will he be able to walk? Think? Talk? Sometimes I have a half-waking vision of his voice being obliterated, the moment he is in fading, and I cannot grab hold of him, his presence becoming tinier and tinier until it is lost in the collapsing stars. I've seen this vision since the day we fell in love. Perhaps Bob is also worrying about his age. Though he hides this, there is a new urgency about his love for Israel. Maybe he feels, and maybe it is only unconscious, that this is the only chance he has to bring what will probably be his last son to his own father's beloved Holy Land. Never mind that this son is not yet realized, sometimes the idea of something is as strong as the reality.

I have felt fine: confident and busy, walking across the park every day with the movie critic Molly Haskell to our studio in the old Harlem Savings Bank building. Inspired by the Writers Room, six of us share the rent in the communal space, which is so conducive to work that I turn out two to three new pages of my novel daily. I have set to work on the house, wiping off the baseboards, steam cleaning the rugs, sweeping the ceilings, and washing the dogs in preparation for the coming of

"Caesar." Once the baby is born, we won't be traveling to Israel anytime soon.

On December 17, 1983, we board a plane to Tel Aviv. I squeeze into the airline seat and feel as if I were incubating a whale. How lucky I am, however. A woman a few seats down has gone into contractions, and another goes into a panic because she thinks the compression in her ears has formed air pockets in her uterus. I shuttle between them, trying to be comforting.

We arrive and ride to the famously massive King David Hotel, which is decorated in biblical motifs that evoke the palace of its name-sake; from our window I can see Mount Zion and the walled Old City, a daydream of illuminated minarets, towers, and domes. But that night, I am so big I can't sleep on one side and I can't sleep on the other, so I end up on my back, tracing the stains on the ceiling. Once asleep, I dream that the baby is taking over my body, crawling up my intestinal tract, filling my lungs. I wake up wheezing and have to put a towel over my head and breathe steam from the hot faucet.

We soon find ourselves traveling through the blooming desert to the Negev, where we sip tea in the living room of the legendary Israeli warrior Ariel Sharon.

"Arik loves to see pregnant women," Uri Dan told me, blowing ciga-rette smoke in my face—something of an Israeli rite. "It makes him think of the future generations he's fighting for."

Sinking into an easy chair in his den, I take in the clutter of photo-graphs ranging from his first wife and son, who were killed in accidents, to him with equally legendary figures like Menachem Begin and Jimmy Carter. For two hours, he explains he had to lead Israeli troops all the way up to Beirut in 1982 to root out Palestinian terrorists. For his efforts, he was terminated as defense minister and assigned the post of minister without portfolio. He is so frank that like Arthur's, my fingers are itching to record his words, but I have promised not to; he still has not spoken to the press since the previous year's invasion.

He folds his hands on his substantial ski-jump belly. I love to hear his thick but softly lilting Hebrew accent. His detractors have called him loud and strident, but he seems surprisingly calm, optimistic, and buoyant for a public official—he had been condemned by the Kahan Commission for his role in the Lebanese massacre—who has been humiliated into accepting a job that has no portfolio.

"I refute the commission's findings, I absolutely deny them! They are libelous, completely and utterly false. I sued *Time* magazine for saying I was behind the massacre, and I won."

"Arik, you are a revered war hero who has spent his life fighting for Israel. People claim that war is in your blood," I say, in journalistic mode now. "Do you think that this is what circumstances have forced you to be?"

"What?" He looks at me quizzically.

I have forgotten that his English is not fluent, especially when you speak circuitously.

"Are you what they say you are? A warmonger?"

He chortles. "I am a peacemonger! People don't know this, but I secretly negotiated the 1979 treaty with Sadat. I let it go, the Sinai, for peace with Egypt. The entire holy land of Sinai, this vast historic land that the Israelites crossed against great hardship in order to gain their freedom, this land we gave away is twice the size of the rest of Israel. We have given away miles and miles of land to the Arabs. We must be tough and we also must give way, and we must know when to do one and when to do the other."

"Arik, your troops . . . oh!" I feel a sudden jolt. I had never heard of a baby who kicks so hard it echoes through your body. "When will they withdraw from Lebanon?"

The general shrugged. "You see, you get peace in different ways. Lebanon is not Egypt, because there's no sitting down with the PLO."

"Of course you had tried to negotiate with the Palestinians, yes?" I ask.

"Ha!" Sharon tips his head back. "How many times we tried. As many times as the hairs on my head. We tried and for nothing. Yasser Arafat is a liar. A cowardly liar. You can't deal with someone who has different faces but the real one wants to destroy you."

He sighed. "We got rid of eighteen thousand PLO and thirty thousand Syrian troops massed on our border, but then we also got me thrown out of office." He laughed. "But I'll be back."

"That's wonderful, the people of Israel need you. But how, after all this, will you return, Arik?" asked Bob.

"Uri Dan says that one day the people will just have to swallow and accept me as prime minister."

His wife, Lily, gives us a lunch of Middle Eastern salads, and then Sharon shows us around his farm, joking with the Arab workers who tend the sheep and the vegetables. I am wearing a red silk top that fits tight around my watermelon belly. He keeps looking at me, smiling slightly, and I wonder if it is because he is confused by the new close-fitting maternity clothes popular in America, so different from the old-fashioned smocks worn in Israel.

He stops and talks with his Arab workers, and Bob tells Sharon he is impressed by his camaraderie with them.

Sharon grins. "Now you can see that I don't eat Arabs for breakfast."

A sheepherder snaps a picture of Bob and me with Arik, his arm around me, and Lily leaning against a fence. All of us are laughing; Arik and I are standing belly to belly. When we return to New York, I blow the picture up and hang it in the hall, where anyone who is secretly anti-Semitic can enjoy it.

When the Dans take us out for a Yemenite feast, I sit up stock-straight because otherwise, with my stomach scrunched into a corner, the food would have no place to go.

Bob grins at me. "You look regal. The queen!"

On Christmas Eve, we make a pilgrimage to Bethlehem. It is a fascinating mélange of the honky-tonk and the spiritual. Coming up from Jerusalem, dark and deserted on this particular holiday, we come over the hill to a blast of flashing lights in the shape of crosses on the rooftops, souvenir shops declaring, "Jesus is here—buy him now," an enormous tree so piled with tinsel that its natural green is rendered invisible. Manger Square is teeming with thousands of people from different cultures—dour-faced monks with hands tucked in sleeves brushing against women from Iowa in fur-collared coats. The nuns bow their heads over rosaries, ignoring the splashes of whiskey that land on their habits from Swedish teenagers happily passing the bottle. I hold Bob's hand tightly as we push through throngs of Arab Christians pulling tight their burnooses against the bitter wind from the Judaean Hills. We warm ourselves with Turkish coffee from an open flame and buy lamb's wool hats to protect our ice-red ears.

"Smell the smells! Lamb roasting and water pipes and that grape alcohol the Israelis drink," I say, trying to remain cheerful in spite of my disappointment at the tinselly crassness of Christians at this holy time in this holy city.

"And there's something else," Bob says, looking at a woman with a steeple headdress jangling with coins climb out of a limo.

"That dates back to the Middle Ages. It's where an engaged woman carried her dowry," I say.

"Looks like she's got another engagement tonight," Bob snipes.

I feel humiliated at the defilement of this holy Christian city on this holy day. Would the Jews do this on Rosh Hashanah? Or even on the festival of Sukkoth, where they say blessings every morning in their ceremonial huts, which are covered not with neon lights but with tissue paper leaves?

Then we make our way to the Church of the Nativity, and for the first time I see Bob, if reluctantly, enter a church. I know he does this for me. We move quietly down to the grotto below the altar. Everything changes. The crush of worshippers kneel before the shepherd's cave where Mary and Joseph went when there was no room for them at the inn; here is a mystical hush. The cave is lit only by candles, and some people weep; others kiss the silver star embedded in the floor, the exact spot where Jesus was supposedly born. Across the way is the manger, where a procession led by the much-loved mayor Teddy Kollek will lay a Jesus doll swaddled in old clothes. Marble, silver, gold, and mosaics have replaced the humble stable that I was taught to love, but still, as we leave the church, I feel a lightness, the kind of floating feeling I felt when I prayed as a child, as though I were being carried down the basilica on a gentle breeze. I have stood at the place where the son of God was born. I look at Bob, and to my surprise his features have also softened. He looks tenderly at me. A choir echoes forth with "Silent Night." The church bells peal, and strangers from all corners of the world smile and hug each other. We are joined together, for we have all partaken, on this Christmas Eve, of the belief in miracles.

At this moment I feel at one with the Lord. I am to be reborn in my own child. A child within a child. I will teach him, or her, the secret that is hidden beneath the bright, wonderful things he loves about Christmas. The joy that is far deeper than the slender pleasures of bells and carols and spiced cider, of the ancestral stories about Great-Grandpa Leavitt in a Santa suit, picking up children in his homemade sleigh, or Great-Grandma Franks sewing sequins on ornaments with her painful arthritic hands.

We will say prayers together. He will know that the celebration of Christ's birth occurs not outside him but within; that all goodness comes from Jesus and that he will hold him when he most needs to be held; that his own love of God and the work it takes to attain that love is a feeling that will spread inside him.

Each year, the ancient story of Holy Week will be imprinted on his mind as it was so long ago on mine. On Good Friday, we will look at images of the cross and talk about the sacrifice of Jesus, so difficult for children, for anyone, to understand. And then, on Easter Sunday, we will celebrate the joy of his resurrection into everlasting life, the hope and victory over death that it brings us. I will teach him about forgiveness and redemption. And if he cannot fully understand, as I don't, why Jesus had to suffer to save us, he will come to understand it in his heart.

•

On our way home from Bethlehem to the King David, I scribble in a notebook to try to capture what we've experienced for a piece in the *Times* travel section. "Nothing is working," I complain to Bob, handing him my lead paragraphs. "It's totally simplistic."

He reads it aloud: "Christmas in Bethlehem. The ancient dream: a cold clear night made brilliant by a glorious star, the smell of incense, shepherds and wise men falling to their knees in adoration of the sweet baby, the incarnation of perfect love."

"It's simple but it's beautiful," he says.

The following Christmas Eve, Cardinal O'Connor, his voice resounding through the magnificent St. Patrick's Cathedral, starts his sermon by quoting my words.

•

Back in Tel Aviv, I begin interviewing Moshe Arens, who became minister of defense earlier in 1983. I have no trouble getting entrée because the prospect of appearing in the powerful *New York Times* makes politicians giddy. I follow Arens around, Bob often with me, riding in his limo, attending his meetings, visiting his haunts.

We fly home just before New Year's Eve. I deplane and promptly lose my equilibrium. Everything that looked rosy has turned umber. It is as though I can foresee that our lengthy Lamaze training has been a farce and I will suffer a labor both interminable and frightening. I try to write the Arens article, but it is like swimming through a bottle of Robitussin. Poor Bob doesn't know whether he will come home to a wife in black humor or one in a state of high excitement. I might as well be wearing the two Greek masks of drama: the laughing face of Thalia, the weeping face of Melpomene. I ponder this and wonder if I am somehow acting out my mother's fitful moods. Am I capriciously, vagrantly greeting my husband in the way that she greeted me?

My child, like magic, behaves as compliantly as I did in the face of maternal fickleness. When I am fretful, he goes still, as though to soothe me, and when I am happy, he kicks, punches, and plays tap-tap-tap inside my stomach.

But I do long for her, my poor, unhappy mother. I miss bringing her rare joy, seeing her gaze at her first grandchild; her second chance; the glory of reversing her history, purging her guilt. I miss decorating the nursery with her, shopping for mobiles and crib mirrors. I miss being able to pick up the phone with swollen ankles or scary twinges and hearing her say, "Oh, that's nothing. That happened to me."

It is known that mothers are transformed when presented with the children of their children. Often, from witches emerge indulgent, patient, playful, near-saintly creatures. Thus was my grandma, who was a terrifying mother but understood me when no one else did. Both Bob's and my mother are dead. This baby will have no grandmothers, no refuge, no place to go when his parents inevitably fail him. How will we compensate for the loss of this right, this gift?

•

January 10

Annie had a New Year's Eve party, and I have never felt more close to my stepchildren. Bobby kissed me and said I was glowing; Eddie Rothschild kissed me on the lips, whispering, "You look so beautiful"; Bob Ascheim said I had the most beautiful belly in the room; and Bob's sister, Joan, who is a doctor, said in her aristocratic, nasal voice, "You are much bigger than normal."

Daddy calls every day to see how I am. He asks when he should come down or what he should do, trying, I think, to make up for my having no mother.

Bob has felt him! While he was singing, with his hand on my tummy, he actually saw the baby bulging out toward him. I think Bob's singing has made him into a musician. Sometimes he plays the xylophone on my placenta, a little rat-a-tat-tat, sometimes a glissando, and then boom, boom, boom, no doubt a timpani of toes. I play Vivaldi and Bach at a high volume these days.

We visited Bob's old friend Franklin Delano Roosevelt Jr., sixty-nine, on his horse farm in Millbrook. FDR's son has had four wives and seven children, one of whom is fairly young. Franklin said, "Bob, welcome to the Older Fathers' Club!" He looked and sounded eerily like his father, long, aristocratic face and voice so plangent it might have been coming out of a radio.

•

I'm finally up against the clock, with just enough time to put together the Arens piece before the baby comes. This is how I write best: poised on the edge. Looking at my notes, I become excited: I had forgotten that the Israeli defense minister had dropped a gold nugget right in my lap. I had gone into the interview wondering why President Reagan's defense secretary, Caspar Weinberger, virtually leaked hostility toward the tiny Jewish homeland. I found out that Weinberger, though racially Jewish, was a committed Episcopalian and that he had worked for an anti-Semitic company, Bechtel Corporation, before becoming the man who could essentially decide Israel's fate. I asked Arens if he thought Weinberger harbored a revulsion for Israel, and he rolled his eyes. I asked if he thought him anti-Semitic. He replied that Weinberger was a Jew who denied his own Jewishness. "He needs a psychiatrist," Arens snapped.

When the *Times* hears that Israel's defense minister has publicly declared the American secretary of defense in need of psychiatric care, it schedules the article for the cover of the magazine.

•

I have finished the piece three weeks before the baby's due. Foolishly, I assume I can rest up for the event. A week later, I naughtily eat two chocolate croissants at the Writers Studio, toddle home, and go to bed at 11:00 p.m. Just after dawn, I ignore it when my water breaks; the baby isn't due for another two weeks. Then I am seized by a strong cramp and grab the phone. "Contractions," my doctor says, yawning. "Go to the hospital when they're ten minutes apart." I shake my husband, who has attended Lamaze classes with me and will be my breathing coach. "I'm having labor pains!" I shout.

He looks at his watch. Six in the morning. Then he turns over. "Okay, let me get some sleep. It's going to be a long day."

I sit up, dumbfounded. Well, he has been through it five times, nothing novel. But that the imminent birth of our baby is all about his own sleep? It reminds me of our friend Pierre Leval, who, when his wife, Susana, went into labor, promptly threw out his back.

The cramps are growing more severe. As they increase, I briefly consider waking Bob with a glass of water in his face.

·

When we finally arrive at Mount Sinai Hospital, I'm told to walk around with the other women there who circle each other, clutching their stomachs and moaning through their contractions.

In the middle of a contraction, I am abruptly led away for an "urgent phone call" at the nurses' station. On the other end of the line, the *Times* copy editor starts barking away at me. They are putting the story to bed, and they need last-minute clarifications. Through the contractions, I answer his questions crisply, from memory. Finally, he asks me what Arens was wearing when he made the Weinberger comment.

The cramps are getting more intense. "Gray suit . . . blue tie."

"Do you have that quote on tape?"

"Nee-yo," I breathe. An arc of pain is sweeping over me, and I drop the phone.

"What'd you say? Hello . . . hello, are you there?" I hear a tinny voice.

I am half carried and laid out in a single room where my doctor and a resident are watching *M*A*S*H* on television.

My doctor comes over and pats my hand while Bob intones, "Breathe, breathe, breathe." Then they attach me to a fetal heartbeat monitor, which the doctor warns sometimes malfunctions.

But Bob is fascinated by the wavy line that tells him Josh is healthy. And after ten hours of labor that is getting me nowhere, I have become rather a whinnying bore, even to myself. I finally consent to an epidural injection—giving up the possibility of pure, unmedicated natural childbirth—and I am staring at the ceiling, adrift in my painlessness. At my urging, Bob leaves my side for a more important job.

He becomes the protector of the heart. Hours go by. I'm still not dilating, and I get more injections. And then, in a blur, Bob moves to the TV and quietly tells the doctors, "The heart has stopped." They hoist themselves up and shout orders, and I find myself on a gurney being raced to the delivery room. I pass Bob in the hall, and his tawny skin is dead white, a sight I will never forget. Soon, I hear a lusty wail. But there are no announcements. Perhaps it is another woman's baby. "Is it alive?" I finally whisper.

"Oh, yes, yes!" A merciful intern comes over. "A nice healthy boy."

Bob comes in and rests his damp cheek on mine. "That damn machine malfunctioned," he mumbles. "But I called our pediatrician, and he's on his way over." They bring the baby to us: bronze skin like Bob's, huge blue eyes, strands of dark hair arranged around his head like a crown. It is a little after 11:00 p.m., March 2, 1984.

Bob brings bottles of fine French wine, duck pâtés studded with slivers of pistachio, goat cheeses, Saint-Andrés, and caviar for our dinners. To the consternation of the nurses, I won't let Joshua Franks Morgenthau out of my sight. When he has to be bathed, they do it in the room. Bob looks on happily, content to be the observer he is. Each time I try to put the baby in his arms, he blocks me and shakes his head. Finally, I simply deposit Josh on his lap, pleading for a break. When I return, Bob is holding the baby gingerly, but on his face there is a smile of indescribable delight. Caesar has arrived.

15

It takes just a single moment for a journalist, justly or unjustly, to lose her credibility, to watch years of hard work disappear like a balloon in the sky. On Sunday, March 25, with my baby three weeks old, my article on Arens runs in the *Times*. There is instant outrage from the Defense Department and talk of Weinberger's holding up a supply of U.S.-made fighter planes to Israel. Arens reacts by denying that he ever said Weinberger needed a psychiatrist. The *Times* reacts by publishing a front-page story about the controversy. Unluckily, I did not tape the exchange, which took place in a car, but luckily, Bob had been present. "I was there when Arens said it," he told the newspaper, and *The New York Times* wrote that it stood by its reporter's story.

Just as quickly as I had fallen, I had been redeemed and was able to make my new life with Bob and our son.

April 6

Will I ever be the kind of mother he can love? Or will I be the type you read about in the newspapers, whose son holds her off at knifepoint while he eats a box of hidden cookies?

I have given birth to a night creeper, waking every two hours, wanting to socialize or eat. I say let's just take him into our bed, but Bob says what if we roll over on him?

·

Bob and I smile constantly, like idiots. Before you have a child, life is, in large, predictable. Enter a child and nothing is ever predictable again.

You are drunk with delight one moment and hungover in despair the next.

One day, I am bathing Josh, absently trickling water down his back, simultaneously trying to hold him up, keep the water warm, and maneuver the soap, when without warning comes a thunderbolt, shifting the prism, abruptly stopping the clock, bringing forth a sight such as I've never seen before. This baby, this baby unbearably beautiful: you know that you will long for this moment for years after it is over. The soap swirls unattended as he goes absolutely still, like a tableau. Who is this? Where did this marvel come from? His creamy glistening skin, the light coming through his tissue-thin ear, the enormous blue eyes, wide and wishful, fixed on me, his world.

At one month old, he is like a stand-up comic, expressing frustration by running a hand down his face, curiosity by cupping it under his chin, anger by looking rather like Henry VIII, dangerously displeased with one of his wives.

Bob has moved Josh's cradle next to him and tries to solve the sleep problem by holding his hand through the twirled slats. Sometimes he sings "Give My Regards to Broadway," which makes Josh, who first heard it in utero, flap his arms in recognition. I wake and see my son's chubby little fist holding tight to my husband's long, sculpted finger. Yesterday, when we thought the baby asleep, Bob said, "Lucinda, are you scratching my back?" I wasn't, but Josh, reaching through the cradle, was. When we peered over at him, he had a look of sheer delight.

April 10, 1984
Western Union telegram
Grandma died in sleep Monday. Funeral Kankakee yesterday. Thought you too busy with baby. Buried next to your mother. Inform Penelope. Yours, Bill.

I crushed the yellow rectangular paper in my hand. Grammy. Gone. Just like that. Without a goodbye from me, without ever seeing her only great-grandchild. Laid in the ground before I even knew it.

Uncle Billy, my mother's brother, had disliked all children, but he had particularly loathed Penny and me. Once, under duress, he took me to

Kresge's for a root beer float. He watched me, glowering, as I sipped very carefully; I was sure that if I dribbled once, he would have got up and left me there. Our Waterloo occurred when Penny was six, and I was twelve; we carelessly threw our wet bathing suits over the braided arm of his favorite chair. He told my mother he never wanted to see us again. Still, she perpetuated the myth that deep down this troubled personality, which she must have recognized in herself, loved us with all his heart.

Gram's favorite opera was *Tosca*, so I put it on the record player and call Penny. I haven't a friend that comes close to her; there is no one who understands me better, no one I know so deeply.

"He didn't even phone? He used a telegram!" Penny cries.

"He might be insensitive to us," I reply, "but he was devoted to Gram, and she to him, and at least we can be grateful for that."

"He let Kathleen take care of her," Penny says darkly. "He didn't do a thing.

"All the friends we know of hers in Kankakee, her bridge club, that woman who taught her Chinese paper weaving, what will they think about us not even coming to her funeral!"

"I wonder what *she* thought?" I reply quietly.

There is a silence. "Cindy, are you going loony on me?"

I am and I hang up because I hear a faint tremolo above Renata Tebaldi. It gets louder, and my hands go icy. Gram is here, I can hear her, I can feel her. She was an opera singer in Chicago when she was young, and now I see her but don't. That stolid powdered shape, bosom like the prow of a ship, silky dress of roses, white wispy hair. The smell of lavender. Her spirit taking shape behind a screen. Her mouth is pursed in a little smile, and her eyes are bright. I weep; "I'm sorry, I'm so sorry, Gram. I never came to see you when you were sick."

"You were there," she intones in her glottal Victorian voice.

"You didn't even see your first great-grandchild!"

"But I did." She smiles. "I see him now."

A gentle wind caresses my forehead and Gram is gone. Her scent lingers in the room.

•

Not long afterward, Bobby, now living in his own apartment, comes in our front door quietly. Renia peeks into the living room and sees him leaning over the old brass cradle that once rocked his great-grandfather, talking softly to his new brother, letting him suck one of his fingers. This makes me inordinately happy.

May 5, 1984

Our lives have been taken over by Joshua. If I go out of the house, I come home in a panic, desperate to see him. Bob works hard as usual, but part of his mind is devoted to making up stories and songs for the baby. He comes home early now to see the spectacle of his son winding up for his evening meal: Josh snorts, makes an O, and crosses his eyes before diving into the nipple. Bob is amused. Delighted that Josh has inherited his big appetite, he holds him and sings, "I am a pig, a very big pig, and I don't care who knows it. All I do is eat, eat, eat, 'cause I'm a barracuda."

•

Bob likes to carry Josh in a blue sling, wearing him proudly, like a medal. We take the baby everywhere, to parties, to workplaces, to restaurants. That August in the Vineyard, we go to a cocktail party at John and Margery Oakes's. Bob, a man who lives by his own rules, gives the baby sips of his beer. John is horrified: "What are you doing? He's an infant! That's got to be bad for him, not to speak of the fact you are breaking the law." Bob grins and gives him more.

Not every experience out on the town is so jolly. We go to a trendy Chinese restaurant called Pearl's with a straitlaced couple—the man, a city official responsible for the DA's budget—and a Morgenthau cousin who approves of neither our marriage nor our baby. Josh must have sensed her animosity because the spring rolls have barely been served when the baby starts screaming like a mynah bird. Nothing can induce him to stop. Finally, Pearl comes running over and throws us out. We laugh all the way home.

•

May 10

He stares at me with his big blue silver-dollar eyes, then runs his hand down me so lightly, it is like a feather blowing past. We are woven together as tightly and as intricately as the threads of a tapestry. When he laughs, so do I, and when he cries, I am close to tears.

In my arms, he picks the petals off the apple blossoms, crushes them up in his little fist, and offers them to me. Suddenly it begins to drizzle, and we run as the clouds go ashen, light shimmering beneath them over the mountains, grass waving, Josh laughing, silver light borne on the wind.

When I try to hand him over to Renia, he tilts his head back and closes his eyes and yells, "Mama, Mama," in deep desperation. I take him back. I am the center of the universe.

•

Bob smiles when he sees us together. But I should know something else is lurking inside. We used to discuss our days when he got home in the evening, but now we only discuss Josh's day. Companionable cocktail hours have given way to eating dinner over reruns of *Murder, She Wrote* with Josh nearby in the cradle or cuddled in my arms.

We usually go to bed together about eleven, but lately, at eight, he gets up and announces, "Josh and I are going to bed now." Then he picks him up and processes down the hall like a page bearing the king's crown. This has been happening for a while.

"Oh, I'll come too," I say the other night.

"You don't need to, love, go ahead and watch Angela Lansbury, take a break."

I give him an indulgent smile because I'm glad he is asserting his needs. But as the TV drones on, I sit there, feeling deserted. We have not acknowledged this new struggle over ownership of the third person in our marriage: like three young teens, one of whom vies to steal away another, we compete to make the threesome a pair. Our little world of two has been breached: we are not a couple anymore.

"Bob," I say one night, "I know how you hate psychologizing, but we've got to analyze what's happening to us."

"What?"

"I think we're competing over Josh. I think that's why you take him up and go to bed so early."

"You have him all day. I need some time with him too."

"But I don't feel you have any interest in me anymore."

"Well, you have no interest in me."

I laugh and put my arm around him. "We're acting like children. We're jealous of each other like we used to be jealous if our siblings got more than we did. And maybe we're even jealous of Josh, which one of us he wants."

He nods slowly. "Then maybe we should start acting like grown-ups."

"Uh-huh. And start remembering that our first love is for each other, that we're a team."

•

We close ranks sooner than we thought we would, thanks to a loner named Bernhard Goetz. On December 22, 1984, Goetz, who had once been mugged, rode a Manhattan subway, took out an unlicensed .38-caliber Smith & Wesson, and shot four black teens who he thought were about to rob him. That some scared, angry New Yorker would take the law into his own hands was inevitable. Even though Bob briefly helped bring it down from 1980 to 1983, violent crime remained a serious problem. Fifteen hundred citizen crime watches have been organized to help quell the fear of a population leery of becoming victims.

Goetz is quickly lionized as the "subway vigilante," "Thug-Buster" T-shirts have been produced en masse, the Guardian Angels hold out their red berets for defense fund money, and even CORE, abandoning its mandate to protect black civil rights, is rallying for the thirty-seven-year-old man. The city, three to one in favor of letting Goetz walk, is going crazy. And my husband has to decide the shooter's fate.

Murphy's Law has asserted itself. This all is happening on the eve of Bob's reelection campaign in the fall. We become as obsessed with Goetz as the rest of the city and give Josh over to Renia so we can concentrate on the case. The District Attorney's Office has already arraigned Goetz on four counts of attempted murder, four counts of assault, one count of reckless endangerment, and four counts of carrying an illegal weapon. Now, do they go the distance and indict him?

The assistant DAs are split on the question, so Bob and I systematically pick apart the case. He's told me the whole story, the undisclosed facts that the public doesn't yet know. For once we are on the same political side; we don't think Goetz should get a free ride, as it were. But we decide to role-play.

I am devil's advocate: "Bob, put your ear to the ground and listen to the people. Don't commit the folly of ignoring this great city!" I throw up my arms like Clarence Darrow. "The election will be here before you know it. You've run unopposed for ten years, but now you've already got at least two candidates denouncing you. You've got Catherine Abate talking about becoming the first woman DA and that Vernon Mason guy declaring he will become the first black one. Do you like being district attorney? Well, just picture what will happen if you indict Goetz: the whole city's gonna carry you out of office at the end of a rope!"

Bob puts down his head to hide his smile. I tell him not to break character, and when he looks up, his face has become so austere, so unforgiving, so scary, I shiver. "I don't prosecute on the basis of mobs. I don't do it for political advantage."

"But look at the case. Goetz's four muggers slam him into a glass door and give him permanent knee injuries. They're hardly punished. He was angry, and I don't blame him."

"Anger is not self-defense."

"This guy is gentle, shy; he won't even talk to the press. He was just trying to protect himself! Maybe he freaked out a little, but those thugs weren't panhandling him; I bet you dollars to doughnuts they were going to rob him. You've already decided you can't put them on the witness stand; one of them is up for armed robbery! People are going to riot when they learn this."

"I'd rather that than practice bad justice," he says quietly. Bob pauses. "There's no doubt in my mind that Goetz was out for revenge. After he shot all four, he stood over Darrell Cabey—and he'd already wounded him—and shot him again, severing his spinal cord. He'll be a paraplegic the rest of his life."

"Wow, a fifth shot? You didn't tell me that!" I say, a bit too enthusiastically, as if I were going to shout it down Park Avenue.

"Remember, this is all confidential, Lucinda," he says, scowling at me. "And if the office presents it to a grand jury, our discussions are finished. Unless you want us to be charged with a felony for leaking grand jury minutes."

I already know this. "I'm more and more convinced you should go for the max," I say. "I mean, it's so clear what the right thing to do is. You don't rise up and blast four people nearly to death because they ask you for five dollars. He was already prepared; he had his hand on the gun under his Windbreaker is what you told me."

"Yes, but it's a little worrying, all this hysteria."

"The Irish call it common bloodlust," I remark. "But in this case, the mob happens to be wrong."

I hold his hand and smooth down his hair, noticing that it is much whiter, its thinning strands aloft on his head. "You will win, love, just because you *are* going to indict this shooter. The people know who you are. Even the Goetz supporters have to concede that you're the real thing amid a bunch of phonies. They know you protect the victim, that you're someone ethical beyond ethical . . . incorruptible . . . fair . . . scrupulous . . . honorable . . ."

"If I'm all that, lucky I married my alter ego."

"Thank you, love. I think we both live by Kant's categorical imperative: the obligation to do one's moral duty because it is moral, not because it leads to other ends."

He runs his finger down my cheek. "I think that's right. Except you're more intellectual than me."

On January 25, 1985, the case is presented to a grand jury. The twenty-three jurors indict on three of the weapons counts and dismiss the rest. They have broken the precedent of grand juries doing what the DA wants. Some jurors wait in line afterward to receive Goetz's autograph. Bob, forced now to put the thuggish victims on the stand, presents it to a second grand jury; after hearing testimony that Goetz, when he fired a fifth shot at Darrell Cabey, said, "You seem to be doing all right, here's another," they indict on ten of the most serious charges. Appeals courts affirm the indictment, throw it out, and then reinstate it. The process is grueling, taking two and a half years of the courts' time and at least that much off Bob's life. A trial ends the case where it began—with Goetz getting off on all but a weapons count.

Through it, Bob would often walk through the door as though he were carrying a boulder on his back. I could cheer him up, but Josh saved his sanity. When he saw his dad, he galloped over on his hands and knees. Bob would shed his coat and pick him up, and I would watch the boulder roll off.

"We're flying, we're flying," he sang in a voice like Ernie the Muppet. As Josh swung back and forth through the air, I don't know which one of them was laughing louder. The poker face of the city's district attorney had disappeared. "Look, Mom," Bob shouts, "we're flying!"

16

Bob was so flustered that after eating his bran flakes, he put on his beloved baseball cap backward and then later proceeded to drop it in the gutter.

He was mad at *The New York Times*. C. Vernon Mason, a black lawyer, had come forward to challenge him in the upcoming 1985 campaign for district attorney, and the man had become the press's darling. Bob felt hurt and abused by the city. He had served its people for a quarter of a century, and Mason was a minor Harlem figure, often criticized for his rashness and questionable ethics. But morale in the city had dipped; street crime and police brutality were high; earlier that year there had been the acquittal of six transit policemen who were said to have beaten to death Michael Stewart, a young subway graffiti artist who became an international symbol of a decaying New York.

"Robert Morgenthau is neither a leader nor a creator," Mason proclaimed as he announced his candidacy. He described himself as a man of the people and said his opponent "was born into aristocracy and wealth . . . and lives in insulation and isolation speaking to the power elite and speaking for the power elite . . . He takes a limousine to work." Mason, on the other hand, drove a gray Mercedes.

Jim Gill, a prominent attorney, echoed much of the white establishment when he wrote to Bob, "I think it was very kind of Mason to remind everyone of . . . the power which you wield."

Bob knew that C. Vernon Mason actually represented drug dealers and often didn't show up in court at all.

In recent years, Bob's pedestal *had* been shaken, and he was under relentless attack by the media. First there was the bitter rivalry with Rudy Giuliani, who had worked at Bob's former law firm and in 1983 stepped into Bob's old job as U.S. attorney. Rudy busted up organized and corporate crime, as Bob had done, but Rudy was flamboyant. "He had cops burst into a brokerage firm and handcuff a bunch of junior managers right in front of their colleagues, and then he paraded them in front of the cameras. They were weeping," Bob said, seething. "He didn't care whether they were innocent or guilty. He's a publicity hound. He's raised the perp walk to an art form." Moreover, Rudy would also steal away Bob's cases, including the bribery charges against the powerful Bronx Democratic leader Stanley M. Friedman, after the DA's Office had done all the investigation work, on the grounds that federal prosecutions of federal crimes trumped prosecutions by local DA offices. He would often talk about Rudy at the dinner table.

Ironically, much later, when Rudy became mayor, he praised Bob's talents effusively. And one day, Bob began speaking fondly of Rudy. "I'm human. I forgive my enemies," he said with a smile. "And I suppose I'm susceptible to flattery. Especially since the mayor will provide the majority of the DA's budget."

Then there came the racially charged cases, one after another. Though Bob had tried to nail Goetz on murder charges, part of the public was angry at him for the high court's ultimate acquittal of Goetz on all but gun possession charges. And the not-guilty verdict in the trial of the policemen who manhandled Michael Stewart earlier that year was considered an even worse travesty of justice. Bob was perceived as having twice failed to persuade a jury that black men had been victimized by white ones.

The Stewart case, a labyrinth of vitriolic contradictions, was bugled throughout the world. Under tremendous pressure, Bob remained cool and ostensibly above the hullabaloo, declaring to me that Mason didn't worry him.

I wanted to believe him, wanted not to recognize the worry in his eyes. I wanted badly for this inconvenient interruption in our lives to go away. I might have subliminally given him that very message—Don't disappoint me.

The fact that our August vacation was just a few weeks before the mid-September Democratic primary, which would decide the election, somehow didn't bother me. It was easy to take advantage of his undemanding nature.

After eight years of marriage, I still hadn't learned how to read Bob. I took him at face value. I couldn't see that subtle tightening of the lips, the flattening of the normally expressive voice—those little signifiers that he was feeling something that perhaps even he didn't know he felt.

"Look, if you won't come to Martha's Vineyard, I'm going anyway," I told him in July. "I'm worn out, and the baby needs sun and fresh air."

Bob didn't blink. "That's fine," he said. "Go."

"Great," I replied and went off to make ferry reservations to the island.

·

The Vineyard: as always, a sanctuary of pleasure. Every day, Josh and I climb the little hill to Quansoo Beach and watch the big waves roll in.

We like to sit alone, so we go far down the shore where Josh's favorite thing to do is to toddle off and explore. I sit there proudly and watch his chubby little body go farther and farther, picking up handfuls of warm sand. When he becomes too tiny, I go fetch him, ignoring the disapproving looks of the mothers who don't let their little ones stray from their umbrellas. I wish Bob were here to see this show of Josh's sovereignty. We decided to give him independence early so he would grow up to be a man with a free and mighty spirit.

I call my husband every night, and Josh screams "Dada! Dada!" when he hears his voice. Then he gets upset because he can't also see him. Bob sounds busy when he talks to me, so I pick up the *Times* in the morning in hopes he'll be in it. Today he is on the front page of the metro section, affably listing the healthy state of his vital organs—prostate, heart, lungs. He looks buoyant and sexy, and I feel a stirring inside.

I decide I could do something for the campaign, even here. So I try to put together a Women's Committee for Morgenthau. I call some of my writer acquaintances—Nancy Milford, Nora Sayre. But Nancy, whose son Bob once hired for a summer job, stumbles about: "Ah, I have some political differences with Bob." Nora Sayre says she's too busy: "I'm unfortunately on a deadline." Mary Breasted says it would compromise her objectivity as a reporter. My cleaning lady, however, obliges. So counting myself, I have a women's committee of two. I won't tell Bob of my failed efforts—or the pathetic loyalty of my friends.

One day, I learn that Bob's campaign headquarters have been broken into. Though nothing has been taken, his people suspect it's the work of the other side. This time the photograph of him in the *Times* is almost pitiful. His cheeks are sunken, and there is something odd in his aspect. As if he were uncomfortable in his suit. Has he seemed this way on the phone? No, he's just spoken in a clipped voice. Clipped? Suddenly I feel dizzy. What am I doing here, lolling in the warm breezes instead of by his side, pounding out the miles of a political campaign worker. Perhaps I've been too selfish or maybe I just couldn't face the attacks and witness the stress it was putting on him, coward that I am.

I throw a few things into a suitcase, grab Josh, and then wait in the ferry line for hours to get off the island.

When I get home to New York, he is getting ready for bed, turning down the covers, in silence. I come up from behind and throw my arms around him, making him jump and whirl around.

"Sweetheart, it's me. I'm back! I deserted you. Please forgive me."

"Nothing to forgive. I've been fine."

"I left you alone to fix your own dinner. No one to talk to, to share the day's events, sleeping every night in a cold, empty bed."

"You do warm things up," he quips. "In fact it's a little like sleeping with a furnace." He looks around. "Where's Josh?"

I retrieve him from the living room and put him in his father's arms. "Actually," he says hesitantly, "I have been a little short on support. Even Charlie Rangel won't return my calls. I guess his constituents have forgotten me; they're so excited about having the first black DA. He's too scared he'll lose his seat in Harlem."

"I wouldn't worry about him. He's one person."

I recall Charlie's respect and love for Bob, all the dinners we had with Charlie and his wife, Alma, eating a feast at their home in Washington. One night, we locked ourselves out of the car, and the congressman took a hanger and had it open in two minutes flat. Bob was amazed:

"Where'd you learn to do that, Charlie?" Rangel laughed his gravelly laugh: "How do you think I survived growing up in Harlem?"

All those years of friendship and now Charlie turns his back on Bob . . . just as I had.

"I left you too," I say guiltily.

He picks up Josh, and the baby excitedly pats his father's cheeks. "No," Bob says. "I didn't particularly like you leaving—and taking Josh with you." Josh's little arms were tight around his neck.

"Bob, you *are* upset. Will you be straight with me, please, just once?"

Standing there in his underwear, he suddenly looks unprotected. He falters. "Everyone has turned off me, and you weren't there," he says thickly. The words are spilling out slowly. "Even the people I've considered my friends—Ed Bradley, Charlayne Hunter-Gault—they're going over to Mason. You don't know how it's affected me. I've had no one to talk to."

He's telling me I've hurt his feelings?

"Oh, sweetheart, I'm sorry. If only you'd told me! I'm so selfish, and I really didn't think you needed me."

"Well, you were wrong. I did." As I rest my cheek against his lips, I feel a trembling. His chin.

Don't move. Don't say anything. Don't say it's okay to be vulnerable. Just hug him, hug him till he can't breathe and he will know.

"Daddy, Daddy, what's the matter?" Josh is staring at him with alarm.

"Your mother. I can't breathe!" Bob pries my arms from around his chest.

The moment has passed.

"I'm staying right here, by your side," I say.

He strokes my hair, but Josh still looks upset.

I put my arms around the two of them: "Family sandwich! Daddy and I are the bread, and Josh is the ham." Josh giggles. Everything is all right again.

•

Dearest love, you must have felt desperate. You are so cautious, shy, secretive, closed, and you turned yourself inside out in front of me.

But I know that it stops here and now. You will not return to your

*emotions. You have pried a feeling out like a pearl from an oyster. No
more pearls tonight; you are standing safe on your sandbar.*

*For such a long time now, I have waited. My hopes have been my ex-
pectations. Each time you managed to express a feeling, an emotional
need, I would think, "Ah, this is it. Finally, he will become how he feels; I
will know his emotional life." But the big reveal has never come. All I have
known, and will know, is emotional moments like these. But how to connect them? To know when they are coming and when they have left and to
fill the spaces in between?*

*Your philosophy of laissez-faire is a generosity, but it is also a form
of tyranny. You have protected me from the tough stuff. Since you won't
bother me with your problems, I don't bother to ask. I have exploited your
reserve, going about with my work and my baby, fulfilling my own needs.
I have ignored the fact that beneath your absence of demands lurks a moral
imperative. Guilt stirs below the surface of my resolve. No matter what you
claim, I really do know what you need. And I believe that somewhere
you expect me to act not on what you say but on what you don't.*

•

Being caught in the midst of this nasty campaign is hell. Each day, it
seems some negative story comes out. The media who yesterday loved
him have turned on a dime. They use adjectives to fit the angle of their
stories. His hair is not thinning but "wispy"; he's not thin but "frail."

One day as I am reading *The New York Observer* in the bathroom,
I tear out a page declaring that "Morgy is too old, too tired, too washed
up" and flush it down the toilet so my incoming husband won't see it.

This ageism, inspired by Mason, is poisonous for me and for Bob.
It has worsened our mild but mutual hypochondria. "My left ankle is
swollen. Think I have heart disease?" or "My head aches; I hope it's
not a brain tumor" is the kind of bedtime conversation we often share.

As soon as Josh enters the fray, the tide seems to change. Suddenly
the incumbent candidate is carrying a little ham who smiles and gives
the victory sign for the cameras. It's as if the baby knows what is needed
even when I don't. The press loves it; now Bob has an aura of youth
and vitality, the young-as-you-feel father of an eighteen-month-old.

I distribute leaflets at subway stops, brazenly making people stop
and smile by shouting, "I'm the wife! He's a powerhouse, I should know!"

I go to Democratic clubs, chat up everyone, and earn tender looks from my husband.

On election night, his campaign workers, wearing "Morgy" pins that display a widely smiling head shot, fill his headquarters. The news trickles through slowly. Morgy is getting a huge two-thirds of the vote, and finally Mason concedes. The phones are ringing with congratulations. Even Charlie Rangel calls.

His older children and his extended family are present on January 6, 1986, when he is sworn in to his fourth term as New York's district attorney. It is a solemn ceremony that takes place in the elaborate marble Surrogate Court Building. As Bob raises one hand and puts his other on the Bible, he swears to uphold the law and then adds his own ending: "without fear or favor."

People are quiet, moved. Until they are rudely interrupted by Josh's climbing off the pedestal and running around, waving at one and all. Before I know it, he's at the other side of the oval, wandering about, looking like a boy from a Renoir painting. Some people giggle, but afterward others soundly criticize me for not controlling my son. Ahh, laissez-faire, how wonderful it is.

Alas, my favorite stepson, Bobby, delivers the unkindest cut of all. "Would you please stop dressing my brother like Little Lord Fauntleroy?" he asks, looking at Joshua's lavender velour suit.

For Bob and me, the election victory has a Pyrrhic quality, for although Bob won by a substantial two-thirds of the vote, Mason, his first challenger since he was elected, took a big chunk. And we will not soon forget the unprecedented viciousness of the press.

As for Mason, he never again ran for public office and in fact was eventually disbarred for misconduct as a lawyer. He became a social worker and, ironically, later offered to help Bob with the black community in any way he wanted.

•

Tired out after the November election, we set off to rest up in Provence with Josh and Renia in tow. We stay in a spectacular old, semi-crumbling mansion with a huge park in back. The hills of light lavender, van Gogh's magical sunlight, snails slithering up the front steps, with Joshua the only one daring to pick them up, all of us walking up a hill of sunflowers to peek at the home of Picasso's daughter. Everything is glorious, but beneath it all Bob and I feel somber.

Finally, I bring it into the open. "We should be high as kites, but do you feel scared? All that nastiness about your age. Does it mean it'll be even worse the next election?"

"I don't know. I'll be a septuagenarian."

"But, sweetheart, you couldn't lose, could you?"

"Yes, I could lose."

"But not *really* lose. In the end, given who you are and what you've done, you'd win, wouldn't you?" I am taking in as much air as I can, but I can't seem to get enough. "Who could possibly be as good as you?" My heart is beating in bunches. Gurgling. A drumroll so loud, how can he not hear it? Am I having some kind of heart attack?

"Bob, I think I'm having a heart attack," I say, and he tells me not to be dramatic.

How could Robert Morgenthau, the DA of the World—that's what newspapers have called him—be virtually wiped out! He's been in law enforcement all his life. What else could he do? It was impossible; it was terrifying.

He turns away. Oh no, if I saw a tear, just one, roll down his cheek! All these years I've complained about his silence, his stoicism, but I have also counted on it. If his power was taken away, how could I keep his spirits up? I'd become one of those wives of early retirees who have nervous breakdowns. And he would walk about with eyes of glass.

"Do you think you could do something else?" I try to sound calm. "Take up some other job?"

"I guess I could stay home and read the *Times* and the *Post* and the *News* and *The Wall Street Journal*," he says. I smile in spite of myself. He knows how much I hate his mess of papers that creep over every surface of the house.

He also knows I'm the one who worries for us both, who takes the pressure off him so that his only concern is to comfort me: "I could scatter them around the house so you could easily find them," he adds. "And I'd never throw any out, that is, if you didn't want me to."

17

The "Boss" returned from our French vacation to cheers from the office staff and ADAs. The twelve hundred men and women he had hired loved him. He had expanded staff and crime bureaus, hired scores of women and minorities, instituted paternity leave, still rare in the 1980s, and extended maternity leave. He delighted his lawyers and staff by drifting into federal jurisdiction, pursuing impossible cases that the U.S. Attorney's Office ignored; he would often win these cases and create new legal paradigms.

The DA's Office approved of Bob's quirky ways. He was known for having the best group of ADAs in New York City—from celebrated figures like John F. Kennedy Jr. to less celebrated ones like the boy who wore sneakers with holes. He chose his lawyers by shunning boilerplate interviews about hypothetical cases and instead asking the applicants about life in their hometowns, their sisters and brothers, their pets. And uncannily, his judgment was almost always right. He often overruled his hiring committee. Once, it rejected a new young lawyer because he was sloppily dressed with ratty sneakers. Bob called him in, and he arrived at the interview similarly dressed. After a few questions, Bob hired him on the spot. He turned out to be one of the best lawyers in the office.

Back in early 1982, seven years after he took office, Bob was feeling particularly daring. He decided to sue the chief judge of the highest court of New York. He deemed that Judge Lawrence Cooke, who set up a rotation system that effectively stripped the supreme court (where most of Bob's cases were tried) of its best judges, had violated the constitution and laws of New York State. Suing Cooke, in the community of lawyers, was like suing the pope.

I was usually a cheerleader when he had these brash brainstorms, but this time I was nervous. Ida Van Lindt, who he always said knew more than his ADAs, was not particularly reassuring. "It's just never been done, anywhere, must less thought of. He's got a lot of chutzpah, the Boss."

So many lawyers warned him off it that one night he simply said, "You know, if nobody thinks the case can be won, I better try it myself." I said, "Well, okay, great," fully aware that he had never tried a case as DA.

But on May 4, 1982, after poring over documents spread out on the dining table for about eight weeks, he did. Before going into court, he grinned and said, "This is the kind of fight I love. It brings me back to my roots, to the days when I bucked the Bronx Democratic machine."

Ostensibly, Cooke had hatched his plan to move judges around between the lower and the higher courts to promote fairness and reduce overcrowding in the Manhattan court system, but in effect he was playing politics. Judges would be assigned no longer on the basis of merit but on a basis that would benefit the Democratic organization. The illegality that Bob homed in on was that Cooke had not gotten the approval of the panel of administrative judges required under the constitution and the laws of the state. The autocratic chief judge had simply made this dramatic change by fiat.

When Bob began arguing his case in front of the court of appeals, he looked up and was startled. There, staring down sternly at him, was his uncle Irving Lehman, once the chief judge himself. "It was a formidable oil painting, and I asked myself, would Uncle Irving have approved of what I was doing? I decided he would and I proceeded."

Watching him in his trim gray suit stand before the panel of black-robed judges, his voice hitting every resonating word, I felt my heart turn over.

"Supposing a judge named Benjamin Nathan Cardozo assigned to the supreme court had been rotated down to a lower court that handled misdemeanors!" Bob boomed, referring to the eminent judge who eventually became justice of the U.S. Supreme Court.

Supposing the judge was a DA named Morgenthau and the court

was the sidewalk, I thought, noticing that my knuckles were turning white from gripping the spectators' bench. I recalled the public remark of one of Cooke's assistants that "if it had been anybody but Morgenthau who brought this case, they would have been laughed out of court."

The verdict was returned. All six judges on the court of appeals—the seat of the seventh, Cooke, being vacant—had voted for Morgenthau.

I wanted to jump up and hug Bob when he left the court, but I patted the sweat off his forehead instead. "Whew," he said. "If I'd lost that case, I'd have been up the river without a paddle. The criticism and the repercussions would have been enormous." I was thinking that maybe the repercussions would be enormous anyway, Cooke being such a powerful figure. But then I thought, maybe not so powerful anymore.

As time went on, his ADAs saw him become more relaxed, more quirky, and more inclined to sophisticated but outlandish humor. "People sometimes don't know how to respond when he says something because they can't believe he's said it," the ADA Peter Kougasian told me one day when I was visiting the office. "For instance, this data-processing guy from outside came in to give the Boss and our computer expert instructions in using a new processor. The guy went on forever, using such arcane, incomprehensible terms that even our computer expert was confused. After he left, everyone was silent. And then the Boss nonchalantly said, 'What I want to know is, is it good for the Jews?'"

•

After the election, I was the beneficiary of Bob's happy relief. I could do no wrong. I could burn his soup and he would smile indulgently and give me a cooking lesson. I could be a half hour late and he wouldn't complain. He would smile if I had a little fit of temper over something. My temper. Only if I touched his ten belongings did I have to beware.

Although we could have won a contest for bickering, we would laugh and make up within hours. We had become more honest, and we saw our periodic two-week estrangements as thoroughly pointless since we usually forgot what caused them. "We're never going to do it again," I pronounced. "Never." He agreed: "That's a promise."

We passed into a slow, sweet togetherness. Sometimes we missed the passion of our early years, but now that desperate longing seemed pointlessly thin. Now being together was more profound, more complex, for we had time to take in the idiosyncrasies of our bodies: the poignant curve of spine, cool breath against flushed skin, the fragile honeyed fragrance of a woman, the man's loamy smells, the beauty of constancy.

•

With the excitement of the election behind us, I got restless.

"I'm lonely, sweetheart," I said one night. I had gotten so bored that I had started to live on the edge, flirting with disaster: I had begun to cook. That day I had made veal scaloppine, which Bob loved and which, to my delight, didn't turn out too rubbery. I also put tulips on the table and lit candles all over the house.

"I don't have any adults to talk to until you get home," I complained. "And you know how I get when I'm not doing something useful, and currently I'm not, unless you count the odd magazine article and a dozen Popsicle-stick houses."

"Watch that Val-Kill piece!" Bob exclaimed. "Let's put all this fire out now; it's dangerous." Red wax was about to drip over his heirloom end table, the one Eleanor Roosevelt had made at her little furniture factory. I blew out the candles and sat with arms folded.

"Why don't you get out more, make some women friends?" he suggested.

"But I do have friends. I was elected president of the Writers Room board! I'm good friends with Nancy Milford. We've been there for dinner; you gave their son a summer internship."

"Nancy is not your friend."

"Well, it's true I don't see much of her, but I don't see much of anyone. I've crawled into this shell with you and Josh."

"I repeat, Nancy Milford is *not* your friend."

Crickets gather in our terrace garden, and now their rhythmic sound is like an execution drumroll. "Why do you say that?"

He looks down. "At the Writers Room fund-raiser, your welcoming speech was great. I saw Arthur Gelb giving you a big hug afterward. But Nancy and that Andrea woman were rolling their eyes the whole time. I think they're envious of you."

"Oh." The old childhood tune begins to play in my head: Nobody likes me. "Well, I'm shy with people. I never know whether they really like me or they're just pretending, just sucking up to me because of you."

We undress for bed and I surprise him by rubbing his back with olive oil. He has wide shoulders, shiny, flickering with candlelight.

"Mmm, that feels nice," he says, and drifts off to sleep.

I go to the living room and do some yoga, resting in Child's Pose. I most always do what Bob advises, but this time I'm nervous. How am I to find a loyal friend? By megaphone in Central Park? I don't even want to leave my apartment. My astrological sign is a crab, and a crab is a homebody. Bob could never putter about inside like me. He exists in the universe, his family a backdrop behind which he can retreat.

•

Writers are like bucks. They generally have their horns at the ready. Before you can see it coming, they ram you in the back. More than once I have been robbed of an assignment by some ambitious, politically skilled operator. At the *Times*, I had friends, but our connections, though they could be close, mostly revolved around office gossip: who was on Abe's shit list today; who Arthur would pick to do the death of Nelson Rockefeller "in flagrante delicto." Journalists are more interested in cultivating their professional stature than in companionship. And they were always being transferred to different cities, different countries, or different positions above you. Even the deepest of our friendships were fungible.

Worse than journalists are authors. Rivalry is often the left arm of comradeship. Wendy Gimbel, a fine writer, a soul mate who seasoned me with her intellect and her humor, once imparted this piece of wisdom: "They may not admit it, or even know it, but not all your friends wish you well."

Still, I had to move away from my tiny nuclear family, and ironically it was through Josh that I finally did. Jill Comins, a cheery, outgoing blonde, and I were the only two mothers who lingered to watch our children through the viewing window at a music program for tots. As they waved around colored scarves and tambourines, we chattered away about everything from the dangers of being too attached to your children, to the absurdity of President Reagan, shot by a mail-order gun, coming out in favor of them. As our children grew, so did our comfortable and intimate friendship. Jill had helped me solve problems with my stepchildren, and her advice was so good that I persuaded her to go back to school and become a therapist. We even shared confidences about the eccentricities of our husbands. For the first time, I was secure in a friend whose loyalty and honesty I could count on.

That it should have amazed me how complex women were was testament to my naïveté and solitude. They were such cogent thinkers, intuitive analysts, emotionally sensitive, multifaceted beings! Once I really knew them, I realized it was no fun living without them. I needed women to go places where most men did not or, more precisely, could not.

As time passed, I became rather particular about choosing my friends, avoiding those who wooed me not for who I was but for what Bob and I could give them.

•

Bob was happy about my connections with women, even if he didn't understand them. He was accustomed to female friends who conducted themselves with a modicum of restraint and decorum. The first time he overheard me telling Blair Hoyt, "I love you too . . . I'm going to miss you so much," he was startled. I didn't explain why I used such tender words on Blair, words he had laid claim to. I much preferred to tease him. Then, one day, he saw Lila Meade, who is a hugger like me, come into the house and hold me in a long embrace. He gazed at us, looking confused.

"We haven't seen each other in a week," I explained over her shoulder. He turned away.

Once happily possessed by him, I had found an undiscovered capacity in myself—that I could have loving liaisons with people of the same sex. I knew he was pleased that I had gotten out of the house and found friends, but I suspected he was also uneasy. Finally, as we were resting after playing tennis at the farm, I turned to him and said, "Sweetheart, I'm not gay."

He scowled at a can of tennis balls.

"Women can love each other in a way men don't." I pointed out the passionate attachment in the letters between his mother and Mrs. Roosevelt. "You've told me that you think those letters indicate an affectionate friendship, nothing sexual."

"That's right."

"Well, if you don't think your mother was a lesbian, why would you wonder about me?"

"I don't," he said. "C'mon, let's go down and get some lunch."

And we never talked about it again.

•

Meanwhile, to our amusement, Josh was growing up to be as eccentric as we were. He was sensitive and proud. He had learned to talk in Renia's Jamaican lilt, punctuating his sentences with "Listen here, mahn."

He was loving and without judgment. One morning, I was complaining that I was getting fat, and he piped up, "Well, if you're fat, fat is beautiful." He disliked my singing, however. When I took up my guitar and sang mournful folk songs, the same ones that had brought me applause and a few pounds a night at a London pub long ago, he would say "Stop!" and put his hands over his ears. "It makes me feel like I'm dead."

•

When it came time to send Josh to nursery school, which was just around the corner, I panicked. The room was cramped, the teachers looked like teenagers, and the kids were running around like mice in a maze.

I was unable to leave him. I mean, I didn't budge from the room. Initially, the teachers allowed me to sit in a corner of the classroom, then they had me move back toward the door a few feet each day. I was the only mother in the room, and finally Josh came over, patted my arm, and said, "Try going out for five minutes, Mama. Just try it." So I did and I never came back inside.

But I missed him. I could hear the children at Dalton out in the playstreet. I was sure I could hear his voice, echoing like his father's. And inside, the silence resounded. In order to exorcise, and understand, my lingering emptiness, I decided to write about the embarrassing problems I had in relinquishing Josh to the teachers.

To my surprise, this slim little tale became a classic, reprinted and distributed each fall in nursery schools throughout the country. It seems that although much had been written about the effect of school separation on children, nothing had quite brought out the distress of mothers like the chronicle of my sorry display at Dalton.

When Bob laughed and talked about the piece, to me and to others, I was moved. Between Josh, my new girlfriends, my passion for jogging, and my writing, I had lost sight of my husband. But he had not lost sight of me. He had been watching. I looked back at the trips abroad we had taken in the last few years; they had always been Bob's suggestion. He began to make unilateral decisions to take me to a museum or the movies—without our son.

It would mark a major change in our marriage-with-child. We had sentimental candlelight dinners at Gino's, where we had had our first date, and if we took Josh, he let us alone, amusing himself by making concoctions of salt, pepper, and shreds of napkin in his water glass. We collected art catalogs and went to Sotheby's auctions just for fun. Bob loved to go back in time; he was still stirred when he saw paintings similar to those that had hung on his parents' wall.

•

When Josh was about four, we watched the Oedipal phase draw to a close. He now saw me in a more human light—giving me some sass—and transferred his affections to a little blond, blossom-cheeked playmate named Ariel. Most of all, he began to emulate his father. He started getting down on the floor and flinging his arms up and pumping his legs. "What's this?" I asked. "I'm doin' Daddy's Canadun Air Foss exercises!"

Unfortunately, his father couldn't do them as well as he used to. Once, Bob, as always, was carrying Josh, now a big five-year-old, in a big metal-framed backpack, when he suddenly put him down. "You'll have to take him," he said, and from then on I did. I had been dreading those words. I had been dreading seeing my husband walk up the lawn to our house so much more slowly. He was seventy now, and though he had the health and stamina of someone much younger, every little glimpse of his mortality still haunted me.

I was not the only one. When he was about to turn six, choosing just the right moment, as children do, Josh asked a heart-stopping question. I was hurrying into the elevator, already late for an interview. "Why did you marry Dad?" he asked. I stopped short and let the elevator go. "Why do you want to know?" I asked as casually as I could. "But why did you marry an old man? Why do I have to have a father who looks like a grandfather?" he replied.

"Because sometimes," I said, "love just catches you by surprise and there's nothing you can do about it."

I knew he adored his father, but he was clearly being teased at school. I supposed I had blocked it out until now, but our children would also grow up in the shadow of our achievements. It was chilling to think of the many kids of exalted families, Franklin and Eleanor Roosevelt, for example, who had had problems because they feared living up to their forebears. We worried about this but then we considered our children both independent and persevering souls, and after all, we were just their parents.

·

My father was coming to visit from Massachusetts more often because somehow, at only five years of age, Josh got hold of his number—was it from my Rolodex?—and invited his grandfather himself. At night, they would put a moth trap up in the yard that my dad had made from a washbasin and two ultraviolet light tubes. Josh would come running out in the morning to find big green lunas, white arctics, and brownish noctuids. Grandpop, having reassured Josh that the moths would feel no pain and that they only had a two-week life span, would put a pin through them. Then they would both mount the specimens on cork and label them in tiny black writing. The two kept a meticulous moth log.

Josh slept curled up to his father now. Once he kept pinching him. "Josh, stop pinching me. I don't like it," Bob said. "Well, I like it," Josh replied. "What did you just say?" Bob asked. "I really don't know. The words came out so fast I can't remember," Josh said. "Josh, you are a character," said Bob, and Josh, slapping his hand on his forehead, replied, "Let's just go to sleep, Dad."

18

And then I decided I wanted another child. On August 20, 1990, Amy Elinor Morgenthau was born. We were elated. She was so lovely, with brown eyes so deep and contemplative, it was as though she were trying to fathom her universe. Josh was beside himself—a new playmate delivered right to his door. Bob was fascinated by her uncanny awareness; having a new baby to fall in love with met his profound need to cultivate and watch the blossoms unfold.

•

December 14, 1990

My baby girl, you are as serious as a judge, you are the DA reincarnated. You have that scowl, which mirrors your dad's, it makes all of us laugh.

It thrills me: after living with two men, I have a little girl! It thrills me—to be made of the same stuff, just us acting alike, thinking alike, getting our feelings hurt, leaping for joy, being all the things women will be. You have pale skin and chubby cheeks, like me, but your mouth, the shape of a perfect heart, is all yours.

The world can wonder why you haven't yet smiled, but I see that you are too busy. Your hands play across my face as if it were a piano. Will we be artists together? You are precocious. You have been on earth just four months and you do not say a word, but you point to the moon every time you see it. You stare at the shadows and the light it casts, I'm sure of it, trying to figure out what it is and where it belongs in the world.

•

At six months, Bob leaned over Amy's crib and did his unique trick that had worked on every one of his children. He made a sound like an airplane and shook his head back and forth so fast his wide elastic mouth slapped from side to side. Amy's eyes widened, as though she might have been afraid. He did it again. Then, for the first time in her life, she smiled this huge smile and bubbled with laughter.

"Aah!" Bob's voice echoed throughout the apartment. From then on, Amy would laugh at the littlest provocation. At Josh blowing his cheeks up with air, at Peter Rabbit, the cat, leaping from a chair, and at herself when she put her hands on my antique washstand pitcher, squealed, and hoisted herself up to stand. The fact that Amy was such an observer, rather than a doer, made it especially poignant to witness her first step, her first word, the first time she brought a spoon of food to her mouth. The more independent she became, the happier she seemed.

But not all the time.

From the beginning, Josh thought Amy was the most fascinating toy he had ever owned. He would toss her up in the air and catch her. He would smother her, tickle her. But she adored him, so she took being treated like a pet gerbil in stride. It was only when he began to mercilessly scare her that she rebelled. At night, when she was about three, she would be cuddled up in her little bed, sucking her thumb and drifting off to sleep, when she felt a series of thumps beneath her. "I'm a dinosaur and I've come to eat you," Josh would say in a haunting whisper. She would scream, and in I would come, soothing her after what I thought was a nightmare. Even when she was much older, Josh enjoyed playing a good joke. He was especially thrilled when he took string and draped her room with morels he had dug up on the farm.

She never tattled on Josh, but one day she figured out a way to return his favors. They would be playing, and for no reason she would suddenly begin bawling in a startling Wagnerian contralto. Then she would falsely accuse Josh of hitting her; I would believe her and send him off to his room for confinement. Once, when he was nine and she was four, he spent weeks building a complicated Lego city; she took it apart piece by piece so that when he came home from school, he found his city had become a miniature quarry. He detested cockroaches, so for his sixteenth birthday she presented him with a nicely wrapped jar in which one of the giant bloated insects crawled.

Still, they never stopped being close. By the time she went off to nursery school, she was a true beauty—silky light brown hair, huge eyes, a perfect radiant smile. Once Josh began staring at her with complete awe. "Mom, she is *so* cute, how can somebody be so cute!" he breathed as though E.T. had arrived and he didn't know what to do about it.

As the kids grew, we became a close foursome in more ways than one. At night, Bob and I would be drifting off when two little bodies came wriggling in between us. We didn't have the heart to kick them out, much to the disapproval of my friend Jill Comins, who by now had become not only a therapist but a psychoanalyst. She argued that it was inappropriate, and I countered that in southern Europe they did it all the time.

Josh and Amy fought to get a place beside me. One time, we were all settled down when Josh reached over Amy and tickled Bob's head. "Stop it!" he said in such an absurd growl that the mischievous child in me popped out and I reached over both kids to tickle him myself. Assuming the culprit was Amy, he got up to carry her to her own bed. "No, no, Daddy, please!" we both wailed. "You promise not to do it anymore?" asked Bob as he gently put her back in the middle of the bed. "I never did it, Daddy," she replied.

•

Amy was an old soul, wise beyond her years; she never did the expected. When she was three and we were walking down the sidewalk, she abruptly ran out in the street. I grabbed her up, held her by the arms, and sternly told her she could get hit by a car and never to do that again. She cocked her head. "It must be hard to be a mom," she said, before she began to cry.

The love I had for each of my children was almost overwhelming. When she was little, Amy and I did things only girls could do together—we danced around half naked in the rain, we wrote poetry together, reveling in each other's imagination. On Easter morning, we would take a walk through the orchards looking for signs of spring. Soft, mild air, a medley of squeaks and creaks and trills, Amy saw a rabbit chewing the head off a dead dandelion, I pointed out a formation of geese clattering back from the south, Amy said it looked as if a magician took off the winter rug of brown and slipped on a green one instead.

When we reached the second row of McIntoshes sprouting their baby leaves, she would begin to hunt for the little gifts I had left there nestled against the trees. Then we would sit on the dewy grass and watch for fairies hidden in the twirling leaves.

With Josh's help, she painted a watercolor of a Venice canal in fluid salmons and blues that has hung on the wall for years. Some people asked if we got it at a gallery.

Susan and Bobby's children, Harry and Martha, were close in age to our kids, and they formed a lively bond, often visiting the farm for weekends. Harry and Joshua would troll the stream at the bottom of the farmhouse, catching small fish with their hands and sometimes purposely slipping into the water. Amy and Martha were a duo, loyal and unwavering; they confided in each other, they had each other's backs. When they were navigating the tricky currents of adolescence, you could hear whispering and peals of laughter from upstairs. Susan's sense of blithe mischief captivated them. Susan loved to organize games of hopscotch down our long hall. And if she and Bobby babysat while we went away, I'd more than likely come home to find my furniture rearranged and covered with sheets, the kids squealing delightedly within.

Amy entered kindergarten at the challenging primary school Nightingale-Bamford. We went roller blading together to school every morning, with Amy doing complicated jumps, and garnered dubious smiles from some of the stuffier educators there. Tutors helped her with what they diagnosed as dyslexia, a learning difference that often occurs in bright children.

Bob thought the whole thing was hokum. He simply didn't believe she had any learning issues, just a lack of confidence. He would cite the evidence of her power of observance over and over: one evening, she could see both the sun and the moon, a faint foggy ball, when no one else could. In nursery school, the teachers had said she didn't know her colors, so Bob had read her a book; he pointed to a purple balloon and said, "Look at that pretty yellow balloon," and she said, "Dad, that's a purple balloon, silly."

Getting Amy to do her homework was a challenge. Everyone agreed how smart she was. But she was turned on by the arts, and dry factual essays were not her thing. And what she didn't like she often blanked out on. She got nervous during tests and hated them. When she was diagnosed with dyslexia, I put her into a plethora of learning programs and got a range of tutors. The pressure on her must have been great and probably canceled out my attempts to reassure her that she was bright and wonderful and we were going to prove it.

I was furious that in third grade the children had to write papers that contained a thesis, several backup examples, and a conclusion. With increased competition to get into the leading colleges, the curricula of private schools in New York were advancing so fast that grade-schoolers were forced to learn college-level material.

I tried to help her with a "thesis" paper and was caught out; her teacher nearly accused us of committing plagiarism. After that, Amy played a game of psychological chess with me. I nagged her to do her English essay, she said she was doing it, I offered to help her, she said not on your life, I asked how she was doing, she said she was done, I came in to look at it, and off she stalked with a handful of blank pages. Checkmate. She was so sly and canny—a bit like her father—that at times I felt as if I wanted to run my fingernails down a chalkboard. Nevertheless, her struggle to live up to her teacher's expectations, and her frequent success in doing that, made me proud of her. I still hurt for her, for her sense of frustration and disappointment at school, but I had to smile at how it had built her character. She had become persevering and stubborn.

When she began to go on the school stage, she impressed even the sternest teacher. In junior high, the whole family, including my stepchildren, came to see her play the important role of Puck, the mischievous, quick-witted, and capricious sprite in A *Midsummer Night's Dream*. She frolicked and swept her arms up magically and charmed the audience into a standing ovation, as she did when she played a disturbed girl in a two-person show. The way she walked, fell on her knees, imbued her words with misery, was haunting. Everyone was impressed, with the possible exception of the director, who nearly went crazy when she altered her lines, rendering it impossible for him to direct.

That director thought her brazen, but the word did not fit. She might have put on an air of detachment—for instance, when her classmates laughed at her for misusing words, instead of retreating, she laughed along with them—but behind it all she hid an acute sensitivity.

Amy was so attuned to her environment that she would pick up people's feelings before they knew they were feeling them. "That person's unhappy," she'd say, looking at a smiling neighbor who we later found out had just lost her job. On the other hand, sometimes she saw emotions that weren't there. Especially with me, her mother, who had changeable and occasionally unfathomable facial expressions. "What's the matter, Mommy?" she'd ask in alarm when I was in fact pondering some entirely pleasant memory.

I first discovered the painful acuteness of her senses when she entered pre–nursery school. She refused to participate in a class band, with the boys banging the drums and the girls blowing kazoos, and instead went into a corner and put her fingers in her ears. The concerned teacher thought it was a psychological issue, but I knew my daughter.

I would always see her writing, and one day, while tidying her room, I caught sight of a plethora of journals she had secretly written, stacked up as high as the old *Encyclopaedia Britannica* might have been.

I wanted Amy to feel that unquestioning attachment to Jesus that I felt as a little girl. We began to go to a small Episcopal church near the farm, where she could kneel and be blessed at the rail, and at night we said prayers together and then sang hymns; our favorite was "O Savior Sweet."

We liked to play "the switch-off story game"; I would begin a narrative and then stop in the middle so she had to continue it. But if she saw Nerissa, the Caribbean housekeeper who had replaced Renia when she retired, she'd stop whatever she was doing. There was nothing she liked better than to lie in wait and then leap out when Nerissa came round the corner. Nerissa obliged by collapsing on the floor, moaning with terror, while Ivan the Terrible barked gleefully.

When she was little, Amy would write me love notes like this one: "Dear Mommy, Every time I look at you your eyes make me giggle. I would never trade you for a billion dollars. You're my mommy, no one else. I love you so much, Amy."

When she reached twelve, she was already developing her father's wry sense of humor. One handmade card had a dog barking, "What is she doing?!" Across the top, Amy had written, "Sometimes you can act way beyond weird . . . ," and inside it read, "But there's no one better than you to cheer me up!" On the opposite side, sharks and dolphins swam around laughing, "Haar, harr! Ha hoo ha!"

I'm glad I saved all the notes, tacking them on my bedside wall, because in what seemed like a few weeks but was only a few years, I had fallen from grace. Just as Josh's adolescent rebellion was ending, allowing me at last to let out my breath, hers began.

She came home one day—she was about fourteen—and announced that God wasn't real. "You deceived me, Mom. Now that I've grown up, I can see it clearly. There's no god. I believe in a random universe without intelligent design. If there was a god, how could he let children starve to death in Ethiopia? How could he let poachers nearly wipe out the black rhino?"

"Some kind of higher power, some god had to make the world," I said, and she huffily replied, "Then who made God, Mom, who?"

We debated the issue endlessly until I noticed the prayer books we had made were no longer visible in her room. Her Bible had vanished. She refused to accompany me to church. The closer you are with your children, the more rigorous their separation from you has to be. Amy's was difficult for both of us until one day, an eon later, she came to the table, mature, sweet, newly achieved. Bob and I had regained our stature as passable human beings.

•

The very thought of the death penalty had always made me ill. In 1974, when Bob first ran for DA, a good many New Yorkers disagreed. Homicides were at a record high, and the polls showed that the majority supported the New York State statute providing for the electric chair. In fact, the death penalty was hardly an issue; the public use of obscenity by entertainers and the frequent power blackouts were far more crucial to the sophisticated people of New York City.

Bob was then a friend, and a news source and I suggested he condemn New York's death penalty statute. "I know it would take a lot of courage, swimming upstream. Especially when all people want to hear is they'll get back their supply of electricity."

He thought for a minute, then joked, "I'll do it. I'll say that I'm against it because of the power shortage."

"I think that would be a bad idea," I said, giggling.

He did come out against the death penalty—skipping the black humor. It was basically abhorrent to him as well because of the events of

World War II. "I saw how easily a civilized government could commit genocide, and I don't believe we should give the state the power to take away life," he said publicly on one campaign stop. With that, he became the first public figure in the city to publicly oppose government-sanctioned execution. And when he was elected, he remained at the vanguard.

New York's death penalty laws had been abolished and reinstated several times throughout history. The death penalty had even been abolished accidentally in 1860 when the legislature repealed hanging as a method of execution but provided no other means of carrying it out.

In 1972, the U.S. Supreme Court had invalidated all death penalty statutes nationwide, but a year later New York rewrote its statute to get around the Supreme Court's decision, passing a mandatory death penalty for murdering a police or corrections officer.

But in October 1976, Bob refused to seek capital punishment for a cop killer, Luis S. Velez. "The death penalty statute," Bob declared, in explanation, "may be unconstitutional." This inspired a public outcry from conservatives like the U.S. senator James L. Buckley of New York, who called the DA's decision "an affront to every policeman." Thirteen months later, however, New York's high court of appeals, decided that, as applied in a Westchester County case, the statute was indeed unconstitutional, and a 1984 ruling effectively abolished New York's death penalty.

From 1978 to 1994, Governors Carey and Cuomo had vetoed death penalty legislation, but in 1994, George Pataki had run on a promise to reinstate it. Only eleven days after he took office in January 1995, he extradited a New York prisoner to Oklahoma to be executed. Bob and I were outraged.

"If the officials who sentence people to death got up from their desks, went into the death chamber, and watched an electrocution up close, I wonder how they'd feel then," Bob said with disgust.

When the New York legislature began considering Governor George Pataki's proposal for a strong death penalty bill, Bob decided to write an Op-Ed piece for *The New York Times* about "the dirty little secret prosecutors know"—that capital punishment actually hinders the fight against crime.

We brainstormed the editorial together, concentrating on the fallacies of the death penalty law: that statistics showed it did not reduce crime rates; that it cost the government two million dollars to execute a person; that this money took away resources that could root out recidivist career criminals and get the young ones in rehab programs; that innocent people are often executed; and that the dehumanizing effects on society of putting people to death cause more murders than they prevent. In other words, violence begets violence.

Ironically, Bob was a Jew who increasingly lived by Christ's tenets more than anyone I knew; he held charity above personal glory, he valued and helped the poor and the afflicted, he was incorruptible, and at bottom he was an unusually humble and kind man who lifted people up. He even appeared to perform miracles, such as single-handedly raising the bulk of money in two days to build a museum and thwarting the victimization of hundreds of immigrants by setting up an unprecedented immigration unit in the DA's Office.

When those irritating marketers called in the middle of dinner, he was patient and polite with them where I just peremptorily hung up. He brought to mind Christ's parable of the tiny mustard seed that grew into a tree so mighty, birds found a resting place in its branches.

I wondered whether I had found the reason for Bob's refusal to discuss his religious beliefs. Perhaps he simply didn't know if there was a God.

The sermons I had heard in Temple Emanu-El on the High Holidays often talked of the Lord as a concept, the spirit of possibility, for instance, in the heart of man. I felt Judaism was a religion based not on blind faith but on a search for godliness through doing good works. "I think it's a matter of how you live your life," Bob once said.

But in spite of his reticence about his spiritual beliefs, I pressed for him to put God in his piece. "Maybe something about only he has the power to giveth and taketh away?" I suggested.

"Uh-huh," he replied thoughtfully. " 'Vengeance,' " he began, then looked with relish at the food on his plate. He took a bite of roast guinea hen. "Mmm, this is good. Renia *can* cook fowl."

"Yes, you were saying 'vengeance'?"

He chewed the bite slowly.

"Bob, finish your sentence!"

"'Vengeance is mine, sayeth the Lord.' That's how I'll end the piece." And so he did. To my satisfaction, this argument was continually quoted. Though it didn't stop Pataki, Bob's piece was one of the most read Op-Eds that he had written. It established him as the only district attorney in the state, save the DA of Erie County, to oppose the governor's statute before it was enacted.

The death penalty law was a prime example of how Bob wove in, out, and around the system to get what he wanted. Rob Johnson, the Bronx DA, publicly declared he would not seek the death penalty after the statute was reinstated and was soon embroiled in an ugly confrontation with the governor. Bob did not outright defy him, which could have led the governor to supersede him with a special prosecutor; he just did it quietly. He appointed a committee of six senior assistant DAs to review the case of every murderer eligible for capital punishment. Never once did it recommend a death sentence, because it would find mitigating circumstances or loopholes in the law. In the nine years that the death penalty was in effect—from 1995 until it was struck down in 2004—Bob never sent anyone to the electric chair, even criminals who had shot cops. Moreover, before he made a final decision, he would consult the families of the victims, and most, like Gerald Levin, head of Time Warner, whose son was brutally murdered by students he had tried to help, didn't want the killer to be put to death. The governor was reportedly reluctant to challenge a politically skilled powerhouse like Bob.

In 2004, the death penalty in New York State gave a dying gasp when the state's highest courts declared the 1995 statute patently "unconstitutional." The ruling freed four death row inmates, though, since the legislation was passed, no one had been executed. This was in part due to Bob's work for the previous thirty years, both publicly and behind the scenes, against capital punishment.

"I don't think any judge or jury dared go near electrocution," Bob said. "You'd hate to go down in history as the first one to execute a man in New York since 1939." At public hearings on whether capital punishment should be reinstated, Bob testified that "death is different . . . it is the most irremediable and unfathomable of penalties." He talked about the horrors of "hanging" judges condemning innocent men and noted that even though he had imposed no death sentences since he took office in 1975, Manhattan's crime rate had plummeted by 86 percent.

In 2008, New York's death chamber would be padlocked by Governor David Paterson. I remember the day clearly. I remember how Bob and I toasted each other. "To God's justice," I said, raising my glass and then putting it down and hugging him tight. I couldn't remember when I felt more in love with him. He was good and great, and he had allowed me to make him greater. I had brought him a little closer to God. The circle that had started with our talk about death and the Almighty had ended where it began.

19

In the late winter of 1996, we gave notice on our rent-stabilized Park Avenue apartment, which was put up for sale at an exorbitant price, and bought a smaller place near Central Park. It was actually two contiguous apartments, each with a series of tiny, drab rooms, and you could hear the roaring wheeze of the buses below. Bob was dubious, but he also had a budget—we were land-poor—and this was cheap. I thought it a sleeper with big potential.

I didn't have an architect—I wanted to do it myself—but I found a creative Greek contractor, Renos Georgiou, who helped me transform the spaces. The first day, Renos's son Steve battered the wall between the two apartments with a sledgehammer. I took a swing, and with chunks of plaster flying about, the air snowy, I made a hole into the other side. It was like peering through Alice's looking glass into a beautiful warren of rooms in the opposite image. Then we took down walls until there were big open spaces.

I found an independent craftsman in Vermont who made a bed with a headboard that swept to the sky, and carved elaborate double doors between the apartments, replicas of what I remembered in my grandmother's grand Victorian home. We made closets where there could be no closets, halls too tiny to be even classified as halls; we squeezed every inch of usable space from the relatively small apartment. Mindful of Bob's having to pay a mortgage and rent at the same time, I went into one of my hyper-focused frenzies, running about the city twelve hours a day, finding just the right light fixtures, choosing moldings, and even discovering a white Georgian marble fireplace that was in pieces at an urban warehouse outlet. I mixed the paint for all the rooms myself. I wanted everything to come right out of my dreams, and I wanted it in three months.

I met my self-imposed deadline. In March 1997, we packed up and moved. I was exhilarated but so exhausted that for days I just lay on our new velvet viridian sofa and gazed up at the cascading crown moldings made by Renos's cousin. Everyone was excited about our new apartment that was at once cozy and spacious; we would sit in the living room, which looked like a British don's study, eating Renia's shepherd's pie by the elegant fireplace that the workers had assembled beautifully.

"Daddy, tell a joke," Amy said one night. She was six.

"Yeah, Dad, tell one," said Josh, now thirteen.

"I can't remember any."

"What about Pedro, Dad?"

"I can't tell that in front of Amy," Bob said, softly chuckling.

"Yes, tell it, Daddy, tell it!"

"She won't understand it anyway, Dad."

"Come on, Dad!" we chanted in unison. We never got tired of hearing Bob tell the same jokes, because he told them in an expressive basso profundo voice, doing his eyebrow trick, moving them up and down for emphasis.

"Well," began Bob, with mock resignation, "it was a hot, dusty day in a Mexican village, and Pedro was walking down the street passing the local church, and the padre said, 'Pedro, where are you going?' 'I'm going to the market, Father.' 'What do you have there, son?' 'Buttercups, Father. I'm going to trade them for a tub of butter.'

"The padre said, 'Pedro, you're a very stupid peon. You can't get a tub of butter for those buttercups.' Pedro said, 'Just wait, Father, I'll be back.' About an hour later, Pedro came walking back on the hot, dusty street with a tub of butter over his shoulder. The padre just stared at him. Next day, Pedro was carrying a bunch of flowers, and the padre said, 'What have you got there, Pedro?' 'Father, I have cowslips. I'm going to the market to get a cow.' The padre said, 'Pedro, you are a very stupid peon. You can't get a cow for a bunch of cowslips.' Pedro said, 'Wait, Father, you'll see.' About an hour later, Pedro came back leading a cow. The padre watched him with disbelief. The next morning Pedro passed by the church with a bunch of flowers, and the padre asked him what he had and where he was going. Pedro said, 'Father, these are pussy willows, and I'm going to the market.'

"The padre said, 'Wait, Pedro, I come with you.'"

Even Amy laughed, though she could hardly have understood the story. "That's your best joke, Daddy!"

•

Life in our new home couldn't have been more perfect, but perfect is perfect because behind it there's the unspoken. How can you not resist the rush of pleasure that comes with the belief that at last, at last, everyone has his place, everything is as it should be. We labor under a temporary illusion: happiness when you are happy seems immutable, the natural permanent state of life. We are sewn together; all the bad that is going to happen has already happened. We become children who lose our common sense, who believe the magician's illusions, believers in the Angel of Light until Satan slips out from behind him. Or the Jesus of ancient Docetic Christians, who passed from Mary's womb "like water from a tube," never to be what he appeared to be. We close our eyes to the lessons of history and believe that our good fortune is the essence of our fate. The way God wanted it. Surely he will always hold in his hand the way we are now.

In April 1997, four weeks later, our perfect world came to an end.

It happened on a cloudy Monday. Jill and I were having coffee in the kitchen when Bob's dermatologist called. She was a tough, all-business doctor, but now she sounded upset. "This growth on his nose, I took a routine biopsy, and it came back this morning malignant. I've never seen a melanoma look like his."

"Oh God," I said, crumpling onto a chair.

"Could you call and tell him he has a melanoma?"

Sure, Doctor, I'd love to. Bob had been worrying about the bump, but I hadn't. I thought it was some innocent flesh-colored wart. I had forgotten that against all odds, innocence will reveal itself as evil. I felt this sudden wave of fatigue. My coffee cup was as heavy as a bowling ball. Jill left and I called Bob. He was clearly stunned, wordless.

When Josh was a toddler, he was plagued by hives and hay fever, so when he was stung by a bee, I yelled for Bob to get the epinephrine pen while I watched him for signs of anaphylactic shock. By the time I had tweezered out the stinger, Bob was still standing there, paralyzed. Later, he got on the phone with the pediatrician, investigating all possible reactions, but the parameters were set. I was the quick one in an emergency.

Now I shook off the weariness and whipped into action, just as my mother would have done. I called around for the best melanoma specialist and persuaded his secretary to schedule a quick examination—as well as a probable surgery. I phoned him: "It's all fixed, sweetheart. You go in tomorrow, 8:00 a.m."

When he came home, I sat him down and rubbed his shoulders. I thought he'd want to talk about it, but he just picked up his *Forbes* and started reading. I didn't want to ask him if he was frightened, for fear it would make him so. But when he was taken into surgery two days later, at the age of seventy-seven, not knowing whether the disease had spread, he was placid, even jocular. Jenny and I were walking beside his wheelchair when a Catholic nun appeared and asked to say a prayer over him. "Sure," said my husband, the passionate Jew, startling me. "I'm happy for any help I can get." It occurred to me later that he might have enjoyed all the attention. He had been having more trouble hearing, and though he never complained, it must have increased his isolation. If, for instance, one is the honored guest at a party and he can't hear what people say, they tend to ignore him.

During the operation, I prayed constantly. I was in the middle of my umpteenth Psalm 21 when the doctor strode out and said his cancer had been contained with no lymph node involvement. It might have been the first time Jenny and I laid hands on each other.

Bob went to work as soon as the bandages were taken off, having refused entreaties by the plastic surgeon to operate on his somewhat misshapen right nasal lobe. I agreed, for I didn't want him to go under the knife again and, besides, I thought his new nose looked rather cute. I got him his favorite oysters and soft-shell crabs and generally tried to fill the house with a nice gestalt. I looked for opportunities to reassure him, but if they were offered, I missed them. In fact, he never talked about the experience again, except to say that nobody seemed to have noticed the change in his nose.

I think I was just relieved it had turned out all right. Like the women whose men came home at the close of World War II, I just wanted to get on with our lives.

Until three months later.

It was on a sunny Friday morning in late June, while Bob was count-ing out his vitamins. I found a lump the size of a marble in my breast.

It had seemed to come from nowhere. I asked Bob to feel it. He did, very gently, and then I probed it more thoroughly, and he yelled for me to stop touching it. "It could just be a cyst," I said, hyperventilating. "But you think it's something, don't you?" We had always reassured each other about the symptoms of our occasional hypochondria, but this time my concern didn't seem unfounded. He told me to have it checked right away.

I got an emergency mammogram the same day. I remember that evening clearly, when Bob came home and found me in the kitchen. I was bending over the fridge, and I mumbled to the yogurt that the doc-tors thought it was breast cancer, maybe mid-stage. "What? How do they know, how can they tell so quickly?" he said almost angrily.

I was becoming more alarmed, so I told him not to talk to me any-more and retreated to my study. I, myself, was amazingly calm, easily distracted. I took down one of my favorite comfort books, A Moveable Feast, and soon I was sipping crystal glasses of Pernod and ice water in the Café de Flore, flirting with Hemingway, Dos Passos, and my other pals from the Lost Generation. I ignored the banging about Bob was doing in the other room, kind of like a dog who clatters his dish around when he wants you to know he's hungry. I supposed I should have in-vestigated Bob's anger, which was an interesting show of emotion un-der the circumstances. But whatever it was about, I couldn't deal with it. My eyes got heavy, and before I'd even had dinner, my head went down on the Salvador Dalí that Gertrude Stein had just hung on her wall.

My lazy equilibrium continued, perhaps because I hung on to the shred of possibility that the tumor would be benign when they operated on Monday. That weekend, we threw our annual Fourth of July bash at the farm, featuring illegal fireworks obtained from the Chinese black market. As he always did, Bob went around quipping, "It's my responsi-bility as DA to destroy them by burning." The party was a tradition that Bob loved, and I wouldn't let him cancel it. We hung up his father's flag and put out the picnic tables and the citronella candles, but before the hot dogs and butterfly lamb had been cooked, word of my plight had crackled through the crowd. Word had apparently been spread by Bob, and I could have killed him. This person who was me but didn't feel like me brushed off the expressions of sympathy, ignored the tactless alarm stories, and put on a nonchalance and a dazzling smile for everyone. I said "Oh, it's nothing really" so many times my tongue hurt. After the last bottle rocket and Roman candle and lingering guest went off, I collapsed into bed without saying good night.

•

When we told the children, we made light of it. As soon as they were reassured I'd be all right, they went back into their own worlds. But I knew it wasn't all right, at least between Bob and me.

The Monday after the Independence Day party, I was scheduled to have the lump removed under sedation at a New York Hospital outpatient center. Bob went with me, of course, but I asked two friends, Sage Sevilla and Linda Hanauer, to come also, fearing that this would unmoor Bob. After the operation, he and the doctor were standing by my gurney and told me the mixed news: the tumor was cancerous, but it seemed to be contained. I went into a cubicle to dress, feeling moderately hopeful, until a snippy researcher with a clipboard asked me my name. Then I silently wept. When I came out and Sage saw my white face, she immediately took me in her arms. Bob must have been there, but I don't remember him at all. A gate had slammed down between us; throughout the ordeal I had the impression I saw a person who looked like him but wasn't.

A few days later, however, when I went into the hospital for a precautionary operation to find out if there was any residual cancer to be removed, he came with me. Jenny came to be with Bob and give me moral support before the operation. Afterward, Annie visited me, gift in hand. Penny sent me a teddy bear, Jill brought me Chinese food, and Marina slept on a chair to be with me the first night after surgery. As for Bob, when he came in and saw all the tubes and drains, he seemed to shrink. He didn't even get too close, claiming he was afraid of dislodging the apparatus. And he stayed less than half an hour.

After I was discharged, my stepdaughter Barbara stepped up to the plate. She had gone from being a shy fifteen-year-old to being a doctor's assistant who worked with breast cancer patients. She knew how to inter-pret results and advise me.

We were waiting for a fax from the New York Hospital pathology lab, and as it began to come in, Bob disappeared into the bedroom. I ripped out the report. It said that though the tumor was of moderate size, there was no spread into lymph nodes or cells outside it. "Hey, this is great!" I shouted, waving the fax. "I'm clear!" Bob peeked his head out. Barbara took the report from me and studied it. "It's not entirely great, Lucille," she said gently. "The tumor is listed as estrogen nega-tive, not positive, and that means it's aggressive." Bob retreated. "You may have to have chemotherapy."

Barbara said I should go to an oncologist at Memorial Sloan-Kettering, arguably the best cancer center in the nation, the place where a surgeon had successfully operated on my mother when others thought it hopeless. The only thing was, the Lauder Breast Center was so over-whelmed, they couldn't see me for at least a month.

My husband suddenly jumped in to help; he was not without good friends. He found that Sloan-Kettering's best oncologist was the emi-nent Larry Norton, who indeed wasn't taking new patients. But that made no difference to the man no one could say no to. One call to the hospital's chairman of the board, and I had an appointment with Nor-ton in a week.

I asked Barbara to go with me, which must have relieved Bob. When we entered Norton's office, we shook hands with a slight, balding man who reminded me of Bob's mild-mannered accountant. Then he opened his mouth and out shot raw, point-blank words more appropriate to a neo-Nazi biker. He ruffled my lab report and said it told him noth-ing conclusive and in fact he found it hard to believe; my type of tumor had to have deep roots. I told him, just as belligerently, that this is not what the New York Hospital doctors had said. Barbara, seeing Norton's eyes narrow, swiftly played the good cop: "Lucinda, calm down, Dr. Norton is just trying to help us, we want the truth." Norton replied that we should get the complete report from the New York Hospital lab, in-stead of this little summary, and his own pathology lab would analyze it.

So Barbara and I ended up running several blocks to New York Hos-pital in the heat of a July day to get the complete pathology notes before the lab closed early. We got there just in time and then raced back to

Sloan-Kettering, where, sweating, we gave it to a nurse who promised she'd give the new, complete report to Norton.

We held our breath, expecting to be called in to his office at any moment.

The moment became four hours.

We turned over and over the possibilities of what Sloan-Kettering's own lab would find. I imagined having my breasts removed. I began to mentally put my house in order, mentally write instructions for my funeral. I wondered if the pastor I grew up with was still alive and willing to see me. I remembered the moaning of my mother as she suffered excruciating cancer pain for months ("There is no other pain in the world like it," her friend helpfully told me). I felt the dry, peeling skin on her feet and tried to soften them with Eucerin lotion. Would Bob and Barbara and Josh and Amy be there to hold my hand, rub my feet?

Just when I thought I couldn't stand the waiting anymore, Barbara suddenly cocked her ear and hushed me. She listened to a faint voice coming from behind the door to the medical offices. It sounded to me like tinny gibberish, but then she said, "It's all right, I heard Norton's voice talking to a pathologist, and he said, 'She's all clear.' He was talking about you. Stop asking me how I knew it, I just knew."

And she was right. In another two hours, Norton called us in and affirmed the tumor had just sprung up unattached. I silently thanked God, and I also expressed my appreciation that he had sat us by one particular door, that a doctor's telephone hung on the other side of it, and that Barbara had such sharp hearing.

Because my type of malignancy was so aggressive, I had grueling courses of chemotherapy and radiation. Doctors had told Bob he was clear of cancer, but after my bouts of treatment they told me only that the prognosis was good. Some cheering literature I had read there claimed you never "got over" breast cancer, the cells were always floating around—it was just a matter of keeping them under control.

My preventive treatments weren't easy. The needle slipping under the skin of the hand, the quarts of toxic chemicals pumped into my body, were bearable. But when the radiation began, it was like being the victim in a horror movie. First I was warned that this six-week treatment could increase my chances of getting heart disease or lung cancer, then I was led into a room of blazing lights with the odor of what seemed like embalming fluids drifting through. Finally, I was pressed between two heavy pieces of steel and zapped. When they let me off the table, I began to sob and I couldn't stop. It had just been too much. "I'm being a baby," I said to a nurse.

"You're not alone," she said reassuringly and put her hands on my shoulders, trying to get me to look at her, to talk about what it had been like for me. But I couldn't. "I want my husband," I whispered.

She offered to call him, but I said no. Frankly, I was afraid he wouldn't come. I got out of there as fast as I could.

I had a powerful desire for Bob. I wanted to be held, made love to. I needed so badly to know that this part of my life had not been gouged out also. Did he see the body that he had loved now mangled, as though run over by a train? Was it hard enough to feel the same desire for a woman you had fallen in love with twenty long years ago, much less one who now had a deformity? Had I become undesirable?

Please, Lord, I prayed, let him get used to the way I am now.

He had been afraid to touch me while I was healing, but I healed fast, and now, only three months after my early July operation, my scars were hardly noticeable.

That evening, I waited anxiously for Bob to come home. I never wear makeup, but that night I put on blush and a touch of lip gloss. I evened my hair with fingernail scissors; I put on the turquoise blouse that he loved because it brought out the blue of my eyes. I couldn't just crawl into his arms these days. I needed to do everything just right.

When he came home that night, I waited until he loosened his tie and told me about his day. Then I finally interrupted. "I had my first radiation today; it was awful . . . so demeaning. To see this big X-ray machine coming down and filling you with what amounts to fallout from the atom bomb."

"Oh, I forgot!" he said. "I'm sorry." He patted my hand. I waited for more: a question, a hug, a few soothing words. But he abruptly changed the subject to a potential death penalty case he was struggling over: the student who had committed the premeditated torture and murder of Jonathan Levin, son of the head of Time Warner. The tragedy made my experience seem puny.

I went into the bedroom and put on the semi-sheer nightie I had bought for our tenth anniversary. I draped it with a new creamy silk shawl. It wasn't exactly like the white poncho he had claimed to fall in love with, but it was the best I could find. As I walked back to him, my pulse was so fast, and I hoped he wouldn't know how nervous I was. I thought of the risk I was taking. I couldn't stand it if he rejected me. I had to do this right.

He was sitting in the den watching Channel One, papers spread across his legs. Confidence: that is what men like. So with gossamer nightie swinging, I strode into the room like Bette Midler and surprised him by popping a square of Ghirardelli dark chocolate into his mouth. Then I ran my fingers through his hair, kissed his chocolaty mouth, and sat down on his lap. He didn't seem to notice the nightie, only the papers that he held on to for dear life. "Bed?" I asked, cocking my head and giving him the apple-cheeked smile he had once fallen in love with.

"I'm sorry, sweetheart, I have to get through this work." Then he touched his lips to my cheek and said, "Night."

I went back to the bedroom and threw my nightgown across the room. Then I edged to my side of the bed, rolled myself into a ball, and cried until I fell asleep.

At about 2:00 a.m., I woke with a start. The mattress was shaking. Was it the tremors of an earthquake? No, it was Bob, tossing around, tugging the covers, apparently in the midst of a bad dream. For weeks, he hadn't slept well. I felt so angry with him that I might have pushed him off the bed, but I tried unsuccessfully to wake him instead. Then he began kicking and shaking the bed all over again. I spent the night half-awake, dreaming that I was in an old livery cab, bumping up and down through the potholes of Madison Avenue.

20

Weeks and weeks went by. We had dinner with friends, but I was afraid they would sense our alienation. I could hear the gossip: "You should have seen the Morgenthaus the other night! This perfect marriage they are supposed to have after twenty years, well, you should have seen them, taut, silent, *American Gothic*."

It was better going to the farm every weekend, where we let no one poach on our privacy. The dirty half-light of winter matched my mood. A hard, stony season, with umber grass stamped down from last fall, the muted, truncated trees throwing up bony limbs, the earth battered from its suffocating spell beneath the snow. Even the tractors looked rusty as they stood idle in the barn.

Depression and weariness would overcome me, and I still felt a bit sick from the treatments. Since the sheer-nightgown debacle, I hung around in baggy work shirts and ate éclairs and mashed potatoes and put on weight. Who cared what I looked like? Not Bob, apparently, not the kids, to whom I was the same mom no matter what I wore.

I was always tired. I lay like a bag of wet earth all morning on the somnolent old couch in my little study. I became superstitious: Did my fatigue mean that cancer was breeding inside my cells, coming together again like an invading army? Was Bob worried about himself? His melanoma was less serious, less likely to spread than my breast cancer. He didn't have to have treatments like chemo or radiation, but still, though the doctors said they had gotten it all, how could they be sure?

In the afternoon, I would graze the stores, compulsively buying things I'd never use, which would make me feel better—for a while.

Then the terror would return, and the omens: Bob knew everything, and without his reassurance could I keep the disease at bay?

One day, the bills arrived, and Bob gave me a mighty scowl: "We're spending too much money!" It brought me a wave of relief. He hadn't exactly said the words "You are not going to die." But if I *was* going to die, he wouldn't have barked at me so heartlessly.

He poured his energy into the children. Cooking was love for him. He would make pancakes for the kids on Sunday, piling them on until Amy held her stomach and begged him to stop. They were our buffer, and we came together as a family, giggling and clowning around, aping each other or playing games of telephone. Josh's thick, wavy hair, his extraordinary sky-blue eyes under dark brows; beautiful Amy, with her Alice in Wonderland smile and her deep eyes as big as they were when she was a baby. The children were our comfort, our compensation. Sometimes, when the kids had left the table, Bob would cheerfully make me an egg, poached hard, just as I liked it. But I would find myself eating it alone.

We were coming home from a drab dinner out one night, and there was only one rather small parking space left on our street. I was an expert driver, a killer at dodging in and out of traffic with centimeters to spare, but at parallel parking I was hopeless.

I started backing the Volvo into the space slowly.

"Pay attention, you're about to take the bumper off that car!"

Squeal. My tire had hit the curbstone. "Did I back in too sharply?"

"That's an understatement. Straighten it out again, and then back in, slowly, slowly. Now turn your wheel, turn it *now*! The other way, for God's sake!"

By the time I had backed a quarter way in, he had made me so nervous I had bumped into the curb again.

"You're hopeless," he said. "Pull out and try again."

"Heck, Bob, this is good enough. Let's just leave the car where it is."

"Are you kidding? You're almost perpendicular to the curb!"

That was it. I slammed the gear into park. I got out of the car, strode to our building, and didn't look back.

•

How close we had been before the cancer scares! Everything was done together: eating, sleeping, cheerfully sparring. We had even enjoyed brushing our teeth at the same time. We liked to look into the mirror, laughing to see who could dribble the most foam. We'd examine who had the longest neck, the biggest head, the widest torso. We looked out for each other, sensed each other's moods, stepped in to soothe a wound.

But now he didn't go into the bathroom until I had left. And when he put space between us, I would return the favor. He would kiss me hello, and if I had a buoyant response, he would quickly detach. So the next time he came home, I wouldn't even come in from my study to greet him. He would go through the motions—a dry joke, a polite smile here and there. Even a rare compliment, and this is what I hated most because not only did I have to ask for it—how does my dress look?—but I could predict his response. It was never "You look pretty" but a serviceable "Fine."

What was happening to us? Our lives were dangling on meat hooks. We had both just had cancer. One of us could be dead in a month. The kids stole wary glimpses at us. Josh looked worried when we were together. Amy clung to each of us more than she had before.

Why was Bob so alienated from me? He had never before turned his back on me in times of trouble. So I waited for the reconciliation that didn't come.

Outside, it was cold and bracing, little white lights were looped over the branches of the trees, pink ones blinking against sunny brick. But inside our overheated apartment, it was always dusk.

Perhaps this was the way we were destined to become. Together, but apart, our oneness riven. We all know that we are ultimately alone anyway, in life and in death, and our only solution is to embrace it. The Sufi poets of the thirteenth and fourteenth centuries knew the value of solitude. Rumi told of a man who called out to Allah every day and finally, after a long time, received a response: "This longing you express is the return message." In other words, our hunger is what makes us human. In a similar way, Hafez warned, "Don't give up your loneliness . . . Let it ferment and season it." Being alone can be bountiful. I had only to remember my paralyzing dependence when first married to know that alone we can create that which would be extinguished if shared with another.

One night, my stepchildren came over for dinner. The first thing that Paul Grand, Annie's husband, said was "What you two have been through!" He shook his head. "You must be completely wiped out."

"Oh no," I said automatically. "I'm happy! I'm just so grateful that we're still alive and that everything turned out all right."

"But you've been through two big traumas. It's okay to be depressed."

"Oh, not at all," I heard myself say. "We're just fine. Let me take your jackets."

After they had left, I realized he was right. Maybe we had closed down because we were too afraid to face the trauma. We *were* depressed. If we got too close to each other, then we might get too close to what had really happened to us.

•

Kriya Yoga was my favorite form of meditation. I hated living with ambiguity, and this one was supposed to give you insight, the truth, really, behind a specific problem. I closed the door to my study, lit a candle, and asked myself what had made Bob and me so angry at each other. Then I forgot the question and went deep inside myself. I pictured my hospital room, big and dark, filled with the presence of the mother of one of Amy's playmates come to take me home. But all she seemed to do was examine the medical equipment, the bandages, asking me what the heart monitor did, why there was an IV there. What was my operation like? And then she watched me pack up. "Where is Bob?" she asked. I couldn't exactly remember. He must have been at the farm, because when I got home from the hospital, the house was empty. Had I been disappointed at the time? Angry? Kriya meditation is supposed to bring you peace and oneness, but what I felt now was anger.

All this time, in reaction to Bob's incurious attitude, I had also stepped away. Some of his actions had pushed me further. What husband doesn't pick his wife up at the hospital? Had I really forgiven him for that?

Candlelight helps me think, and I lit another one of aromatic sandalwood. I suddenly realized something. I was no longer fixated on Bob's death. Since I had been married, the fear would catch me unawares, at breakfast, while writing, in the hot sweat of the night. If I saw so much as a hair whitening on his head, a cold panic could run through me. And then, one day, it was I, not he, who suffered the dreaded sickness that had no cure. It was my own health that I found myself concerned with now. The doctors hadn't told me I was cured as they had told Bob.

He might outlive me. At that moment, I felt nothing for him. But when I caught sight of his picture on the piano, smiling roguishly at my camera, my throat tightened.

The sight of couples in a restaurant who ate their food without sharing a word had always disturbed me. What were they thinking about? Their stopped-up drains or their stopped-up hopes? Were they bitter about lost loveless years?

Would we be?

Finally, I bundled up and went to Central Park, to a place that never failed to calm me or present me with new ways to look at my troubles. All I needed was my favorite rock in the wildly thicketed underbrush of the Ramble and my book of ancient Greek philosophers. Plato, especially, with his Socratic parables, has lifted me out of many a dark night. His stories organize my chaotic mind, each one explaining another absurdity or contradiction. He had taught me what was behind much of human frustration: the imperfection of the senses colliding with the perfection of the idea. That made me think about the unreality of my idealistic expectations.

I grew up believing that human experience was static. When I was young, my mother used to call me Sarah Bernhardt. Whatever befell me was high drama. And each drama seemed immutable, fixed, a shadow of the last that would be a shadow of the next. My world took place in a single Sisyphean moment. Everything changed and everything stayed the same.

Women are the ones who are adept at redemption. They have the vision and are willing to take the emotional risks. But if, deep down, I still believed in stasis, how could I redeem our marriage?

Brooding on that depressing thought, I began flipping aimlessly through the writings of other Greek philosophers. I was stopped short by two fragments from the work of Heraclitus: "Nothing endures but change" and "He who does not expect the unexpected will not find it."

It was February 1998. I had a choice: I could try with everything I had to save our marriage, or I could simply live expecting the expected. But I couldn't figure this out alone: I needed help.

A friend recommended a psychotherapist named Laura Pancucci as one of the best and most knowledgeable in the city. I feared a tough, aloof woman, but when she opened her office door, she welcomed me warmly. She was a spirited woman, no pretense of grandeur, and clearly accessible.

Over several sessions, she learned the details of our predicament. I was often reaching for the box of Kleenex she kept on the floor next to my chair. One day she gently asked, "Do you think it's possible that your husband has post-traumatic stress disorder? What we call PTSD?"

I held my tissue in midair. That was the last thing I expected her to say. "Uh . . . like Vietnam veterans?"

"Yes, like the Vietnam veterans who came back from the war traumatized. I'm not saying this is the case, but it's worth exploring."

So over the next week, I read exhaustively about PTSD to see if I saw something I recognized. To my surprise, I discovered that the mental disorder that followed trauma could hit ordinary people as well as soldiers, especially if they faced one of life's major blows, the death of a spouse being number one. I remembered Bob telling me that he cried every day after his first wife's death and Renia saying he wouldn't come out of his room for weeks.

Although Bob knew she was very sick, Martha's chief doctor at Sloan-Kettering had been upbeat, giving Bob the illusion that she would beat the odds. Another doctor was not as sanguine, however, but Bob was often blind to bad news. I thought it likely that when Martha finally died, he had gone into a state of shock similar to that suffered by war veterans.

After her death, symptoms of PTSD that seemed to fit Bob included irrational self-blame. I knew somehow that Bob had survivor's guilt and a feeling of detachment from others (he avoided seeing friends after her death). He also tried to avoid remembering the event (making it clear to Steve Kaufman he never wanted it mentioned).

Then I read about what happened to a PTSD sufferer if the trauma was repeated somewhere down the line. The symptoms included "psychological distress at an event that resembles the original event . . . persistent avoidance of people that arouse recollections of the trauma . . . numbing of responsiveness to them . . . nightmares . . . inability to participate in previously enjoyed activities or to feel emotions associated with intimacy, tenderness, and sexuality." "The duration of the disturbance," the book said, "could last for an undetermined time, especially without treatment." I was so startled, I read it over twice. I found other books, and they described the same thing.

At my next session, I nearly ran into Laura's office. "It's him! The books describe him, even down to his restlessness at night."

She nodded. "You know, one other risk factor is experiencing still another trauma that happened even earlier in life. Do you think there was something traumatic in his childhood, his early youth?"

"The war. World War II. He was sunk by the Germans in one ship and hit by a kamikaze 550-pound bomb in another.

"He watched his men die. He saw . . . God, he saw horrible things."

Laura said nothing. She must have seen on my face what was happening within.

"I feel so upset for him, but I'm also kind of upset for me. Maybe his past-past is wiping out his present-past? Maybe he doesn't love me anymore, 'cause I got sick?"

"I think he loves you plenty, but if he's a victim of PTSD, it must have been hard for him when you contracted the same disease as his first wife. It wouldn't be a safe place for him."

At that, I bristled. "So he can just throw away twenty years of feeling safe and passionate and totally attached because of a bunch of bad memories?"

"It's a disease, a condition, Lucinda. It sounds like he's depressed and doesn't yet see that his reactions to you are connected to his traumas."

"Well, he can't express his feelings, and then they poke out in little bursts and go right back in again. The other day, we were trying to clear a clogged drain, and his head was under the sink, and out of the blue he said, 'No, I had cancer too. And you told me it was nothing, but it wasn't nothing.' He had blamed me all this time for giving him false hope."

"Why don't you encourage him to talk about it? If you are kind and nonjudgmental, and know it's not about you, you might help him."

I tried to follow Laura's advice, but he would always cut me off. Then I had the idea of using his own language—arid attorney talk—to present the ultimate repercussion. One night, insisting that we talk, I sat across the dining table from him. I calmly said my piece: "Bob, I think we're proceeding toward an end neither of us wants. As we discuss this, I don't want to misunderstand or misrepresent you. You say that my breast cancer hasn't driven you away, but I think you're a deeper person than that. This is a moment of reckoning, and I want to be as honest and clear as we can. We need to be aware of the issues as we take the next step in our marriage."

He looked vulnerable for the first time in months. "You sound as if you're going to leave me."

"I'll never leave you. But I want the truth."

"I've told you. I have no sense of pulling away from you. I depend on you."

"Sweetheart, please answer this question as truthfully as you can. Have you been feeling depressed?"

He looked down, pulled off a loose thread from his button, looked up, and said, "Yes."

"Really? For how long?"

"Oh, since I got cancer, I guess."

"Have you been scared?"

He nodded. "It was a very serious kind of cancer; it can spread to the intestine, anywhere in the body. I remember going up to the Amherst reunion and talking to the president, and when he saw those early red scars, he said, 'Oh, that's terrible. A woman on our staff had a melanoma and she had it removed, but it spread down her face and she's walking around completely disfigured.' It scared the hell out of me."

"Oh no, just what you needed. You never told me about that. And all I've been doing is focusing on my own cancer. Have you been mad at *me*?"

"No, no, not at all. I've been upset, disturbed, depressed, but I never thought of being angry."

"But I'm aware I've been ignoring you," he reluctantly added.

"Why?"

"I don't know." He looked so hapless, I felt sorry for him.

"I can imagine the terror you must have felt at Martha's illness. And even guilt. And now, with me, it's happened all over again."

Something began happening to Bob. His forehead was moist; his face had gone pale, slack, tentative. "Radiation wasn't as sophisticated as it is now," he said, taking out his handkerchief. "She was very badly burned, and she was confined to the hospital for months. She never talked about dying. It was very difficult for everybody."

I swallowed. "God, what a double whammy. Two wives with breast cancer.

"Bob, I understand why you've been abstracted." I touched his shoulder lightly. "People who've come out of a war might hear a log crack in the fireplace and relive the gunfire that killed their buddies. Well, people in peacetime can relive a life shock when something happens to bring it back. Do you know what I'm saying?"

"Yes."

"Breast cancer kills your wife, and then it happens to me. Do you think it was so traumatic that you went into a kind of post-traumatic stress disorder?"

It was as though he knew already. I didn't have to convince him.

"Doctors say that full-blown PTSD begins when you have a second shock that is just like the first one," I said.

"It wasn't the second shock, more like the third. The fourth, the fifth, really."

"How do you mean?"

He looked at the wall. "I had to put my father into Bloomingdale's; that was a place in Westchester for people with psychiatric problems. I went to see him every weekend."

Henry junior had met and married a Frenchwoman, Marcelle Puthon Hirsch, not long after Elinor died.

"But then he got hardening of the arteries, and he hardly knew who or where he was half the time. He would do things like go around in the middle of the night, waving a gun and shouting, 'Where is that Charles de Gaulle?'"

"Your father? Oh, Bob, and you so revered him."

"I was the only one of my siblings to come to see him. I came every weekend and longer at the end. He had his leg amputated. He had circulation problems. He was sick, physically and mentally."

"So you had to take him to a psychiatric hospital."

"Marcelle wouldn't let him come home," he replied. "She didn't want him around, so one day I just picked him up and brought him back.

"I took care of him until he died in 1967, and a year later Martha got breast cancer."

Bob got up to get some water. I could hear him sniffling in the kitchen. This was so hard for him. I knew I wouldn't have his attention much longer. I had better get to the point. But when he came back, he was already talking.

"Then before that was the war. When the *Lansdale* sank, my men were in the freezing waves fighting to stay alive. We tried to save the ones we could, but there were sailors who were wounded or were just overcome, and those went down for good. When I came home, I would wake up screaming every night."

"Oh, Bob, you've never told it to me that way. It's got to have been horribly traumatic for you. And on top of that you had to have the inevitable survivor's guilt."

"Yes, I think I did."

"Do you remember how you felt when they told you I had breast cancer?" I asked.

He nodded. "I felt bad. I was scared." He hesitated. "I thought, 'Here we go again: my father, Martha, me, now you.' I didn't want to end up taking care of anyone else. I wanted someone to take care of me."

"And look what I went and did. You married a young girl and it backfired. You must have resented me."

"It wasn't your fault. How could I have resented you?"

"Then why have you stayed as far away as you could from me? You haven't always been there when I wanted you."

He looked surprised, hurt. "Maybe I haven't been there every single time, but I've been there at the critical moments, when you really needed me. Don't you remember when I went with you once to chemo? I was there when you were operated on."

"You never went with me to the doctor."

"I have an office to run; I can't easily wait in waiting rooms."

I tried to suppress a smile. That is, unless you are faced with competition. When I had follow-up tests after my cancer treatments, I told Bob that my friend Blair was accompanying me. I had barely met her in the lobby when Bob showed up and told Blair she could leave.

"I wish," I continued cautiously, "I wish that you would just have comforted me a bit."

"I thought I *was* comforting you. I also thought maybe you didn't want it. You don't really like sympathy."

"If I don't, I married the right husband," I said under my breath. But

I thought about what he had just said. He was right, to a degree. My father would put his arm around me and tell me things would be okay when they wouldn't. But my mother had been a fixer. She tried to solve the problem, to make it disappear. That was her comfort. So now, if people pitied me, I would automatically think things couldn't be fixed.

"I know it was hard for you," I pressed on, "but all I wanted is for you to put your arms around me and tell me everything was going to be okay."

He seemed to go paler. He started to get up.

"This is upsetting for you."

"I don't like talking about it, no."

"Bob, I just need you to answer one more question. Why wouldn't you just reassure me?"

"Because I'm not a good faker. I couldn't be near you and say it was okay. I'm pessimistic about cancer, and I . . ." His voice shook. "I wasn't sure you would be all right."

A fist tightened inside my chest. In other words, the man who's always right is scared I *won't* be all right. The tables are turned. "Well, I'm not going to die on you," I said, managing a smile. "I promise."

He got up, and for the first time since I was diagnosed, he kissed my lips. Then he held me, and I nestled into the hollow of his shoulder, and I thought it was my tears that tasted salty, but it was his. "I'm sorry, sweetheart. I really am sorry I didn't support you enough. I'm sorry you felt I haven't been there for you. I just didn't know. I guess I never know."

"It's okay," I said, wiping his eyes with my sleeve. "We understand each other now."

He let go of me. "Let's get some fresh air," he said with a smile, affectionately giving me his suede jacket to wear.

We headed for the park, where the forsythias were budding and crocuses struggled to emerge from the warming March ground. As we stood in front of the tall, starkly lonely Egyptian obelisk, I asked, "Did you feel detached, did you have trouble concentrating after the melanoma and breast cancer? Those are PTSD symptoms."

"After the *Lansdale*, when I was on the *Bauer*, I never slept. I was executive officer, navigator, and director of the CIC—Combat Information Center. I never left my post for close to a year and just dozed in a chair whenever I was exhausted." He laughed. "One time, the captain was giving me instructions, and I nodded off while he was talking. I guess you'd call that detached.

"I had a deal with my men on the *Lansdale*," he said haltingly. "If anything happened and people were lost, I'd go see their families. So I remember going to see George Haines's widow . . ." Bob stopped on the path and began to choke back tears.

Then we started walking again, and I saw he was holding his jaw tight. "But then there were the men on different ships," he went on. "The *Paul Hamilton* in our convoy was blown up the same night as the *Lansdale*, and 580 men died. I got all kinds of mail from parents of those sailors, but I didn't know anything; I didn't know their sons or what had happened to them. I couldn't do anything for them, and it was very upsetting. I ended up giving them to my father to answer."

I squeezed his hand. "No one could have cared so well for those people you tried to save in the water. I read a letter Mrs. Roosevelt wrote to your mother sympathizing about her 'poor boy having seen too many horrors.' It seemed like you had one trauma after the next."

"Then after the war," he continued, "Judge Patterson asked me to go to Buffalo with him. I had accompanied him on every trip for four years, but this time I told him if I went with him, I didn't think I could finish an important brief for the U.S. Supreme Court. He told me to stay and finish it.

"The day before he was scheduled to return, there was a blinding snowstorm. I looked out the window and thought what fool would fly in a storm like this.

"The judge had. He'd moved back his reservation. And it was the birthday of the pilot of this American Airlines Convair, and he wanted to get home. He got home all right, but not the way he had planned. The plane crashed into a building in Elizabeth, New Jersey. No one survived."

I felt sick at the thought he might have been dead instead of walking beside me. He had turned his face away. Perhaps he didn't want me to see the grief that still came over him almost fifty years after Patterson's death.

Then, suddenly, we were jolted out of our somber mood. A man came up, smiling widely, sticking out his hand. "Mr. Morgenthau? Is that Mr. Morgenthau?" an older man asked, stopping in front of us. "I just want to thank you, sir, for the wonderful years of service you've given this city."

Three more strangers waved or nodded at Bob, and he gave them big smiles and sometimes stuck out his hand.

"Who do you think you are, Bruce Springsteen?" I asked, trying to lighten his mood.

"Who is he?"

"The best rock singer in the world, that's all. You've got a lot in common. They call him the Boss. You know, I think people think you've just enjoyed success after success. They idealize you; they don't realize you haven't had a charmed life."

"I'd been so used to getting bad news I began to harden myself. Now I just skip over it.

"People asked me if I missed the U.S. Attorney's Office, and I really didn't. They ask me if I'm upset at losing a big case, but I'm never upset for long.

"You know what I say when these writers, editors, publishers, have asked me to write a book. I'll never do it. I just don't have what it takes to pull it all up again and again, editing and adding and going back over my life."

"You're too sensitive underneath to do that; I think you couldn't take it. You're so like my dad. So determined not to be laid open, not to let yourself go.

"I understand now why you sweep things under the rug," I added.

"I don't want to hurt people, be a burden. I don't want them to have to live with my problems. I also think if you bring things up when people have tried to stop thinking about them, you're liable to hurt them all over again."

"As well as hurt yourself," I said, smiling. "How do you maintain the discipline?"

"I *did* get pretty good at suppressing things," he replied. "I've been in the war, lost friends, my mother and father and Martha were sick for so long . . . I've learned never to look back. I don't have anything at stake anymore."

"So you've eliminated the possibility of your suffering, and you try to stop others from suffering. You sound like the Dalai Lama."

"I thought you said I was like Bruce Springsteen."

"Ha. You're both. A public star and a private Buddhist."

I thought about his habit of removing himself from an emotional argument, putting away unsolvable problems, forgetting the complaints and resentments that others harbored against him. That is why he could call me a nasty word one minute and then the next sweetly designate me his "pet." He had disciplined himself into an ancient Eastern state of mind—live in this present moment and obliterate the one that came before.

I put my arm around his waist and looked up at him.

"What?" he asked, smiling back and smoothing down my hair.

"Oh, nothing. Just this moment, that's all."

•

I breathe in, and the air, as though trapped, is propelled out of me. Is it the first spring pollen? The perplexing beauty of your confessions? Or my own regret? I've not known you before. You've sat maddeningly silent beside me, and until now, I never knew why.

Lord, let me always remember his suffering.

It feels as if our marriage has shifted today, for you have finally been explained to me. After two decades, you risked taking me to a place you've kept hidden, sometimes even from yourself. It was a place where you did look back, where you did relive the wounds of the past, where your truest self prevailed and your grief was deeply felt.

•

On September 11, 1997, John Cardinal O'Connor, trailing brilliant red robes, arrived to address a thousand people before the soaring hexagonal Museum of Jewish Heritage that Bob had worked for years to create. Bitter winds came off the Hudson, whipped past the Statue of Liberty, and set the great tent bucking. From the moment he took the first step to the podium, the cardinal's head was bowed, his back curved, bent almost to a right angle. I was afraid for him. I was afraid something was wrong with him.

The decision to invite the cardinal to open the museum had been controversial. Now there were some grumbles and polite but less than enthusiastic applause. Nobody in the audience seemed to notice he wasn't looking up at them but kept his head so low that he might have been paying obeisance to the pope. Then he softly uttered the words that had never been heard from a Catholic leader before. "I am grateful," he said, head still bowed, "to have the highest honor of seventy-seven and a half years of life on this earth: the humbling privilege, publicly, as a Christian, to ask forgiveness for all Christians who helped in any way to make the horrors of the Shoah possible."

Many in the crowd gasped. It was the first apology from a church official since Pope Pius XII signed a concordat with Hitler and let two thousand Roman Jews at the foot of Vatican Hill be taken to Nazi death camps.

It was tantamount to the pope himself standing before a representation of Jews, many of them survivors, and saying he was sorry. In fact, O'Connor surely had the pope's blessing, for some time later John Paul II himself issued an official church apology.

When the cardinal finished his speech and walked off the stage, standing upright now, the applause this time was considerable.

That Morgenthau had chosen a representative of the ecclesiastical Goliath that collaborated with the Nazis outraged some of his board members on this historic occasion. They said the beautiful new museum in Battery Park deserved someone better.

One of the four founders slapped his hand on the table and said, "Disinvite him!"

"No, this is who we are going to have," insisted Bob. "We don't want to be talking to ourselves. It's important to have a broad range of people of all religions visiting the museum. The cardinal is the Vatican's figurative liaison in the Middle East, and he's very sensitive to Jewish affairs."

Governor Pataki, Mayor Giuliani, and Elie Wiesel, the author who was a survivor of Auschwitz, all spoke passionately. Then Bob got up and told the story of his grandmother's first cousin who could not be saved from the gas chambers, even though the influential governor Herbert Lehman and his brother Chief Judge Irving Lehman intervened. Eva Lehman Thalheimer, told she was going to a retirement home, was gassed in Treblinka at the age of eighty-six.

"This museum is important for young people to understand what happens when criminals take over the government," Bob told the audience.

Then the six-sided, eighty-five-foot-tall museum, designed by the prominent architect Kevin Roche, was opened to the guests. The sides represented the six million in the Nazi genocide and the six points of the Star of David.

"God in heaven," said a survivor of Dachau, holding her cheeks as she saw an exhibit of the album that she kept at the camp. There were ancient photographs, kiddush cups, wedding dresses, children's shoes, and videotaped testimonies by some of the last survivors still living. All together, they described the rich Jewish life before the Holocaust, the resistance during it, and the renewal afterward. Some survivors wore placards with the names of their ghettos or concentration camps in hopes of connecting with friends and relatives. Many danced to the music played by a Yiddish folk band. In the entry hall were etched the words REMEMBER . . . NEVER FORGET. THERE IS HOPE FOR YOUR FUTURE.

"You did wonderful," I said as we gazed up at the towering edifice on the water. I knew he was thinking of his father: the museum was his private tribute to Henry junior, who had not been fully appreciated for helping to win the war against Hitler. I asked him how his dad would feel today.

"He would be pleased, proud," Bob said, a catch in his voice. Fifteen years earlier, Bob had agreed to help lead the Koch commission to build the city's only Holocaust museum. Indeed, he had been thinking of his dad: "I wanted to complete what he had started.

"He would have wanted this museum so that succeeding generations will always know about what the Nazis had done," Bob said.

He added that it wasn't widely appreciated that Henry's Treasury Department had been responsible for the gigantic preparation of America for war: the building up of the military and the creative decision to issue war bonds to let ordinary Americans participate in its financing. But perhaps when the war was won, guilt was mixed with his relief.

"He did what he could to save Jewish refugees, but he couldn't do all that he wanted to do, because we needed to win the war first," Bob said.

It was the government's discovery of the extent of the Nazi genocide that inspired Henry junior to propose the controversial Morgenthau Plan. I had thought the proposal had been rejected from the start, but it was actually greeted enthusiastically by FDR and other cabinet officials. I'd found an obscure book that Henry junior had written, *Germany Is*

Our Problem, in 1945 after the Nazis' unconditional surrender. I had read about the final war conference in Potsdam, where Truman, Stalin, and Churchill had signed off on the plan that Germany be deindustrialized and turned into an agricultural country. My own research showed that indeed this deindustrialization had been implemented—shipyards were blown up, and heavy manufacturing was converted—and continued for several years until it was gradually ended by pressure from the new German leaders. Truman, who finally fired Henry junior, argued that the United States needed Germany to be an armed bulwark against Communist Russia. The incarnation of Henry junior's plan for Germany was quickly reversed.

Bob saw his father as a visionary: one of the first American politicians to realize, or admit, what Germany was doing to the Jews. "In August 1938, Daddy took Henry and me to Europe. When we got to the Swiss side of the Rhine, across from the Black Forest, Henry said to my father, 'Bob and I want to cross the bridge to see Germany,' and my father said, 'Why in the world would you want to do that?' Henry replied, 'So we can say we've been on German soil.' Daddy said, 'Henry, you are never going to want to say you've been in Germany.' "

•

The completion of the museum in September was a beacon in the horrible year of 1997. It was a celebration of triumph over tragedy in more ways than one. Publicly, the beautiful museum, as it grew over the next months, hailed the defeat of Nazism and the continuation of the rich life of Jews, and secretly it represented Bob's and my triumph over cancer and the near ruin of our marriage. After Bob recognized that he had had the symptoms of PTSD, we talked about it many times, and I think it gave him some relief. Now we stood reconciled, hand in hand at the fence as the breeze from the Hudson aimed itself at our backs. "We fought hard, didn't we, Tart?" I said, putting my head on his shoulder. "Nobody will ever find us eating on trays in separate rooms."

"No, they won't," he replied, putting his arm around me, shielding me from the cold, "because fortunately for me, you never run out of things to say."

•

"Where's my wife?" he would invariably ask as soon as he walked in the door, even if he had been gone for an hour. "Lucinda! Where are you?"

"Here," I would shout, and he would impatiently reply, "Where is here? I don't know where here is!" I would stride quickly out of some room and welcome him home.

When I talked to my friends, that was a signal for him to claim ownership. He'd make noise, make faces. One night Lila Meade and I were talking excitedly about the runaway success of the Vassar Haiti Project founded by her husband, Andrew, and her. They had been buying paintings and crafts from Haitian artists, selling them at fairs in New York, and then using the profits to help a village in the ravaged country.

"We've built them a school, and now we've raised so much we'll be able to start on a medical clinic!" Lila exclaimed.

I giggled. Bob, sitting on the couch across from us, was wiggling his eyebrows at me.

"You look so handsome, Tart!" I couldn't ignore his attentions any longer.

Lila looked at him. He looked back straight-faced.

"Do you think *I'm* handsome?" I asked him.

"You're very cute," he said.

"Well, you're very, very cute," I replied.

"You're very, very, very cute," he said, grinning now.

Every so often, he suggested we go out to a nightclub and dance. So off we went to Doubles, had a glass of wine, and hit the floor. I had tried to teach him to dance, and what he could do was pick up one foot and then the other, but with perfect respect for the rhythm, thus providing me with a foil to let go, hair flying, hands clapping to the hot beat of "Disco Inferno" or the cool one of "Little Red Corvette."

Still, underneath all the jollity we consciously worked to create, we felt beaten down by the events of the last two years. And then, one day, the head deity, undoubtedly getting tired of our obsession with ourselves, engineered a series of exciting and sometimes bizarre twists in our lives that must have amused him and certainly woke up our fighting natures.

This is what would happen to Bob: he would wage a lonely fight for restitution of Nazi loot to Jewish owners and turn the international art world on its head; he would convict two murderers where there was no body; and he would indict a rapist who was not present or even identified. Each of these cases made legal precedent.

This would happen to me: for *The New Yorker*, I would write about my sister's baby, who had serious birth defects but the mind of a genius; I would fly through Africa with Hillary Clinton and get an exclusive interview with the First Lady about the Monica Lewinsky affair, revealing that the president's weakness for infidelity was connected to his abuse as a child; I would finally persuade my father to tell me the details of his work as an undercover agent and write a memoir that became a modest bestseller and broke my writer's block for good.

And so came our years of plenty. They began in 1998 and lasted more than a decade. One moment we were sunk in bleak gravity, and the next we were whirling through a rush of stars. Though we were taken over and thrust in different directions, we no longer felt responsible for each other's every mood. At last, as in my everlasting dreams, we were on parallel paths, knowing that our lives would intersect, and often.

21

On January 7, 1998, Bob got a strange call from the niece of a Holocaust survivor who said the Nazis had stolen an Egon Schiele from her aunt; the family had been trying to get it back for more than half a century. Within a day, Bob had retrieved it from the Museum of Modern Art. What was fascinating to me, as the case unfolded in our dining room, was the story behind the story.

The fallout began with Ronald Lauder, the genteel billionaire who had been a Pentagon official, a Middle East negotiator, and an ambassador to Austria and was a cosmetics heir and a real estate mogul with his name on buildings throughout Manhattan. Now he was the august chairman of the city's Museum of Modern Art, and after the seizure of the Schiele, he strode awkwardly into Bob's office, chin thrust forward, jutting brows casting a shadow over eyes luminous with indignation.

The DA, having no precedent, had seized the exquisite *Portrait of Wally*, which was a star in the museum's exhibition of the works of Egon Schiele. The DA had, in fact, slapped a subpoena on Lauder's museum a day before it planned to ship the painting, which was a rendering of Schiele's mistress, out of the country. Lauder was in shock. The work had been a particular favorite of his and one destined to skyrocket in value.

"It doesn't even belong to us!" Lauder said during this private meeting. "We borrowed it from the Austrian government, and we have to give it back."

"It doesn't appear to belong to Austria," Bob replied evenly. "It appears to have been stolen by Nazi looters from a Jew."

That Jew was one Lea Bondi, Schiele's supporter and dealer, who, after the war ended, had been trying for much of her life to get back the exceptional canvas.

Lent by the state-owned Leopold Museum, this work of the artist, who was the harbinger of Expressionism in the early twentieth century, had had a journey through time as twisted, grotesque, and deathly as one of Schiele's figurative portraits. If Lauder loved the work, it had also been cherished by Bondi, who had hung it in her living room before it was confiscated by a Nazi and eventually passed on to the government of Austria.

Lauder was a passionate Zionist, an active supporter of the right-wing leadership in Israel, but on this day he was less an advocate of Jewish rights than a collector of famous paintings.

"Austria would have returned the Schiele painting to its rightful owners, but you have now made it much more difficult," said Lauder, the son of Estée Lauder.

"Austria would never have returned the Schiele," Bob countered coolly. "Their laws favor the buyer, and you know this.

"It seems to me you have a conflict of interest in this case," Bob added, referring to the MoMA board's dismissive treatment of the Bondi heirs, who had pleaded with them not to ship off the Schiele.

"Well, I guess I do wear two hats," Lauder admitted, suddenly subdued.

"I'd say you wore four," Bob replied. "You are a collector of Schiele paintings that have no provenance, you are the chairman of MoMA, and being its former U.S. ambassador, you are a friend of Austria. You even chair the Commission for Art Recovery that confines itself to persuading governments and museums alone to make restitution."

"You're going to ruin the art world," Lauder said. "People won't be able to enjoy art exhibitions without lending between museums, and no museum will turn over their best art if they might not get it back. There are rules of lending between museums worldwide. Are we supposed to break them because you decide we should?"

"It's not my decision; it's the law. We did extensive research, we obtained affidavits, including one from the world's leading Schiele expert, before we moved against you."

A disgruntled Lauder left the office, but at home a landslide of vitriol began to bury us. The phone rang incessantly, and we were inundated with irate letters from board chairmen of the New York Public Library and every museum in New York, including the Jewish Museum. The first epistle came from Bob's friend Arthur O. Sulzberger, the mighty chairman of both the New York Times Company and the Metropolitan Museum of Art:

> Dear Bob:
> The Metropolitan Museum, its Board, staff, donors, and lenders are all . . . deeply disturbed that your office would issue a subpoena to The Museum of Modern Art involving it in a criminal investigation and forcing it to violate contractual obligations to return works on loan to the lender.
> . . . During the past year, the Metropolitan hosted 24 loan exhibitions helping to attract 5.4 million visitors. The Glory of Byzantium brought together 268 works of art from 23 countries . . . An economic development survey found that these visitors spent $184 million, generating tax revenue of $18 million for New York City and New York State. In the course of the year, the Metropolitan borrowed approximately 1,642 works of art . . .
> . . . The action which your office has initiated has put at risk the ability of the Metropolitan and other New York Museums to obtain loans essential to their exhibition programs. We urge you to resolve this matter as expeditiously as possible.
> Sincerely,
> Punch

I was spellbound on January 7, 1998, as Bob told me what he had accomplished in a matter of hours. It began with that call from Lea's niece, who said Bob was the Bondi family's last chance. She said that the U.S. Attorney's Office and the State Department in Washington had brushed them off, and with time running out, she decided to try this man Morgenthau, who was known to be a maverick who sought justice whether he had jurisdiction or not.

Then, predictably, hearing of Morgenthau's interest, the feds jumped back in. "You can't do it," Bob quoted an assistant at the U.S. Attorney's Office as saying. "That's our territory, and we're investigating the claim. You can't touch it, Bob."

"You know there's nothing that gets my blood up more than being told I can't do something," my husband recounted to me over the phone. "But I have to do it fast, and there's the small problem of New York law. There's a statute that says cultural properties on loan in New York are indemnified from seizure and must be returned to the lending institution."

"Why don't you get hold of Judah Gribetz"—he was an expert on Nazi looting and former counsel to Governor Carey—"and tell him to drop everything and try to find a little hole in the law that you can crawl through."

So that is what he did. The clock was ticking—they only had twenty-four hours—but Bob's friend Judah found a loophole. Although it was open to interpretation, the statute protecting art-lending institutions seemed to be confined to civil actions, not criminal.

But would the courts rule for the DA? Bob always hedged his bets. "I called Ray Kelly, and he urged me to act and told me if the courts ruled against me, Customs would take over and stop the painting from going anywhere," Bob told me. "He accused me of being a hound with a ham bone. But I had to be. I knew the feds wouldn't act against MoMA."

"You are amazing!" I cheered. I thought of how hard Bob was working to raise money for the museum, how steeped he was in the plight of the Holocaust survivors. Now he had been presented with an opportunity to seek retribution for one family of victims.

"If your husband wins this," Judah said, "he will have set a precedent. A huge amount of stolen art has been wandering around Europe since the war. Most Holocaust survivors have been resigned to having lost everything. They just didn't think they could ever get it back. I don't think there's been another case like this anywhere in the world."

Meanwhile, a variety of art mavens, especially friends of MoMA, began attacking Bob for his motivations in the case. One widely copied story, in *The Boston Globe*, hit a raw nerve. In a piece titled "The Haunted Memories of Robert Morgenthau," the paper accused the DA of trying to avenge his father, who had called the State Department "satanic" for suppressing news of the Holocaust and blocking a congressional mandate to rescue Jewish children in Europe. Henry junior went on to set up the War Refugee Board, but by then he was only able to save 200,000 Jews.

"That's a bunch of bull," Bob said, slapping down the article. "I received evidence that art had been stolen, so I abided by the law. I've prosecuted stolen art cases before: there was a drawing stolen from the Louvre, artifacts from Italy. Schiele was a routine case."

Routine? Watching Bob's paradoxical, even illusory nature in action was fascinating. Deep empathy for Holocaust victims was ingrained. It wasn't just his father who saved victims; his grandfather Henry Morgenthau had sponsored and paid for dozens of Jewish families to seek refuge in America.

Indeed, when the Austrian government finally agreed to let go of *Portrait of Wally*, the ceremonial return of the painting to the Bondis would take place at the Holocaust museum that Bob had been commissioned to build.

Other newspapers wrote editorials speculating that Morgenthau might be responsible for shutting down smaller museums and galleries that depended on borrowed art. The Austrian press was the worst, with their anti-Semitic ramblings. One accused him of making "heists," typical of his race, and of forcing "the art world into a banana republic."

I was worried about the effect the attacks would have on Bob. One day I asked him how he was feeling about them. He thought a minute, said "fuck 'em all," and resumed opening a bottle of my favorite port. Other times, however, he got somber. With many of the city's powerful figures, newspapers, and museums arrayed against him, he felt as though he were fighting behind the Alamo. "It's upsetting," he admitted.

"They'll respect you in the end," I said. "Why don't you have a press conference discussing the morality as well as the legal standing in the case? That way everyone will know what's really happening." So Bob did. After that, public opinion ceased to be unanimous against the seizure.

The case languished in the federal courts for nine years until finally the Leopold Museum settled with the Bondis by buying the painting for a wildly inflated price of nineteen million dollars. The agreement stipulated that *Portrait of Wally* be displayed at Bob's Museum of Jewish Heritage for three weeks before being returned and be hung with the story of the painting's deceptive, peripatetic provenance on the wall.

"Justice requires patience," said Bob in a speech to members of the Bondi family and the guests who attended the museum's unveiling of the 1912 portrait of Schiele's red-haired mistress, which had been in storage for eleven years. Andre Bondi, Lea Bondi Jaray's grandnephew, spoke of his gratitude to the DA, wiping tears away.

Bob's actions as a prosecutor caused a revolution in the international art world and had as far-ranging permanent effects as anything he had ever done.

"Everybody's thinking more about provenance today than they were yesterday," said Philippe de Montebello, director of the Metropolitan. Representatives Charles E. Schumer and Nita M. Lowey of New York drafted a bill requiring art purchasers to do background checks to see if the art was stolen or face losing the work in court. It also provided fifteen million dollars for organizations that helped locate looted art. Museums began to willingly return artworks to their rightful owners. Panels were created to help families trace their losses, wartime archives were opened, conferences arranged, books and documentaries produced. Even the Austrian government joined the rush. It gave 250 works of art worth a hundred million U.S. dollars to the Rothschild family, which had been stripped of its treasures after Hitler annexed Austria.

Within a year, the United States had signed the groundbreaking Washington Conference Principles on Nazi-Confiscated Art; governments and museums in forty-four nations pledged to repair the damage Nazi looters had done to Jewish art owners.

•

If you asked our children, Bob was the perfect parent. To him, the basic requirement of one was to put on a happy face. Calm, steady, and consistent, he taught Amy and Josh by example. Though I had been very close to our two and taken a much larger share in raising them, Bob had always been nearby, solving issues, reassuring me.

As teens, both kids began to come to their dad with their confessions and their problems. It amused me to see Bob, who had little respect for psychiatry, treat them as though he were a Freudian analyst. He didn't judge and rarely betrayed his reactions. To them, he was accessible and easygoing. The few times he got angry, he had only to scowl and level his smoky-blue eyes at them to make an impact. Me, I could shout all night and they would pay no attention.

When things got hot, however, Bob stepped out of the line of fire completely. He was experienced enough to know that it is always the mother who gets it. All the child-raising books say never contradict a spouse while he or she is disciplining a child. Therefore, this was exactly what Bob did.

Take the case of the brass doorknob. I was blasé when Josh had girls in his room and shut the door. I would smile indulgently when I found they had spent the night, ending up fully clothed, in a pile on Josh's bed. But when I heard about seventh graders in some schools having sex in the bathrooms, I began to have thoughts about sending Josh to a seminary.

The libertarian philosophy of parents who came of age in the 1970s had created rather entitled children. Josh and his friends, for instance, locked their doors, as though their parents were trespassers in their own home. Moreover, Josh began entertaining so often that his bedroom had become party central.

We decided to finally set down a few rules: his door could not be locked, especially when he had girls over, and we were to have free access. Josh protested mightily. Then, two days later, we found the heavy, tightly fitted doorknob to his room had vanished. Screwdrivers, a wrench, a ruler, a can opener, and other "tools" were scattered on the hall floor. But no doorknob. Josh had removed and hidden it so only he could get into his room; in essence, he had found the loophole: he didn't need to lock the door if there was no doorknob.

Bob knelt down and examined the plate, tried to figure out how he had engineered this, and finally gave up. "He's really done a job," he said with the hint of a smile.

"I don't believe this, I just don't believe it," I said. I was particularly irritated at the admiration on Bob's face. Did he identify with Josh the mischief maker, having been one himself?

When the little villain appeared, clearly proud of himself, I was fuming.

"You ruined that precious antique doorknob I searched the city for!" I yelled, my vow to be a sunny, insouciant mother having vanished.

"How did you do it?" asked Bob curiously.

"It's why he did it that matters!" I barked. My son had made me do what I vowed I'd never do: act and sound like my mother. This made me angrier, and I picked up the hammer and absurdly waved it in the air, having no intention of using it on anyone.

"Lucinda, calm down," Bob said, alarmed. "Let it go."

"This is a joke to you, Bob? Lawbreakers, criminals, they start just like this. Practicing at home, vandalizing property, disrespecting their parents. Do you know what juvenile detention is like, Josh?"

"Sure. I'd rather be there than live with the inmates in this asylum."

"If you don't produce that doorknob now, you're grounded for a month."

"For God's sake, Mom," Josh laughed.

"Lucinda, leave him alone."

"We're padlocking your door. You won't have the last word on this." Josh was taking my house apart, and Bob thought it was cute. I felt as if I were at the Mad Hatter's tea party, where wrong was right and right was left.

Josh retreated behind his door. We heard him put on the doorknob. "You're insane, Mom," he called.

"Did you hear what he said to me?" I asked, looking at Bob.

"Josh, you shouldn't talk to your mother like that," he crooned, in the same tone he had used when asking his erstwhile dog Rennie not to pee on the rug.

"Oh Lord, the two of you are revolting!" I said, turning on my heel.

•

The next evening, Bob and I walked around the reservoir, watching the sun turn gold on the water.

I confronted him about his reinforcement of Josh's behavior: "Never mind me, think how Josh is getting mixed messages from his two parents—he'll never be able to figure out what is right and what is wrong unless we act as a united team."

"I think he already knows the difference," Bob said. "He's just act-ing his age."

"But do you think it's right for me to be scolding him and you then to start scolding me?"

"I don't do that."

"Yes you do! You do it all the damn time. You don't know how infu-riating it is for you to leave the discipline to me and then, when I do it, you pull the rug out from under me."

"I made you soup yesterday, cut articles out of the paper for you."

"What?"

"And now you're complaining about me."

"What does that have to do with this argument?"

"Last weekend I took the kids to the farm so you could stay home and finish that *New Yorker* article."

"Bob, you're talking about apples in the middle of a conversation about oranges."

"Look at the birds flying around the water," he said, pointing. "I wonder what kind they are?"

I didn't speak for the rest of the walk, which I knew drove him crazy. He hated any member of his family to be mad at him.

•

Two days later, Jill Comins, my psychologist friend, and I were having lunch at Sarabeth's, a sunny restaurant with a Scottish bakery. We ordered big healthy salads, since we were both trying to take off a few pounds. I told her about my argument with Bob, which still upset me.

She laughed. "Men generally don't know how to defend themselves in a woman's style of arguing. They get flustered. Bob, he just landed in the soup, so to speak."

I giggled, then waved away the waiter with the bread, which was the last thing we needed. "You know, there's no one like you who I can laugh with and learn from, both at the same time," I said.

"Maybe what he was trying to tell you is that he feels like he's being taken for granted. He's answering your complaint with one of his own. He doesn't want to be overlooked. He may be saying, 'I need you to recognize what it meant for me to get you soup, babysit the kids, all that . . .' Or maybe he has been harboring hurt feelings—that you don't appreciate the things he does for you."

"Hmm, while dismissing me and the critical issue I brought up. Very convenient.

"You know," I said, "the blueprint for our dynamic was set the first day we met. That rainy afternoon when I tried to get a story out of him about Nixon's crooked cronies, it was like pulling grass out by the roots. He ducked and diverted. But still, I suspected then that he hadn't given away anything he didn't want to. Shall we splurge, get dessert?"

"Oh, why not," Jill said merrily. "I think you should remember that it's often hard for men to say they're wrong. I imagine Bob is no different."

"Like a little boy."

"Men *are* boys, haven't you heard?"

We giggled some more, and I moaned with exaggerated pleasure as a creamy bite of crème caramel rolled down my tongue. "You know," I said slowly, "you're making me think. I'm realizing that my hubby is very skilled at nuance. He says what he wants to say in very few words, words that are . . ."

"Cryptic," Jill said, dreamily eating her slice of moist dark-chocolate cake.

"So maybe, in his weird Middle-earth world or whatever dimension he lives in, nuance is everything. What do you think of all that? You're leaning back with this Freudian look on your face."

She smiled. "What I'm thinking is how did you, who're such an extrovert, end up marrying the introvert of all introverts?"

I looked at her blankly.

"I'm teasing," she said, grinning. "Opposites attract all the time."

22

One day in early March 1999, I got a letter on beautifully bonded stationery. Hillary Clinton's people were inviting me to accompany her on a trip to North Africa, implying that she might give me an exclusive interview. I nearly dropped the letter. Half the reporters in the nation had been trying to get to the First Lady. The president had just been acquitted of congressional impeachment charges, but the Monica Lewinsky scandal hung on—and Hillary seemed to be getting the brunt of it.

I couldn't imagine the humiliation she must feel. Or what it would be like asking her about it. I showed Bob the letter.

"Exciting," he exclaimed.

"I'm not so sure," I replied, through my own excitement. "Why would she even discuss Monica Lewinsky? The woman who publicly cuckolded her."

"Cuckqueaned. Only a man can be cuckolded."

"How'd you get to be so smart?"

"You're stealing my line."

"Can you be serious for once?"

"Look, don't worry, you can get anybody to talk," Bob said dryly. "I should know."

I had been writing for *The New Yorker*, whose editor was the formidable Tina Brown, and now I was joining her as she left to start her own magazine, *Talk*, designed to be a glossier version of *The New Yorker* with photographs.

Why had the First Lady chosen me? Did she think I would have a sympathetic ear, write something favorable? Or did she remember my solicitous treatment of her the night Princess Diana had died?

A few weeks later, on March 20, I boarded the shuttle for Washington, giving Bob a long hug; the trip with Hillary would be some three weeks, and we'd never been apart that long.

I found myself at Andrews Air Force Base deposited in a plane full of White House reporters. For the first three days of the trip none of us shared a word with Mrs. Clinton: she was kept away from us; from a distance, she looked embattled, her face puffy, her skin drained of color.

Hillary's press corps was a clubby group of reporters and photographers, mostly women, employed by the Washington media. When I introduced myself as a correspondent from the new *Talk* magazine, they gave me blank stares. How did some worker bee from a talk radio station get on board? I didn't enlighten them; I wanted to keep a low profile.

In Egypt, during a lively Bedouin feast of lamb tagine with prunes and apricots, Hillary and I were among the few who looked disheartened, who didn't dance. But she never got near me, and I finally asked one of her press agents about seeing her privately. Not now, the agent warned, adding that I was not to tell anyone about an interview with her. This was mildly comforting; if there was a now, there was bound to be a later.

I was known in New York for my journalism but not in parochial Washington. Candy Crowley, a star at CNN, befriended me anyway. When she became my pal, I relaxed enough to enjoy myself. I had never been to Africa, and when I could finally contact him, I told Bob about the towering ruins of Luxor and the fluid, rhythmic dancing of the natives, the exotic eating and riding on camels, and the odd, colorful cultural mores. Everywhere the First Lady went, not only was she not vilified, but she was adored; the people cheered wildly for "Hillaree, Hillaree."

This is just what she needed, I thought, to see the plethora of poverty-stricken women who worshipped her, the people she had helped by championing microcredit loans that allowed them to start small businesses. This was probably why she got out of Washington, out of a country where a good many blamed her for not asserting her militant imperative. Feminist that I was, I wondered what the First Lady of the nation was supposed to do—get on a platform and wave a placard demanding Bill's head? I personally admired her for her dignity and restraint, for putting aside her pride for the sake of the president of the United States. Hillary was like Bob: she knew the right thing to do.

I couldn't say the same for a couple of the reporters on the plane who seemed irritated by my presence. I wondered what their fantasies about me were. Did they think I was a spy in disguise? Well, actually, in a way I was. Did they think I wanted to sneak in a one-on-one with Hillary? Well, actually, I did.

One day, we got the news that Hillary was about to make her first trip back to the press bay. Everyone bustled to their seats. I saw someone's leg come out but not quick enough, not before I had fallen flat on the floor. I managed to get up and settle myself into place before the First Lady appeared at the door. She strode confidently down the aisle, nodding, saying bright hellos, a queen dispensing acknowledgment to her subjects. Rubbing my knee, I pasted on a happy smile. When she got to me, she stopped. "Everything all right?" she asked, patting my hand. "Oh, fine!" I chirped, and she continued on. I don't know which of us was the better actor.

Her minions, meanwhile, kept me hanging. By the last stop, in Marrakech, they were giving me an enigmatic conspiratorial "shh" whenever I asked about this elusive interview. There must have been some reason I was there. Was it Hillary who was stalling? Did she have something to say but was reluctant to say it?

For the next months I kept being invited to accompany the First Lady here and there. I certainly was collecting color, vital for any kind of story on her. Once, the two of us were in the back of a limousine, and she was talking away about social policy. She had put on a crisp beige suit, her hair styled to look windblown, and clearly, behind her chatter, she was thinking about something else. I wondered how she couldn't have sensed my anxiety; it seemed so palpable to me. We were on drastically different wavelengths. Bill's behavior seemed the furthest thing from her mind (or maybe it wasn't), and I sensed if I brought it up now, I could blow it.

The ring of her car phone startled us both. She took it from the mount on the window frame and spoke emphatically: "Do the plastic leg braces hurt? Oh, good. Well, I plan to come out to see him when all this is over." When she hung up, I raised my eyebrows questioningly and she hesitated. Then she said an emphatic "Okay, I'll tell you, but I don't want you to write about it, because I don't want him to be deluged by reporters." Some time ago, she recounted, she made a speech to disabled children and their parents: "There was this little boy with big brown eyes looking up at me and he was just irresistible, so I picked him up. I couldn't believe how heavy he was, and then I saw the metal braces on his legs. I didn't want to put him down, though I thought I was going to do something worse and drop him. Which I didn't. We became friends, and I paid for polyurethane braces and several leg operations. I go to visit him as often as I can." Her voice was wavering.

Because she was a probable Senate candidate, I was startled that she would wave off publicity that would contradict her image as cold and calculating. "I won't have him deluged by reporters," she repeated. There was a brilliant intensity in the eyes of this Wellesley grad who couldn't be ruffled.

Bob, as well as Tina, was astounded that I hadn't yet nailed the interview. "Sounds like they're playing with you," Bob warned. "You're going to lose the exclusive," Tina weighed in. This had never happened to me in my decades of journalism. I was flying without a parachute, at the mercy of the Clintons. I didn't even know the rules.

Finally, at the very last minute, I pounced. Two months after her trip to North Africa, I was accompanying her to Northern Ireland. The woman had reinvented herself: svelte, clad in Oscar de la Renta, hair bobbed, a youthful bounce in her walk. After being praised in Belfast for helping bring peace to the province, however, she repaired to the plane and immediately took to her bed.

Oh no you don't, I thought; it's showtime, Hillary. I took a deep breath, insisted to a factotum that this was my last chance to interview her, and then stood by her bedroom door until she came out. I could see rumpled bedclothes inside, but she greeted me graciously, pillow marks on her cheek, circles under her eyes. We sat down side by side across from her press people, and I turned on the tape recorder; because of the roar of the engines below us, no matter how they cocked their ears, they didn't seem able to get a word of our conversation. I like to think she planned it that way, for if they had heard what she was telling me, they surely would have stopped her cold.

We sipped tea in silence for a few minutes. Then I got into it slowly, telling her about my father's addiction to alcohol. "How did you deal with that?" she asked. I told her I hadn't, really, and elaborated on all the frustration, longing, and sense of failure. Then I asked her how she was dealing with her husband's addiction.

She paused and considered. "It makes me angry. It makes me really angry," and I could see the anger in the set of her mouth. "Were you mad at your father?" she asked. I told her I was, my whole life. "Well, I don't want to be angry all the time, but this was such a shock. I thought Bill was cured. We talked to so many professionals; we went to a psychiatrist."

She was controlled, and her sentences were simple and unadorned, so different from the lavish way she talked to her audiences. I asked her when she thought Bill's sexual addiction began. Did she know about it when they married?

She shook her head no and then became more animated as she started to talk about his mother. She sat up and looked at me with a disarming intensity. "She was a doozy. Did you ever see her? . . ."

"Did she influence Bill?" I asked.

"In ways you wouldn't believe."

"What do you mean?" I replied.

"He was abused. When a mother does what she does, it affects you forever . . . I am not going into it, but I'll say that when this happens in children, it scars you . . . you keep looking in all the wrong places for the parent who abused you."

•

Later, we talked about her marriage. "Will you stay with him?" I asked.

"Yes, there's love between us, still. But how we'll stay together, I don't know. He's responsible for his own life, and he's going to have to live it the way he wants. I can't be part of that anymore," she said crisply. "He can live his life, and I'm going to live *mine.*"

So this was how Hillary was going to deal with Bill's betrayal. This was how she could accept it and put it all back together.

This addictive act by him, it wasn't about them, Bill and Hillary, but about this other thing outside them, this dysfunction that happened long ago and haunted him still, this calamity of which they were victims. She had spent all this time reasoning it out, and it had a certain validity. Using me, she was closing the Monica narrative in her own way, before she stepped out into the voyeuristic electorate and ran for the Senate. And after all, the last word belonged to her.

But I knew she had told me more than she should have.

As Hillary talked to me, her face had been a prism of competing feelings—anger, determination, compassion, even some native Midwestern naïveté. It had been assumed she knew about Monica long before the public did, but I found her look of bewilderment genuine.

I saw her mind working, watched an idea form. What she really seemed to want to do was forgive Bill in front of the world. And at the same time, be forgiven herself; regain the respect she had lost when, in her humiliation, she did not leave him. She was finding a way to take them both off the victim list.

Though she had strongly implied Bill's childhood abuse, she had not given me concrete examples. Had the national mania about Bill's adultery—fellatio in a bathroom near the Oval Office, the stain of his semen on Monica's dress, all the intimate details no man, surely not the president of the United States, would want plastered over every newspaper in the world—run its course, I would have wanted to publish my whole interview with Hillary. But in the current climate, the impact of what the First Lady had said could be considerable. I was having doubts.

I had hardly gotten off the plane in New York when I found out that Hillary's people had called Harvey Weinstein, the owner of *Talk* and its parent company, Miramax, and pressured him to kill my story. Well connected in Washington and bound to be shunned by Bill's friends over this article, to Harvey's everlasting credit, he refused.

I thought about the impact of what Hillary had said about Bill's mother. She had declined to give me details. Moreover, abuse is a nonspecific concept that can refer to any number of behaviors, some more severe than others. In any event, it was not Bill's memory; it was Hillary's— and she wasn't even there.

So, for the article, I wrote up only part of the interview that she had given me on the plane and described the abusive atmosphere in the president's childhood home and the constant conflict between his mother and his grandmother over him.

•

On August 3, 1999, while the family was vacationing in Paris, Bob walked to the news store, paid for his *Herald Tribune*, and then saw my name in the headlines of every paper on the shelf. He rushed back to our rented apartment with *Der Spiegel* and other magazines.

"*Talk* is out," he said, giving me copies of *Der Spiegel, Izvestia, Oggi.* "Your interview has been picked up everywhere." He turned on the TV, and there was a newscaster interviewing Tina Brown about the cover article. Of course, though I had a multitude of interesting quotations from my many interviews with Hillary, the "abuse" paragraph, demurely buried in the middle of the article, was the one seized upon.

"You better go home!" Bob exclaimed.

I didn't really want to go. I had been drawing cows with their swishing tails at a château; France was lovely and languorous, and I didn't want to jump back into the hurricane that would now be my New York.

"Go," Bob repeated firmly. "Not tomorrow. Now!"

So I did and was met at the airport by *Good Morning America.* For days, it was a constant round of congratulatory media interviews of all sorts—from national TV to college radio stations.

The magazine sold a million copies. "Your article has put us on the map," Tina said. "And it's only the first issue."

But what happened next was inevitable; the media are kingmakers who have to bring down the king. Once the press got over their admiration for my coup, bloggers from all colors of the political rainbow started bashing me. Some liberals complained about my portraying the First Lady as an antifeminist, thereby damaging her chances in the upcoming race for senator from New York, and others thought I was a servant who had done her bidding.

One prominent online magazine headlined its hatchet job "Will Tina Fire Lucinda? . . . Re: Franks Scandal." And then came the deepest cut of all, from my journalistic home, *The New York Times.* The editorial page editor, Howell Raines, though presenting the highlights of the article almost admiringly, condemned it as "militantly laudatory and unanalytic." All I focused on were those two derogatory adjectives. Then my well-meaning friend Gene Anderson, husband of Bob's daughter Jenny, sent me a plaque with the *Times* editorial embedded in metal typeface. "Not many authors generate *NY Times* editorials," Gene wrote, in his big generous scrawl.

For days, I sat in my hot, empty apartment, certain that I had become a pariah in my profession.

I knew that if my full interview had been published, which made Bill's weakness for a certain kind of woman more understandable, Hillary's words might have seemed less like a lame excuse for her husband and the article might have been more compelling. Still, I did not regret the judgment call we had made.

In the end, Hillary's press spokesperson confirmed the veracity of my story, and the president himself didn't deny what Hillary had said. Even better, my family returned. The kids brought noise and hugs and long narratives about what I had missed in Paris. And Bob rescued me. "It's all bullshit," he said. "They're jealous; they're trying to undercut you. You got the only interview she's given about Lewinsky. People like to shoot the messenger. They might take exception to what Hillary said, but you reported it—what you could report—accurately."

Still, the nasty blogs kept coming, and I was drawn to them like an insect to the jaws of a Venus flytrap. Finally, my husband lost patience.

He stole my computer.

For days, I was cut off from the e-mails of my supporters—and my tormentors. I heard that some of the Clinton people were whispering to reporters that I might have fabricated what Hillary had said. They wanted me strung up.

The denouement to my little drama came several weeks after publication. It was late August, and I was walking through a heavy fog on the beach in Martha's Vineyard. All of a sudden a chocolate-colored Labrador retriever bounded out from the miasma, and holding the leash was Hillary Clinton. We both stopped dead. Although I had talked well of her to the media, I had never heard from her about the article. Finally, she smiled at me.

"Well, we've both been getting a lot of publicity, haven't we?" she said pleasantly, and we both laughed. And then, following the pull of the Labrador, she was gone.

23

"Watch out!"
  "I saw the car, sweetheart."
  "There was no indication of that," he growled.

•

I love to drive, and you love it too because it allows you to let your secret autocrat out for air. I hold my tongue. I can't snap back at you now. You are depressed, and I am alarmed. You almost never do depression, invested as you are in being calm and even-tempered. Seeing you sinking is like watching the Titanic going down. With me on deck. You are my strength, my anchor.

  I have been behind the wheel just an hour, traveling north out of the city, to Buttermilk Falls Inn—that is, if we can find it. We always do something special for our anniversary, and tomorrow, November 19, 2000, will be our twenty-third. We should be enjoying the cool fresh air, the mellow voice of Cat Stevens cradling us in our old blue Toyota, but the car just feels stuffy.

  The rare times you are out of sorts, you don't moon about as I do; you become churlish, cranky. You won't seek comfort from me, for I am the only place where you can put your displaced feelings.

  I feel what you feel . . . as well as gnawing remorse. I set you off. First, there was the impassable mound of wet towels on the bathroom floor, which didn't go unnoticed, and of course our nighttime battle over the temperature in the room.

  Me: I couldn't sleep; I was too hot.

  You: No you weren't.

Me: Oh, were you inside my body?

You: Unfortunately, no. But it was below sixty in here. You couldn't have been hot.

Me: I was hot, Bob.

You: You weren't hot.

Me: Oh my God, whenever you want something to be true, it is true.

After that, a weekly newspaper was delivered, and in it a journalist we didn't know had called you "frail, slow and out of touch with the people."

"You are not frail," I said. Screw that lousy reporter. "You've got a big chest and good biceps. I ought to know. And the violent crime you've reduced. How many people who would have been murdered ten years ago are living 'cause of you? Five hundred twenty-five, is it?"

"Five hundred thirty-six."

After that, things got even worse. Your new hearing aid went on the fritz. Now voices came through to you as if through a tunnel, the words blending together. Poor you, you asked me to repeat things twice, even three times, and I lost my temper and barked it out or enunciated extremely slowly as if I were a schoolteacher with a toddler. You winced and I felt like an asshole.

When this kind of exchange would happen, I'd keep my vow never to react like that—until I didn't keep it and the cycle would begin all over again. "You act like I'm purposely not hearing you," you would say, and you'd be angry. "You think I like not being able to hear what people say?"

What was wrong with me? I had learned to be patient with the deaf people in my family, but something about your hearing loss is different, more threatening. As though you were taking a step away from me.

I would do anything to lift you up now.

·

"That reporter must have been some enemy with a grudge," I said as we barreled across the Newburgh–Beacon Bridge on Route 84. "By the way, I've been meaning to tell you that my girlfriends have been confessing they have crushes on you. Really. Jill thinks you're unbearably cute, Lila said you're smarter than anyone except her husband, and Blair, well, Blair thinks you're very hot," I said. "And she loves your creative way of getting the bad guys. She thinks there ought to be a statue of you in Riverside Park, next to Eleanor Roosevelt."

"That's the last thing I want."

"Well, sweetie," I said, turning off the music and making my voice loud and clear. "No one deserves it like you do. Just think of the innocent children whose lives would have been ruined without you. The pundits who criticize you for ignoring street crime for white-collar crime, they're idiots. They don't get the picture; they don't know that closing down banks that trade with big narcotics dealers protects schoolchildren. And the terrorists you've caught! Those you uncovered while investigating BCCI, for one thing. Then there are all those guys on death row, innocent guys, who didn't go to the electric chair because you found ways not to charge them with murder one. You—Bob Morgenthau, one man—have set a million legal precedents because you wouldn't be intimidated."

"Are you writing my obituary?" he asked dryly.

"In the words of your father, nobody likes a wise-ass, or I should say a W.A.," I teased.

"For God's sakes, keep your eyes on the road! You're riding the shoulder."

•

Maybe I can go through the details of some of your best cases, be a mirror for the success you really are. You always refuse to tell reporters your favorite case. You say, "Each one is important to the victim." But I know what things you particularly hate: rape, elder abuse, and being told you can't win. This year has been a particularly good year for all three.

•

"Just look at the impossible prosecutions you did this year," I said, as my speed leaped over the limit, "the Kimes murder convictions and the indictment of a rapist's DNA footprint. The cases are so symmetrical. One without the body of the victim and the other without the body of the criminal! As though Balanchine had choreographed it or Ovid had put it in an ode. 'It's a beautiful thing,' as Lila would say."

"Okay, okay," he groaned, but less strongly. He loved my exuberance; the sillier I got, the better.

"I'm just so proud of you; I want to pull over and put my arms around you."

"Don't!"

He leaned over. "There's Route 32. Take a left."

"I'm in the process of doing that. And I know where we're going."

"Ha," he grunted. "You've gone steaming through intersections in every town from Bordeaux to Athens. Remember Alsace, when we went thirty miles out of our way? And the county in the west of Ireland where we almost drove off a cliff into the Atlantic Ocean?"

I started chuckling and didn't stop, and then he grudgingly started too. "Nobody knows what I have to contend with in my personal driver."

Then his smile turned to a frown again. He bit into a fresh Stayman apple picked from our trees. "No, it was really terrible." He gave a little shake of his head and kept munching.

"Who are you talking about, sweetheart? Not me?"

"No!" he said. "What they did to this Irene Silverman."

"Oh!" That was the "no body" conviction. A mother-son team named Kimes had murdered and stolen their way across the country, and nobody had been able to catch them. Then they came to New York, wormed their way into the life of an eighty-two-year-old lady named Irene Silverman, and killed her for her money. Unfortunately for them, their "perfect crime"—they had disposed of the corpse so well, nobody could find a trace of it—landed in the jurisdiction of my husband, who loved such impossible cases.

"What really went on in the office on that one?" I asked. "No, really, I can't remember the details."

"We didn't have a case. There was no body, no confessions, no eyewitnesses, no bloodstains, no overturned chairs or weapons in the drainpipes, no physical evidence at all. Some in the office didn't want to indict the Kimes duo. They seemed like reasonably normal people who just didn't know where Silverman had gone."

"So how did you persuade everyone again?"

"I knew they'd killed her," he said, talking with a little animation now, "but we had no way of proving it. We searched for a body in every disposal site in four states. Nothing. I put four assistants and seventeen detectives working full-time, and they found stun guns, duct tape, handcuffs, knockout pills, and records of offshore bank accounts. The circumstantial evidence was wild."

"Oh yes, yes, it was so strong," I pealed.

"The Kimeses had convinced the old lady's staff to give them her Social Security number, then they got her ID and credit cards and forged her handwriting. Sante Kimes dressed up in a red wig and frilly nightgown and told a notary she was Mrs. Silverman," Bob said, laughing. "So he stamped the document, and all at once they held the deed to her eight-million-dollar town house. That property was what they wanted, why they killed her."

Bob's ADAs had interviewed four hundred witnesses—from the notary to friends to maids—and they got a unique verdict. From how I saw it, it was a homicide proved entirely by inference.

"The public didn't know it, the newspapers never got hold of this, but the FBI nearly ruined the game. Halfway into the investigation, they decided to butt in and question the witnesses we had gathered. If a witness like the notary told one story to the DA and a slightly different one to the FBI, he'd be thrown out of court. I called Louis Freeh, you know who he was, the director of the FBI, and Freeh told FBI New York to 'stand back.'"

•

He was better, my poor baby. But I was still so nervous—would it last?—I felt as if I had nothing under me but the gas pedal. In fact, I'd just run a red light; fortunately, he hadn't noticed.

•

"How much time did they get?"

"Kenneth Kimes got 130 years to life and his mother, 127½ years to life," he declared.

"It led to a landslide of convictions, right? Letting the worst murderers, the ones smart enough to erase all the evidence, know that they'd go down anyway."

"Some time later," Bob said, nodding, "we had a doctor who had thrown his wife out of a plane into the ocean. He remarried, relocated, had a child, and thought he was scot-free. It took us twelve years, but we got him. We had at least twenty-two more cases like that."

"Wow, your memory always astonishes me, much better than mine."

"No, you're wrong. I can't remember half what I used to."

•

You are feeling your age. But you are determined to stay alive. No more steaks, no more pasta, only a tiresomely healthy regimen to keep yourself trim and well. People become impatient with your partial deafness, but what is it like for you to hear not a thing at a crowded party and to even be unable to join the conversation at small gatherings because you don't know what people are talking about? I can imagine you working so strenuously to hear the strategic nuances of your bureau chiefs' debates and thanking God that you will be able to guess what they are going to say before they say it. Working harder than anyone else, only to read a news essay headlined "Is Morgy Really Up to the Job?"

I wanted to go out and announce to the city, "He's sharper than any of you."

•

"You know you're the only one in the family who's always right," I said. "You know that, don't you? It doesn't matter whether it's directions to an inn or a criminal case, it's uncanny—the way you not only do the right thing, morally, but you get the little daily things right."

"I'm not smart. You're the smart one."

"Why would you ever think that?" I asked.

"Because I'm stupid, that's why," he said, his voice again taking on the timbre of Eeyore.

I started to hyperventilate. "Sweetheart, did you forget that you set a second precedent? Like getting a rape indictment against something you can only see through a laboratory microscope?"

"You mean the East Side rapist? I suppose so."

In March 2000, Bob's office brought the first case against a rapist known only by his "DNA footprint." The tool of DNA became widely used by prosecutors in 1994; it not only convicted criminals but freed the innocent. This rapist, who had terrorized the city's East Side and victimized at least sixteen women in five years, had left his DNA all over the place. But nobody could catch him or even identify who he was.

"We had the DNA evidence for a conviction but no suspect to pair it with. And you know, there's that five-year statute of limitations on most rape in the state of New York that I've been trying to get changed for years; I was afraid it would run out before the rapist was caught. So I indicted the DNA." He finally looked pleased with himself.

"Wow, yes, how brilliant."

"Well, it just infuriated me that murder, kidnapping, major drug sales, and even arson, they're A felonies with no time limit on prosecution, but rape, which is one of the worst of all crimes, is a B felony with a short statute of limitations."

"The rape statute is sexist. And damn unjust." He was over it. He was high now, and so I was high too.

"We argued that rape did more permanent damage than any crime except murder and that if we indicted this rapist now, that indictment would stand no matter when he was caught." And the grand jury agreed.

"I'm so proud of you for that, Tart. There's no one who sticks up for women like you. I love you even more than I did twenty-four years ago."

"You don't think I'm an old fart? Past my prime?"

"Are you kidding? You're eighty-one going on sixty. That's what your doctor says."

And after we arrived at the inn and climbed into our regal Victorian bed, the doctor would have been gratified to see he was right.

That afternoon, we went down to the lake to sit back in the Adirondack chairs, Bob to read *Barron's* and me to crack open *The Screwtape Letters* by C. S. Lewis.

•

Oh hell, I can't read this boring Christian character study of the devil. I believe in Christ but I also consider myself a Jew who aspires to do good. I'm hankering to dip into my latest spy novel. But what is this? Your chair is empty! Where are you, why didn't you say where you were going? The minutes crawl by. Now it's almost an hour. I can't concentrate on Red Gold *and the exploits of Furst's hero, Jean Casson, either. What if you are still depressed, what if something terrible is happening to you that you didn't want me to see? I feel panicked, hands turning to ice . . .*

Oh, there! There you are! Coming down the hill. Very slow and deliberate . . . bowlegged . . . like a cowboy. Surely, that isn't a gun in your hand?

But you're getting closer, and now I see it's a bunch of wildflowers! Blue salvia, white blooms like daisies, ferns, tall curvy grasses, and something with scarlet berries.

•

"I picked these for you," he says with that shy little smile that slices into me. It is a beautiful wild autumn bouquet. He sees my face. "Don't worry," he says quickly, "I'm fine. Thanks to my wife." He is pleased, happy, himself again. Thank God. Leaning into him, I can feel the blissful warmth of his body, and he knows it will become my warmth too.

•

One day not long after our anniversary, my father came to the farm. He sat at the dining table, blowing smoke rings for the benefit of the kids. He was taking his time telling us how he crept through the enemy-infested jungles of Guadalcanal. "The men in my unit were following the sound of these faint screams, which got louder and louder until we saw what was happening in a clearing ahead. They were women, screaming. The Japs had tied these women to trees and were using them for bayonet practice." My father looked down for a minute, and when he looked up, there was the pain, the same pain I saw when not so long ago I would walk out of a room to avoid him. Jarring pain for such a dead-pan face: a plea in his furrowed brows, his silvery-blue eyes swimming behind his thick glasses, the half-moon of his smile gone dull. "They were nuns and they were naked, some dead and some still alive, and they were covered in blood. We were only ten . . . we were outnumbered . . . there was nothing we could do about it but watch."

Then he slapped his tobacco pouch angrily down on the table. "I'd never heard of anything like this. These weren't the goddamn enemy; they were nuns!"

Everyone was silent. The kids looked dazed; I should have seen the gruesomeness of the story coming and told them to go outside, but I was obsessed with knowing every detail of what Dad had done in the war. And the rare times he felt like talking, you just had to freeze where you were and listen.

I started to ask a question when Bob interrupted. "I had some experience with that," he said quietly. "We had a perpetrator who raped this nun repeatedly and then took a nail file and carved twenty-seven crosses on her body. She was so psychologically damaged—nightmares, phobias—that she was under constant psychiatric care."

"I hope you got the monster who did it," Dad said.

"Oh, we got him all right," Bob said, an uncharacteristic tremor in his voice. We all stared at him. I couldn't help but think of the story he always told reporters: "I never get emotionally involved in a case."

"We wanted to spare her the trauma of testifying," he continued. "So we plea-bargained. He was sentenced to ten to twenty years and was publicly registered as a sex offender for life."

My father nodded slowly at his son-in-law. "You can't forget it when you see a thing like that, Bob."

At eighty-seven, Dad was still a tall, straight, poker-faced gentleman who, like my husband, was a protégé of Zeno's. Stoics both, they were men who never shared what was bothering them, and with only six years separating them, they got along like brothers.

That was fine with me because the last thing I wanted was to feel my father's pain. Unfortunately, I had to see it on his face anyway as it was almost exclusively directed at me, the furrowed entreating brows, the longing in his big eyes. He wanted what we hadn't had since I was a child: a real relationship.

But I couldn't. I would avoid him, drifting out of a room as soon as he came in. I would lie in bed in the morning and listen to him talk to Bob until he'd say "Where's the sleeping princess?" and I knew I had to make an appearance. When alone with him, I felt I was talking to someone behind a glass window on one of those maximum-security prison phones. I tried to be friendly, affectionate, but I just couldn't do it. He hadn't been there for me since adolescence, when he was seldom home and never present when he was home.

I felt that he loved me for my money. After his steel business went belly-up when I was in my early twenties, he became an alcoholic and spent his savings not on rent, utilities, or nutritious food but on booze and boy toys—the newest Glock pistol or .25-caliber handgun for his championship silhouette shooting. We had a cycle going. He would let his bills pile up until his lights were cut off or he was about to be evicted so I would have to rush in and save the day. I was his enabler, no doubt about it, and I loathed the role. One day, I found all the news articles and notes I had sent him for years unopened. He had apparently just tossed them aside. I realized much later that though he loved my successes, they made him feel even more of a failure.

I felt that the order of the universe was upside down here; the father I was supposed to have was in actuality my child.

I had become intrigued, however, when in 1990 my father confided that he had helped liberate Ohrdruf, the first concentration camp discovered by the Allies. He had told a friend that what he had seen there he had never gotten over. Bob and I persuaded him to give testimony to Bob's Museum of Jewish Heritage. Hundreds of survivors had made taped confessions of their experiences for the museum, but few Christians had stepped up, and they were the Holocaust witnesses who would be judged as particularly impartial and believable.

But then I forgot about Ohrdruf until one day I was helping Dad clean out the cartons that had remained unpacked in his apartment since my mother had died fourteen years before. Under the pastel silk nightgowns Mom loved to wear, I pulled out strange things—a yellowed, old handwritten silk map, a trick compass, and then a military cap with skull and crossbones, a symbol of the Nazi Party.

I was completely confused. Had he been a Nazi sympathizer? Had this been the reason for his mysterious, detached behavior at home?

He stubbornly refused to talk about them. "I took an oath of silence," he would say over and over again, like a POW telling the enemy only name, rank, and serial number. This set me on a six-year quest to find out who he really was. I took out all my reporter's tricks and strategies to tease information out of him. It became a contest between us—one that ironically brought us emotionally closer. I put things together: his deadpan demeanor; his ability as a crack marksman who won trophies into his eighties; his photographic memory; his ability to quickly master languages and any new skill; his fluent German; the guns he had hid around the house, even one under my bed; the game of "writing smaller" we had played that he had learned as a secret courier delivering messages so small he could swallow them if threatened with capture.

I was so consumed by this process of reinventing my father, of revising my history of him; in one sense he had balanced out my life, even saved it, the only person who was consistently kind and accepting of me. But I knew the flaw that had led him to fail in life had condemned me too; no matter how much I had succeeded outside, inside a bad egg begets a bad egg. But perhaps neither of us was bad inside at all.

It was a race against time. After years of abusing his body with alcohol, pipes, and cigarillos, my father had gotten both Alzheimer's and lung cancer. He was losing his short-term memory while remembering events of the past clearly and in detail. I drove the three hours to Milford every weekend to visit him, often bringing Amy, whose intelligence, huge smile, and Alice in Wonderland hair he loved. She was the only one who could get him to shed his holey bathrobe and don street clothes. It was she whom he now called "my little princess."

Bob did everything to help me in my quest. He got Dad's military records through Congressman Charlie Rangel to see if he had been assigned to the areas where recorded sabotage missions took place. Then, armed with information, I would try to find evidence of his spy activities in the National Archives.

I eventually found out he had been an intelligence agent attached to different spy agencies, mainly the OSS, the nation's chief World War II intelligence agency. He had taught the French Resistance about guns and explosives, posed as a Nazi and shot a German guard, broke into Gestapo headquarters and stole secret documents, and, another little detail that shocked me, was an assassin. When he finally forgot that he was supposed to forget, the missions tumbled out of him, and we sat side by side, my head on his shoulder, as I scribbled away.

I was flabbergasted. How could my father ever have gotten over doing what he did during the war? He had been made to witness and even commit atrocities no human being should. He kept it all a secret, protecting his family as well as his oath of silence. Those guns around the house were not the work of a paranoid but a way of safeguarding his family from threats of reprisal.

I visited him nearly every weekend as he descended into Alzheimer's, ministering to him, cuddling up to him. It was the first time since I was thirteen that we had been this close, shared the love we had missed all those years. Our alienation from each other, which had lasted from my adolescence through my adulthood, slowly fell away. I became that child in his arms watching the stars through his big white telescope, falling in love with him all over again. Starved of my respect for so long, he eagerly embraced my attentions. We spent the last two years of his life together. It was more than just a resolution of our relationship; it was a resurrection, too spirit-driven, too circular, to be accidental. My early passion for Jesus Christ, the gentle friend of children, the maker of miracles, rose up from the weakness of my faith. He had been buried deep within me, much as my father had. When Dad finally became real, almost sacred to me, so God did in a way he never had before.

•

When, in 2001, Dad finally entered a hospital and then a nursing home, Amy, eleven, and Joshua, seventeen, visited him often, talking to him tenderly, responding respectfully to his nonsense sentences. At the end, besides me, they were the only ones he recognized, the ones for whom he clumsily tried to flap his hands like wings. How could he forget the little girl who could persuade him to do anything, who now would bring him her teddy bears, or the little boy who every morning raced with him out to his washtub moth trap to see if they'd caught a great willow-green luna? Josh was a talented art major at Yale, and he did a series of line drawings of him that so brilliantly captured Daddy's confusion and pain, as well as his love for us, that the best one still hangs on my study wall.

When he died, God must not have cared a whit about his atheism. His eyes were a hauntingly bright blue, and they were trained on something in the distance. I had never seen him look so surprised. And after he drew his last breath, the hint of a smile, a trace of happy irony, settled on his inscrutable face.

On the phone, my sister and I decided that Dad would not have wanted a funeral, just a simple cremation. When I hung up, my husband gave me a grave look. "We're going to give him a proper send-off." So, as I looked on in surprise, Bob called up the commander of the *Intrepid* navy carrier, docked in New York Harbor, and planned a full military funeral on the ship.

Penny came out for the service, and we had a rabbi say Kaddish—I thought my father would like that. There were pictures of him in dress uniform and wearing fatigues in various combat zones. Patriotic songs were taped in, and at the end the mourners, composed of our friends and a few of Dad's, stepped outside on the windy deck. Salute rifles were slowly fired by marines ten times, report after report echoing off the water, a bugle played a rich, poignant taps, and the American flag was folded and presented to me. I turned and gave it to Penny. Tears were streaming down our faces as a wreath of flowers was hurled overboard and made its way out to the Atlantic Ocean.

Bob's love for my dad was never more abundantly or publicly expressed. He had even arranged a burial at sea. A Coast Guard boat took us out to the Statue of Liberty, where we opened a bottle of champagne and toasted him for the last time. We said our goodbyes, and then Josh and my nephew Luke emptied the urn over the turbulent water. My father, stubborn to the last, came sailing right back, covering the boys in a gritty gray powder. Once our horror abated, we began to laugh. Daddy's humor, still at work.

Earlier, I watched as his still-warm body was zipped into a rubbery black bag and hoisted over the funeral men's shoulders like a sack of potatoes. I began to feel an agonizing wave of remorse for all those years I shunned him; my lazy failure to give him a second chance, to find out who he really was until it was almost too late. Walking to my car, I thought what a waste it was—I would never see him again.

I got into my Volvo, turned on the ignition, and my CD of Bob Dylan came on. He was singing "Girl from the North Country," a ballad about lost love that was Dad's favorite. As I pulled out of the hospital parking lot, gulping back tears, all at once I slammed on the brakes. There was Dad, incorporeal, sitting in the passenger's seat, rhythmically tapping his knee. He grinned at me, and I heard him say, "Remember how I used to play this song over and over? Until I couldn't work my tape player anymore?"

An indescribable warmth spread through me. He had returned, or at least that's how it felt. For several weeks, Penny and I both felt his presence, and we were inexplicably happy, oddly forgiven. We had the sense he wasn't letting us mourn him. The very opposite of the anger and guilt we felt when our mother died.

Now, more than a decade later, sometimes when I'm driving—an activity Dad and I both found relaxing—I feel, rather than see, a rainbow at the left corner of my windshield. It is always followed by the impression of a smile, a voice: "Don't worry, I'm watching over you."

Are these visions spiritual? My father really talking from the beyond? Or are they the voice of Bob, his earthly presence beside me? For nearly half my life, Bob had schooled me in accepting myself, in trying to purge the useless remorse that comes from looking back. It has been through him that I grew to recognize my father, to listen and learn from him as Bob had done.

As time clutters the mind, cause and effect are blurred. You forget why you hate, why what happened, happened. Is the voice of my dad a dream, a salmagundi of memory, a commingling of the living and the dead? Or do I even need to know?

.

"Wow, look at this!" I held up an old blue letter, tissue thin, sent to my mother from abroad. "He did love her after all! See, the whole page is covered with 'I love you, I love you.'" I was beside myself at the discovery of a bundle of war correspondence to Mom hidden in his closet. When a child, in vain, I had made prayer books promising God perfect behavior if he would bring them together. Though a little late, my prayers had been answered.

I couldn't stop reading the letters aloud to my husband. "He's a different person in these letters! I think this shows that Dad had some kind of post-traumatic disorder after the war. He was totally different before— jolly, full of ambition, playing pranks. He even carried an iguana named Oscar on his shoulder! The war! World War II! That's why he disappeared inside a shell, like you, except his was a lot more severe."

"Okay, I'm trying to eat my oatmeal without a lot of talk," Bob said.

"But don't you see that this *proves* the war changed him? It took away that joyousness that is in these letters."

"I have a project for you. Write a book about him."

I smiled and nodded. I had already thought of this. I had decided over time that I could turn this very private discovery into something that might help people understand the veterans of World War II who had never talked about their crippling experiences and lived repressed, often haunted lives. I had even asked Dad to give me his blessing. "Why me?" was his response. "I didn't do anything more than what others did." It was the stock answer of these humble World War II veterans who had sacrificed everything for their country. I argued with him until finally he gave in. "Oh, all right," he said with a half smile. "You'll do what you want to do anyway." He was right.

24

On September 11, 2001, at 5:15 in the evening, Bob walked through the door and time stopped. Smudged with smoke and soot, he dropped his pile of files, and I put my arms around his shoulders. We held on to each other in silence.

"There was a cloud of debris and dust just sitting in the middle of our street, I don't know why," Bob began. "Sid Asch had come in with debris in his hair, in his eyebrows . . . he was completely disoriented. We put him in the shower, cleaned him up, and had the detectives drive him home." Poor Sid, he was the man who had married us.

I peeled off his coat as Bob talked incessantly, so unlike him. The state courthouse was only a third of a mile from the Twin Towers, as were the federal courts. "The feds ordered the courts closed, but we got air purifiers and we stayed open, that's why I'm so late. I wanted to send a message to looters. It wasn't going to be open season."

"You must be exhausted," I said, giving him a glass of water. "Sit down, sweetheart. Tell me everything."

And so he did. Story after story of heroism that emerged from the disaster.

"A great ADA named Karen Friedman, she was trapped on the fourth floor of her apartment building directly across from the towers, with her two four-year-old twin boys. The electricity was off, the elevator stopped, the staircases blocked. The air was thick with debris; there was the sound of explosions. She called the fire and the police departments, who couldn't help her, and then she called her father in Oregon to say goodbye," Bob said, close to tears. "Her father was a Holocaust survivor and told her not to give up, the family were survivors. Then she thought of calling another ADA, Micki Shulman, who rushed over through the blinding white smoke and got her and the children out. Micki is not much taller than about five feet."

If Bob was seeing redemption, I was seeing death and destruction. Like so many Americans, I remained upset for weeks about the mind-numbing event in lower Manhattan. At first, I was fixated on images of big planes coming in droves to topple apartment buildings. I volunteered at the Compassion Center, comforting families, some of them Muslims, even helping them tack pictures of their kin on telephone poles in the vain hope someone had seen them wandering about dazed. Though the people of the city had made it a gentler place, at least for now I felt sick and anxious most of the time. Nothing helped.

Until one day when I was on the Lower East Side buying the chewy homemade bialys Bob loved and saw a man in black robes. Suddenly I remembered the case of the extremist rabbi Meir Kahane, who was murdered by an anti-Israeli terrorist. I remembered Bob told me something about the World Trade Center in that case, something that had been suppressed, that the public didn't even know about. I hurried home and took out of my file cabinet the journals I had filled for years, peeling off the rubber bands that held them together, spreading them out, and finally locating a notebook labeled "Terrorism—1989–1991."

I began skimming and stopped when I came to two entries.

December 1991

Bob has lost an important slam-dunk case. An Arab terrorist named El Sayyid Nosair killed Meir Kahane, the crazy ultraconservative rabbi, on a street in plain sight and was acquitted of murder. Bob is complaining bitterly about the FBI and the police department. Apparently, in Nosair's apartment, they found dozens of boxes full of really damning documents and tapes indicating a big Islamic conspiracy, including vitriolic anti-American tapes by a blind sheikh named Rahman who's a big leader in the conspiracy. There are blueprints and plans of how to bomb U.S. landmarks, including maybe the Twin Towers. But the FBI seized the boxes and wouldn't allow the DA's Office to put them in evidence at Nosair's trial. The police and the FBI kept saying he was just a "lone gunman," and Bob says that's absurd.

The FBI is playing down the significance of all this incredible mate-rial in the boxes. Bob has been trying to get the feds to at least listen to the Rahman tapes, but they're dismissing them, and they haven't even had them translated. The up-to-date DA's Office has an Arabic translator, of course, but the FBI says it doesn't. Bob is furious.

February 1993
    It's happened. The World Trade Center has been bombed. A nightmare. A van in the garage of one of the towers exploded, and six people were killed and many others injured. And the horror is that if the FBI had ever looked in Nosair's boxes and found all the blueprints of places they wanted to blow up like the World Trade Center, this could have been prevented. Un-believable. Is our government just incompetent, or did we have it right in the 1960s? Maybe we weren't silly and paranoid; maybe there really is some dark multinational conspiracy. The FBI should be exposed. Would love to write an article, but of course I can't, with Bob's involvement.

Goose bumps on my arms. I put the notebook down. Had the same terrorists who did the 1993 bombing also committed the mayhem on September 11? Had they upped the ante over the years, systematically exploding targets around the world until, with visions of the Evil Em-pire collapsing, they carried out their supreme act? I did some research and found that the violent Arab bombers and terrorists during the last decade of jihad were all linked. Different groups in Egypt, Saudi Ara-bia, and other Arab countries sometimes fought each other, but mostly they were a united front against America, the baton passing from uncles to nephews, cousins to cousins, fathers to sons. The terrorists who had made the deadly attack on the USS *Cole* in Yemen in 2000 were also involved in the 1993 garage bombing at the World Trade Center. No-sair, though acquitted of murder but convicted on weapons charges in connection with the Kahane assassination, helped plan the bombing from his jail cell.

Most people knew little back then about al-Qaeda and the number and passion of anti-American Muslims. But guess who did? The CIA and the Defense Intelligence Agency (DIA). It started when the agencies gave millions of dollars to Islamic extremists, many from Saudi Arabia, who were supporting the mujahideen trying to oust the Russian-backed regime in Afghanistan. The Islamists were told by the Saudis that if they did a good job, they would be admitted to the United States. When they came to America in the 1980s, still carrying some of the intelligence agency money, the Islamists used the al-Kifah Refugee Center in the al-Farouq Mosque in Brooklyn to build a terrorist cell. Meanwhile, the CIA and the DIA recruited a mounting number of them as informers. The only problem was that many of those informants were to participate in the very bombing attacks they informed the CIA about. The al-Kifah cell grew wiser and more powerful until it had the wherewithal to carry out the 1993 World Trade Center attack. You could say that the U.S. intelligence agencies had become inadvertently complicit in the terrorism they were supposed to be preventing.

What exactly was in those early Nosair boxes? I was flipping through magazines at the library, trying to find articles on terrorism, when I did a double take: here was the most damning of revelations—made by my husband. When he came home, I told him what I had found.

"Of course, if they had listened to you, the Twin Towers tragedies might never have happened," I said to him.

He stared at me, puzzled.

"Remember the Nosair case?" I asked as we sat down to dinner. "Those boxes in his apartment the FBI ignored, the ones that had tapes of the leader of that Egyptian terrorist organization Omar Abdel-Rahman, who urged the bombing of the World Trade Center?

"It was the CIA that ordered the police and the FBI to suppress that evidence, right?" I added.

He shook his head. "The FBI didn't need any encouragement to ignore the boxes. They weren't focused on domestic terrorism. They didn't even have any agent who spoke Arabic. We had hired an Israeli Arab policeman who translated the material."

"I spent two hours researching it, and my head is reeling. I keep imagining this chilling thought. Maybe there are as many terrorists reporting to the CIA as there are to Rahman."

Bob, bent over his soup, kept eating, and I leaned toward him, like the lonely hypotenuse of a right angle, straining for answers he didn't want to give me, a tableau not uncharacteristic of our marriage. He knew his silence would just get me more and more agitated until I gave up.

Why couldn't I just keep my cool? "In fact," I said, steely. "There are hints that Rahman himself was cooperating or pretending to cooperate with the CIA!

"Really, Bob, tell me, didn't the CIA influence the FBI not to examine those boxes in Nosair's apartment? And to put out the false story that Nosair was a lone gunman instead of part of a larger terrorist conspiracy?"

"I don't think the CIA had anything to do with it," he replied dismissively.

"Well," I said quietly, picking up a printout of an article in *New York* magazine of March 1995. "Here you were quoted as saying, 'The FBI lied to me. They're supposed to untangle terrorist connections, but they can't be trusted to do the job.' Then you went on to suggest that the CIA put pressure on the FBI to divert attention away from the terrorists."

"I don't remember saying that." Was he prevaricating or suppressing? Then he added, "I remember the interview; they never even checked the quotes with me."

"The magazine didn't fact-check your quotes?"

I had stumbled on a scoop of mammoth proportions, and I couldn't write about it. In fact, to my knowledge it was never written about, at least not in the mainstream media.

"Bob, I've gathered information about how the intelligence agencies were in bed with al-Qaeda, how we unwittingly encouraged its growth, and how this led to the mayhem at the Twin Towers! And you aren't even interested in talking about it?" I stabbed at my meat but didn't eat it.

"I can't remember all the details!" Bob shot back. Bob's memory was formidable. What was going on? "Call Pat Dugan down in Williamsburg. He tried the Nosair case."

So I left the table and called Dugan.

Dugan confirmed many of my findings. A slow-talking, thoughtful retired ADA, he began by asserting that the Kahane assassination was the beginning of jihad in America. Then he told me more precisely what was in the boxes, claiming he went through seventy-five to a hundred, not the widely printed forty-seven. They included the following:

- CIA manuals on explosives, military tactics, and the use of significant large weapons. Materials to make a bomb that was later found out to be similar to the bomb used in the 1993 World Trade Center bombing.

- Audiotapes, both originals and duplicates, that were distributed throughout al-Farouq of lectures by Rahman about holy wars and the destruction of landmarks, including the obliteration of America's "high buildings."
- Photographs of the World Trade Center at every angle. Tourist shots, pictures looking up, some far away, some from Liberty State Park in New Jersey.

Later, I was to find out that in another of the cartons were instructions for forcible entry into big airplanes.

I asked Dugan if he thought there was a relationship between the earlier World Trade Center attack and the recent one. "That's the million-dollar question," he said, sighing. "The FBI's behavior in ignoring the Nosair evidence definitely led to the '93 bombings. But whether it's possible to then connect the dots to September 11, I just don't know."

I went to the periodical section of the library and found evidence that Nosair, Rahman, and one Ramzi Yousef, who directed the 1993 bombing, and Yousef's uncle Khalid Sheikh Mohammed, the mastermind of 9/11, were intimately connected. In fact, Nosair and Rahman were linked to the Kahane killing as well as the subsequent 1993 World Trade Center bombing. Though Yousef and Nosair were in jail for the latter crime and Rahman was imprisoned on other terrorist charges, it was hard not to draw the conclusion that they, along with other al-Qaeda terrorists, knew about plans for the September 11, 2001, Twin Towers disaster. Indeed, a scheme to use fueled planes to explode government buildings—and specifically CIA headquarters—was found in Yousef's apartment. Rahman, who first urged the bombing of the World Trade Center, had been referred to as the "spiritual leader" of 9/11. A major reason why so many of those conspirators took the risk of communicating with each other is that they knew they could skirt detection by speaking on the telephone in obscure Arabic languages, impenetrable by ill-equipped U.S. intelligence agencies.

The dots connected all right. At least in my mind. The 1993 bombing of the towers, barely investigated by government intelligence agencies, led directly to the terrorists' great denouement—the massacre of three thousand innocent Americans and the extinguishing in seconds of one of America's leading symbols of dominance.

That Bob seemed to have amnesia or be in denial about this outrage bewildered me. His placid insouciance was beyond frustrating.
"You never listen to me. You never concede that I'm right even when
you know I'm right!" I said.

Bob did admit that while the federal government was muddying the
waters in the case against Nosair, the CIA was also vigorously blocking
his investigation of the Bank of Credit and Commerce International
(BCCI), perhaps the biggest case of his career.

His investigation into BCCI began in 1989 when Jack Blum, an in-
vestigator on Senator John Kerry's staff, tipped off Bob to the crooked
dealings of a multibillion-dollar Arab-owned bank with branches in seventy countries. He brought Bob stacks of impossibly complicated records and such allegations against the sprawling bank that even Bob's
best investigations assistants balked at the case. But Bob relished the
decoding of this bottomless well of evidence that indicated the most
massive bank fraud in history. At first, he was the only one who could
understand the labyrinthine trail of documents, but after explaining the
broad outline of the fraud, he spelled it out to John Moscow and his
special international crime unit. When they got to the bottom of endless layers of money laundering, out flew nests of terrorists and drug
dealers.

They never suspected that people more powerful than Bob were
working against him.

The U.S. Justice Department, it turned out, knew a great deal about
BCCI and set out to impede the international probe.

Bob complained to me almost every night. "Justice refuses to give
us access to informants, evidence, documents," he said one time during
our cocktail hour. "They lied about having taped witnesses. It's a mess."

"No, *they're* a mess, not you," I replied. "You're the master at finding
ways to maneuver around the power structure. Smash them under your
feet."

But the screws tightened—all over the world. The Bank of England
(it later cooperated), the Serious Fraud Office, and other British institutions also closed their doors. One night, before he had even taken off
his coat, Bob gave me a little smile and said, "So today I got a call from
the CIA liaison in Justice. He was very oppositional. He asked me why a
local crime buster was pursuing an international bank case, and I told

him that it was because of the drug dealers. He said, 'I'll give you one hundred drug cases if you'll stop your investigation.' I refused."

I gave him a thumbs-up. "Why is the CIA ordering all this opposition, Bob? Maybe it's coming from the White House."

On July 29, 1991, in spite of all the obstacles, the DA's Office succeeded in indicting BCCI and its two principal Pakistani officers, including the president, Agha Hasan Abedi, for bribery, money laundering, financing illegal Iran-contra operations, and trafficking in arms and nuclear materials. They pleaded guilty and received huge fines. BCCI was forced to close down. Meanwhile, to cover itself, the U.S. Department of Justice jumped in and put out indictments that simply repeated the DA's. Two other operatives were indicted by the DA's Office, and more indictments were in the works, but then, suddenly, John Moscow's team, under pressure from the CIA, was stopped cold.

Finally, Bob and I were politically on the same page. I even tried to comfort him. "It's beyond your control," I said with disgust. "It's unbelievable that terrorists who are bent on bringing down America and America's protectors are actually old buddies who've joined forces."

Bob, to my gratification, was also outraged. "The CIA not only wanted to protect their informants, and yes, some of them were apparently the terrorists we'd targeted," he said, "they also didn't want the bank destroyed. It was *their* bank. They'd been using it to fund their overseas projects."

Even the former president Jimmy Carter was guilty of questionable conduct in the BCCI case. The bank's president, Abedi, had befriended President Carter and become a regular at White House dinners. "After Carter left office in 1981, he flew around the world with Abedi on the BCCI 707 and introduced him to bank presidents in third-world countries," Bob explained. "Abedi would then bribe them to put their deposits in BCCI.

"Carter also had a BCCI credit card," he added.

•

Although I had finally tired of railing about it, I could never forget finding out that our government allowed a conspiracy by a handful of terrorists at a Brooklyn mosque to grow and finally become U.S. headquarters for al-Qaeda; that the CIA had helped set the terrorist ball rolling so that it couldn't be stopped; that the cells grew so large and were so accustomed to being given a free pass, it was no surprise the massacre at the Twin Towers went off without a hitch.

The obvious conclusion in my eyes, in late 2001, was that personnel from many levels of the U.S. government had been implicated in one of the biggest American horrors in a century.

Why would Bob, who knew a decade earlier that the CIA had enabled anti-American terrorists, simply dismiss this moral and political, even criminal action?

There was a fundamental difference between us. Where I still raged against such official Machiavellian perfidy, he seemed to look upon it as just another aspect of life, a construct that held no larger meaning. Did he have greater wisdom than I about the existence of evil, greater acceptance of light and dark and the human failure to change it? Or was it that he simply refused to become emotionally involved or lose his objectivity about any case? Now I think of all he achieved after 9/11 and how he achieved it. If he had kept brooding about what he hadn't been able to accomplish, he wouldn't have had the self-confidence to accomplish anything more.

Just when I had reconciled myself to Bob's silence, he began to speak: "You know, I *was* very upset about the attacks. The CIA and FBI knew about terrorist intentions and did nothing! But I don't talk. Especially about secret national security information with a reporter who happens to be my wife. I just quietly decided that if the big guys are going to look the other way, then I have to work that much harder."

I sighed, relieved. Perhaps we weren't so far apart after all.

25

In 2003, I sold the proposal for my memoir on Dad, the wartime spy, to Miramax Books. To my good fortune, the new publisher, Rob Weisbach, a respected trailblazer in the book world and a gifted editor, took an interest in my memoir and gave me the reassurance I needed to begin the book in earnest.

I flew through my youngest years, faint memories taking on color: Daddy and his little girl, our sweet concordance almost too much to bear; watching at the window, my cheek pressed against the glass, puzzles unopened, dolls untouched, just watching, until the sun went down and the sky grew violets and I heard the swish of his trench coat coming through the door. I knew that I alone could put the light back into his somber face.

Writing so easily, I became cocky, sure that my old blocked creativity was history. And then I came to my adolescence, when I broke with Dad, and my fingers froze. If I was going to write about our breach, I had to know why it happened. So off I went to the National Archives outside Washington; the last resort when you can't produce is to turn to an activity that feeds your creativity—the soothing exercise of research. At the Maryland facility, I sorted through huge boxes of intelligence reports, travel vouchers, officers' orders, expecting at any minute to find Lieutenant Thomas E. Franks engaged in a daring mission. But he was nowhere. Not once could I find a mention of his name.

I went home and listlessly flopped down on our Stickley Morris chair. Maybe he lied; maybe the undercover stuff was a fiction designed to impress me.

"Don't give up, he was telling the truth," Bob said firmly. "Why would a regular navy man, even one attached to the marines, be sent to examine the first concentration camp discovered by the Allies? He was an intelligence agent; he wrote a report that helped convince Eisenhower to finally visit Ohrdruf."

"You're biased, Bob. You didn't know Dad's devious personality like I did," I said with a sigh. "But then again, your bullshit meter is near perfect. You can judge character so quickly; that's why you have a staff of ADAs who're the envy of the city."

"Look, just pay attention to what your father was like. He was a big, strong man. He spoke fluent German, could pick up any language in a week, was an expert marksman, expert fisherman, expert bird-watcher, expert bridge player, expert pool shark, and on and on. He could master anything in record time. He was a natural to be picked for undercover work."

The next day, as though sent by Bob or some divine intervention, a navy buddy who served with him in Guadalcanal finally returned my call and told me Dad used to vanish for days; one time, he showed up in a PT boat with a big hole in the side.

So I was off and running again, back to my computer, back to the archives, which again yielded nothing. This frustrating cycle of disappointment and hope went on for months as I was blown one way and then another. My father was a spy; my father was not a spy. But Bob kept prodding, even motivating me with clever surprises: he took me to the opening of a special Holocaust exhibit at the museum, leading me through collections of artifacts and original pictures of Nazi atrocities until we reached an oval room where he sat me down. All of a sudden my father's voice surrounded me. I was startled, panicked, and then I saw him. Big as life, on a screen above, talking of the pits full of blackened bodies. It was the first time I had seen the video testimony that he had given the museum fifteen years earlier. Nearby, inscribed on a silver plaque of Righteous Gentiles, was his name: Thomas E. Franks.

As I held my husband's hand, I saw the pleasure in his weathered, stately face, and I was stirred. This man who at eighty-seven was still moving mountains, still making subtle changes in the ethos of the city, was proudest of all that he had made his wife so happy.

Now I was spurred on by Dad's image, by my husband, and by Rob, who used a multitude of clever strategies to get me to finish the book. But when my buddy the respected novelist Hilma Wolitzer sent me *The Artist's Way*, things really began to happen. Rather skeptically, I did what the author advised: I prayed. I called on God to send me the words. And he did. They began to come faster than I could get them down. Through dinner, at dawn, in the middle of the night, my fingertips kept hitting the keys. I didn't hear my family's voices, didn't feel hunger or fatigue. Nothing could enter my space. No longer was I simply making a book; I was reinventing my childhood—erasing history, living my dream, enjoying the peaceful life I had prayed for. I threw out my hands in bewilderment. *Now* you're answering my prayers? Well, apparently. Had I forgotten that God has his own clock and works in his own way? My last months with Dad, I stretched out into a lifetime, experiencing him as the man he would have been without the horrors he had seen and done, without the PTSD and oath of silence that had crippled him.

In the fall of 2006, four years after I had begun researching and writing it, I put the last period on the last sentence in *My Father's Secret War*. I had hardly gotten out of my chair for months, and now, with a rush of well-being, I rose—and couldn't stand up straight. A lumbar disk, in protest against my endless immobility, had tightened around a nerve, pinching it, painfully and perilously. There was the rush to the hospital, the walk through the halls bent over like an old lady, the emergency surgery to free the nerve.

I was on crutches for three months, and when Christmas came, Bob, my true love, surprised me when I shouldn't have been surprised. Knowing I had inherited my mother's love of making a festival of the holiday, the one time when everyone was good to each other, he went out and got me a big Fraser fir. The kids hung it with the sequined felt stars and bells made by my grandma Franks, but since they were now a sophisticated twenty-two and sixteen, they sniffed at the little Victorian women in muffs skating on an oval mirror and the china carolers with hoopskirts singing round a tea shop, as well as the other beloved tableaux that I relished imagining myself into. Sadly, my children, in some ways miniature Bobs both of them, thought the joyous winter scenes excessive. "Mom, you're being too dramatic," one of them said with a sigh. Thankfully, our devoted Nerissa, the Caribbean housekeeper who had replaced Renia when she retired, put them out herself.

While we would always miss Renia, Nerissa had her own strengths, with her loving nature and quiet dignity. She was nanny to the whole family and had her own zany charm. She was in her thirties, energetic, and liked to break out in a little jig, limbs akimbo, while vacuuming. She was unflaggingly loyal to us, stepped up to a crisis, was brilliant at doing errands, and never missed a day of work. She liked to spend her time shopping and talking to vendors who, to her delight, called her "the black Mrs. Morgenthau."

•

On November 11, 2001, Renia had died of complications from diabetes. We had all gone to see her during her long ordeal in the hospital, but when she finally slipped into a deep coma, Amy lingered outside her room until we all had said our goodbyes. Amy was the last child Renia had helped to raise. She wanted to have the last conversation with her. I could see my daughter from outside the door, talking animatedly and lifting her hands as though she could raise up her beloved nanny. She was recounting the latest happenings in her life and the family's, as though the two were cuddled up together as always, as though Renia were listening to her with all her heart. And maybe she was.

I told Renia's son and grandchildren not to spare any expense for her funeral. I wanted Renia's little Brooklyn church to be filled with flowers of their choice. I requested only one flower: a white lily, to represent the one that I had given her on an Easter long ago, the strange everblooming plant that had prophesied I would become Mrs. Morgenthau.

When I walked into the church, I was stunned at the sight of a hundred big snow-white lilies tied with white ribbons to every pew in every row. My eyes filled, and then I couldn't stop the tears from streaming down when I saw the extended family—my stepchildren as well as Josh and Amy—squeezed together in the second row. Even Barbara, with her small daughter, Mimoh, had flown in from her home in San Francisco.

Bob was the first one to speak to the congregation: "After my wife died, I wasn't much use to my two youngest, Bobby and Barbara . . . Renia knew that and she took over. I remember passing her room, seeing Barbara sitting there with her tattered pink blankie . . . I don't know how we would have gone on without her."

After his moving eulogy, he sat beside me and whispered, "I'm sorry I didn't mention you. I know how close you were."

I squeezed his hand. "You didn't need to talk about me." Renia had stood by me, taught me. The love we shared was private. "You said exactly the right things."

Josh told how he would mischievously splash water on Renia in the bathtub: "She would say, 'Careful, child, trouble don't start like rain.' I don't think I knew what it meant . . . but it stopped me in my tracks . . . Renia made you feel like the glass was not half-empty or half-full, but overflowing."

Bobby, who spoke for Barbara and himself, talked of his mother's last words. "She said, 'Could I have some of Renia's applesauce?' . . . She gathered us up and shepherded us into adulthood. That's how I think of her now. More than anything, Renia was a shepherd."

•

On July 4, 2008, we were looking forward to our annual Fourth of July barbecue. Bob had this Houdini-like knack of plucking the main point out of a complicated argument and expressing it with astonishing and sometimes exasperating simplicity. Often, this skill would pop up in his private life. Since Josh's graduation from Yale in 2006, Bob, who had been teaching his son about farming since he was a toddler, began to teach him how to run the operation. Josh, an artist, planted hundreds of new trees and organic vegetables and acquired laying chickens that wandered free around the trees; the rolling fields and fruit trees unfolded like a stunning Grandma Moses painting. Bob soon made Josh manager of the sizable Fishkill Farms Store, where we sold our produce. Bob had given Josh a lot of power and responsibility in a short time, but Bob also made the big decisions when he wanted to, often, as was his wont, without telling anyone he had made them.

As Independence Day approached, Bob and I decided to move the party, which had grown quite big, from our home up to the store, whose patio overlooked the farm that Josh had re-created. Bob, however, forgot to tell Josh this, and when Josh found out the week before, he was understandably put out.

"How could you guys do this without asking me?" he said. He was leaning against the kitchen counter, arms folded. Bob was leaning against the fridge, and I was sitting a little ways away at the table.

Bob graciously took the fall for both of us. "*I* decided we should have it up at the store. I wanted everyone to be able to look down and see the terrific job you've done."

"But, Dad, you didn't even consider my side of things. All the things I'll have to do—close the store for the party, get our staff to clean up afterward . . ."

"Well, I thought people should see what you've done, the new plantings, the chickens . . ."

"You know, the staff work long hours, and the store is the store, not a party hall."

"I wanted people to be impressed by how you've changed the farm."

"Aren't you listening to me? You should have consulted me!"

"I did it for you. I wanted people to see all that you've accomplished here."

At first, hearing Bob repeat the same answer over and over, I became alarmed. Could he not hear Josh? Was he losing it?

"I wasn't trying to hurt you; I did it *for* you," he said again, and suddenly I burst out laughing. And then Josh started to laugh too. I knew what Bob was trying to do. Letting Josh shine in front of a hundred people was the only important part of this. The rest was dross.

And the following week people crowded onto the patio to peer out over the orchards and couldn't stop marveling at Josh's handiwork.

26

We were heading home from the farm, zooming down the parkway with hardly a car in our way, when we ran into them all at once entering the Bronx. It was the kind of traffic jam that made us want to just abandon the car and walk the remaining fifteen miles to the city.

We were sorely tempted. Our ten-year-old Volvo, heavily dented due to my issue with parallel parking, wasn't particularly comfortable, and Josh and Amy were hot, cranky, and nauseous in the cramped backseats. "Let's play Who Am I?" I suggested.

"Okay," Josh said. "I'm it. Start guessing. Amy, you go first."

"Are you a famous politician?" she asked coolly, as though reading Josh's mind. Yes, he was. A woman? I asked. Yes. "Are you a female dog-catcher?" Bob ventured, eliciting a family groan and a polite request from Amy to stop being silly.

"I was perfectly serious," he said, adding, "Is it Ruth Messinger?"

"Daddy, you're cheating. You only get one question at a time."

"Bob, Messinger is yesterday's news. Josh's is a current politician," I said. "Oh, pee-yew, who did that?" I opened the windows as Josh and Amy quickly blamed the dog, a placid white fluff ball whom Bob had christened Ivan the Terrible. I was physically and psychologically allergic to dogs, but Amy, who worked as subtly and effectively as her father, had finally managed to talk me into getting a hypoallergenic bichon frise. Everyone but me constantly fed him scraps, after which he would sit on Bob's lap and fart away for ninety minutes from the farm to the city.

The game moved on until it was established that Josh was a female politician who had run against a prominent man for a prominent Manhattan office.

It was Bob's turn. He thought and he thought: "I don't know. I give up. I can't think of anybody like that."

Josh began chuckling. "He won't say her name! Right, Dad? You know the answer, but you've blocked her out. It's Leslie Crocker Snyder!"

Bob looked straight ahead, unsmiling.

•

During the 2005 campaign for DA, Bob had had his first serious opponent since the Mason challenge twenty years before. She had a following among right-wingers and extreme feminists, who had visions of Manhattan's first woman DA. Like now, he seldom referred to Snyder in anything but the third-person pronoun. At the beginning of the race, I chided him as harboring a tinge of sexism.

"I'm not against women, just this woman," he replied acidly.

Snyder was a judge handling criminal cases and a death penalty advocate so tough she once told a defendant that she would personally give him the lethal injection if she could.

"She's been a correspondent for NBC News; she wrote an autobiography while she was a judge inappropriately titled *25 to Life.* She's even done cameo appearances on *Law & Order.*"

"Well, that's interesting, since the show was modeled on your office and the DA character, Adam Schiff, on you. How many times did Sam Waterston pick your brains about playing the chief DA?"

"She thinks of herself as a star."

"Sounds to me like she's a star fucker."

"She'd go after the high-publicity cases and ignore the rest of the city's crime," Bob said, slapping down his newspaper. He mentioned that the next day he was going to start visiting the district Democratic clubs, whose support was vital. "Would you like to go with me?"

"Oh, gosh, that's the night of my writers' group at Hilma's. Michael Cunningham and I are supposed to be reading from our novels in progress."

"Don't bother, then, it's not that important."

But it was. Since the Mason campaign, when I had, at first, failed him, Bob, just by being Bob, had given me a bigger conscience, robbed me of some of my selfishness. I could no longer conveniently ignore what I well knew: that often Bob says not what he wants but what he thinks you want him to say. By the end of the day, I had canceled on Hilma.

The next night, we were getting dressed, and I had helped Bob find his toothbrush and the missing money clip given to him by his father, and now I was rubbing a spot of dinner off his lapel. "Stand still," I said, and then I took a deep breath. "I think it's important I come tonight."

"No, I told you it was fine if . . ."

"You want me to come. Say it."

"I want you to come."

"So do I. You need me to watch your back. From now on, 'whither thou goest, I will go.'"

I kept my vow; I was with him all the way through the campaign. I hurt when I saw that he hurt; when he was scared, so was I; his little triumphs became mine. What was important to me was more than just winning the election; it was that his dignity and self-respect were preserved, that he did not go down in humiliation.

Snyder was using the media to push him to the brink. Journalists want their stories to be read, to be praised, to be so much better than their competitors' that they themselves will be written about. And Snyder's constant colorful slurs made good copy.

Like Mason twenty years before, she went after Bob's age like a coiled cobra. "He's too old, stale, decrepit," she chanted. To my frustration, she managed to revive my old fear that Bob would die on me; I was afraid that he would be as affected as I was by these intimations of his mortality, so I'd slip the newspapers into odd places. Of course, he always found them.

When you judge someone not by who he is, his character and achievements, but by *what* he is—short, black, young, old—it's some kind of global *ism* we haven't yet got a word for. While many columnists refuted Leslie's claims that Bob was over the hill, others took her at her word, failing to examine what he had done in the last decade. Ironically, at eighty-five, Bob was at a peak of his career and frequently dubbed the leading prosecutor in the country: Who else had changed the paradigms for convictions? There was Schiele, Kimes, the DNA rapist, and the continuing ripple effects from his prosecution and closing down of BCCI (which was known in London as "the Bank of Crooks and Criminals"), a favorite bank of terrorists.

Snyder criticized him for spending too many resources pursuing useless white-collar crime like the recent Tyco scandal, where the CEO, Dennis Kozlowski—with the six-thousand-dollar shower curtain and parties in Sardinia—looted the company of millions. The conviction was an early message, a warning: the greed of financial high rollers would all too soon cause the collapse of the economy.

"She's blowing these accusations through her nose, isn't she?" I asked Bob one night when we were proofing some campaign literature. "She knows that banks launder money for drug dealers, which ends up as cocaine or heroin in the backpacks of our kids."

When Bob spoke, I always sat in the front row, smiling and nodding. During a particularly grueling debate, Leslie snarled that he had brought no innovations, no energy, to the office. Bob ticked off the thirty-four new units and bureaus he had established and the dramatic drop in Manhattan's crime rate to 10 percent of what it was when he took office in 1975. The citywide police department had its new programs, like putting more cops on the street, but of the city's five boroughs only Manhattan enjoyed the drastic drop in murder and violent crime. The reason? The office's prompt and tough prosecution of small-time offenders, like turnstile jumpers, who had traditionally been let off. The office correctly deduced that they were usually the very ones committing the murders and rapes. Having destroyed Snyder's claims, he gave me a triumphant wink, which made the pages of The New York Times. Thank God I was there. Who else would he have been able to wink at?

Snyder kept criticizing him for being out of touch, for abdicating responsibility to the top ADAs who established little fiefdoms. This accusation had a modicum of validity. Bob had his hand in the most significant cases, but with thousands of prosecutions a year he had to rely on assistants whom he had extensively tested, who had won his trust. His hands-off philosophy had garnered him gratitude and loyalty; it had helped him build what was considered the most talented law enforcement team in the city. But it occasionally left him with a legal mess.

Perhaps his biggest vulnerability was the Central Park jogger case.

Back in 1989, Manhattan was saturated in crime; there was a murder every four hours and the sound of gunfire was common. Then, on April 19, 1989, a white woman taking a night run in Central Park was raped and almost fatally beaten. The city was outraged; the police quickly got confessions from five black teenagers who were said to have been on a "wilding spree" that night; the DA's Office, led by Linda Fairstein, the prominent head of the Sex Crimes Unit, obtained a jury conviction on assault charges, and they were sent to prison. Later, the defendants claimed to have been coerced by overzealous police interrogators. The convictions unleashed protests and cries of racism from the black community.

More than a decade later, and after the young men had served their sentences, one Matias Reyes, doing life for serial murder and rape, came forth and confessed that he had been the one who raped the Central Park jogger. He first wrote and then talked on the phone to the Innocence Project, which ended up taking no action. He then told prison officials, who contacted Morgenthau, who did take action. Bob got samples of both Reyes's DNA and the DNA found on the victim: they were a perfect match. Morgenthau then led a months-long reexamination of the evidence in the Central Park Five case and, against the vehement protests of Fairstein and the NYPD, decided the verdict should be set aside.

As for Reyes, because he was already serving a life sentence, he was not tried for his rape of the Central Park jogger.

The police and prosecutors had grossly bungled the Central Park Five case.

The debacle unfolded this way.

Two days before the jogger rape, Reyes had committed a rape in the same area of Central Park. Passersby had interrupted it and Reyes had gotten away. The female detective who was looking into the earlier rape and the male detective handling the jogger case were sitting right next to each other but never exchanged information or apparently even noticed what the other was doing.

Then there was the Manhattan chief of detectives. He took home the forensic pictures of the Central Park jogger crime scene and kept them. Maybe he figured he would write a book about the case, complete with the exclusive photos.

Faced with investigating a case with this key evidence missing, Bob raised hell, called the citywide chief of detectives, and demanded them back. The photographs were returned, and the offending Manhattan chief of detectives was taken off the case. This led to even more damage to the people's case since there was then no supervision or even coordination of it.

In the earlier Reyes rape, the rape kit gathered after the assault ultimately disappeared. So even though detectives had obtained the name of her attacker—Reyes liked to chat up his victims before he pounced— the case was closed by the police after six weeks.

"This was unprecedented," Bob said. "To just prematurely throw the case into a cold file in spite of having so much proof against a perpetrator!"

"You have to bring this out," I urged Bob. "If the Reyes case had remained open, someone, someone like *you*, would have linked it with the jogger rape."

But he refused, saying that this was not the way he did things.

The NYPD and Linda Fairstein reacted furiously to Morgenthau's decision to consent to vacate the convictions. Eager to save their reputations, reluctant to admit they had committed egregious errors, they demanded a public hearing.

But Morgenthau wouldn't budge from his decision to permit setting aside the convictions from the young men's records. No more investigation, no more hearings, no more stalling. The victim, the defendants, and their families had suffered for too long.

Bob figured that the NYPD wanted a hearing to plant doubt about Reyes's story by implying he had lied. "They hoped they could show he had wanted to make a deal for leniency," Bob told me, "or even that he could have been an accomplice of the Central Park Five."

When Linda Fairstein left the office to write mystery novels, which were based on her cases in the Sex Crimes Unit, she thanked Bob profusely in her books. But her attitude changed. Suddenly Bob fell from grace. To this day, she shuns her beloved "Boss." In fact, upon the death of her husband, the lawyer Justin Feldman, she failed to invite Bob to the memorial service. Bob was visibly hurt: "Justin was one of my closest friends."

•

During the election fight with Snyder, Bob kept from the press a number of unsavory facts about his opponent. Her reputation as a criminal court judge, he told me, was less than sterling: she arrived at the bench at a late 10:00 a.m., took long lunches, and favored certain lawyers.

While Bob kept refusing to do negative campaigning, Leslie kept slinging the mud. When she told the press that Bob "had to be trotted out and propped up for news conferences," I wanted to break her neck. I wanted to cut off all her dumb blond hair and grind her preppy suits into the muck and pull out her sixty-two-year-old pink teenybop finger-nails. Bob, to my amazement, just smiled. "That's politics," he said. Nothing, however, prepared either of us for the blow that was to come.

You think life is proceeding sensibly and relatively sanely, that up is up and down is down, and then, in an instant, you find yourself inside a Dalí landscape where the clocks are dripping and ants are crawling over everything. This is what happened to me the morning I opened *The New York Times*, my home away from home, the abiding supporter of my husband, the liberal publication that abhorred the death penalty and long prison sentences; when I saw that this revered publication had endorsed Leslie Crocker Snyder, I thought someone had played a malicious joke, substituted the real *Times* for one of those fakes manufactured in Times Square.

Within days, however, while I remained hurt and angry at the paper, Bob found a way to explain the editorial and put it away. "You can't predict the *Times*," he told people. "After all, in 1940, the most crucial presidential election of the twentieth century, with Hitler having overrun Europe, the paper opposed the reelection of Franklin D. Roosevelt. The publisher liked Wendell Willkie, a lawyer who had no government experience."

The night of the election, Bob and I, our family, and our closest supporters crowded into a mustard-yellow hotel room. His principal assistants, Dan Castleman and Jim Kindler, planted themselves behind computers, calling out the numbers as the voting results of each election district came in. Trying to be useful, I stood and redundantly shouted out the numbers after they did.

Finally, Dan stood up and with a giddy grin hollered, "It's Morgenthau, three to one!" Campaign workers began clapping, jumping, whooping, slapping each other on the back. Their pleasure transcended the vicarious. Each one owned the victory; each wondered whether it was his efforts that tipped the scales.

Everything after that was a blur. I remember the state senator Eric Schneiderman, our steadfast supporter, ushering us into some room with a microphone to stand before the press. We were dazed. "Make a victory sign!" Schneiderman whispered several times until finally he raised both our arms for us. The picture was on the front page of all the New York newspapers.

•

During the campaign, Bob had ignored Snyder as she hammered away at his eighty-six years and "questionable health." He had made public his doctors' medical reports on the excellent state of his heart, lungs, liver, blood pressure. But after it was all over, a kind of survivor's backlash set in. When you enjoy a victory over another, you are prone, at least subliminally, to magical thinking: in some unknown way, you will have to pay it back; the balance will have to be righted. One way to cause yourself misery is to fear for your life. A sudden pimple, a bruise, a cough, there is hardly a thing that doesn't present itself as a portent.

And then, one day, Bob's worries were eclipsed by an obsession that ran much deeper. I assumed it was my fault. I assumed I had caused him to break the promise to himself that had helped make him the finest prosecutor in the nation. I caused him to look back, way back. And I was scared.

27

Sometime in 2006, the mountains of material on my father, the World War II spy, began spilling out of my small study. So I moved the research for my book into the dining room, where I banged the keys, sometimes exclaiming at the discovery of yet another harrowing undercover adventure of my phlegmatic father.

Bob loved Dad, was fascinated by all his talents, and skillfully drew war stories out of him. But Bob would seldom reciprocate. Most veterans had never talked in depth about their roles in the war. Bob, for instance, was Byron White's best friend at Yale Law School. "I talked to Byron White every day, but we never discussed the war," he said. "After his death, I found out that his destroyer had been right near me in the Pacific."

I was approaching the end of my book, or so I thought, when I began getting calls from Dad's war buddies. They had previously divulged very little to me, but now, suddenly, they wanted to talk, clearly needing to expunge all that they had kept secret these long years. They were joined by thousands of veterans in their late seventies and eighties who came out in television, print, and Internet interviews, ready to reveal the dramas of those most enthralling and terrible years of their lives.

Then, one day, Bob decided he could truly risk reliving what happened more than sixty years before. Cautiously, he began to speak, not just to me, but also to old friends who told mesmerizing stories of being marine pilots or captains in famous battles.

Meanwhile, Bob began to read monthly military magazines, and I noticed him occasionally leafing through my World War II histories and memoirs, which had articles about the sea battles in the Pacific and the Mediterranean. He soon became fascinated with anything about the war—army, marine, air force—for he had missed most of it; confined to his destroyers for long periods, he hadn't watched newsreels or heard accounts, had never known what was happening elsewhere in Europe and the Pacific. He collected the works of World War II historians like Stephen Ambrose, created special exhibits on the war at the museum, and relished books about the Resistance and the Jewish underground. Soon he had almost as many volumes as I did. The bloodiest war in history had taken over our bedroom.

He organized reunions of *Lansdale* survivors, engineered a museum exhibit detailing the thousands of Jews who, far from submitting to the Nazis, became fierce saboteurs.

He had shared scraps of war memories with me before, but it was when he began to recount grisly stories of sea battles in detail, those that had weighed on his mind and kept him separated from others for so long, that I began to worry. For half a century, he had functioned by keeping these terrifying things that happened to him locked away; could he now, at his age, bear to bring out so many of these deeply suppressed memories?

He was known for his unusually precise memory, never forgetting a date or a name or a place, remembering details and whole conversations better than those half his age. People were captivated by Bob's stories, which ranged from tales of crazy ship captains to the seventeen kamikazes his ship shot down at Okinawa. I could listen to them over and over, for each time he told them, I knew him a little better.

He would tell me—in little isolated flashes—the stories behind his stories: the promises he made to "the Almighty" when he spent hours in the freezing waters of the Mediterranean, giving his life belt to an injured sailor, not knowing whether he would live or die; what it felt like to see kamikaze planes coming at you, larger and larger, like meteors from the sky.

One morning, when I was halfway out the door heading for the compost pile, he came down from our bedroom in Martha's Vineyard. He looked like a homeless waif, one eye closed, hair sticking up, barely holding his ground on the red-painted floor. "Where's my fuzzy bathrobe, the one like yours? Did you take it?" he rasped.

I put down the garbage.

"I had a bad dream," he said. "The *Lansdale* was sinking again. The gunners, the mess attendants, sailors I hardly knew, were trying to grab hold of me, but they couldn't, and one by one they were sucked down into the swells."

"Oh no." I put my arms around him, felt the damp of his T-shirt come through my muslin beach dress. "How long have you been having these dreams?"

"Off and on," he said, sitting down on the round seat of an old chair at the kitchen table. "Shhh," he whispered, as though addressing his nightmares. "Look out the window." There was a ruby-throated hummingbird, revving its wings like a tiny plane, poking its long beak into our purple buddleia blooms and sucking out the nectar.

"I really was badly shaken after the war," he said. "Maybe you're right; maybe it did change my personality as an adult." He was meticulously peeling off strips of bacon and ever so slowly laying them side by side in the skillet. It was like watching a plant grow. Much more efficient just to dump them all together and occasionally toss them around.

"After I came home from the Pacific, there were things I was afraid of, afraid to do." He held up the spatula and scowled at me, as if I were to blame. "Working in Judge Patterson's offices on the forty-second floor of One Wall Street was hell. If there was a high wind that came and rattled the windows, I'd have to go down to the lobby."

"It's more of the PTSD, sweetie," I said gently. "You're letting the trauma out, letting it go, little by little, dream by dream. Every memory you talk about is a memory that loses its power." Or at least I prayed that it would.

"I guess, but when will it stop? I don't think I ever told you, but after we sank, the captain committed himself to a mental hospital. The ship's doctor went home and didn't come out of his house again. We went to see him, but he wouldn't answer the phone or the doorbell. He never married, had no friends, saw no one. He lived the rest of his life as a recluse as far as I know. There were a number of officers and sailors who refused to ever go to sea again, some whose lives were ruined. They called it battle fatigue in those days, and the VA paid no attention to the victims. As soon as you looked normal again, they sent you back to war."

I went over to the stove and rubbed his shoulders. "Now I know why you hate the Oak Bluffs fireworks," I said gently. "You should have told me. It must sound like the world is exploding in gunfire."

The garbage was gathering flies, but I ignored them. Since I convinced him he had PTSD around my breast cancer, since we had reconciled, he would bring it up, but only rarely. Now he was in a confessional mood, and I knew he was never finished talking about a subject until he was finished. I forced myself not to speak. To interrupt him would be to lose something priceless.

"I had had too many near misses. When I came home from Okinawa, the navigator on the USS *Lawe* asked me to help him and I refused. I thought my luck had run out." He liked his milk heated. I dipped my finger into the little pan, warm enough, and I put it in his coffee. He took a large sip.

"For fifty years, I couldn't remember the name of that ship I came home on. Fifty years!

"When they let me off in Seattle, I was in a daze. The ship put me off in Seattle, and nobody met me, no parades, no welcome wagon hostesses. No cabs. No hotels. I had to lug a sixty-pound canvas seabag, which contained all my worldly belongings, up a steep hill to find one. There was nobody at all to help me.

"After the judge's crash, I was even more afraid my days were numbered . . . I know how the veterans from Iraq and Afghanistan must feel," he added, leaning next to the stove. "Nobody ever appreciated what we did."

"I do. I appreciate what you did," I said, stroking his hair. I was also in awe that he had continued to remember and discharge these psychic injuries, that he was essentially giving himself PTSD therapy. Perhaps it hadn't eased his mind, stopped his nighttime terrors, but we both agreed that it had freed up something inside him.

Every time he talked about his war experiences, he changed a little; he was able to let go of the reins he had held so tight. After that morning, for the second time in the last several years of our marriage, he seemed to put away his stern persona and extract some of the high spirits from his youth.

It was as though a phantom captain had finally said, "At ease." Gone was the iron set of his face; instead, it became vulnerable, full of a range

of emotions. He could look hurt or confused or moved or goofy; his famous scowl took on an aspect of thoughtfulness rather than displeasure,
and displeasure was often expressed by sheer goofiness. If I was su-
premely crabby, I would be subjected to "There was a little girl, / Who
had a little curl / Right in the middle of her forehead. / When she was
good, / She was very, very good, / But when she was bad she was horrid."

He seldom laughed at my jokes—I was the only one in the family
who thought them funny—but now I had his full attention, and he
chuckled easily. If I snapped at him about the inexorable creep of his
papers across every table in my beautiful orderly home, instead of pretending he hadn't heard me, he declared I had hurt his feelings.

I had always assumed that the fulcrum of Bob's life was his work; I
had both respected and resented this. I never imagined that one day he
would tell me that really it had always been me. And when he would
choose the office over me, he would surprise me by apologizing. One
night, after he had missed a speech I had made, I came home late and
flopped into bed, only to feel something crinkling under my head. On
the back of an envelope he had written, "It was bad of me not to come.
I am sorry. I love you. I get frantic when I think of all the work undone
at the office."

Once, we were examining the Macouns in the orchards as it began
to get dark. He was more at peace with his war memories now, but I still
had visions of his enduring the icy Mediterranean suffered afterwards.
"You didn't do what so many trauma victims did," I said. "You didn't go
berserk or become a hermit or get cynical like some of the others on the
Lansdale. You went on to live a normal life and function brilliantly. I
suppose it's because of the work you do, how important it is."

He stared at me, and in the dimming light his eyes were like blue
crystal.

"My work, yes, but mostly it's been you," he ran his finger down my
cheek. "When have I had time to get discouraged?"

•

Sartorially, Bob didn't need me anymore; his clothes looked neat and
trim. The only problem was that he liked gray. It was so woven into the
fabric of his being that in his eyes this overcast hue seemed to masquer-
ade as every other color except itself.

"Be sure and get a *lively* shade," I would say before he reluctantly went shopping. "A nice deep blue. Maybe with a tiny little stripe."

He would come home with a big smile and a suit the color of lead. "You've bought gray again!" I'd cry.

"No, it's not. Look at the little red threads," he'd reply defensively.

"Oh, baloney. You look beautiful in blue or tweed or even charcoal, and instead you want to look like the inside of a pencil!"

"I wouldn't talk," he would say vaguely.

That would stop me. For years, a line of buddies had tried to teach me how to dress, but I still didn't get it. I'd put on a stylishly ragged sweater, whimsical earrings, and masses of bright beads and hop happily off to a fancy cocktail party. Perhaps that accounted for his conspicuously neutral attitude toward what I wore.

Nevertheless, when we caught sight of ourselves in the mirror, we would still laugh: Mutt and Jeff, the Bohemian and the Old Bear. Physical opposites; moral comrades. With our radically different ages and styles, people still asked if I was his daughter, and each time it would startle us. We might as well have sprung from some dimension of No Time; we had no sense that we came from different generations. We were thoroughly compatible; we thought the same way. We both had either great sympathy with certain people or no sympathy at all; we liked and disliked similar types of movies, restaurants, parties—and these days even politics. Bob might dress like a banker, he might be conservative about the Middle East, but with his passionate stand against the death penalty, his promotion of women, his giving of himself to the underprivileged, his dozens of radical prosecutorial decisions, he was as soundly antiestablishment as I was. We represented the perfect meld.

•

As I was finishing up my book, Bob was trying to change a law he loathed—the state's five-year statute of limitations on rape. "Murder, arson, kidnapping, and major drug dealing all have no statute of limitations," he would say. "Rape is as serious as murder because the psychological damage is so severe; the woman can never lead a normal life."

Bob felt so strongly about this that he repeatedly warned me not to go into the park at night. "That's when it happens," he would say. "That's when they'll get you."

When he first came into office, one of the first people he saw was an articulate rape victim who said she had not only been forced to reveal the details of her past sex life but been pushed around and forced to relive the attack again and again; she had been questioned first by two sets of detectives and then by two ADAs. This was because the Indictment Bureau, which had its files in an old kitchen, had mislaid the first indictment, necessitating another ADA to go through the process all over again. This inspired Bob to make his first big change in the office: vertical prosecution. To an uproar of criticism, he abolished the Indictment Bureau and the Homicide Bureau. A crime, according to his new system, would be handled by one ADA from start to finish rather than passed from one bureau to another, each of which handled a separate phase of the prosecution.

Thirty years later Bob began lobbying the legislature to remove the five-year statute by making it a class A felony, but the Defense Bar—its members often defended rapists—was a powerful lobby opposing it. The state senate and the governor had eventually been convinced of the need to change the rape law, but the one holdout was the influential Speaker of the Assembly, Sheldon Silver, a practicing lawyer himself.

Bob asked for a meeting with Silver. He brought back that first rape victim, who had moved to California, to accompany him. The woman told the assembly Speaker the poignant story of her rape, and Bob, who had been backed by feminists and other DAs, argued that the new DNA "footprints" stored in computers could indisputably convict a rapist after the five years had run out. Silver was finally convinced.

In May 2006, flanked by Bob, Silver announced a new law that would make rape a class A felony, wiping out the statute of limitations. Bob considered it one of the biggest victories of his career. But when he stood beside Silver, looking somber, I knew he was thinking about all the women who had suffered rape before and the ones who would be raped in the future. At least they would no longer be haunted by visions of their attackers running free, raping others.

•

Another crime that incensed Bob was elder abuse. He once got a call from Annette de la Renta, wife of the fashion designer, who emotionally recounted that Brooke Astor was being abused and tormented by her son, Tony Marshall.

We had both met Mrs. Astor, the charming matriarch of high society and philanthropy, before she developed Alzheimer's disease. When I was president of the first Writers Room, she made a generous donation, even though the organization was young and unproven.

Annette, a striking and distinctly ethical woman who had become like a daughter to Mrs. Astor, told Bob that looking good, wearing the latest couture, was Brooke Astor's passion. However, Tony falsely told her she couldn't afford new clothes. "Meanwhile," Bob said with disgust, "he apparently removed one of her favorite paintings, a valuable and historic Childe Hassam. Annette said that when she had last visited her, she was very unhappy. She was lying on the couch in a puddle of urine."

As bad as the abuse sounded, Bob had to weigh whether to investigate it. Prosecutors were generally reluctant to handle family disputes involving the treatment of the elderly. It was messy and hard to prove who was actually the one who committed a crime.

"What would you do?" Bob asked me.

"Go after him," I replied strongly. It was particularly execrable to me when children turned on their parents. "If the accusations are proven," I said, "it could set a standard and stop prosecutors from looking the other way when the old and helpless are being victimized." He agreed.

During the succeeding days, I talked a bit too much about the horrors of elder abuse: the sadism that went on in nursing homes, how we took the old out of their own homes and warehoused them with people who sometimes feel only contempt for them. I finally realized that my screeds weren't designed to persuade my husband to take the case; he had already made up his mind. What I was trying to do was personal: to reassure him that this would never happen to him. I would always love him and be by his side, no matter his age or his condition.

In 2009 Tony Marshall, eighty-five, and his lawyer, Francis X. Morrissey, were convicted of defrauding Mrs. Astor, then 104, of millions of dollars and valuable property, including paintings by Tiepolo and John Frederick Lewis. During the nineteen-month trial, the prosecution had thousands of exhibits and seventy-two witnesses, including the butler, the housekeeper, Henry Kissinger, David Rockefeller, and Barbara Walters, who testified about her mistreatment. Marshall and Morrissey were sentenced to state prison for one to three years. They appealed, but the conviction was affirmed by the appellate division of the supreme court.

Bob was both pleased by the verdict and saddened by the case. "It's a hidden crime. Elder abuse will still go on without anyone knowing about it. Not every incapacitated old person has friends like Mrs. de la Renta."

28

On a December day in 2008, a gale whirled through the orchards. Our weeping willow was swinging back and forth. "Oh, wow, look, it's doing hip-hop!" I exclaimed, but Bob, who doesn't like storms, was sitting looking at the refrigerator. I, who love them, sat facing the bay windows. The wind bent the tree so far to the left, its long leaves puddled like a mass of hair on the ground.

Suddenly, with a tremendous crack, the old tree broke in two and dangled perilously over the glass. "Get back! It's going to smash through and land on our heads!" I cried.

"Do you think I should retire?" Bob asked. I almost tipped over in my chair. I didn't think it was by accident that he had chosen this tumultuous and distracting moment to blurt out the question that had caused us both to privately agonize for so long. In truth, I thought it was time, but what if he disagreed? I couldn't make this choice for him. The DA's election was less than a year away. If he ran, it would be his tenth term. He would have to declare soon. He slowly moved his chair forward to sit next to me.

"Reporters have been asking me the question for years, and I've always said, 'I'm too old to retire.' But now I wonder if I really am too old."

"I'll support you whatever you decide," I said, a lump in my throat. "You must be feeling a lot of pressure."

We hashed over the advantages and disadvantages. There was not, of course, anyone out there who could do what he had done—rid the city of terrorists, white-collar and street criminals, and murderers. Would crime skyrocket without him?

"But I'm going to be ninety. What I don't want is to be incapacitated in the middle of my term," he brooded.

"No, that wouldn't be good at all. Bob, I think you've already made up your mind. I know it's hard because, ironically, your last years as DA have been your best."

He nodded.

"You want to go out when you're on top."

"Yes, that's right."

He told no one else of his decision; he didn't want to be a lame duck. Indeed, as late as six months before, he had quipped to the *Daily News*, "If I broke both my legs, I might not run; if I broke one, I would run."

But his devotees feared what he was thinking, and they didn't want to lose him. His mind was like a cleaver, and his energy and boldness still embarrassed the younger and the less spry. His campaign committee had already raised $750,000, and its members were urging him to stay on.

"People have gotten together, asking me to run for DA again." He chuckled. "They already have a slogan: 90 in '09."

•

On February 27, 2009, Bob and I walked down the long dark hall from his office to the press room. He was calm, even joking, but I felt heavy in body and mind. I tried to brainwash myself, repeating the mantra "You are not going to cry in front of the press."

As his top assistants looked on, visibly upset, we sat down. The bulbs flashed wildly, blinding us. Bob stumbled, but then, recovering himself, he gave the press a nervous little smile and told them that this was his last term as district attorney. I just kept smiling.

The press began yelling out questions, and I whispered the ones he couldn't hear into his ear.

"I've been the conductor of an extraordinary orchestra," he said, speaking and gently looking more vulnerable than I'd ever seen him in public. "I've served twenty-five years past normal retirement age, and I decided I wouldn't press my luck any further."

Magazines, papers, and blogs rushed to make him the big story, awarding him the moniker "the world's district attorney." They filled pages with time lines of his cases and a variety of photographs depicting the last fifty years of his career: Bob with Martin Luther King; Bob with Bobby Kennedy; Bob opening a fire hydrant for underprivileged youths who would play and cool off in the hot streets of New York.

The New York Times was effusive: great pictures, glowing panegyrics, deferential headlines. The *Times* lionized him as "a legend . . . his legacy assured . . . the last of an era of great men in American history."

At first, hearing him called a legend over and over gave me a headache. It smacked of a children's fairy tale. The Legend: Quasimodo in love with a Gypsy, a Headless Horseman, an Imaginary DA. As for the "end of an era," I certainly wasn't ready for that. For sure, there were more eras to come.

At least once a week, he was honored and roasted at dinners, presented with trophies, some of them nice enough to display—a huge cut-crystal Tiffany bowl, a big bronze copy of the famous Jo Davidson bust of Franklin Delano Roosevelt. On the one hand, the attention was exhilarating. Unlike so many great men, who had to wait until after they were gone to be honored, Bob got to enjoy this cascade of accolades in his lifetime.

•

There was something beautiful and terrible about these endless encomiums, much like attending your own memorial service. "How did I get to be this old?" he would sometimes ask at the end of the evenings. "I don't feel entitled to all this fuss," he said. "I haven't lived half long enough yet for these honors."

For me, the parties were transformative, particularly those thrown by his old assistant U.S. attorneys; the funny and adoring stories I couldn't have imagined. My tears came easily. The bedrock of the man I thought I married was cracking, and I felt myself falling down through the fathoms of his life to meet him anew. I was in love with him all over again. I internalized how the world saw him, dressed not in a tattered undershirt grumping about the house but stepping placidly into his masterful persona with a silk scarf round his neck and a jaunty cap on his head. He had no need to rein in his multitude of assistants for, like the Greek god Argus, he knew exactly what they were up to.

During his final months as DA, he had become more than ever a prosecutorial swashbuckler. In the last month alone, he had uncovered two European banks engaging in lethal activities. Using Israel's Mossad and the global intelligence network he had developed long ago, he had caught Credit Suisse and Lloyd's of London red-handed. Not only had they violated U.S. sanctions against Iran; they had laundered a billion dollars for the enemy, which, incredibly, used the money to buy contraband in the United States designed for building nuclear weapons. Thanks to these "friendly" Western banks conspiring against us, Iran was building the atomic bomb America was trying to prevent—with *American* components. President Ahmadinejad of Iran must have been laughing all the way to his uranium enrichment facilities.

The U.S. Treasury Department attempted to impose only civil penalties on the banks, but Bob stepped in and threatened Credit Suisse with a criminal indictment for felonies it had committed in Manhattan. As a result, the Swiss bank settled with the DA's Office for a $536 million fine. Lloyd's had agreed to pay $350 million.

It didn't surprise many people that Bob had pulled off a settlement unique in the annals of prosecutions. And, as many times before, Bob had been the first, the precedent setter. He recognized long before the U.S. government that Iran had no intention of negotiating or giving up its nuclear advancements. In fact, Bob was the one who alerted the CIA that Iran had terrorist agents all over the world and was giving major funds to anti-Israeli terrorist organizations like Hezbollah. Iran, his sources revealed, was, in actuality, a terrorist nation.

As retirement nears, we grow closer, lighter; we touch each other and feel only the present moment.

Feathers fall from nowhere, and we make a pillow of them . . . then all we know disappears, and what we don't is here within the gold-blue hollow beneath our heads.

•

After dinner, we watch movies on the DVR. Tonight, as often happens, Bob stretches out his arm, and I cuddle into his shoulder. We have just seen Margaret Rutherford solve the wealthy uncle's murder in a delicious Miss Marple antique. "After thirty years of marriage," I say, looking up, "this is pretty sweet, don't you think?"

"Someone gave me some chocolate today," he says and pulls a big box out of his briefcase. It is covered in crinkly gold foil with raised red rosebuds on top. "Who?" I ask. He shrugs. Little mystery gifts often appear on his desk from assistants who imitate his practice of not taking credit for his deeds.

"Want to share it?" he asks, smiling shyly, as if we were on a first date. I nod, smiling back. His face is soft and open, his body bending toward me like a newly planted scion. "Let's each have one," he says, choosing a sugarplum shaped like an unfolding flower. He carefully peels back the wrapper, observes the chocolate, then puts it in my mouth. As we bite into them, we look at each other with surprise, strawberry cream sliding around our tongues but not tasting like strawberry at all. Instead, it manifests itself as a rather odd array of spices and liqueurs. He breaks another in half, popping part in my mouth and part in his own, and we suppress laughs as the rich, uniquely tasty goo slips down his chin.

·

A few weeks before he was to relinquish a lifetime of power, Bob and I were having one of his favorite meals, Cornish hen with gravy and peas. The meal was sticking in my throat: Would anyone listen to him when he was no longer DA, when he had become an afterthought? What would happen to his ego, his active mind? What could he possibly do at age ninety? Just as the fluttering inside my stomach was reaching a high, his booming voice came through the silence.

"I'm going to accuse the president of using dope."

I stopped eating. Then I waited patiently until he had cleaned the meat off his wing bone. Lately, he had aimed some parting salvos at high public officials. He had, in fact, publicly accused the mayor of not wanting "anybody around who doesn't kiss his ring or other parts of his body."

Bob finally pushed away his plate. "The reason I'm going after Obama is that I'm worried. Iran has the capacity to fire long-range ballistic missiles right into the middle of Jerusalem. Everyone's dropped the ball on the sanctions. We could be headed for a third world war.

"Obama thinks he'll get further if he makes nice to them. Meanwhile, they'll be firing missiles into Israel. The president must be high on something, and that's what I'm going to say."

"Uh, I don't think that's a very good idea, sweetie," I said, though I'm usually the one who urges him to step out of the box. "You can't insult the president that way."

But he did anyway. On December 26, 2009, he had the president smoking pot in *The Wall Street Journal.*

29

Five days later, on December 31, the last day of his term and well after the clock struck 6:00 p.m., Bob Morgenthau walked out of the DA's office for the last time.

On that night and the nights to follow, we sat together, hypnotized by reruns of *Law & Order*. As I look back, I see that it worked on us as a drug, a dirge, and a perfect channel for emotional displacement. We got furious about the long-departed but still-missed Adam Schiff, the district attorney based on Bob. Why on earth had he been eclipsed by Dianne Wiest, who, oddly enough, reminded us of Leslie Crocker Snyder?

Everything changes; nothing stays the same.

•

As ever, we were each other's counterparts, and I tried not to veer from his side. Sometimes, we were just idle, taking in the smells and sounds of the city: the distant traffic, like the rush of water over stones . . . the rich aroma of beef bourguignon turned to a simmer . . . the spine-tingling scream of tires, praying that shattering glass and crumpling metal wouldn't follow . . . the *bump bump bump* of boys' blocks hurled from the floor above our heads . . . and the secret setting of the sun, fast obliterating twilight's glow.

During the day, he did what has always been his favorite pastime. There was not a room in the apartment where I couldn't hear his booming voice on the telephone. I adore that voice. And I was grateful that he had this outlet, raising money for charity, brainstorming, or just chatting with Steve Kaufman, Judah Gribetz, his children. Yet when he hung up, even if he had secured a hundred thousand dollars for PAL or the museum or gotten a job for a former ADA, he was subdued.

He was unwinding. "When I came home from the war, I was physically, mentally, and emotionally shot," he said. "I slept twenty-two hours a day, would get up to eat, and then go back to sleep. I couldn't even remember the name of the destroyer that had brought me home. It took me a long time to recover. That's what this is like."

•

Sometimes, I see images floating through your subliminal mind. A paper-thin heart, a hand withdrawn, a rose encased in ice. I laugh at the littlest things to keep you smiling. But my laugh comes out of sorrow. You were a king. You were the creator of justice and peace, the inventor with integrity. And there is nothing, nothing at all, that I can do to get that back.

•

"Bob," I said at breakfast one morning, "when I tell you all the great things people are still saying about you, when I tell you how proud I am, right in this moment, it doesn't seem to affect you."

"Huh," he said and smiled. "Maybe I don't believe you."

"What? You think I'm lying!"

"No, but it seems unlikely people are paying that much attention now."

I put down my spoon on my plate of berries. "You're very down on yourself."

"I'm let down. I'm at odds and ends," he admitted.

"This is a bitch, love, I know," I said, rubbing his arm. "But you don't have to *do* anything. You don't have to *prove* anything. You just have to be. You have accomplished more than a dozen leaders put together, and that's not an exaggeration."

"It certainly is."

I swallowed. "You know what they say in chaos theory? If a butterfly flaps its wings in Texas, there will be a hurricane in Japan. You are that butterfly."

He gave me a rather indulgent smile.

•

The days go by uneasily. The leitmotifs that run through our life—habits, phrases, familiar gambols—they keep us steady; I depend on them. But leitmotifs are not always melody; they don't always reassure us. Lately ours have been dissonant, uneasy. Wagnerian. Wotan gives and Wotan takes. You are up, I am down. I am down, you are up. I have forgotten my vow to keep you cheered and engaged. I have become just a skip in the record. Die Walküre *playing over and over on the turntable.*

•

I am too busy. There have been the regular stories for Tina Brown's online newspaper, *The Daily Beast*, on Bernard Madoff, the sham money manager to the rich and famous. I had broken a number of exclusives about his Ponzi scheme; for a while, I was the media's leading Madoff expert, reportedly causing even *The New York Times* to express frustration. This, of course, had nothing to do with my scant financial acumen and everything to do with the sources I had developed.

Now my desk is strewn with piles of research on teen bullies for another *Beast* series, manuscripts from hopeful student grads I taught at Yale, Princeton, and Vassar. On a portable easel is a pastel portrait of Amy and Josh; art has become a hobby. My cell phone keeps ringing, e-mails go unanswered, my calendar is full: lunch with an editor, tea with a news source, theater with Christine Connor, my buddy on European biking trips. Bob's secretary, Ida Van Lindt, used to tell people who invited us out that I was harder to get than the Boss.

I need to find a quotation for a novel I've started. Standing on a chair, I reach a dusty *Bartlett's Familiar Quotations* from my top bookshelf, and out fall sheets of yellowed paper. My old poems. Very old. They are not particularly good, but they make me smile at the jelly bean who wrote them. One is dated 1978—a year after our marriage—"For the Duke from the Lost Duchess":

> *Who am I, will you tell me*
> *After having loved you.*
> *I am a wide-eyed fly whirling*
> *Around you, my transparent wings*

Beating in your ear,
Tentatively requesting
An audience.

Since then, we have done a double psychic somersault. How ironic that Bob, the most independent man in creation, is now so dependent on me. Thirty years earlier, I went from being a high-powered writer to a lovelorn girl, totally subservient to him. I would have given anything to have him home with me all the time. Now, though I love the continual surprise of seeing him during the day, I think sometimes I love my privacy more.

An unpleasant word from me can leave him hurt. I have more power over him than I ever did before. And I don't want it.

•

One night I summoned the courage to bring things to a head. "Sweetheart." I inched closer to him on the couch. "We've been avoiding this for too long. You need to let it out of you. You miss being DA, don't you?"

"Not on your life," he replied. "It's a relief. I'm glad not to be doing all that work."

"Bob, I just don't believe you. I think if you talk about your loss, you'd feel better, like you did when you talked about the PTSD. Or . . . is it that you don't want me to feel lost too?"

"Up, up, attaboy," Bob said. Ivan jumped happily into his lap. My competition, the "other woman," so to speak, was a dog. He was also Bob's go-to when he wanted to avoid something unpleasant. Once, I asked Mark Doyle, a top farm manager, if Bob had brought Ivan to the farm store. He replied, "Well, actually, there's a question of whether Bob brought Ivan or Ivan brought Bob."

"Forget bloody Ivan and look at me, damn it," I exclaimed. "Look, you've been used to being the Boss—thousands of cases, constant feedback from what, some five hundred ADAs? Reporters writing adoring pieces. And I've had the privilege of being the DA's wife.

"You know that retirement is one of life's biggest causes of stress. Maybe we're both in shock."

But that was not the discussion my husband wanted to have. Instead, he preferred to talk about our heartbeats. He put his finger to his wrist, took his pulse, and then asked me to take it. Afterward, he double-checked it. Finally, trying to go with the flow, I asked him to take *my* pulse. He did. "Seventy beats per minute," he said happily, dropping my wrist. "We're both fine."

•

And that's all there is to say. Does your pulse signify the pulse of the office? Taking the measure of how much you miss it?

I feel the defined crease of your knuckles, the curve of your thumb, firmly encircling my hand. I keep vigil for definition; I crave it, for it means you are still with me: whole, quirky, mine. You have not begun to slip into that hazy dimension of old age, that flattening out, a free fall into the not here. Counting your heartbeats is a ritual I actually like, feeling the strong throb in your wrist, the cool touch of your hand on my skin.

•

It was mid-January, and I was taking a brisk walk on the frozen orchard ground: dying grass, dying leaves, dying gray sky; no tractors plowing the soil, no Newtown Pippins or newer innovative varieties being planted. The raw wind was making my cheeks red, not a fresh young blush, but a late splotchy irritation; I used my inhaler to ease the bronchial tubes tightened by the icy air.

Summer rushes by like a bullet, reminding us of love's quickness, while winter sticks to us forever: dead, cold, stiff.

In defiance of an injured knee, I picked up my pace, speed-walked, faster and faster until sweat dripped down my neck. When I walked these paths with Bob, it was exercise for him but not for me.

This made me all the more eager to reassure him that he might not have as fast a gait or as strong an arm, but he would live for many more years. We had friends who were over a hundred.

"Sweetheart, age isn't always chronological," I had said to him recently. "You are perfect proof of that. One day you feel ninety, and the next you're fifty. Look at Gram Leavitt. She seemed to be losing touch when she turned seventy-five, and then, when Mom got sick and she was needed, she snapped right back."

If my words were a comfort to Bob, they were not to me. They simply disguised my latest bout of fixating on death, and this time I was not only afraid of losing him; I was afraid of losing myself.

•

From the day we met, we were ageless; we called ourselves twins. We acted as if we had boarded the Trans-Siberian train and it would just keep rolling on and on. We never thought about the last station, but in the haze I see it now. Why can't I simply be happy about your excellent health? You do strength training, aerobics; you are an active father and husband. But I see the other you: the one who may still surpass me in mind and can no longer keep up with me in body.

Share your fears, the psychology books say, which neither of us wants to do; it would only make things worse. Though if I understood your dread, I would try to help you. You never complain. When your body refuses to obey you, you bear it stoically. A scary imbalance on the steps, toes and fingers losing their straight fine shapes. When you are stiff, I know it only by your quips: "When are they going to invent WD-40 for the joints!"

I cannot stop my body from following yours. I have begun walking gingerly over the farm's stony paths. A doctor told you whatever you do, don't fall, so your feet barely skim the ground. I find myself mimicking you, and what happens? I trip and fall. Like now. If I hadn't caught myself when I stumbled on that stone, I would have landed smack on my knees. Once you locked us out of the car, and ever since, like a little old lady, I check and recheck my purse to make sure I've got the keys.

I don't want to be your twin. Old age is after me, and I'm running for my life. I say to myself what Dylan Thomas said: "Do not go gentle into that good night. / Rage, rage against the dying of the light."

Once, I imagined away the fear. But it will never really go. I see the future without you all too well. The echoes of an oboe: your voice. The faint sound of newspapers crackling in your beautiful veiny hands, your wisecracks, your jokes, your exciting ideas. I will eat soup alone at a diner, celebrate Christmas with an empty, treeless apartment, the kids living their lives and I, my own, too numb to lose myself in the little worlds of ice-skaters and choristers. Then, one day, falling sick . . . suffering . . . passing through alone.

Please, God, don't let him die before me.

•

When I got back to the farmhouse, he was coming out the door. He ran his hand over my dripping hair. "Oh, you *did* have a good walk! I hope you were careful with your knee," he said gently. "I'm proud of you."

But his eyes said something different. A wish. An entreaty. He finally passed me by, his back slightly bent, his walking sticks penetrating the earth before him, slowly making his way down the old dusty lane.

He grew smaller and smaller. Before he disappeared from sight, I willed myself to empty my head of all the phobic garbage that had accumulated there. Instead, I chose to see my husband as bold and gritty and ready for anything. I caught up with him, slipped my hand into his. "Can I walk with you?" I asked.

30

On January 19, 2010, looking natty in tweed cap and silk scarf, Bob left the house and, at age ninety, began his second career. I was jubilant. On this day, I vowed to rid myself of the specters of old age and death that had obsessed me for too long. First, I set my bike to high gear and pedaled furiously to the beat of the Pointer Sisters. Then there was the cold shower, scrubbing off dead cells with a concoction of brown sugar in olive oil. Finally, feeling symbolically cleansed, I went to my studio and began a regime of writing fiction, any kind of fiction, for seven hours a day. Shaping imaginary realms was the only way I knew to keep imaginary realms from shaping me.

As the saying goes, "If you want to make God laugh, tell him your plans." The retirement that had undone us turned out to be a three-week illusion—an intermezzo before a prestigious New York law firm gave Bob the chance to undergo an explosion of creativity.

With a sense of dignity and his own office in which to study and think, he gradually opened up the dark hidden places where a new breed of "little guy" suffered unnoticed. He lambasted the U.S. government that he had once pledged to uphold for abusing and deporting the "tired [and the] poor, [the] huddled masses yearning to breathe free," who were once welcomed to our shores with the words inscribed on the Statue of Liberty. He blamed the government for providing little help to the heroic young soldiers traumatized by fighting its wars in Afghanistan and Iraq. He exposed the plight of both immigrants and soldiers with PTSD in Op-Ed columns published in the most distinguished newspapers. His pieces, sometimes coming one after another, in *The*

New York Times, The Wall Street Journal, Newsweek, Reuters, the *Daily News,* turned the thinking of policy makers from New York to Washington upside down.

If I had tried to mirror Bob as a man who had never lost his potential, Martin Lipton made it a reality. A founder of Wachtell, Lipton, Rosen & Katz and a public leader in his own right, Marty hired Bob as of counsel to advise and do pro bono work for the firm. A professor, author, trustee, and financial wizard, Marty had invented an algorithm called the poison pill that prevented quick hostile takeovers of small companies; it had been called one of the most important corporate innovations ever made. If Bob had altered the criminal justice system, Marty had altered the face of Wall Street.

In one weekend, Marty Lipton and Herb Wachtell had walls knocked down and a spacious office created for Bob with sleek blond furniture. In days, plaques and pictures of Bob with the nation's leaders were hung on the wall. A procession of curious young lawyers lined up to meet him, but they had to get by the famous and devoted Ida Van Lindt, who had, upon his orders, come with him from the DA's Office and was now his de facto vice president. He advised the firm's young lawyers and provided moral support. He spoke at prestigious think tanks like the Brookings Institution, warning that nuclear materials were being amassed at our back door by Venezuela courtesy of Iran. He continued to exchange secret information with his Israeli contacts. He again publicly criticized Mayor Bloomberg about financial issues and publicly made up with him. It was clear to everyone that being DA was not what had held him up.

After his many immigration exposés, the newspapers rushed in and began publishing a plethora of stories about the maltreatment of immigrants whom we once welcomed to our shores. His personal outrage was catching, especially by President Obama, who proceeded to issue new reforms. But Bob didn't let him off the hook. The reforms were deceptive, he wrote, and they were simply not enough.

One day, we heard about an intolerable injustice, which brought Bob into the crusade against the death penalty once again. A man from Alabama who was convicted of murder in spite of gross negligence by the state had languished on death row for twenty-four years. Bob asked two prominent prosecutors to join him in a friend-of-the-court appeal to the U.S. Supreme Court to hear the case. The brilliant brief that Bob had helped write landed him on the top half of the first page of the *Times's* New York section. The panegyric, written by Jim Dwyer, was accompanied by a wonderful color picture of Bob grinning in mid-stride through his office. Quoting Dickens, he crisply told the reporter, "The law is a ass." Dwyer began the weighty piece on a light note, making the irresistible observation that the heaps of scattered papers on Bob's desk seemed transported intact from the one he occupied as district attorney. I made fifty copies of the article for friends and family. At ninety, my husband, my hero, the defender of the helpless, was back.

•

Dear Sweetheart,

You are the Erasmus of our day. Almost five hundred years ago, this Christian humanist said what you have said in so many ways: "It's the happiest of men who are willing to be what they are." People sought Erasmus out for the same reason they seek you out now: because of who you are. They want to be on the side of good; they want to absorb what you have. Being near you enhances their reputations.

You have always surprised me, just when I thought things were fixed. I have watched you reinvent yourself from a cool prosecutor to a crusading columnist! Lashing against the system's moral turpitude, as I did one time long ago.

You are still chairman of the boards of PAL and the museum and, in a tough economy, saved them by raising a record amount of donations.

Don't worry about your promise to work only part of the days. It is silly for you to defend yourself by pointing out that you now come home at 6:30 instead of 7:00. Remember that nasty blizzard last winter? You and Marty were two of the only ones who came to the office. You work too hard, and I worry about you. But I have always known who you are. There are some people who work to live and others who live to work.

Love,
Your Tartlette

•

Tartlette,

Thank you for your nice letter. I'm glad you think I'm more important than I am—if you think that, then I think it too. You are right; I feel the

pressure to work, and I know you worry about me. I'm sorry I was so hard
to live with after I left office. You make me happy and secure, and I love
you with all my heart.

    Tart

•

Bob had branched out from immigration to other causes. He had written
about gun control, corporate transparency, and other issues, but perhaps
his most poignant column was about a pitiful victim of post-traumatic
stress disorder. Bob had become so in touch with his own postwar shock
and how it had altered his personality that he wanted to reach out to
help other afflicted veterans. One day he found out from a source about
a Vietnam vet, one Peter Wielunski, who had been diagnosed with severe PTSD at a Veterans Administration (VA) hospital in Queens, New
York. For one year, Peter kept asking for psychological help but was not
given therapy even when he threatened to commit suicide. Finally, he
hanged himself in front of the psychology department.

    I felt sick when Bob told me. And then I got angry. No other media
knew about the case. He had to get this outrageous story out quick before some VA press agent spun it as a minor incident. I was excited to be
part of the process, to bring in my expertise. I coached him on how to
persuade the family to talk and how to get the autopsy reports. He even
obtained the VA's one thousand pages of records on Wielunski. *The
Wall Street Journal* jumped at the story and assigned him Op-Ed space.
Leading the column with the suicide, he gave harrowing statistics and
told how veterans who were not given the chance to talk about their experiences went on to either hole themselves up or become violent, even
murderous. His piece was widely applauded and helped him get private
hospitals involved in treating these men who had sacrificed so much for
their country.

•

He made frequent appearances, including an interview about his war
missions conducted by Tom Brokaw at the New-York Historical Society.
To me, the culmination of his work on immigration came in January
2012, two years after the law firm had hired him. We had been in a state
of agitated excitement for weeks because a top *New York Times* reporter,

the respected Kirk Semple, would be interviewing him in front of some two hundred people at the distinguished Roosevelt House, now a museum and a forum for the top American policy makers.

Bob was at heart a modest man who didn't really believe that he mattered as much as he did. He worked on his words and his graphs for weeks and occasionally wondered whether anybody would even care about them.

I arrived early and sat in the front row so I could allay his nerves with encouraging smiles. I wanted my husband to shine, to hear people say, "I don't believe that man's over ninety!"

He walked in and sat, waiting for the program to begin. Under the bright lights, his eyes closed and his mouth opened in such a grimace that he might be thought to have seen some repulsive sight invisible to the rest of us. I beamed at him and then closed my mouth tightly, hoping he'd pick up the signal, but he didn't seem to see me, though I was right in front of him.

Semple's first question was easy: "What do you think about immigration reform, Mr. Morgenthau?"

"I think we have a special responsibility to immigrants because that is what all of us are," Bob replied. "We are a nation of immigrants who came from all over the world."

Bravo, sweetheart! Then a harder question came: What about the argument that immigrants are taking the jobs of the American people? Bob proceeded to give almost word for word the same answer he gave to the first question. Oh, dear. Sweetheart!

Then Semple praised him for his columns, which he said were being read and taken to heart by the highest echelons of power in Washington. See, sweetheart? I told you!

Now he let it rip. As he noticed me smiling and nodding, a raft of horror stories poured out of him, leaving the audience aghast. Graphs he had put together were flashed on the screen showing that only two out of twenty thousand immigrants were deemed security risks last year. He said that President Obama, while instituting "reforms," bragged that this year they had deported more immigrants than ever before; that immigrants were hauled off the street and deported on the spot for something as minor as a traffic ticket; that it wasn't just the ethnic poor, the Mexicans, South Americans, Asians, but anyone who could be victimized. Even the middle and elite classes. The immigration officials didn't discriminate.

Bob recounted how the daughter of the distinguished Greek-born filmmaker Costa-Gavras, who was living in France, was arrested as soon as she landed in New York to attend a major Greek cultural festival at Lincoln Center sponsored by her father. This was because she had overstayed her student visa by weeks the last time she was here. The Greek ambassador, the French ambassador, and other public officials tried in vain to save her from immediate deportation. Bob just happened to be at JFK Airport and heard what was happening. "I proposed," Bob said in his deep, mesmerizing voice, "that they turn her over to me as a criminal and I would make sure she was on the first plane out after her father's conference. Miraculously, that worked." People chuckled and applauded.

When the questions began from the audience, Kirk had to repeat them to Bob, who became so relaxed about his deafness that each time Kirk asked him if he had heard an inquiry, he would smile and shake his head. Judging by the absurdity of some of the questions, I figured that my husband was not hearing them on purpose.

As for me, I had been sweating under my wool blazer, and in spite of the command of my friend Lila to "breathe, Lucinda, breathe," I had barely done so. Now, mightily relieved, I began breathing long and deeply.

Afterward, at a private dinner, Bob entertained the table of dignitaries with story after story about his career long after dessert was served. When we got home, he was ready for a nightcap, and I was ready to collapse on the floor. "Bob was amazing. I wonder why I'm so tired," I asked Lila.

Now she smiled and said, "Of course you're exhausted. How can you not be—you were holding him."

•

The sun, a lovely July sun, had just set, its colors coming through the wispy clouds—a huge spread of hot pink melting into spirals of lavender covering half the sky. It was July 2012, and we were on the deck overlooking the hills of the Hudson Highlands. "Look!" I exclaimed. Bob was poring over farm planting schedules. "Look, right now! The sunset, it's turning ash purple, like the lavender we picked in Provence, all the colors are changing. It's spectacular!"

"Uh-huh," he said, head down, lost in his reading.

He was frustrating me. "Been there, seen that?" I asked edgily.

"What?" He cocked his good ear toward me.

"If I think something's beautiful, it's guaranteed you won't even glance at it."

"Oh, stop your complaining," he said, taking up the copy of *The New Yorker* I had brought outside.

"Ha, very clever. I'm beginning to realize that's your way of shutting me up . . . Hey, you stole my *New Yorker!*"

"It's our *New Yorker.*"

"It happens to be mine."

"You guys are funny," Amy said, coming out the door. She was on her way down to the waterfall to look for turtles. "Are you sure you aren't sister and brother?"

Amy was an original. Wise and artistic beyond her years, she was a near genius at solving mechanical problems. In fact, she had saved the family last winter from suffocating in a voluminous nonstop of steam from the heating system. No one could plug it up until she accomplished some complicated maneuver in a minute, saying with a sigh, "Well, that was easy." No one ever understood how she had done it.

I took up my pencil and started doing a crossword puzzle. I also surreptitiously looked at my watch. I was betting on ten minutes. He didn't like to be ignored by anyone, particularly his wife and his dog.

It was only eight and a half.

"Look," he said, pointing to the rows of new Pink Lady and Honeycrisp shoots. "They're already growing." He refused to share the sunset with me, so I didn't bother to take my eyes off my puzzle. I had my pride.

"What're you doing there, Mum?" he asked cheerily, as though fighting words had never passed between us. I rather envied Bob's ability to start every moment anew, as though the present were the future and the past never happened.

•

We talked about our children then. One of our satisfactions was the success and well-being of our ever-growing brood. Amy and Josh, who could have languished under the pressure of having two high-achieving parents, had found their own paths to excellence, as had the older children from Bob's previous marriage.

Jenny, Bob's first child, had gone from her job in the city's human resources division to be the executive director of the Fresh Air Fund; she expanded programs, becoming well-known in New York's not-for-profit circles. She married Gene Anderson, a former assistant U.S. attorney under Bob, whom he still called Boss. Similar to her father in age, personality, and ethical values, Gene had founded a firm dedicated to forcing reluctant insurance companies to honor the contracts of their policyholders. Tragically, Gene died in 2010 of double pneumonia. But after a period of mourning, Jenny raised herself up and began a second life, dating and participating in a panoply of social activities.

The second child, Anne Morgenthau Grand, at age fifty determined and hardworking, got her doctorate with honors; she acquired a private practice as a psychotherapist and became associate director of the substance abuse program at New York–Presbyterian Hospital. Her husband, Paul Grand, was still a successful lawyer. The Grands' daughter, Hilary, and son-in-law, Ben Harris, lived in the city with their two bright young children, Sam and Daisy. The Grands' son, Noah, had gone to Russia with us one summer, bringing along a stack of Roald Dahl books and ending up teaching Josh to read. Noah had become a teacher for special-needs children and made his home in northern Idaho with his wife, Ali, a social worker.

The fourth child and elder son, Bobby, had became a top money manager in a respected firm and a trustee of the Museum of Jewish Heritage. His wife, Susan, had taken an increasingly active role as a New York Public Library trustee, organizing special literary panels and sitting on pivotal committees. We continued to be very close to their children: their son, Harry, had graduated from Middlebury College summa cum laude and went on to New York University Law School; their daughter, Martha, was thriving at Amherst and had a flair for ballet dancing.

My youngest stepdaughter, Barbara, married Hanmin Lee, a pediatric surgeon whom we came to love, and they settled in San Francisco. They produced two of the cutest, most gifted children, and I loved them as dearly as I did Barb. Mimoh, nine, and Taemoh, six, adored Amy and were always by her side whenever they stayed with us on the Vineyard.

As for the youngest daughter, Amy, she had been a superb actress, landing all the leads in school plays, and was also a beautiful poet and painter, talents she had always seemed to dismiss, perhaps because her competitive New York schools valued only academics. She had finally decided on a career in the veterinary field, working in a refuge in Georgia dedicated to propagating endangered species from Africa. She volunteered at shelters and ended up getting a job at an animal care center in New York. Her passion for animals soon made her the most popular handler at the center. As her co-worker Jason remarked, "When she walks in, the dogs are all over her; she has a special way with them."

Josh, our younger son, who was also a talented artist, had just become an entrepreneur, managing the New York branch of Good Eggs, an online grocery start-up that connected farmers to shoppers by delivering local fare right to people's homes. Bob had made Josh, at age twenty-four, manager of Fishkill Farms, and Josh had expanded it to include free-range chickens and organically grown vegetables. He even began using organic clay sprays on some trees and had planted thousands of new fruit trees. He had a burgeoning reputation as one of the leaders of the new young growers who were changing the Hudson Valley. When he was twenty-six, he was awarded an honorary doctorate from Mount Saint Mary College across the river. It gave me a thrill to witness the extraordinary closeness between Josh and his father. Bob taught his son about farming at an early age—they had an acre garden near the house—and now they work together and chat about farm matters constantly.

We were proud of the success he was making of the teetering farm, which we had barely been able to hold on to. He worked fourteen-hour days and was exhausted but happy at the growing fans of the orchard. But it wasn't easy. A farmer's life is frustratingly dependent on the whims of nature. This summer's bounty can be next summer's disaster. A spring freeze that wipes out half the lovingly tended apple crop, a tomato blight, a weevil infestation—some seasons could be nerve-rattling.

"When you are as old as I am," I remember telling him, "you'll look back at what you did for your father. You preserved his heritage. The love of the land that your great-grandfather gave your grandfather, which was in turn passed to your father, finally came to you. Look around you, the Morgenthau tradition has lived on. And you made it happen."

•

One weekend, Bob suggested we visit the Garden of Stones at the Museum of Jewish Heritage. A visionary installation created by the famous sculptor Andy Goldsworthy, the sunken garden commemorated the victims of the Holocaust. It was exquisite in its simplicity—huge boulders excavated in Vermont spaced out on a bed of sand—and spiritual in its symbolism. Saplings planted by survivors several years earlier rose from holes in the huge stones, and to me they represented the struggle between life and death: some of the trees were tall and strong on this December day, and others had perished.

Bob was walking around alone, thin in his puffy green jacket, as though he himself were a tree trying to rise from a boulder. I saw a vision of the young sailor that Bob had once been; I saw him as he had appeared in the early home movie his father once took at the old estate in Fishkill Farms. In it, he had been breezy, mysterious, clearly fond of skylarking, and unbearably handsome.

The movie recorded a secret visit made by Winston Churchill in 1942 to huddle with President Roosevelt and Treasury secretary Henry Morgenthau Jr. It was a historic and unique portrait of the three powerful men, but the camera kept wandering back to Bob. I was captivated by how this new ensign flirted with the girls. Not by going after them, but by leaning back, legs crossed, arms folded, waiting for them to be presented to him. Wearing crisp dress whites, he behaved not the least crisply: he gobbled a piece of finger food from the picnic table and then smirked for the camera, swiping his mouth with the back of his hand. Churchill clearly didn't like the mint julep Bob had made, and he slid down in his Adirondack chair, legs spread, stomach protruding, like a plump oyster on the half shell.

By 1945, Bob had returned as the person I now knew, dead cold sober, his lively roguish spirits gone. I felt a longing for this youth I had missed by thirty years, the man he would never be again.

I leaned against the fence near the roiling waters of the harbor and gazed at the Statue of Liberty looming over the garden. The brackish smell reminded me of the boat trip the family had taken in July 2003. It was heavenly. Navigating the *Souvenir* from New York to Montreal. The kids were supposed to sleep on the deck, but it rained constantly, so the four of us stuffed ourselves into two bunks; toes tickled nostrils, smelly boys' feet had to be endured, bodies flopping over on bodies. Bob, then eighty-three, went up and down the bridge lithely, steering through thick fogs, finding narrow channels. Everyone was truly happy: unspoiled, unentitled pioneers who never complained.

Bob came up behind me then. "Remember the boat trip to Montreal," I said, "how we all thought it was the best family trip we've ever taken . . . That's something we'll never do again." I flinched, hearing the bitterness in my voice.

He shook his head. "Can't you stop being negative? Try to enjoy a memory for what it is, something you can look at anytime you want; no, it will never come again, and I don't think it should." He pointed to the boulders. "Look at these trees. Healthy, thriving, and fed only by rock. That's optimism.

"Nothing is set in stone," he went on, leaning against a rock, looking to see if I got his pun.

He looked out at the harbor, the gateway abroad. "I read an article on Portugal in the *Times*," he added nonchalantly. "I'd like to go there sometime."

I gave him a blank look.

"Don't we have a thirty-fifth wedding anniversary coming up?"

"Are you suggesting we celebrate it in Portugal?" Not at ninety-three years of age. We hadn't been to Europe in at least seven years. And even then, not to a country where we didn't know the language or the customs or the quality of medical care.

He regarded me slyly. "It depends on whether we have the right suitcases."

31

Frankie shoots out of the airport like Mario Andretti at the Grand Prix, skims the streets of Lisbon, and comes squealing to a halt before our sedate Belle Epoque hotel. As we shakily disgorge from the black Peugeot we have rented, he looks at his watch and gives us a triumphant smile: "Four minutes exact. A record."

I nod politely at the small-boned driver of medium height and dark hair. Bob rolls his eyes.

Frank Sánchez, a talented photographer who was born in Cuba and immigrated to Spain, turns out to be an ideal guide. He is a translator for us as well as a driver, saving me from doing 150 miles, which is the length of Portugal up to San Sebastián on the Spanish coast.

Bob and I love to visit vineyards, and because I love port, I want to go to a particular port house that makes an excellent glass. When we discover it is located up a long, winding road on the pinnacle of a mountain, I suggest we skip it, but Bob, in spite of his acrophobia, insists we go. How many adventures have there been that I wanted to take and he didn't? This is something I will never know because I'm realizing now that he has kept them a closely guarded secret. He has wanted to make me feel simply happy, not guilty.

During the climb to the port house, the dialogue between him and our breakneck driver is highly entertaining.

"Slow down, Frankie!" he booms as he's jolted along, avoiding even a glance at the canyon below. "Watch that turn!" Frankie, however, cannot hear him because his primitive GPS is delivering adenoidal commands: "¡A la derecha en la ro-tun-da!" So Frankie continues to whip around the hairpin curves, sending his right wheels—and Bob in the passenger's seat—almost over the cliff. The tyrannical woman in the GPS, whom we name Loco Loca, and Bob's reverberating voice make a desperate dodecaphonic symphony.

Hired to simply chauffeur us around, Frankie turns out to be as quirky as we are, and we soon become a little family, spending most of our time together touring, jesting, and eating.

We listen to a woman singing Portuguese fado music—rich, complex, and mournful—go through wine country in the Douro Valley, and end up in San Sebastián, which, with the greatest number of Michelin stars, has become the food capital of the world. We dine at a little restaurant where the grim Basque owner has somehow, thousands of miles across the ocean, heard of Bob and drops his veil of grumpiness to embrace him in a bear hug.

During our week in San Sebastián, Frankie divides his time between Bob and me. He and I wander around eating pintxos, the Basque version of tapas, made from fresh crusty bread topped with delicacies ranging from marinated anchovies and caviar to baby squid to foie gras and figs. Frankie and I spar and joke. Unlike my family, he actually thinks I am "the funniest person" he's ever met. Every minute he seems to be snapping pictures of me with his sophisticated cameras—Lucinda caught off guard looking confused, Lucinda against the mountains with the sun at her back, Lucinda at the exact moment she is cursing an elevator that shuts on her knuckle.

I come alive, soaking in such unusual attention, while Bob sits back and watches with interest, his razor blue eyes missing not a thing. My husband's reaction pleases me as much as Frankie's compliments. I wonder what he is thinking? Is he jealous? I hope so.

But Frankie's admiration does not stop with me. He loves Bob—who reminds him of his Cuban grandfather—and always defers to him. Frankie makes him look young and vigorous. The two of them walk along the river each morning, and my husband takes the pavement with long, fast strides. Moreover, instead of the one mile he walks at home, he walks two miles with Frankie. He isn't going to let this young fellow outdo him. I am astonished. Even more so when, later, we have a Pernod at the Deux Magots and then I, of course, get us lost in the backstreets of Saint-Germain-des-Prés. Bob finally says he'll guide us. He passes me and proceeds with his sticks swinging so quickly I can't keep up with him.

The next morning Bob bangs on Frankie's door, bellowing, "Let's go, time for breakfast. Hurry up," and I think I hear Frankie jump out of bed and frantically rustle around to find his clothes. Bob is taking charge. That afternoon, as we set off for high tea, Frankie puts his elbow out as if to escort me, and before I know it, Bob pushes ahead, places his arm around my shoulder, and leads me down to the dining hall.

Waiting for the elevator, Bob says, "That color you're wearing is nice on you. You look beautiful."

One morning, Bob is trying to get his pants buttoned, lying down on the bed like a model trying to wiggle into an extra-small pair of jeans. "I'm too big for my britches," he gasps.

"You've got to get bigger pants," I say, giggling. "You're not the same size you were when you were married. Well, actually, weight loss or not, neither am I!"

We eat at a three-star restaurant, just the two of us, and consume a lunch consisting of twelve courses, every one presented to us by a different waiter, each with his uniquely comic snootiness. Of much notice is Bob's khaki farm pants and my messy hair held back with honeybees that are actually barrettes. After dessert, we fairly roll out the door and then start laughing about the turned-up noses, the tight mouths, the drawn-out accents, and the meaningful glances of the staff. I don't remember when we've had such fun—as if we were teens in a house of mirrors.

It feels as if something were about to happen; I get a tingling in my fingertips. Are things changing? Has Frankie come into our lives for a reason? Miracles often happen when you're not looking.

Our time together draws to a close. We say goodbye to Frankie and watch him get in the car and roar away.

We go through the rest of our day, expectantly. But we are as we have been. Nothing changes. Nothing happens.

Yet.

•

A few days later, we arrive home from JFK airport and barely get through the door when Bob suddenly shouts, "Hug!" I turn to see an unusual smile—tender, unprotected—and arms stretched out like a boy going after a butterfly. "Hug!" he repeats, and then holds me tight, as though he hasn't seen me in years. We fall back on the couch, laughing.

And that's when I know something is happening.

The following night, with one eye glued to a recipe since I'm such an unpredictable cook, I make his favorite, soft-shell crabs, and, miraculously, they are delicious. The next day he rushes off to tackle the overwhelming amount of work he needs to do. An hour later, the doorbell rings. Sitting outside is a pink orchid. From Bob? But Bob isn't programmed to send me flowers! In return, like a Pavlovian dog, I begin doing things like buying farm-fresh milk for his coffee in the morning and constructing his complex bowl of bran buds, berries, yogurt, and honey. He acts as if I've opened a piñata.

That is how I know that something is changing in *me*.

•

The next night, Bob, who falls asleep when he hits the pillow, flicks out his lamp while I, as is my habit, lose myself in my hero, Lord Peter Wimsey, the dashing, shell-shocked detective who is also a talented lover. But tonight my attention wanders, and I drop Dorothy Sayers to the floor. I want my husband.

I am nervous, but I slide over and press my belly in the hollow of his back. The man likes his sleep. I nuzzle his neck and take in that sweet musky scent, faintly familiar but not forgotten. His hair feels thick and wiry but silky beneath.

I make spirals round his chest, his navel, and trail my fingers downward, to a nostalgic warmth. He stirs and dreamily turns over and touches me. Dreamy, nocturnal love. Then we fall into a deep sleep; through the night, we keep reaching for each other, finding a lost arm, a leg, a hand to be held. The way it should be.

In the morning, I find him sleeping on top of me, his new apnea machine tickling me, swooshing in my ear.

"Did you feel me rubbing your back last night?" he asks, waking.

I put my cheek against his and gently take off his mask. My beloved.

When we finally get dressed, I take out my underwear and find my stockings oddly stretched out. I glance at him. How ridiculously zany was our banter once! Should I take the risk?

In a stern voice, I ask, "Bob, have you been wearing my panty hose?"

He stares at me blankly. Then the sly grin begins. "How did you find out?"

"Just what is it you do with them?" I ask coyly.

"If you think I'm going to tell you that, you're crazy!" His laughter. Not the low slap of a wave, but the sound of a young tide rolling up the shore. Carillons ringing over the drumbeat of horses.

That's when I know things are changing for *us*.

•

We walk in the park that afternoon, holding hands. It is filled with people, different faces, different looks, happy, guarded, shy, aggressive.

"Do you think people are mostly good or bad?" I ask him.

I've asked this question before, but I really want to know. There were two reasons: to bring us together in a common belief, and to provide him with one way to get through hard times. "Look at all this beauty. Do you think God is here, in the trees, the sky, the earth . . . in the people?"

He looks at the boys on the baseball diamond. "They're still playing. What crazy weather."

"Please, for once, tell me what you believe in."

"I believe in you."

"You are so sweet . . . It's because of the Holocaust, isn't it? Why you might not believe in God? Maybe you know this story already, but I love it and it's true. In one of the camps, they made a little boy pull the rope that hanged his father. Everyone had to watch, and the inmates were crying and some of them shouted, 'Where is God?' A lone voice in the crowd answered: 'He is up there in the gallows.'"

•

It is getting colder now, and foggy puffs of air are coming out of our mouths. I take out the wedding snapshot that I found in the leaves of my old *Roget's Thesaurus*, and I show it to Bob.

"Look at us, how young we were! Do you believe those wide grins? I don't think my lips would stretch that far anymore.

"Uh, I was wondering, in Portugal, when I was joking and laughing with Frankie, did I smile as much as I did back then? Did I look a little bit like this? Like the girl you were once determined to win? I noticed you were watching us."

He stops and studies the picture. He takes me quite seriously these days, is more responsive. "I think I did see you that way. It's how I see you now."

"I see you differently too. I see you as a handsome, strong man whom I was so lucky to get, a great man who belongs not only to me but to the people."

"I see a girl with a sparkle in her eyes and dimples in her cheeks. No, don't say that, I don't like it when you complain that you've gotten dimples where they're not supposed to be. I love them all. The more the merrier."

I laugh. "I think Frankie brought out the best in us; in a way, he made us remember why we fell in love. Maybe we'd forgotten that."

"I think we appreciate each other more." He tickles the nape of my neck. Then he sweeps me with a tender eye: my red coat, my cold cheeks. "You're my peony," he says.

I smile, startled. I have never heard him say anything quite like that. Later, I look up the flower and find that devilish but lovable creatures are said to live inside.

•

The following Saturday afternoon, the sky went black, then opened up. I was sitting looking at the window with Amy, who was twenty-two and now my friend as well as daughter. We loved rain; it was exciting, coming at us as it did in pin-sized bullets, then shattering into pieces and rolling down the panes.

"It's funny," she was saying. "Rain is just rain until you look up close at it and then it becomes something new, a kitten or a ballerina or an octopus. I think that's the way we all are; we don't really see other people for what they are." She rolled her eyes. "Like boys hiding what jerks they are."

I smiled and nodded. "Well, you've got a dad who's a hard standard to live up to." Amy and Bob were in the midst of a lovefest, similarly laid-back as they were. "He has a special look he gives you, a special way of making us laugh, like when he said he'd like to wear your little jacket if you didn't want it anymore."

"Ha, yeah. He has this perfect sense of how to lighten the load, at least with me. If I messed up in school, I felt he'd still be proud of me. He's so powerfully conscious of what can happen to you."

"Amy, that's very perceptive. He lets everybody keep their dignity, doesn't he?"

"He doesn't put people in a place where they have to crawl, even though he has all this authority. He keeps them as his equal. He really enjoys just being."

"But when he doesn't, he'll never tell you."

"That's 'cause he knows that his emotions are his own burden. I asked him one time if something was bothering him, and he said, 'Oh, just something stupid.' He didn't want to inflict it on me. He knows if you're feeling bad, and he uses humor to make you feel better."

"Yep, he holds things in, and that's his defense. He's very complicated."

"No, he isn't. Dad's totally straight. You know who he is and what he's going to do. He has his little patterns and routines, and they don't change. It's what makes him trustworthy. I love to be with him because he doesn't require anything of you; there's no pressure, like some people . . ." She looked pointedly at me.

"Well, he never cared about you doing your homework like I did."

Amy looked up at the ceiling and grinned. "He used to *do* my homework. Then he'd show me how to do it. He knew how upset I'd get with algebra. He used to *keep* my math book!"

"Well, that's not so commendable," I said, smiling.

"He's so secure he's not threatened by mistakes, yours or his own. If he spills food on his tie or I spill milk on his newspaper, he just laughs.

"Mom, see how the drops come down quickly and they meet the ones coming really slowly from another direction? I think you and Dad are so different you just miss meeting each other. You think he should be mushy gushy, and he's not that way." In point of fact, Amy herself was so oversensitive to touch she didn't even like people to hug her. "He has a different way he shows that he cares. He makes things very simple, gets things down to their essence. He tries to make people happy as best he can.

"But you guys are all lovey-dovey these days for some reason," she said, amused.

"That's nice for you to see, isn't it?"

"It should be nice for *you*, Mom. He really loves you."

"I know." I was beginning to get a deeper understanding of what had happened to Bob and me to bring us so close. If Frankie had mirrored back a picture of who we had been to each other, Amy, the family philosopher, had put me on the trail of who we could be now.

"I see you getting frustrated if he doesn't talk a lot," she said. "He would ask me to come next to him on the couch, and just sitting there was enough to have the feeling of him. We just chilled out together.

"Listen, Mom, this is what he does when he loves you: You know how he used to make me pancakes? He'd give me one stack and then another and then another, whether I wanted them or not. He was so happy I was eating them. But I was really giving them to Ivan so Dad wouldn't be hurt and I wouldn't feel guilty. All three of us ended up happy."

Then, suddenly, Amy's eyes filled with tears. "I'm so afraid of his age. That he'll leave me. Every year I'm really grateful he's still here."

My daughter, a young woman, so much younger than me, had already learned one of the greatest of human virtues: gratitude. Expecting nothing from the most important man in her life, she had accepted with joy what he had to offer.

POSTLUDE

Sometimes, you have to take a journey back in order to take it forward. If you are lucky, a third force will come to jolt you into awareness and set you on a course you didn't know was yours.

That force can take any number of forms. For us it was Frankie, a man who saw us from the outside and led us back in time. The one who moved us forward was Amy, who somehow brought everything into perspective.

Although Bob and I have contrasting personalities, we thought that we viewed the world from the same lens. Yet there was one essential difference. We had a sense of that difference, but we didn't know what it meant. Nor did we ever really define it. From language comes light; if you know something vaguely and don't put it into words, it doesn't exist.

Love simply looked different to Bob than it did to me. To him it resided in *doing*, and to me it was about *showing* and *telling*. When he met my need for touch, for reassurance, I knew he loved me. If I kissed him and he pulled away before my vision of the kiss was over, I felt alone. But he didn't experience my aloneness. He thought his love was felt. If he served me blueberries in bed, thought up adventures he knew I'd like, made a call on my behalf, these were acts of devotion. But to me, they just seemed expected.

As for Bob, all he needed was some attention, some little acts of love and concern. What he thrived on was quiet affirmation, gentle caring. Love was in the gesture: setting up his sleep apnea machine, buying him a weather radio on sale, being there for him when he needed you.

•

One day, Josh, who had recently been looking for an apartment, told me his dad had suggested he pick a place near our apartment so he could always look after me. Bob had wanted to protect me, without ever telling me.

It hit me like a bomb: all the things he had done, the sacrifices he had made to show me he loved me in the only context he knew how to show me. How he had gone to church when that was the last thing he wanted to do. Enduring the discomfort of eating on the coffee table because I wanted to escape the negative aura of my family's dining table. Drinking red wine when he liked white just to see the contentment on my face.

When my birthday approached, a big one for me, Bob asked me what I wanted, and I couldn't think of anything. Once, long ago, I had told him I'd always wanted a hot rod, but I was certainly too old for that now. Besides, our finances then were stretched, and I didn't want to give him more worry. So this time, I told him what I wanted most was a card with one of his wonderful cartoons and a message inside.

My birthday approached. One morning, I came to breakfast and found a set of keys on my plate.

"Look outside," Bob said. "There's a red devil out there."

I peeked through the window, and on the lawn was a gleaming red convertible sports car.

I stared agape, dropping the keys to the floor. I could barely take in this beautiful piece of art: long, sleek nose, black top, metal spoke wheels, an interior of caramel-colored leather; it looked as if it belonged in a museum. I put my arms around my husband and laughed, then cried. I had received an honor from him, a tribute. It made me shy, humble.

As I was happily wiggling into the bucket seat, I saw him smiling ear to ear and felt such a rush of thankfulness. It was not the car that moved me as much as the love and effort that he had put into choosing it: the reports he must have read on safety ratings, the search for an affordable vehicle with an excellent engine and the accessories he knew I would love—the leather seats, a tough fabric top that could be opened while the car was moving, manual as well as automatic transmission, and most of all the color. He knew I would want it to be a bright tomato red.

•

What a paradox that two people can have loved so deeply for so long and yet, in one sense, have been strangers all their lives. No matter how strong the union, there is almost always something missing, something lingering unfulfilled. We hang on to our ideas of what the relationship should be, and the cost is longing. Having recited our vows, we proceed to fight for what we cannot get. This is futile, of course, for the law of resistance decrees that neither one of us will win.

We look inside our partners for our fathers, our mothers, for the chance to complete what was started but never finished. I wanted badly to know my dad and to be known by him: I tried everything to break through his emotional wall and mostly failed. When Bob came along, a man so like my dad, the challenge was reawakened. Self-will is so strong that we can't stop trying to get what we missed in childhood. And when inevitably our life mates cannot give it to us, we feel rejected all over again.

We don't see what they can give us, and so we waste it. Determined to get what they can't give, we ignore all that they can. We become Plato's leaky jars. In his parable, a person who has too much desire ends up with a jar full of holes. He keeps greedily filling this jar with precious substances, and it keeps leaking, so every time he picks up the jar, it is empty.

This was where our journey forward was taking us: If I could enter Bob's world and recognize and cherish the love that he was able to give me, and if he could do the same for me, how could our marriage ever be the same?

•

I adore my car. It makes me feel free and strong, and Bob has given me that. For just a few seconds, I rev up the six-cylinder turbocharged engine and shoot through the orchards, the car so low to the ground it seems as if we're going a hundred miles an hour instead of half that. It is the warmest December day in New York history, and we've put down the top. I see the little smile on Bob's face as he looks at me in my sunglasses, my hair flying, cheeks flushed, at one with my car.

When he sees me peeking at him, he shouts over the blast of the engine, "You're going to kill us!"

I take my foot off the gas, and all on its own this intelligent vehicle glides to a stop. Bob is taking new pleasure in my fancies these days. It makes me feel renewed, perfect in his eyes.

We have gone to the loveliest corner of the orchard, and because I like the idea of it, we're going to neck. I remember my husband's stories of dallying among the yellow daffodils that reflected the sun behind his house. So this morning, I found a Jetfire daffodil at the florist, and now I pin it on his collar, just beneath his chin. The flower, with its perfect orange trumpet and brilliant petals, casts a golden glow on his surprised smile.

A zephyr sends the leaves left on the apple trees chattering. The sun beats down, warms our faces. We lean back, safe, comfortable. I take in his features, not with the old slumbering eyes, but finely, closely, as fascinated as I was long ago, watching him sleep. Flared nostrils, the sign of a bold heart; gentle mouth and prismatic eyes: lashless, hooded, deeply set, eyes that kept secrets, disguising even their color. They can cast many hues: the shade of a lazy sky or a clear lagoon or jade waters swallowed by the gray jaws of the sea.

He leans over and tries to nuzzle my neck with his. "Is this necking? Is this what you wanted to do?" he asks in a muffled voice.

"No, silly, like this." I plant little kisses around his face, putting one on the tip of his nose and another on his chin. "Just close your eyes and pretend I'm Katharine Hepburn." He loves Katharine Hepburn.

"I don't have to," he says. Then he gives me a long, rather unrestrained kiss that makes my molecules jump up and down.

"Now, isn't necking nice?" I say, lying in his arms. "We're both nice and warm."

I tell him about my thoughts yesterday, my epiphany. "Will you forgive me for complaining so much about you? I wanted us to have deep, earnest talks and share revelations about each other. I know now that this isn't how you are—it probably isn't how any man is . . . I'm afraid I made you think I was disappointed in you."

"I didn't think you were disappointed." He pauses and then points into the distance. "I think you have this ideal out there of what a model husband should be."

"Well . . . maybe I do. Hmm, all those times you seemed preoccupied, maybe sometimes you weren't. Maybe you were sort of getting your own back, because you thought I was just one long harangue?"

"That's true. Sometimes I stopped listening to you on purpose."

"I know. I thought you didn't care about me."

"I thought you didn't care about *me*."

"Oh no," I said, sighing. "You thought I didn't accept you! We've both been so absurd. The more I've tried to pull stuff out of you, the more you pushed me away. We've taken up battle stations until winning the war has been more important than what we were fighting for!"

We are quiet for a while. My eyes are fixed below on a big withering tree. It has stood majestic since the time of my grandfather-in-law. Now there is only a single shriveled apple on its lowest branch. It will be cut down tomorrow.

"I think you're angry at me because I got old."

I'm taken aback. He has finally said it. "What? Oh no, you're, I . . . I," and then the tears come before I can stop them. Alarmed, he takes out his handkerchief, dabs at my cheeks, and holds me. "I think that's why I've been snapping at you. I've been taking everything out on you. It's not your fault you're getting older. I'm just so afraid of losing you. I always have been."

He kisses my head. His chin is unsteady; I can feel it through my hair. "Poor sweetheart, I can understand that. But I'm not planning on going anywhere. I have to stay to keep you out of trouble."

I manage a little laugh, take a long breath, get hold of myself. "It's not rational. If anything, you're getting younger. Look at your stress test, better than last year. And your writing, your memory, a million other signs. And besides, since Portugal, I don't think of you as old."

"We never used superlatives when I was growing up; they didn't mean anything and were considered effusive. But I know you need those words, and in spite of it sometimes I've dug in my heels. I'll try to do better, to be more sensitive and more available to you."

"I haven't given you much peace, have I?"

"Peace is not what I married you for." He paused, trying to articulate what I wanted to hear. "I loved your honesty and your determination to do the right thing. I observed you always thinking of something new to say and to do. And I was sure you would stick by me. No, don't interrupt me. Just listen. I can't think of what I'm saying when you do that. Yes, I'd get mad at some of your offbeat antics, especially in the beginning, when you seemed very young, but then I guess I was also attracted to them."

I fold my arms. "Hmm, I don't steal road signs, but otherwise I think I do the job for you. I'm your surrogate. There's an impetuous man hiding in you, and that's why you got me the hot rod, even though it cost so much money; it's why you call it the red devil. You have a crush on this car!"

He chuckles. "I do like the car."

We sit and watch the golden glow of the sun's last light, the crows spiraling and the hawks gliding high above the trees. I am somber, thinking about how it has taken me three decades to come to terms with the nature of the husband whose nature I deliberately chose.

I think of all the hard work ahead of us, the mindfulness, the concentration, the biting edge of angry exchanges as we change.

The language of love, so different for each of us and for each of us so hard to grasp, to translate. The discipline it will take to understand the nuances, the shades of our desire, to recognize and truly feel our divergent expressions of intimacy.

I know that Bob, no matter what his age, no matter how distant he was raised to be, craves love as much as I do and that he needs me to love him—not in my way, but in his. My mission is to find the oblique paths to his heart. Which offerings, which gifts, will relieve his pressure, will please him, will bring out the depth of his feelings.

I must recognize his own gifts to me. He may not speak the words I expect or want, but I will know that what means little to me often means everything to him.

When he arrives home in the evenings, I will never again dismiss or, being busy, pretend not to hear him call, "Where's Lucinda?" This is his way of locating his love by locating me; he seeks only to be beside me. I will expand my definition of love, watch for the things I once ignored: the glow of acceptance in his eyes; the electricity of his touch as he intentionally brushes against me; the shiver of pleasure I could feel when he runs the tips of his fingers down my hand.

And if, in the end, I myself should need more from him, now I am certain it's only for the asking.

•

I have a strange sense of rising into the air, as I did when I was a child, praying. One day, here on this soil, you will be taken to a place inside me where death cannot reach you. I feel the deepness and the timelessness of our love, the certainty that it expands beyond our physical selves, that it exists outside us, a current coursing through the lives of the ones who love us. We pass its spiritual power on to them. It will be there when we are gone.

•

"*Maxwelton braes are bonnie!*" Bob has suddenly broken into song with the Scottish ballad I love most. His rich baritone has a completely new vibrato, and never has he sung so in tune, his voice soaring, a new voice that has left behind the two or three good notes he had before: "*Where early fa's the dew!*"

As his chest expands, as he lifts his chin and lets forth the almighty "*A-a-a-n . . . nie Laurie,*" the highest and grandest of sounds in the ballad, goose bumps come up on my arm. His voice is so heartrending and his delivery so amusing I want to cry.

Now he takes up "Loch Lomond," and I warble a descant. We drive past the perfect rectangular fields, hay brown, sage, burnt umber; the apple trees, some of them shedding their leaves. Ahead, by the barn, we see Josh talking to Rowan, a jaunty Jamaican who's one of my favorite orchard workers. They're smiling, and we slow up to wave to them. As we pass, I can just hear Rowan saying, "There goes Romeo and Juliet."

ACKNOWLEDGMENTS

I want to thank the people who gave their time and energy to help shape this memoir: Sarah Crichton believed in the book from the start and expertly guided it through the thorny thickets of revisions, more revisions, final revisions, and at last, production and publication; Rob Weisbach, superb agent and editor, gently coaxed me to think more deeply about relationships, to locate the reality behind the reality; Lila Meade, my editorial assistant, worked tirelessly until she virtually lived the book; Laura Pancucci made me see truth where there was illusion and feelings where there were just facts.

Elaine Markson, my former agent and a beautiful person, took me through three decades of writing and publishing. Ruth Gibson illuminated my understanding of spirituality.

Blair Brown Hoyt, editor, Jill Comins, therapist, and Pat Bryne Cosentino, poet, shared their talent and friendship. The wonderful writers Fran Klagsbrun, Hilma Wolitzer, and Wendy Gimbel helped me usher the book into the world.

Carolyn Hessel, head of the Jewish Book Council, has given me confidence and endless support.

The inimitable Ida Van Lindt, my husband's secretary, provided me with much material, as did the lightning-quick Marilyn Bauza.

Susan Morgenthau, my much-loved daughter-in-law, who is a trustee of the New York Public Library, gave me welcome insight, as did Holly Hollingsworth, my opera comrade.

Laurie Lowenthal, Sarah Morgenthau, Ellie Hirschhorn, Sage Sevilla, and Henry Morgenthau III provided me with introductions and inspiration. Pierre Romain, film producer, advised me on any number of issues.

Victor Temkin talked to me many times and at length about Bob, as did Pat Dugan and Peter Kougasian.

Chris O'Connor, Marina and Steve Kaufman, Soma Golden Behr, Alex Hoyt, Andrew Meade, and Howard Stein were there to give me ideas and moral support. Emily Strasser and Robyn Yzelman helped with the nuts and bolts.

My gratitude to the patient and indefatigable FSG team: Laury Frieber, the excellent lawyer; Lottchen Shivers, my publicist; Jenny Carrow and Maureen Bishop of the art department; Susan Goldfarb and Nina Frieman in production; Jonathan Lippincott, the designer; and Marsha Sasmor, Sarah Crichton's invaluable editorial assistant.

I owe a special thanks to the two men who influenced me, coming as they did from a different time and a different place: William Gifford, the first professor who convinced me that my passion for words could tease out my ability, and Edward Hoagland, the nature writer, who taught me my first valuable lesson as a writer: always keep a journal in your pocket.

INDEX

Abate, Catherine, 217
Abdel-Rahman, Omar, 309, 310, 311–12, 313
Abedi, Agha Hasan, 315
A Coney Island of the Mind (Ferlinghetti), 67
Ahmadinejad, Mahmoud, 343
Alcott, Louisa May, 129
Alpert, Jane, 25–26
al-Qaeda, 310, 312, 313, 315
Alsop, Joseph, 183–84
America First Committee, 52
American Agriculturist, 51
Amherst College, 55
An American Tragedy (Dreiser), 162
Anarchist Club, 14
Anderson, Gene, 89, 292, 360
Arafat, Yasser, 179, 203
Arens, Moshe, 206, 208, 209
Arnold, Marty, 95
Asch, Sidney, 122, 308
Astor, Brooke, 37, 338–39

Baez, Joan, 16
Bank of Credit and Commerce International (BCCI), 314–15
Bauer, USS, 267
Beame, Abe, 77
Bechtel Corporation, 208
Begin, Menachem, 202
Belfast, 18
Black Panthers, 80

Bloomberg, Michael, 354
Blum, John Morton, 55
Blum, Jack, 314
Bondi, Andre, 281
Bondi, Lea, 276–77, 278, 280, 281
Boston Globe, 279
Bradley, Ed, 223
Breasted, Mary, 26, 84, 85, 95, 118, 222
Brokaw, Tom, 356
Brookings Institution, 354
Brown, Tina, 286, 289, 292, 348
Buckley, Charlie, 69–70, 71
Buckley, Sen. James L., 243
Buckley, William F., 120
Burroughs, William, 67

Cabey, Darrell, 217
Cambodia, 12, 24
Cambridge (Mass.), 13–14
Cardozo, Benjamin Nathan, 228
Carey, Gov. Hugh, 243, 279
Carlisle, Kitty, 37
Carroll, Mickey, 28
Carter, Jimmy, 36, 139, 186, 202, 315
Castleman, Dan, 329
Central Intelligence Agency (CIA), 310, 311, 312, 314, 315, 316
Cherry Lane Theatre, 61
Chomsky, Noam, 18
Children's Hour, The (Hellman), 176
Churchill, Winston, 54, 273, 362
Clinton, Bill, 176, 286, 287, 288, 290, 293

Clinton, Hillary, 176–77, 275, 286–91, 292, 293
Coffin, William Sloane, 25
Cohn, Roy, 74, 76, 77, 78
Cole, USS, 310
Comins, Jill, 231–32, 238, 249, 284–85, 295
Commentary, 76
Communist Manifesto, The, (Marx and Engels), 13
Conboy, Ken, 61
Congress of Racial Equality (CORE), 216
Connor, Christine, 348
Cooke, Alistair, 183, 184
Cooke, Lawrence, 227–28
Cornell University, 51
Corrigan, Mairead, 142
Credit Suisse, 343
Crewdson, John, 34
Crowley, Candy, 287
Cuomo, Gov. Andrew, 20
Cuomo, Gov. Mario, 243
Curley, James Michael, 29
Cunningham, Michael, 324

Daily Beast, The, 348
Dan, Uri, 164, 177, 178, 179, 202, 203
Deerfield Academy, 55
Defense Intelligence Agency (DIA), 310, 311
DeLuca, Giorgio, 131
Democratic Committee Women's Division, 54
Derry (Northern Ireland), 35, 144
De Sapio, Carmine, 70, 74, 77
Diana, Princess of Wales, 176–77, 287
Doyle, Mark, 349
Dreiser, Theodore, 162
Dugan, Pat, 312
Dylan, Bob, 306

Eichmann, Adolf, 164
Eitan, Rafi, 164
Ellison, Nancy, 176
Emerson, Gloria, 25, 95
est, 31

Fairstein, Linda, 327, 328
Federal Bureau of Investigation (FBI), 17, 169, 298, 309, 310, 311, 312, 313, 316
Feldman, Justin, 328
Ferlinghetti, Lawrence, 67
Fleischer, Ellen, 198
Food and Drug Administration (FDA), 28
Ford, Gerald, 30, 32, 81
Fortas, Abe, 73
Fosburgh, Lacey, 26
Fraiman, Arnold, 149, 150
Franklin National Bank, 27
Franks, Lorraine, 12, 13–14, 15, 16, 21, 23, 30–32, 33, 34, 35, 44–45, 57–58, 100, 114–15, 119–20, 121, 124,126, 128, 148, 169, 183, 207, 213, 250, 307, 319; and cancer treatments, 28, 253, 254
Franks, Lucinda: association with radicals, 7–8, 14–15, 17, 24, 25, 80, 187; and breast cancer, 251–60; childhood, 12–13, 19, 30–31, 44–45, 58, 126, 168, 261, 317, 319; first pregnancy of, 192–210; and Hillary Clinton interview, 275, 286–91, 292, 293; hired by New York Times, 23–25; in London, 14, 16, 17, 118, 133, 141, 233; at MacDowell Colony, 98–101; and marital strain, 255–70; in Northern Ireland, 18, 138, 140–45; and Pulitzer Prize, 14, 21, 137; quits New York Times, 35–36; radicalism of, 12; relationship with father, 19, 44, 45, 46, 58, 72, 100, 128, 158, 159, 163, 168, 207, 303, 317, 375; relationship with mother, 12, 13–14, 30–32, 35, 44–45, 58, 100, 183, 207, 261, 267; relationship with Uncle Billy, 196, 212–13; at Seabrook protest, 107–108; at Vassar, 14; and Watergate reporting, 18–22; and writer's block, 99–100, 137–38, 275, 317; writes book about father, 317–319, 331
Franks, Penelope (Penny), 23, 45–46, 118, 121, 122, 125, 126, 129, 151, 197, 212–13, 275, 305, 306

Franks, Thomas, 16, 19, 31, 45, 46, 58, 71, 72, 96, 115, 119,121–22, 128, 129,155, 163,168, 194, 207, 235, 269, 275, 305, 317, 331, 375; death of, 305–307; and wartime experience, 13, 275, 301–302, 303, 304, 307, 318–19, 331
Freeh, Louis, 298
Fresh Air Fund, 360
Friedan, Betty, 198
Friedman, Karen, 308–309
Friedman, Stanley M., 220
Furstenberg, Diane Von, see Von Furstenberg, Diane

Gage, Nicholas, 26, 28, 95, 110
Gelb, Arthur, 23–24, 26, 27–28, 29, 34, 35–36, 95, 152, 178, 230, 231
Gelb, Barbara, 152, 178–80
Georgiou, Renos, 247
Georgiou, Steve, 247
Germany Is Our Problem, 272–73
Gestalt, 31
Gifford, Bill, 182
Gill, Jim, 219
Gimbel, Wendy, 196, 231
Ginsberg, Allen, 68
Giuliani, Rudolph, 220, 271
Goetz, Bernhard, 216–18, 220
Goldberg, Arthur, 73, 78, 87
Goldsworthy, Andy, 362
Good Eggs, 361
Graiver, David, 147–48, 149, 150, 192
Grand, Anne Morgethau, see Morgenthau, Anne
Grand, Hilary, 106, 360
Grand, Noah, 175, 192, 360
Grand, Paul, 89, 105, 122, 172, 259, 360
Greenfield, Jimmy, 95
Gribetz, Judah, 279, 347
Guardian Angels, 216

Haig, Alexander, 179
Haines, George, 268
Hanauer, Linda, 252

Harris, Ben, 360
Harry F. Bauer, USS, 50
Harvard University, 13, 90
Haskell, Molly, 201
Hays, Rep. Wayne, 34, 35
Healey, Jim, 70
Hearst, Patty, 25
Hellman, Lillian, 94, 176
Hepburn, Katherine, 376
Hersey, John, 93–94, 174, 176
Herzog, Chaim, 164
High, Stanley, 71–72
Hirsch, Marcelle Puthon, see Morgenthau, Marcelle Puthon Hirsch
Hirschhorn, Elizabeth, 61, 191
Hitler, Adolf, 52, 53
Hoffman, Abbie, 18
Hoffman, Nicholas von, see von Hoffman, Nicholas
Hoyt, Blair, 232, 295
Hull, Cordell, 49
Hunter-Gault, Charlayne, 223
Hylton, Renia, 86, 87, 88, 107, 124, 125, 136, 137, 179, 181, 198, 213–14, 215, 225, 233, 241, 244, 248, 262, 319; death of, 320

Innocence Project, 327
Irish Republican Army (IRA), 141, 142
Ivins, Molly, 28
Izvestia, 292

Jensen, Greg, 119, 120
Jensen, Irona, 119, 120–21
John Birch Society, 12
John Paul II, Pope, 271
Johnson, Rob, 245
Johnson, Lyndon, 16, 73
Junior League, 13–14

Kahan Commission, 202
Kahane, Meir, 309, 310, 312
Kaufman, Marina, 87, 118, 121, 122, 131
Kaufman, Steve, 78, 87, 118, 347

Kelly, Ray, 279
Kennedy, Edward, 183
Kennedy, Jacqueline, *see* Onassis,
    Jacqueline Kennedy
Kennedy, John F., 11, 16, 36, 37, 69, 70,
    71, 78
Kennedy, John F., Jr., 227
Kennedy, Robert, 14, 71–72, 74, 77, 342
Kerry, Sen. John, 314
Kimes, Kenneth, 296, 297–98, 325
Kimes, Sante, 296, 297–98, 325
Kindler, Jim, 329
King, Martin Luther, Jr., 14, 46, 342
King, Stanley, 138, 139
Kissinger, Henry, 338
Koch, Ed, 7, 26, 182–83, 188, 198, 272
Kollek, Teddy, 205
Kougasian, Peter, 229
Kozlowski, 326
Kropotkin, Pyotr, 13, 17

Lahey Clinic, 28
Lang, Dan, 94
Lang, Margie, 93, 94, 129, 173, 174
Lansdale, USS, 50, 266, 267, 268, 332,
    333
Lauder, Ronald, 276–77
Law & Order (TV show), 324, 346
Lawe, USS, 334
Lee, Hanmin, 360
Lehman, Herbert, 54, 271
Lehman, Irving, 228, 271
Lehmann-Haupt, Christopher, 182
Lelyveld, Joe, 95
Lend-Lease Act, 52
Leneman, Nan, 82
Lenin, Vladimir Ilyich, 13
Lewis, C. S., 300
Leopold Museum, 277, 280
Leval, Pierre, 63, 78, 149, 209
Leval, Susana, 209
Levin, Gerald, 245
Levin, Jonathan, 255
Lewinsky, Monica, 275, 286, 291, 293
Lewis, Anthony, 197
Liman, Arthur, 77, 78

Lipton, Martin, 354
Little Women (Alcott), 129
Lloyd's of London, 343
Looking for Mr. Goodbar (Rossner),
    193
Lowey, Nita M., 281
Lukas, J. Anthony, 137

Madoff, Bernard, 348
MacDowell Colony, 98–101
Mailer, Norman, 77
Malamud, Bernard, 197–98
Malkin, Peter, 164–65, 187
Marcuse, Herbert, 18
Marshall, Tony, 338–39
Mason, C. Vernon, 217, 219, 223, 224,
    225, 324, 325
Maybe (Hellman), 176
Meade, Lila, 174, 232, 274, 295, 296, 358
Meir, Golda, 97
Memorial Sloan-Kettering, 28, 253–54,
    262
Messinger, Ruth, 323
Milford, Nancy, 221–22, 230
Millett, Kate, 198
Mohammed, Khalid Sheikh, 313
Mollo, Sil, 78
Montebello, Philippe de, 281
Morgenthau Diaries (Blum), 55
Morgenthau, Amy Elinor, 236–42, 248,
    254, 258, 259, 281, 305, 320, 322, 359,
    360–61; assessment of father, 369–71
Morgenthau, Anne, 60, 64, 89, 91, 96,
    107, 172, 207, 252, 360; relationship
    with Franks, 90, 105; and father's
    marriage to Franks, 105–106, 122
Morgenthau, Barbara, 43, 82, 85, 90, 91,
    92, 96, 105–106, 115, 124, 126,133–34,
    172–73, 174, 194–95, 320, 321, 360;
    and father's marriage to Franks, 122;
    and mother's death, 86, 87, 88, 91;
    relationship with Franks, 60, 61, 89,
    96, 106, 124, 129, 173, 252–54
Morgenthau, Bobby, 43, 60, 86, 87, 89,
    90, 129, 171, 172, 213–14, 226, 239,
    321, 360; and father's marriage to

Franks, 104–105, 122; relationship with Franks, 91, 171–72, 173, 207; weds Susan Moore, 190, 191, 192

Morgenthau, Elinor (daughter), 88

Morgenthau, Elinor (mother), 47, 48, 49, 54, 55–58, 59, 88, 265, 268

Morgenthau, Harry, 239

Morgenthau, Henry, 53, 188, 280

Morgenthau, Henry, Jr., 41, 48, 49, 51–52, 53, 54, 55, 96, 97, 188, 265, 272–73, 279, 362

Morgenthau, Henry III, 47, 51, 58, 96, 171, 273

Morgenthau, Jenny, 89, 90, 91, 96–97, 106, 140, 172, 292, 360; and father's marriage to Franks, 105; and relationship with Franks, 172, 250, 252

Morgenthau, Joan, 46–47, 51, 58–59, 94, 96, 171, 191, 207

Morgenthau, Joshua Franks, 194, 201, 209, 210, 211–16, 218, 221–26, 230, 231, 233–35, 236, 237–38, 239, 248, 249, 254, 258, 259, 281, 282–83, 305, 306, 320, 323–24, 359, 374; and family farm, 321, 322, 361, 379

Morgenthau, Martha, 239

Morgenthau, Martha Pattridge, 16, 21, 59, 61, 88, 97, 105, 114–16, 117, 124–25, 128, 135, 136, 137, 266, 269; and cancer, 86–87, 262, 264, 265

Morgenthau, Marcelle Puthon Hirsch, 265

Morgenthau Plan, 52, 188, 272–73

Morgenthau, Robert: appointed U.S. Attorney, 11, 16, 69, 78; and BCCI case, 314–15, 326; and Bernhard Goetz case, 216–18; boat trip with Franks, 157–63; and Brooke Astor elder abuse case, 337–39; and Central Park jogger case, 326–29; childhood of, 46–49, 58; dates Franks, 59–75; 80–85; on death penalty, 242–46; and "DNA footprint" case, 299–300, 325; elected district attorney of New York County, 16; family disapproval of relationship with Franks, 3, 89, 94–97, 102–107, 124, 127; and family

farm, 47, 49, 51, 96, 171, 251, 257, 321–22, 362; fired by Nixon, 18, 21, 87; first date with Franks, 36–41; first marriage, 16, 21, 59, 86, 116, 135–37, 264; Greece trip with Franks, 109–14; hearing problems, 47–48, 49, 63, 71, 184, 250, 295; honeymoon with Franks, 123; on Israel, 139, 164, 168, 170, 179, 186; Israel trips with Franks, 164–70, 193, 201–207; marital strain, 255–70; meets Franks, 3, 19–22; gubernatorial campaigns, 16, 63, 87; on immigration reform, 344, 354, 356, 357–58; and Judge Lawrence Cooke case, 227–29; and Kimes murder case, 296–98; and Mafia, 11, 74; and melanoma, 249–50; and Museum of Jewish Heritage, 188–89, 244, 270–73, 303, 347, 362; and Nazi stolen art cases, 276–81; Portugal trip with Franks, 363–66; and post-traumatic stress disorder, 262–70, 273, 332–35; and rape law reform, 336–37; reelection campaigns, 219–25, 324–26, 329–30; relationship with father, 51, 53; relationship with mother, 47, 49; retires, 340–42; on Ronald Reagan, 184, 186, 187; and Roy Cohn investigation, 74, 76, 77, 78; and September 11 attacks, 308–14; and service in World War II, 49–50, 266, 267, 268, 301–302, 331–332, 333, 334; as source for Franks's reporting, 20–22, 26–27, 28, 38; weds Franks, 5, 118–23; with Wachtell, Lipton, Rosen & Katz, 354–55; and white-collar crime, 29, 79, 148–49, 296, 326, 340, 343

Morgenthau, Susan Moore, 190, 191, 192, 239, 360

Morrissey, Francis X., 338–39

Mostly Morgenthaus (H. Morgenthau III), 47

Moscow, John, 314, 315

Museum of Jewish Heritage, 188–89, 244, 270–73, 303, 347, 360, 362

Museum of Modern Art (MoMA),
    276–79
My Father's Secret War (Franks),
    317–319, 331

Nemerov, Howard, 180
Nerissa (housekeeper), 241, 319, 320
Newfield, Jack, 183
Newsweek, 354
New York Daily News, 140, 341, 354
New Yorker, The, 174, 275, 286, 359
New York Observer, 224
New York Times, 23–28, 29, 32, 33, 34,
    35–36, 139, 219, 231, 292, 326, 329,
    342, 354
Nidal, Abu, 178
Nixon, Richard, 14, 16, 17, 19, 27, 30, 32,
    87, 284; and Watergate, 18, 21–22
Norton, Larry, 253
Nosair, El Sayyid, 309, 310, 311, 312, 313
nuclear power, protests against, 107–108

Oakes, John, 37, 146, 214
Oakes, Margery, 37, 146, 214
Obama, Barack, 344, 354, 357
Oates, Joyce Carol, 180–81, 182
O'Connor, John Cardinal, 206, 270–71
Office of Civilian Defense, 54
Oggi, 292
Onassis, Jacqueline Kennedy, 37, 38
Oughton, Diana, 14–15, 21

Palestine Liberation Organization
    (PLO), 165, 169, 177, 178, 179, 180,
    203
Pancucci, Laura, 261
Pataki, Gov. George, 243, 245, 271
Paterson, Gov. David, 246
Patman, Wright, 21, 70
Patterson, Hon. Robert, 73–74, 268, 334
Paul Hamilton, USS, 268
Pius XII, Pope, 271
Plimpton, Mrs. Francis T. P., 169–70
Plimpton, George, 169

Power, Katherine Ann, 25–26
Powers, Thomas, 15

Raines, Howell, 292
Rangel, Alma 222
Rangel, Rep. Charlie, 198, 222–23, 225,
    304
Ray, Elizabeth, 34
Reagan, Nancy, 183
Reagan, Ronald, 183, 184, 186, 187, 208,
    231
Redford, Robert, 26
Reeves, Richard, 32
Renta, Annette de la, 337, 339
Reyes, Matias, 327
Robinson, Edward G., 73
Roche, Kevin, 272
Rockefeller, David, 338
Rockefeller, Nelson, 4, 16, 231
Rolling Stone, 36
Rollnick, Bill, 176
Roosevelt, Eleanor, 48, 55–56, 138–39,
    171, 230, 232, 235, 268, 295
Roosevelt, Elliott, 57
Roosevelt, Franklin Delano, 40, 41,
    48, 51–52, 54, 74–75, 235, 272, 329,
    362
Roosevelt, Franklin Delano, Jr., 208
Rosenthal, Abe, 25, 28, 35–36, 231
Ross, Steve, 177, 189
Rossner, Judith, 193
Rowan (orchard worker), 379
Rutherford, Margaret, 343

Sadat, Anwar, 203
Safire, William, 76, 197
Sainte-Marie, Buffy, 59
Sale, Courtney, 177
Samuels, Dorothy, 77
Sanchez, Frank, 364–65, 366, 368, 369,
    371, 373
Sandifer, Jawn A., 149
Sardi's, 23–24
Sarnoff, Susan, 172
Sayre, Nora, 99, 221–22

Schiele, Egon, 276–77
Schlesinger, Arthur, 36, 37, 146
Schneiderman, Eric, 330
Schumer, Charles E., 281
Screwtape Letters, The (Lewis), 300
Selma-to-Montgomery civil rights
    march, 46
Semple, Kirk, 357, 358
Semple, Robert, 177
Sevilla, Sage, 252
Seymour, Whitney North, 21
Shulman, Micki, 309
Silver, Sheldon, 337
Silverman, Irene, 297, 298
Simon, Anne W., 130–31
Sindona, Michele, 27
Sharon, Ariel, 177–80, 188, 202–204
Sharon, Lily, 178, 179, 203, 204
Smith, Ray, 180–81
Smyth, Ted, 84, 85, 95
Snyder, Leslie Crocker, 324–26, 329,
    330, 346
Soblen, Robert, 73
Sotomayor, Sonia, 20
Spiegel, Der, 292
Spielberg, Stephen, 189
Springsteen, Bruce, 269
Stalin, Josef, 273
Stans, Maurice, 21–22, 24
Steinem, Gloria, 198
Stewart, Michael, 219, 220
Stimson, Henry, 52
Students for a Democratic Society
    (SDS), 14
Styron, Rose, 94
Styron, William, 94, 176
Sulzberger, Arthur O., 278
Sulzberger, Iphigene, 177

Talk, 286, 287, 291, 292
Temkin, Susie, 121, 177
Temkin, Victor, 76, 77–78, 79, 177
Terpil, Frank, 164
Thalheimer, Eva Lehman, 271
The Thin Edge: Coast and Man in Crisis
    (Simon), 131

Thomas, Dylan, 351
Thomas, Frank, 78
Three Days of the Condor (film), 26
Tiny Tim, 68
Trilling, Diana, 94, 176
Truman, Harry S., 52, 53, 273

Ulster Volunteer Force, 142
Uncle Tom's Cabin (Stowe), 13
United Press International (UPI), 14,
    16–17, 18, 35, 118, 141

Vanderbilt, Gloria, 181
Van Lindt, Ida, 228, 348, 354
Vassar College, 14, 54
Vassar Haiti Project, 274
Velez, Luis S., 243
Vietnam War, 11–12, 14, 23, 24, 25, 30,
    32, 183; and draft, 14, 17, 30, 139
Von Furstenberg, Diane, 37
von Hoffman, Nicholas, 18

Wais, Pauline, 55, 118
Wall Street Journal, 226, 345, 354
Wallace, Henry, 49
Walters, Barbara, 338
Warhol, Andy, 77
Warner, Sam, 49
War Refugee Board, 52, 279
Washington Conference Principles on
    Nazi-Confiscated Art, 281
Washington Post, 34
Watergate, see Nixon, Richard
Waterston, Sam, 324
We Are the People Our Parents Warned
    Us Against (von Hoffman), 18
Weatherman, 15, 81
Weinberger, Caspar, 208
Weinstein, Harvey, 291
Weisbach, Rob, 317, 318
Weiss, Ted, 180
Wellesley (Mass.), 12–13, 17, 28, 93,
    119
Wellmet, 13–14

Welty, Eudora, 182
Wenner, Jann, 37
Werner, Nan, 93, 94, 130–31, 132, 133, 173
Whalen, Philip, 67
Whitely, Horace, 28
White, Theodore, 182
Wielunski, Peter, 356
Wiesel, Elie, 271
Wiest, Dianne, 346
Williams, Betty, 142

Williams, Roger Neville, 17–18, 22–23, 30, 31–33, 36, 39, 41–42, 63, 65, 68, 100, 139
Willkie, Wendell, 329
Wilson, Woodrow, 41, 53, 54
Wolfson, Louis, 71–72, 73

Young, Rep. John, 34
Younger, Irving, 76, 77
Yousef, Ramzi, 313